Meditations for Women
Who Do Too Much

Meditations For Women Who Do Too Much

ANNE WILSON SCHAEF, PH.D.

HarperSanFrancisco
A Division of HarperCollins*Publishers*

FIRST HARPERCOLLINS CLOTH EDITION PUBLISHED IN 1992

Library of Congress Cataloging-in-Publication Data

Schaef, Anne Wilson
    Meditation for women who do too much / Anne
Wilson Schaef.
        p.   cm.
    Includes index.
    ISBN 0–06–250784–2 (hard : alk. paper)
    1. Women—Prayer-books and devotions—
English   2. Devotional calendars.   I. Title
[BV4527.S27   1992]
242'.643—dc20   92–3658
                                                      CIP

---

92 93 94 95 96 K.P. 10 9 8 7 6 5 4 3 2 1

This edition is printed on acid-free paper that meets the
American National Standards Institute Z39.48 Standard.

ᢒᕋ Acknowledgments

I want to thank so many people who have helped bring this book into being. Let me thank first of all, my agent, Jonathon Lazear, who called one day and said, "I have just sold a book you didn't know you were writing." "Oh no you haven't," I fired back. Then we discussed it. Jan Johnson at Harper and Row was very convincing, and I remembered that way down deep I had wanted to write a meditation book years ago. I also have finally come to believe that I am a writer and I was ready to "try my wings" on some challenges. So I said yes. I loved the process, and I thank Jan and Jonathon for challenging me.

Then there are the people who backed me up. Diane Fassel and John Reed at home gave me constant support and feedback and helped gather quotes. Linda Lewis worked hard to gather excellent quotes. Mary Ann Wells, Linda Crowder, and Gwen DeCino typed and put things together. Ann Sprague did the tedious, time-consuming, and very important work of checking the quotes, checking the typing, making content and editorial changes (as well as great personal comments, such as "I like this one," "Ugh," and so on), and generally whipped the book into shape. My grown-up kids and son-in-law added the needed peppering of encouragement.

We made a great team, and I am more and more convinced that no book ever comes into being through the efforts of only one person. I have had a wonderful time working on this book. It has stretched me as a writer, organizer, and thinker. Perhaps we will do a sequel for women who are *recovering* from doing too much. Who knows?

Most of all, I want to thank the wonderful women whose quotes and lives make up the substance of this book and the Twelve Step Program of Alcoholics Anonymous, without which the clarity for this book would never have been possible.

❧ Introduction

This is a meditation book for women who do too much. When my publishers first suggested doing this book, we talked of the need for a book for women workaholics. Yet, as we discussed the need for such a book, we began to explore the many different kinds of women who overwork and do too much and agreed that many of us would not initially define ourselves as workaholics. However, there are many of us who do too much, keep too busy, spend all our time taking care of others and, in general do not take care of ourselves. Many of us have crossed over the line to compulsive, addictive, self-defeating behavior and need to make some major changes in our lives. Hence, I decided to write a book for women who do too much regardless of where we do it or how we do it. This is a book for women workaholics, busyaholics, rushaholics, and careaholics. I hope that it will prove interesting, challenging, and helpful to a range of women.

I decided to use only quotes from women. This does not mean that there are no tempting, exciting, and useable quotes from men—there are. However, I found so many wonderful quotes from women that I decided to use them exclusively. I have used a variety of quotes from women. I have tried to use quotes from women of different ages, cultures, disciplines, and perspectives. I have used quotes from famous women, women at intensives, and women who just said something important in passing. This gathering of women's quotes has proved to be a rich and enriching experience for me.

In preparation for this book, I returned to several novels by and about women that I had read in the sixties and seventies. What a wonderful rediscovery! I met old friends (the heroines) who had rested dormant in my soul and again came alive as I returned to them. Some of them re-emerge on these pages. I hope you enjoy them as much as I did.

This book of meditations is not only for women, even though it is written from a woman's perspective, in the female idiom and is viewed through the eyes of women. Several men have read the manuscript and found it very helpful. I am happy to share these meditations with anyone who finds them useful. I know that there are many of us who are working ourselves to death and still not making our contribution. Life does not have to be that way.

In some ways this book follows a usual form for meditations and in others not. There is a meditation for each day of the year. Each day begins with a quotation, which is followed by a meditation on it, and ends with a few words for the day. Since I assumed women who do too much would not take much time for meditations (and probably usually take none!), I tried to make each meditation brief. In addition, I have added several "extra" meditations at the end of the book. If you do not respond to one on a particular day, look at one of the extras.

These meditations do not tell you what to do, they do not tell you how you should be, and they are not answers. They are intended to stir up some feelings, get you thinking, and precipitate possibilities for change which will add to the quality and vitality of your life. These meditations can be experienced as an open door or a direct hit to the solar plexus. Make of them what you will.

❧ January 1

RUSHING/FRENZY

Anything worth doing is worth doing frantically.
—New proverb

We women who do too much find the ending of an old year and the beginning of a new year to be a difficult time. There is always the temptation to try to "tidy up" all our loose ends as the old year closes. We fall into the trap of believing that it is possible to get our entire life "caught up" before starting a new year, and we are determined to to do it.

Also, there is the temptation to set up an elaborate set of resolutions for the coming year so that we can, at last, *get it right.* As workaholics, we tend to be very hard on ourselves: nothing less than perfection is enough. Hopefully, on this first day of the year, we will be able to remember that we are perfect just as we are.

I HOPE for the willingness to live this year in a way that will be gentle to myself . . . one day at a time.

ॐ January 2

POWERLESSNESS

We are powerless over our workaholism and our busyness, and our lives have become unmanageable.
—Modified Step One, Alcoholics
Anonymous

Me? Powerless? No, never! The very word causes me to curl my lips and to have grave suspicions of any creature who would suggest it. As a woman, I will never be powerless again. I may be expected to be, but I won't be!

But wait a minute. This step does not say that I am powerless as a human being. It clearly states that I am powerless over my workaholism and my busyness. Now that's a different matter. I have indeed felt a little ragged around the edges, and I am concerned that my relationships and other aspects of my personal life have been taking a beating lately.

Even when I try to stop, I find I can't really. Maybe I need to be willing to take a look at this "powerless-over" idea. My life does need something.

JUST BEING *willing* to take a look is the first step. I can take that step.

ᘒ᙮ January 3

Excuses/Choices

So at an early age I witnessed the fact that work was of the first importance, and that it justified rather inhuman behavior.

—May Sarton

Workaholism, just like other addictions, is intergenerational. Many of us have learned it at home from our mothers and fathers, and we cannot even imagine any other way of being in this world. Work took precedence over everything in our households and families. We could only have fun after the work was done, and the work was never done. We could only relax and take care of our personal needs when the chores were completed and the house had been straightened up. And when that was done, we were much too tired to do anything else. Cleanliness was always next to godliness, and many times godliness seemed very far away.

Work was always tied to the necessities of life, getting ahead, and the American dream, and these ideals justified anything, even cruel and inhuman behavior in the family.

We learned our lessons well, and now we have the opportunity to break the intergenerational chain of workaholism. We have a chance to be different. We have choices.

LET ME NOTICE today how many times I use work as an excuse for my inhuman behavior.

HUMOR

Time wounds all heels.

—Jane Ace

We lose the ability to laugh *at* ourselves and *with* others.

Humor is so healing . . . and it's fun too. We find that humor is one of the first human gifts to disappear when addictive diseases set in.

We lose the ability to laugh *at* ourselves and *with* others. We feel insulted if someone pokes fun at us, and we personalize everything, seeing it as a put down. The more our disease progresses, we make Scrooge look like a stand-up comic. Indeed, instead of being heal*ers* we have become heels . . . heels without souls.

Good humor is very inexpensive. It is one of the pleasures in life that is relatively free. I'm sure, if we try hard enough, we can remember a part of us that used to laugh and be playful.

HUMOR doesn't die, thank goodness, it just goes underground sometimes and digs caverns for our "serious" selves to cave in to.

CRISIS/EXHAUSTION/CONTROL

> *The sky is falling! The sky is falling!*
> —Chicken Little

Living our lives like Chicken Little can be quite exhausting. Yet so many of us live from one crisis to another! We have become so accustomed to crisis and deadlines that we feel almost lost if we are not putting out some kind of fire. In fact, if we really were honest, there is something dramatic and exciting about handling a crisis. It makes us feel as if we have some modicum of control in our lives.

We have, however, on occasion wondered if all these crises are normal and if there is another way to live life that might be a little less exhausting. Even though we are exhilarated in handling these crises, they do leave us feeling drained. Could it be that these things don't just *happen* to us? That we have a hand in their creation?

As we begin to work on our recovery, we see others around us who do not live from one crisis to another, and they seem to do just fine . . . they're even serene.

CRISIS and my illusion of control are not unrelated. I hope I will allow myself to be open to noticing the relationship between the two in my life today.

ಶ January 6

Self-Deception/Illusions

We live in a system built on illusions and when we put forth our own perceptions, we're told we don't understand reality. When reality is illusion and illusion is reality, it's no wonder we feel crazy.
—Anne Wilson Schaef

All addictions are built on illusions. The illusion of control, the illusion of perfectionism, the illusion of objectivity. Dishonesty and denial are the building blocks of addiction. When we participate in any of these illusions, we are deceiving ourselves, and when we deceive ourselves, we lose ourselves. Why is it that we find self-deception and illusions so much more attractive than honesty? It could possibly be because we are surrounded by a society where illusion is the name of the game. Denial runs rampant at every level of our society, and there is not much support for "truth speakers."

Yet, we are the only ones who can deceive ourselves. We are the only ones who can refuse to acknowledge our perceptions and lie to ourselves. The choice to deceive ourselves is ours.

THERE IS an old saying, "Conscience is a cur that will let you get past it but that you cannot keep from barking." Sometimes our awareness makes funny noises to get our attention.

ॐ January 7

RIGIDITY

Changes [in life] are not only possible and predictable, but to deny them is to be an accomplice to one's own unnecessary vegetation.

—Gail Sheehy

Part of the crazy thinking of addictions is that we will be safe if we can just get everything in order, everything in place, and keep it that way. Much of our energy is spent trying to contribute to the calcification of our lives. Unfortunately, calcified beings are brittle and break easily.

When we become rigid about anything, we lose touch with our life process and place ourselves outside of the stream of life—we die. As Lillian Smith says, "when you stop learning, stop listening, stop looking and asking questions, always new questions, then it is time to die."

HAVE I already died? Am I one of the walking dead? Rigid isn't stable, it's just brittle.

ॐ January 8

NEED TO ACHIEVE

Some of us are becoming the men we wanted to marry.
—Gloria Steinem

Getting an important position in a good company is an exacting feat. Many of us have worked long and hard to get where we are and we are proud of our achievements.

Success demands sacrifice and focus, and we have learned how to do both. We have put our work before everything else in our life. We have learned to compete and compromise. We have learned to dress like men and hold our own in a circle of men. We have learned to be tough and to "come on strong" when we need to. We wanted to make it in a man's world, and we have. We have learned to play the game.

It is time to stop and see what has happened to us in this process. Are we the *women* we want to be?

I WONDER if I have really become the man I would want to marry? Would my clear and healthy woman want to marry me?

❧ January 9

ANGER

Anger as soon is fed is dead
'Tis starving makes it fat.

—Emily Dickinson

Anger has not been an easy emotion for us. We get angry when we are passed over for promotions. We get angry when no one listens. We get angry when our ideas are not heard and even angrier when these same ideas are declared "fantastic" when one of our male colleagues presents them. We get angry when we are so strung out and exhausted that we find ourselves yelling at those we love the most. Then we become angry about being angry, and we try to "control ourselves."

It is important to remember that feelings are just that . . . feelings. It is normal for us to have feelings, and it is normal for us to feel anger. Anger is only harmful when it is held in and "starved" as Emily Dickinson says. When we hold it in, it builds and we find ourselves exploding on innocent people in the most astounding circumstances. Then we end up feeling bad about ourselves and getting anger backlash from others. We need to find safe places to let our anger out. We can respect our anger. It is our friend. It lets us know when something is wrong.

ANGER **is not the problem. What I do with it is.**

❧ January 10

Juggling Projects/Negativism

I don't give myself credit for what I do get done because I have so many projects hanging fire that I haven't done.

—Chris

We workaholics are the type of people that see a glass half-empty instead of half-full. It is much easier to see what we haven't done than it is to see what we have done.

Often, if we just stop and take stock, we have really accomplished quite a bit. In fact, we probably have been a wee bit close to the edge of working wonders.

Unfortunately, we miss the opportunity to marvel at our wonders because we have so much set up still to do that what we have done pales into insignificance in relation to what is (always!) yet to be done. Ugly is in the eye of the beholder.

TODAY is awareness day for what I *have* accomplished. Celebrations may be in order.

ᏎᏇ January 11

CHANGE/SECURITY

People change and forget to tell each other.
—Lillian Hellman

How tenaciously we cling to the illusion that we will get our lives in order and they will stay that way! How resistant we are to the normal process of change! We often feel personally attacked if someone near and dear to us changes without clearing those changes with us first. We have somehow come to believe that security and stasis are synonymous.

Change is the manifestation of our ability to grow and become. When it occurs in those nearest and dearest to us it is an opportunity for celebration. When it happens in ourselves, it allows us to share ourselves on a new level. When we try to protect others from the awareness of our changes, we are being dishonest. No one can care for who we are unless they *know* who we are.

THE ONLY constant is change.

❧ January 12

CHOICES

> *To gain that which is worth having, it may be*
> *necessary to lose everything else.*
> —Bernadette Devlin

Sometimes we become very dramatic with our lives and believe that if we are to get what we want, we have to sacrifice everything that is near and dear to us. The "excellence" books tell us that if we want to get to the top, we have to be willing to sacrifice spouse, children (having children), hobbies, and anything in our lives that is not related to work in order to "make it." Some of us have tried to do that. We have become workaholics and in that process lost ourselves. Without ourselves, we ultimately have little or nothing to offer. We have tried to shut out our need for closeness, friendship, rest, and leisure, believing in the rightness and nobility of our decision.

We have sacrificed for our work. We have fulfilled the romantic dream of giving our all. We have excelled.

IT IS NEVER too late to re-examine our choices. Re-examination is wise. We always have choices.

❧ January 13

COMPASSION/RUTHLESSNESS

*And beyond even self-doubt no writer can justify
ruthlessness for the sake of his work, because being
human to the fullest possible extent is what his work
demands of him.*

—May Sarton

What May Sarton has written is not just true for
a writer. No one can justify ruthlessness!

We are told that one has to be ruthless to make
it in the world of business. As women, we have
believed that we have to be even more ruthless than
men just because we are women. Many of us have
achieved success, but at what price? We don't like
who we see in the mirror.

One of the characteristics of the addictive process is that we progressively lose touch with our
own morality and our own spirituality. We progressively lose touch with our humanness. Recovery affords us the possibility of reconnecting with our
compassionate self.

MY ABILITY to be compassionate and experience the beauty of my humanness has not left
me. It was only buried under layers of addictive
garbage.

৽ January 14

BELIEF

*Why indeed must "God" be a noun? Why not a verb
. . . the most active and dynamic of all?*
—Mary Daly

Some of us have difficulty with the concept of
God because we have seen God evolve into something or someone who is static, a mega-controller,
and frankly someone who is not that nice to be
around. Traditionally, we have tried to make God
static so we would feel safe. That is our problem, not
God's.

What if we see God as a process—the process of
the universe? What if we begin to understand that
we are part of the process of the universe? What if
we realize that it is only when we live who we are
that we have the option of being one with that process? Trying to be someone else, who we *think* we
should be, or who *others* think we should be ruptures
our oneness with that process.

IF GOD is a process and I am a process, we have
something in common with which to begin.

ॐ January 15

GIFTS

Make good use of bad rubbish.
                                    —Elizabeth Beresford

It's really up to us what we do with our lives. We may have been battered, beaten, molested, incested, spoiled, or over-indulged. All of us have feelings and memories we need to work through. None of us had perfect families. In fact, dysfunctional families are the norm for the society.

The question for us is how have our experiences affected us and what do we need to do to learn from our experiences, to work through those lessons, integrate them into our being, turn them over, and move on?

When we get stuck in our blame, anger, hurt, and denial, we are the ones who suffer. It is up to us to "make good use of bad rubbish."

IF MY LIFE resembles a garbage dump, it is up to me to sort it through, turn over the soil, and plant flowers to make use of all the natural fertilizer.

FREEDOM

Learning moment by moment to be free in our minds and hearts, we make freedom possible for everyone the world over.

—Sonia Johnson

Freedom begins within. Addictions are the antithesis of freedom. By definition, addictions are anything that have control of our lives and are progressive and fatal. Being addicted to doing too much is no different from being addicted to alcohol or drugs. We are hooked, and we can die from these workaholic behaviors.

Freedom from addictions is an important first step toward personal freedom. In Twelve-Step circles we often hear that "These addictive diseases are the only fatal diseases for which recovery is guaranteed if we do our work." When we are addicted, we have lost our minds and hearts to the disease. As we start to work a recovery program, we begin to have a new appreciation of the word *freedom.*

MY RECOVERY work affects others, whether I know it or not. Freedom *is* a possible dream.

ও January 17

THINKING

To achieve, you need thought. . . . You have to know what you are doing and that's real power.
—Ayn Rand

Thinking sometimes takes a bum rap in some circles, and it is over-exaggerated in others! As a society, we have become so lopsided in rational, logical, and linear thinking that many of us have become confused about the process of thinking. We are very dualistic in our thinking about thinking.

We have come to believe that we must either be cold, calculating, logical, rational women, or we must throw all thinking out the window and carry the load for all the feeling, intuitive aspects of our society. Either of these solutions results in a languishing lopsidedness that leaves us wanting.

There is nothing wrong with thinking. It's the *way* we do it. Often, when we lead with our logical, rational minds, we have not allowed them to be informed by our being and our other thought processes of intuition, attention, and awareness. It is in the synergy among all these aspects of our mind that true thinking begins.

MY BRAIN is a great gift. Using all of it increases its value.

ॐ January 18

LIVING IN THE MOMENT

Love the moment, and the energy of that moment will spread beyond all boundaries.

—Corita Kent

We women who do too much have a terrible time loving the moment. We are always making lists and eyeing the tasks that are just around the corner when we need to be busy working on the task at hand. Hence, rarely does anything get our full, undivided attention. Because of this subtle distractibility and lack of presence, we miss a lot.

When we really can be in the moment, the very process of being in the moment radiates into the crevices of our life and begins to dust out the cobwebby corners.

PRESENCE is such a gift ... to myself and others.

CONTROL

> *People who try to boss themselves always want (however kindly) to boss other people. They always think they know best and are so stern and resolute about it they are not very open to new and better ideas.*
> —Brenda Ueland

We workaholics are difficult to be around. We are hard to work with and hard to work for. Our core form of functioning is control. We often do not know the difference between getting the job done and getting the job done well. Our belief is that if we can just control *everything,* we are doing our job and doing it right. Our illusion of control is killing us. We find ourselves exhausted and burned out.

Unfortunately, control is costly. In trying to realize this illusion of control, we are destructive to ourselves and others. Also, in trying to maintain this illusionary control, we find our field of vision becomes more and more constricted (as do our blood vessels!) and we are no longer open to new and better ideas. In fact we are not open to any ideas at all.

WHEN, in my controlling behavior, I do unto others as I do unto myself, we all lose.

❧ January 20

CONTROL

She was a "what if" personality and because of that she never really happened.
—Anne Wilson Schaef

We addicts are "if" people. We use our "iffing" to try to control our past, our present, and our future.

If only we had been more assertive, we would have made the promotion. *If only* we had been more intelligent, we would have done a better job.

Our "as iffing" tries to cope with the present. We act *as if* we know what we are doing. We act *as if* we are calm and relaxed. After all, we have developed *some* skills!

Yet it is our "what iffing" that really keeps us paralyzed and feeds our illusion that we are in control. We try to imagine every possible exigency and prepare for it before it happens. If I just cover every base, I will never be caught wanting. My "iffing" has resulted in my never being present to my life.

WHEN I QUIT "iffing," I may just start living.

❧ January 21

FEAR/DISHONESTY/DENIAL/CONTROL
STEPS ONE, TWO, AND THREE

*The liar in her terror wants to fill up the void with
anything. Her lies are a denial of her fear: a way of
maintaining control.*

—Adrienne Rich

Our fear is like the first tile in a string of domi-
noes. Our denial of fear causes us to lie, to cheat, and
to become people we don't even respect in order to
maintain our illusion of control. We lie because we
are fearful, and we are fearful because we lie. It is
a circular process and we feel stuck in the middle of
these raging feelings.

What a relief it is to admit our fears! What a
relief it is to admit that we are powerless over our
fears and they are making our life unmanageable!
This opens the door to admit that if we return to our
inner process, our power greater than ourselves, we
can feel sane again.

ALL OF US are afraid sometimes, that's human.
When our life is ruled by fear, that's addiction.

❧ January 22

OBSTACLES

In the upper echelons of the corporate world, it helps to be good-looking . . . but only if you're a man. If you're a woman, attractiveness can be a handicap.
—Diane Crenshaw

Sometimes it's difficult to accept that the obstacles in our life are there for a purpose and that we have something to learn from them. Some of the obstacles seem so unfair . . . and they are! There still are many double standards operative in the world of business (and elsewhere!) What works for men often doesn't work for women in the same situation. And it isn't fair . . . true . . . and we resent it . . . right . . . as well we should. And while we are trying to change the situation, it is important to see what we have to learn from these unfair obstacles and move on. We don't like them, and it is up to us what we do with them.

OBSTACLES often are not personal attacks; they are muscle builders.

HONESTY

When a woman tells the truth she is creating the possibility for more truth around her.
—Adrienne Rich

Honesty is contagious, just like dishonesty is contagious. We need more honesty in the world.

Many of us have prided ourselves in being honest. We have always tried to be honest and have believed that we were. It has been frightening when we have been told that we are "too honest," or when we have been told that we will not be able to get ahead if we insist on being so "brutally honest." Slowly we have learned to "compromise." We have learned to say what is expected of us and not to offend. We have lost touch with the awareness that we are being dishonest when we go ahead and agree to do something that we really do not feel right about doing. We have come not to expect honesty from ourselves or from those around us. We are even surprised when we encounter it.

IF WE WANT to heal, we have to start getting honest with ourselves and others. Creating the possibility for more truth is up to each of us.

Intimacy

> . . . *just a tender sense of my own inner process, that holds something of my connection with the divine.*
> —Shelley

Intimacy, like charity, begins at home. If we cannot be intimate with ourselves, we have no one to bring to intimacy with another person.

Intimacy with ourselves takes time. We need time for rest, time for walks, time for quiet, and time to tune in to ourselves. We cannot completely fill up our lives with activities and become intimate with ourselves. Nor can we just sit quietly indefinitely and become intimate with ourselves. We have to have the time and energy to *be* our lives and to *do* our lives in order to establish an intimate relationship with ourselves.

Surprisingly, as we become intimate with ourselves, we discover our connection with others and with the divine. Neither is possible without intimacy with ourselves.

INTIMACY . . . In/to/me/see. It won't hurt to try it.

LETTING GO

> *When I am all hassled about something, I always stop
> and ask myself what difference it will make in the
> evolution of the human species in the next ten million
> years, and that question always helps me to get back
> my perspective.*

—Anne Wilson Schaef

"Little things mean a lot," especially when we
focus all our attention on them, obsess and ruminate
about them, and can't let them go. Sometimes, when
we are in our disease, we just keep turning disturb-
ing thoughts over and over in our minds, believing
that we will surely figure out some solutions if we
just think about them long enough and check out
every angle.

When we engage in this behavior, it is a sure
sign that we are in the addictive process and thinking ourselves to death. I have always found that
when I am in my addictive process, I have lost perspective. I suddenly become the center of the universe, and my problems are the only ones in the
universe.

It always helps me to step back and realize that
whatever problem I am having is probably not of
universal proportions. This perspective helps me to
see that I am powerless over my crazy thinking, and
that it is making my life insane. At this point I can
get back in touch with my knowing that a power
greater than myself can restore me to sanity, and I
can turn this problem over to this greater power.

ONE of the things we lose in the addictive disease process is perspective.

January 26

FINANCIAL SECURITY

Humans must breathe, but corporations must make money.

—Alice Embee

It's okay to make money. It's even okay for corporations to make money. Unfortunately, money addiction is so rampant in this society that we have lost all perspective on making money. We have become addicted to the *process* of making money. The money itself has become irrelevant. It is the process of accumulation that has us hooked. No matter how much we have, it is never enough. The same is true at a corporate level. More is never enough. We have developed a frantic obsession around accumulation of money. We gather, we spend, and we hoard. We have forgotten that money is not real. It is symbolic. It is legal tender. It is a form of exchange. It has become so real for us that it is more real than our health, our relationships, or our lives. Money addiction and workaholism often go hand in hand.

FINANCIAL SECURITY is a static concept that is illusionary and expands exponentially as we reach our former static goal.

FORGIVENESS

It is very easy to forgive others their mistakes. It takes more gut and gumption to forgive them for having witnessed your own.

—Jessamyn West

How we hate to be seen as our most naked selves! We feel noble when we forgive others their awful mistakes, yet we become paralyzed with guilt and shame when we realize that they have caught us in our worst moments. It is so tempting to try to find something wrong with them and take the focus off what we have done. The best defense is a good offense, we have been told. How hard it is to let ourselves claim and own our mistakes! Yet, also how freeing.

We have the possibility of not only forgiving those who have witnessed our mistakes but also of embracing them as a gift to help keep us honest.

SOMETIMES my gifts are so well-wrapped I have difficulty recognizing them as such. As I unwrap myself, I can unwrap each present.

❧ January 28

EXPENDABLE/CONTROL/FEAR

When I was sixteen, my mother told me that I was expendable and if I didn't work hard, companies could just get rid of me. I work sixty to seventy hours a week, never take time off, and my husband and I haven't had a vacation in twelve years. I'm a workaholic, and I love it.

—Anonymous Woman

Whew! Need I say more? This woman has bought the whole package.

Like her, many of us believe that we can control what we perceive as our expendability by making ourselves indispensable. What a sophisticated illusion of control! Obsessive working is different from a passion for our work.

Usually people who are truly passionate about their work are also passionate about their play and their time for themselves. Workaholics are not. We work out of fear and try to convince ourselves that we love it. Fear and self-abuse go together.

AM I expendable to *me?* That's the question.

ಕ್ಕ January 29

POWERLESSNESS
STEP ONE

> *In the face of an obstacle which is impossible to overcome, stubbornness is stupid.*
> —Simone de Beauvoir

Some of us do not like to hear this, but there are some things in our lives over which we are powerless. In fact, when it comes right down to it, there are few aspects of our lives that we can really *control!*

Certainly the areas of our lives over which we are truly the most powerless are our own addictive, compulsive working, rushing, busyness habits. In fact, that is one of the definitions of addiction. An addiction is anything that controls our lives, over which we are powerless, and which is making our lives unmanageable. Our inability to stop killing ourselves with doing too much certainly fits into this category.

KNOWING when to quit may be my greatest victory.

ठ~ January 30

Awareness of Self

Human beings are an untidy lot. They'd lose their arms and legs if they weren't joined on right.
—Elizabeth Beresford

Our addictive functioning requires of us that we tune out our bodies. In fact, often the purpose of our addictions is to put us out of touch with what we are feeling, what we are thinking, our awarenesses, and our intuition. Addictive working or rushing around leaves little time or energy to notice what our bodies are telling us about our feelings and our health.

We have come to think of our bodies as nonexistent and often experience little below our necks. Some of us even spend most of our time "out of our bodies." Instead of seeing our bodies as our allies and sources of important information, we have come to see them as vehicles for the practice of our addiction, and we use them as objects. We have forgotten the way our bodies move and the way they feel moving.

I BETTER pay attention to the messages from my body. If I don't, it will get my attention, perhaps through extreme and painful measures.

❧ January 31st

GIVING OURSELVES AWAY

Somebody almost walked off wid alla my stuff.
                              —Ntozake Shange

As women, we are often so generous, especially with ourselves, that we give little pieces of ourselves away, to almost anyone who asks. At the time, we hardly notice. Sometimes the pieces we give away are so minuscule that they really seem unimportant . . . a favor here . . . letting something go by that we know is wrong there . . . swallowing the anger from an injustice done to us somewhere else. We can handle each one individually, and we are unaware of the cumulative affect of years of giving away little bits and pieces of ourselves.

We sit up and scream, *"Somebody almost walked off wid alla my stuff!!!"* We have allowed ourselves to be almost devoured by those around us.

GIVING MYSELF AWAY and being stingy are not my only options. I can share myself. Yet to share myself I have to *have* a self to share.

❧ February 1

FREEDOM

How is my own life-work serving to end these tyrannies, the corrosions of sacred possibility?
—June Jordan

Sometimes, when we stop and reflect, we need to believe that the work we are doing has a meaning beyond the tedium of the everyday. In fact, if we cannot see some larger connection in what we are doing, we often experience a feeling of loss or emptiness.

We know, somewhere deep inside us, that even if *what* we are doing doesn't exactly have a great cosmic meaning, the *way* we go about it and the interactions we have with others around our work can give it meaning beyond itself. Regardless of what we do, we do have an opportunity to make it sacred work.

I ALWAYS have the freedom for a sacred possibility.

৯ February 2

HAPPINESS

It is not easy to find happiness in ourselves, and it is not possible to find it elsewhere.
—Agnes Repplier

We are the wellspring of our own happiness. Our happiness resides within us. No one else and nothing else can give it to us. We may try to find all kinds of things outside ourselves to fill us up and make us happy, but they are all short-lived. We think success, recognition, respect, money, and prestige will do it for us. They're nice for a while, *and* the feeling lingers that something is missing. This does not mean that a happy person cannot have all these accouterments of success—she can. Happiness, however, is not a *result* of these symbols of success.

Happiness is ethereal. It only dwells within, and when we seek it, it becomes even more elusive.

I HAVE the opportunity to open myself to the happiness that is mine today and not try to fill myself with happiness substitutes.

ᚠ February 3

ALONE TIME

And when is there time to remember, to sift, to weigh, to estimate, to total?

—Tillie Olsen

Such a little thing: finding time alone. We have often felt that if we took time for ourselves, we were taking it away from our children, our spouses, or our work and therefore it must be a perversion.

So many little moments during the day are so precious to us. Those few moments after we have sent everyone else off for the day and we can breathe . . . those times alone in the car or on the bus or subway when no one around knows us or can intrude . . . those sighing times in the bathroom when nobody is there . . . even those stolen moments alone while doing the dishes are precious to us.

IT'S ALL RIGHT. Moments alone and our need for them are not a perversion, they are a life-giving force.

৪ February 4

GIFTS

Problems are messages.

—Shakti Gawain

I always believe that the intensity of the whack alongside the head that life has to give us in order to get a lesson through to us is directly proportionate to the height and breadth of our stubbornness and illusion of control.

Problems give us the opportunity to learn something. If we don't get the learning the first time around, we get another chance, and another, and another. If we miss the learning completely the first time, the next whack will be a little harder, and then the next time even harder. We get many opportunities to learn the lessons we need to learn in this life.

Obstacles are gifts for learning. We never really know what we have learned until we have learned it. Then we are ready for the next learning.

I HAVE the opportunity for many gifts today. I hope I see them.

❧ February 5

EXHAUSTION

Whatever women do they must do twice as well as men to be thought half as good. Luckily, this is not difficult.
—Charlotte Whitton

Although some of us hate to admit it, it is probably true that we "have to do things twice as well as men to be thought half as good." And it is probably also true that we can produce at a level that boggles the mind.

What we tend to ignore is the cost. Working as hard as we do and as long as we do is exhausting. Sometimes we dread becoming aware of how tired we are. Sometimes it almost seems as if the marrow in our bones aches.

Women have a tremendous fear of feeling our tiredness. We are afraid that if we let ourselves feel it, we will never get up again.

MY TIREDNESS is mine. I have earned it.

❧ February 6

BELIEF
STEP ELEVEN

Neither reproaches nor encouragements are able to revive a faith that is waning.

—Nathalie Sarraute

Faith, in the last analysis, is a personal process. One of the problems that we as women face in accessing our spiritual self is all the things we have been told that we *should* believe. We have tried to swallow beliefs from outside. Rarely have we taken the time and effort to go inside and start with our own awareness and understanding of God or a power greater than ourselves and let ourselves trust our own knowing. In our busy lives, it is easier to reject than "wait with" our knowing. It is easier to move on than it is to "be with."

No one else can give us the answers about our spirituality. Reading and thinking cannot provide the solutions. Our spirituality is experiential, and it is intimately connected with who we are.

SOMETIMES beliefs have interfered with my connection with a power greater than myself. It is time to "wait with" my knowing.

DEADLINES/STRESS

Tension grew at home, and my work suffered as I committed to tighter and tighter deadlines.
—Ellen Sue Stern

One of the myths about workaholics is that they are very productive and they do good work. Myths are confusing because we often act as if they were true, even when we know that they are not.

Contrary to popular belief, we workaholics and rushaholics are often not very productive, and we often do sloppy, uncreative work. Our overextended deadlines become more important than the quality of our work. We suffer, our work suffers and our families suffer.

Another myth about workaholism is that it is just stress and burn-out and can be controlled with stress-reduction techniques. Every drunk has wanted to blame something else for her/his drinking and has fervently wanted to believe there was a way to control it, often with disastrous results. Workaholism is an addiction. It is a progressive, fatal disease that rules our lives. Fortunately, an addiction is the only progressive, fatal disease from which recovery is guaranteed if we do our work.

MAYBE it is time to check out a Twelve-Step meeting.

CLARITY

Well we start out in our lives as little children, full of light and the clearest vision.
—Brenda Ueland

When we begin our recovery from our addictive doing-too-much, we may have little or no experience of what clarity or sobriety from our addictive behavior is like. We have muddled around so long in these addictive thinking patterns and behaviors that they almost seem normal to us. The last time we experienced clarity may well have been when we were children.

After we have admitted our powerlessness over our addictive, compulsive work behavior, and after we have begun working the program for a while, we may suddenly have a moment of clarity. It surges through our consciousness like a meteor and scares us to death. Yet we sense that whatever we experienced is something of extraordinary importance. It is like a lullaby sung long ago. The words are faint, and the melody reverberates in our being.

CLARITY is not unfamiliar to us ... we have just forgotten what it is like.

❧ February 9

SUCCESS/GRATITUDE/
CLIMBING THE LADDER

*Though a tree grow ever so high, the falling leaves
return to the ground.*

—Malay proverb

Many of us work for and aspire to professional success. We have worked hard and long to get where we are, and we deserve the rewards of our position.

It is important that we periodically take time to take stock of *where* we are and *who* we are. Do we judge ourselves by our accomplishments? Does accomplishment mean worthiness in our book? How have we been able to get where we are, and do we feel good about the way we did it? Do we need to make amends to some people and express our gratitude to others?

It is important to recognize that our achievements not only speak well for us, they speak well for those persons and forces, seen, unseen, and unnoticed, that have been active in our lives.

SUCCESS offers me the opportunity to reflect on those who have given me much and to be grateful for their gifts.

❧ February 10

COMMUNICATION

Some people talk simply because they think sound is more manageable than silence.
—Margaret Halsey

Women who do too much need to keep busy. One of the ways we keep busy is talking even when we have nothing to say. It's not that we are so taken with the sound of our own voices. It is just that silence seems so overwhelming and murky.

Much of our lives has been spent filling up . . . overeating and filling up ourselves . . . over working and filling up our time . . . overtalking and filling up our shared moments of silence.

As we begin to recover, we find that we do not need our "filling-up fixes." We can be with ourselves in silence.

WHEN PEOPLE TALK on and on, they usually are not listening to themselves.

❧ February 11

ACCEPTANCE/CONFLICT/FEELINGS

*When Peter left me, the negative emotions that rose up
in me and exploded in me were just horrifying. But
God kept telling me that they were all part of me and I
couldn't try to hide them under the carpet because I
didn't like them.*

—Eileen Caddy

There are events in the passage of our lives that
elicit feelings we never knew were there and of
which we believed *we* were completely incapable. A
spouse wants a divorce or has an affair. A boss
passes us over for someone younger, prettier (we
believe), and less-qualified (we know for certain),
and we find that the witches of Endor or the dragons
of old have nothing on us. We could belch fire and
melt diamonds with our breath.

Right, good, so what? It is normal to have feelings like this. It is not healthy to dump them on
others or to hold onto them. They will rot inside us.

WHEN I FEEL these feelings, I have another opportunity to learn something new about myself.
Thank you . . . I think.

❧ February 12

GOALS/COMPETITION

What you have become is the price you paid to get what you used to want.
—Mignon McLaughlin

Was it worth it? Is it worth it? Can we look in the mirror and say to the person we see, "You are someone I trust and really admire"?

We must remember that each step along the road of life is like taking a walk. It gets you somewhere, and steps often leave footprints.

We cannot say to ourselves, "Well, what I am doing is expedient now, so I will go ahead and do it this way. I will deal with the consequences later," and not *have* consequences later. The denials of our life are interrelated.

WHAT I DO becomes who I am. I am working with precious elements here.

Personal Morality

I cannot and will not cut my conscience to fit this year's fashions.

—Lillian Hellman

One of the effects of the addictive process is that we gradually lose contact with our personal morality and we slowly deteriorate as a moral person. It is easy to see how the alcoholic or drug addict is progressively willing to lie, cheat, steal, and even kill or hurt the one she loves in order to get her fix. But women who do too much are not so different. We have moral slippage too. We will withhold information, lie, mislead, or undercut others to get ahead. We are willing to compromise our standards and our morality to get to the top, to "fit this year's fashions." When we compromise our personal morality, we have sold our souls and we are losing the "us which is us."

Part of recovery is to recognize that our personal morality is one of our most precious assets and too important to treat lightly.

ɪ ᴠᴀʟᴜᴇ myself enough to realize that my personal morality is a beacon that demands to be followed.

❧ February 14

EXPECTATIONS

Nobody objects to a woman being a good writer or sculptor or geneticist if at the same time she manages to be a good wife, good mother, good-looking, good-tempered, well-groomed and unaggressive.
—Leslie M. McIntyre

Right! So what's the problem? It's not easy to be well-groomed when we have toddlers running around . . . but we try. It's not easy to be good-tempered and unaggressive when we have deadlines at work and at home . . . but we try. It is not easy to produce children and be svelte and good-looking . . . but we try.

There is probably no group of people in this society who try harder than women to meet the expectations of others. As a result, we are always looking outside for validation, and no matter how much we get, it isn't enough. In always trying to be what others think we should be, we have lost ourselves and end up having little to bring to any relationship or task.

EXPECTATIONS are like girdles. We probably should have discarded them years ago.

❧ February 15

FEELING CRAZY

You can't start worrying about what's going to happen. You get spastic enough worrying about what's happening now.

—Lauren Bacall

Why is it that *we* always seem to be the ones that need the help. We do feel crazy at times, and feelings of being overwhelmed are not unfamiliar. And yet, why does the label craziness (if someone has to be crazy!) always rest on us?

Sometimes, it's a relief to admit that we feel crazy. We do need someone to talk with when we feel isolated. Others appear to cope all right. Why can't we? At least, talking with someone or going to a group with other women helps us recognize that we are not alone in these feelings. Seeking out help and support can be a real turning point. Groups for workaholics are, after all, free.

PERHAPS my inability to cope with an insane situation the way I always used to is a sign of my movement toward health.

✺ February 16

BECOMING/ILLUSIONS

It's our illusions about our illusions that hang us up.
—Anne Wilson Schaef

Our addictions lead us into a life of illusion. They feed our illusion of control, our illusion of perfection, and our dishonesty. Our addictive behavior allows us to deny reality and justify not living our life. We slip along in a mist of illusion, whether they be illusions of romance, illusions of power, or illusions of success—and somehow we miss life.

One of the significant qualities of an adult is being able to separate ourselves from illusion and to nourish ourselves with reality, rather than feed on illusion. Contrary to popular opinion this does not mean that we have to live dull and staid lives. It means we have to *live* our lives.

WHOOPEE! Let's try reality for a change.

AWARENESS OF
PROCESS/CONTROL/CREATIVITY

Living in process is being open to insight and encounter.
Creativity is becoming intensively absorbed in the
process and giving it form.

—Susan Smith

When we choose to live our lives in a process way, we choose to be open to all that life has to offer. Our illusion of control has often filtered out new insights and encounters. We have been so focused upon our goals and the way things *have* to happen, that we have missed the succulent serendipity of chance awarenesses. We have been so afraid of losing our illusion of control that we have missed some of the richest encounters that life was offering us.

When we can participate fully in the process of our lives, we discover new forms of our creative self. Creativity has many avenues. Just living our lives can cultivate our conscious creativity.

CAN IT BE? Is just living my life enough?

❧ February 18

FRANTIC

We have come to a place where frantic and panic seem integral to being a woman, especially a professional woman.

—Anne Wilson Schaef

Women who do too much tend to get frantic over almost anything. Where *did* we park that rental car at the airport and what in the world did it look like anyway? We were *sure* that we parked our own car right in front of the drugstore at the shopping mall. Or was that last week?

Where did we put that bill that simply must be paid today? There must be a way to get the kids off in the morning that could be less frantic. We are *sure* an organized mother could do better.

Where is that pen? Where is that pan? Where are those pants? Probably right where we left them. It is usually our "frantic" that clouds our vision.

FRANTIC AND PANIC are old familiar friends. Maybe it is time for them to move out from our house.

ॐ February 19

JUGGLING PROJECTS

We are traditionally rather proud of ourselves for having slipped creative work in there between the domestic chores and obligations. I'm not sure we deserve such big A-pluses for all that.

—Toni Morrison

Women who work outside the house aren't the only women who are obsessed with work. Women who are home full-time rarely have time for themselves and their creative projects. After all, children are twenty-four hours a day and the house is twenty-four hours a day. There is always something to do.

Our greatest skill is not perhaps in getting things done, it may be in juggling projects so it looks like we are getting things done, so that we feel better. Watch out! Juggling projects is one of the symptoms of the workaholic. Instead of paring down the projects to those that can reasonably be done, the workaholic tries to do it all.

JUGGLERS aren't paid very well, and sometimes they get hit on the head with balls they have in the air.

AMENDS

Make it a rule of life never to regret and never look back. Regret is an appalling waste of energy; you can't build on it; it is good only for wallowing in.
—Katherine Mansfield

Looking back and regretting are very different from taking stock, making amends, and moving on. When we look back and regret, we are indulging in the self-centered activity of beating ourselves over the mistakes in our past.

All of us have made mistakes. When we have operated out of the craziness of this addictive disease process, we have done much harm to ourselves and others. We have neglected ourselves. We have neglected those we love. That is the nature of an addiction. Now we can admit our wrongs, make amends to those we have wronged (including amends to ourselves when we have not been caring for ourselves), and move on.

We cannot build on shame, guilt, or regret. We, indeed, can only wallow in them.

OWNING and making amends for my mistakes affords me the opportunity to build on my past and integrate it. I can start doing this anytime . . . maybe even today.

❧ February 21

Values

> *When women take on a career, they don't discard their female values, but* add them *onto the traditional male values of work achievement and career success. As they struggle to fill the demands of both roles, women can't understand why men don't share this dual value system.*
> —Susan Sturdinent and Gail Donoff

One of the often most painful learnings for women who work outside the home is that the same skills that work in business just do not work in our homes and in our personal relationships. Luckily, we have the advantage of knowing a value system that does contribute to living, and we have only to learn what works at work.

Unfortunately, in the process of learning a career value system, we are encouraged to denigrate our values and sometimes we succumb to this pressure. Our values are not wrong. They are different. And the workplace would be richer with them.

TRUSTING my value system can be a major contribution to my work.

❧ February 22

SOLITUDE

*"Thrice welcome, friendly Solitude, O let no busy foot
intrude, Nor listening ear be nigh!"*
—from *Ode to Solitude* by Hester Chapone

Solitude is such a blessing! Everyone needs time
alone. Often we are fearful of time alone, because
there is no one for us to encounter but ourselves.
How comforting it is to go to ourselves! How much
like returning home to an old friend or lover after
having been away too long visiting places that felt
foreign and unfamiliar.

Our solitude is one of the pleasures that only we
can arrange. It is up to us to see that we regenerate
through our time with ourselves. We have the right,
and we have the power. If we do not model respect
for our own need for solitude, our children will
never learn that they deserve their time alone.

LET ME REMEMBER that I have the right to create
a space of solitude for myself, if only to enjoy the
soothing sound of running water in my own bath-
tub.

HONESTY

Lying is done with words and also with silence.
—Adrienne Rich

As we begin to heal, we have a new appreciation of Jesus' words, "You shall know the truth and the truth shall make you free." Part of the purpose of our addictive behavior is to put us out of touch with ourselves, and when we are out of touch with ourselves, we cannot possibly be honest with anyone. We have to know what we think and feel to be honest with others. In our early recovery, we slowly begin to realize how far we have wandered from ourselves . . . a long way, indeed!

We have been fearful of speaking our truth honestly. We have been afraid of losing our jobs, losing our friends, and losing everything we have. Yet, as we become more honest, we begin to untie the tangled knot of dishonesty, self-centeredness, control, and confusion. We see how our dishonesty has led to our confusion and even when it is difficult, we find ourselves sighing in the refreshing breeze of honesty.

I AM SLOWLY relearning about my ability to be honest. I am astounded with how far I had ranged from myself.

Choices/Responsibility

We're swallowed up only when we are willing for it to happen.

—Nathalie Sarraute

When we talk about taking responsibility for our lives, we must clarify what we mean by responsibility. The addictive meaning of the word responsibility means accountability and blame. When women accept that meaning, they cannot bear to take responsibility for their lives or to see other women do so, because, they assume, taking responsibility means taking the *blame* for where they are and who they are. Unfortunately, this attitude puts us in the position of being a victim and robbing us of our power.

It is only when we accept that we do have choices, and we exercise those choices, that we can reclaim our lives. Inherent in this reclaiming process is owning the choices we have made (all of them!) and moving on. Thus we are not blaming ourselves for our lives; we are claiming them and owning them so we can take our next steps.

I HAVE MADE some bad choices, I have made some so-so choices and I have made some good choices. The most important aspect of them is that they are mine—all of them.

Pᴀɪɴ

Iron, left in the rain
And fog and dew,
With rust is covered.—Pain
Rusts into beauty too.

—Mary Carolyn Davies

Our pain is ours. Some of it we have earned, the rest not, and it is still ours. When we fight our pain, we fight the experience of our humanness, and we lose ourselves in the process. A life without pain is a life of nonliving. Our pain lets us know and come to understand the full meaning of being human. If we fight the normal experience of our pain, we lose the possibility of experiencing the process of its rusting "into beauty too."

We don't need to seek pain, but when it is inevitably there, we have the possibility of something new entering our lives.

ᴍʏ ᴘᴀɪɴ is a possibility. It is not a liability or a punishment.

❧ February 26

NURTURING ONESELF

Just the knowledge that a good book is awaiting one at the end of a long day makes that day happier.
—Kathleen Norris

The art of nurturing oneself is not something that is taught in most high schools or even in a good MBA (Master of Business Administration) course. In fact, the art of nurturing oneself is rarely taught in families either.

Yet, in this high-tech, high-information society, learning how to nurture oneself is absolutely essential for survival. Some good workaholics have found that if they do a cursory job of nurturing themselves, they can work even harder. Unfortunately, that isn't nurturing oneself, that's protecting one's supply.

Nurturing oneself is allowing ourselves to stop, and in that stopping to allow ourselves to know what would be nurturing for us in that time and space, and doing it.

WHAT IS NURTURING at one point in our lives may not be nurturing at another. In order to nurture myself, I have to know myself each moment.

PERFECTIONISM

This is the age of perfectionism, kid.
Everybody try their emotional and mental and
physical damndest.
Strive, strive. Correct all defects.

—Judith Guest

Perfectionism is one of the characteristics of addiction. Perfectionism is setting up an abstract, external ideal of what we should be or should be able to do that has little or no relationship to who we are or what we need to do and then trying to mold ourselves into that ideal.

In trying to be the abstract perfect, we batter, judge, and distort ourselves. No matter what we do or how we try to achieve, it is never enough. We are never enough. Trying too hard and never trying at all are two sides of the coin of perfection. Unfortunately, it is a coin that never pays off.

PERFECTIONISM is self-abuse of the highest order.

LAUGHTER

Laughter can be more satisfying than honor; more precious than money; more heart-cleansing than prayer.
—Harriet Rochlin

How long has it been since you have had a good belly-laugh? Good laughter seems to be a treasure that is in short supply of late.

Most of us are distrustful and embarrassed by our laughter. As children we were constantly told to suppress it. Often it seems almost lost to us. We are afraid to laugh alone, and we are embarrassed to laugh with others. What a state!

Laughter is one of the gifts of being human. We can't force it, but we can sure stop suppressing it in ourselves and in our children.

LAUGHTER is like the human body wagging its tail.

ॐ February 29

Impression Management

And yet, all these years I'd been terrified I would be stoned to death if people saw through the facade.
——Sara Davidson

How much time and energy we spend in impression management! We firmly believe that if we just dress right others (especially men) will think we are professional, intelligent, competent, and in control. We believe that if we just dress right others (usually men) will think we are attractive, sexy, desirable, and worth knowing. We think that if we are just caring, understanding, and constant enough someone will want to be with us.

We have such terror that someone will see through our facade and discover (our greatest fear!) that no one is there. We believe that if people really know who we are, they would have no interest in us. We believe that it is our impression management that keeps us safe.

OF COURSE, if someone falls in love with my impression, they aren't loving me, they're only loving my image.

৯ **March 1**

IN TOUCH WITH PROCESS
GREATER POWER

*We both of us secretly believed in an external power
that one could tap, if one were in tune with events.*
—Robyn Davidson

Living in process is living *our* process and being
one with the process of the universe. Our addictive
disease removes us from our connection with the
living process. Our disease alienates us from our
spirituality and our faith and tells us we aren't safe,
we have to control, and we must try to assure security by making ourselves, our lives, and even the
universe static.

We put so much effort into trying to make our
universe static that we have not developed the capacity to be in tune with events. As we learn to tune
in and participate, we find that living our process is
so much easier than trying to make the universe
static.

WHEN I am in touch with my process, I am in
touch with the process of the universe.

ૐ March 2

FEELING CRAZY

Feeling crazy may be a mark of sanity in my situation.
—Anne Wilson Schaef

Several years ago, after I had written and published *Women's Reality,* I visited an old friend in New York City. After talking a while, she said, "You've changed." (She's an analyst and she always notices things!) "Really," I said, "How?" (I secretly hoped that I had changed. After all, we had not seen each other for several years, and if I hadn't changed, I was in deep trouble!) "You are no longer afraid of being crazy," she observed. "Was I afraid I was crazy?" I asked, somewhat startled. "Yes," she said quietly. "Well, after writing *Women's Reality,* I realize that I have constantly been told that I am crazy by my society when I put forth my clearest, sanest, most precious perceptions. Now I accept that I am 'crazy' in the eyes of an addictive society, and I feel very 'sane' with my 'craziness.'"

WATCH OUT for who is defining "crazy."

❧ March 3

LETTING GO/RESENTMENTS

Wanna fly, you got to give up the shit that weighs you down.

— Toni Morrison

Our old "shit" is so precious to us. We tenderly harbor our old resentments and periodically throw them pieces of fresh flesh to keep them alive. We nurture our anger. We don't do anything to work it through or let it go, we just hang on and nurture it. And we wonder why we feel so stuck and held back in our lives.

When we hold onto old shit, it weighs us down. It is as if our feet are stuck in fresh tar.

There comes a time that we can see that it doesn't really matter what someone has done to us, our holding onto it is hurting *us* not them, and if we want to heal, we had best take our old shit and fertilize the flowers.

THE ONLY WAY to grow is to let go.

FEELINGS/FREEDOM

The white fathers told us, "I think therefore I am,"
and the Black mother within each of us—the
poet—whispers in our dreams, I feel, therefore I can be
free.

—Audre Lorde

We have been trained to shut off and freeze our feelings. We have been told that feelings are weak and irrational and if we want to be a success in this world, we must be able to control our feelings. The models for success are persons who never have any visible feelings.

Yet when we do this, we find that we are making ourselves more vulnerable, not less. When we push feelings down, we never know when or how they will erupt, and we can rest assured that it will be with greater intensity than if we had acknowledged the original "feeling moment."

Also, feelings are our natural, built-in alarm and information system. It is our feelings not our minds that warn us of danger, that tell us that someone is lying to us, and that tell us of subtle nuances that allow us to discern differences and make decisions. Without this internal information system we can never truly be free.

CELEBRATING my ability to feel is a way to be fully free.

❧ March 5

LONELINESS

Loneliness and the feeling of being unwanted is the most terrible poverty.

—Mother Teresa

The feeling of loneliness is not uncommon to women who do too much. We are constantly busy and surrounded by people and still we feel lonely. In fact, it is quite possible that one of the reasons that we keep so busy is that we are trying to avoid our feelings of loneliness and are, simultaneously, frightened by intimacy.

We believe if we just rush around enough, keep busy enough, and surround ourselves with enough important and interesting people, our loneliness will disappear. Unfortunately, none of these things works. Indeed, as Fiona Macleod says, "My heart is a lonely hunter that hunts on a lonely hill." Our hearts are seeking something, and the many things we have tried don't seem to be it. When we have lost the connection with our spiritual beings, we will be lonely no matter how much we have.

LONELINESS is not outside, it's inside.

ဆ► March 6

RELATIONSHIP

It has been wisely said that we cannot really love anybody at whom we never laugh.

—Agnes Repplier

How serious we are about everything—especially relationships! Often in our most intimate possibilities, we forget that our laughter at ourselves and at each other is one of the vehicles that our creator has given us for grounding ourselves in reality. And relationships that are not grounded in reality don't last.

We have to know others very well to be able to see their funny sides and to share in the frivolity of family functions. Let's face it, we human beings are a funny lot. No robot has ever been capable of the antics we can think up.

SHARING my laughter at myself and others is one of the ways threads of intimacy are spun.

SANITY

> *If, as someone has said, ". . . to be truly civilized, is to embrace disease . . ."*
> —Robyn Davidson

One of the by-products of living and working in crazy situations is that our tolerance for insanity increases exponentially. Our ability to discern what makes sense and what doesn't becomes impaired. When those around us continually exhibit bizarre behavior, we begin to question our sanity. Often we are not insane. The situation is insane, and we become progressively crazy as we try to adjust to it.

If "to be truly civilized, is to embrace disease," maybe we need to take a look at what we have defined as "civilized."

I AM NOT CRAZY—it's just that my situation seems to require a crazy person.

ᙄ March 8

SELF-AFFIRMATION

i found God in myself
& i loved her/i loved her fiercely.
— Ntozake Shange

What better place to find God than within ourselves! It is only when we really know ourselves and affirm ourselves for who we are that we become aware of the divinity that we share with all things. We are part of the hologram . . . we *are* the hologram. When we estrange ourselves from ourselves, we also then lose contact with that which is beyond ourselves.

To know "God" and to love her fiercely is to love ourselves. Loving this God is not loving the self-centered "God" of addiction. It is loving the God that is one, that is within us, and beyond us. It is loving God as we understand God.

CONTACT with God is so simple, and we make it so difficult.

ठ॰ March 9

Self-Esteem/Higher Power

Part of my satisfaction and exultation at each eruption was unmistakably feminist solidarity. You men think you're the only ones that can make a really nasty mess? You think you got all the firepower and God's on your side? You think you run things? Watch this, gents. Watch the Lady act like a woman.
—Ursula K. Le Guin

In some surprising way, Mount Saint Helens proved to be an important symbol for all of us. She reminded us of powers that are unseen and uncontrolled. She reminded us that there are forces on this planet and in this universe over which we have no control. We not only had no control over her eruptions, we could not even predict what she was going to do next, even though we applied our best scientific technology and kept her under constant surveillance. She demonstrated to our technocratic society that nature (often identified as female, especially when she's "bad") could not be controlled.

Although none of us wants destruction to occur or lives to be lost, we do need occasionally to be reminded that we are not in charge.

WHEN SHE SIMMERS silently, she is like a woman. When she blows her top off, she is like a woman. We have a range of responses.

❧ March 10

SERENITY

I am suddenly filled with that sense of peace and meaning which is, I suppose, what the pious have in mind when they talk about the practice of the presence of God.

—Valerie Taylor

When we are operating out of the addictive process, we know little of serenity. The word *serenity* is something that we understand in abstract and often not in practice. As we begin to take care of ourselves and recover from our compulsive doing, we begin to experience *moments* of serenity. The first time we experience serenity, it may zip through our consciousness like a meteor and scare us to death, because this feeling of serenity is so foreign to us. After a while, we begin to recognize these moments of serenity as very special, and we try to *make* them happen through rituals, practices, and techniques. We are now not focusing on controlling the world, we are trying to control our experience of serenity . . . back to the drawing board.

SERENITY is a gift. It is available to all of us. It *is* being one with the presence of God.

Straightening the House/Regret

My tidiness and my untidiness, are full of regret and remorse and complex feelings.
—Natalia Ginzburg

One of the greatest gifts that my mother gave me was that she was a *terrible* housekeeper. She wasn't terrible at everything, she just was terrible at keeping the house clean, which she firmly believed that she should be able to do.

She was a published poet, a great writer of short stories, a painter, a talented breaker and trainer of horses, an avid reader, a knowledgeable collector of antiques, a seeker into the psychic and the mysteries of the world, a good mother, a true, loyal, and devoted friend, incurably curious, an authority on American Indian lore, an intuitive searcher for precious rocks, fossils, and old gems, a defender of everyone's civil rights, and most of all a fascinating and extraordinary woman, but she couldn't keep the kitchen floor clean.

I was not at all damaged by the state of our house. I was saddened that she sometimes negatively judged who she was.

IF NOTHING ELSE, I hope I can remember what is important in this life.

ACCEPTANCE/MISTAKES/AMENDS

*Of all the idiots I have met in my life, and the Lord
knows that they have not been few or little, I think
that I have been the biggest.*

—Isak Dinesen

One of the ways that I can reclaim my power
and my person is to admit my mistakes. Sometimes
it is helpful to sit down and make a list of people
that I have wronged (including myself) and to make
amends to those with whom it is possible and where
it would not harm them to do so.

What a clean feeling it is to accept and own my
life and not beat myself up for the mistakes I have
made! How good it feels to let those I have harmed
know that I am aware of what I have done and that
I genuinely wish to own and change my behavior,
and do what I can to live clearer and cleaner in the
future.

ADMITTING our mistakes and making amends
are powerful tools for reclaiming ourselves.

❧ March 13

SPIRITUAL LIFE

We are not human beings trying to be spiritual. We are spiritual beings trying to be human.
—Jacquelyn Small

So often we try to compartmentalize our spirituality and therefore (hopefully) keep it under control. Our spirituality is much more all-encompassing than many of us care to admit. Everything we do flows from ourselves as spiritual beings. When we make decisions, our spirituality is there. When we interact at work, our spirituality is there. When we wash the dishes our spirituality is there. So often we have tried to remove our spiritual selves from our daily selves because we equated spirituality with saintliness, and we did not always want saintliness interfering with our daily lives. It is only when we recognize that all that we do is spiritual, that we can let our spirituality inform our humanity.

NOTHING I DO is too tiny or too tedious to be spiritual.

ANGER

Fury gathered until I was swollen with it.
—Vera Randal

How many of us know that fury that rises like a thermometer within us until our vocal cords quiver and our eyes turn a bright red and then glaze over? Young children and animals always know to scatter at times like these.

Some of us roll up the windows and scream in our cars on the highways. Some of us wait until no one is around and scream into our pillows. Some of us just scream. Most of us have thought we were crazy at these times. We're not. We are just alive and responding to our stressful lives.

A GOOD scream-a-logue not directed at anyone is often much more effective than a dialogue.

☙ March 15

ALONE TIME

When we, as individuals, first rediscover our spirit, we are usually drawn to nurture and cultivate this awareness.

—Shakti Gawain

Alone time is absolutely essential to the human organism. Many of us have been afraid to be alone. We are afraid that if someone else is not around, no one will be present. When we have lost the awareness of ourselves, we try to fill up our time with work, busyness, food, and other people. We have been afraid to sound our own depths. We have been afraid that we would look inside and find no one there.

Yet, when we have that first awareness of "rediscovering our spirit," we know that there is someone there, inside of us, who is well worth knowing.

There is no way to know ourselves unless we have time alone to explore. We need to nurture and protect our alone time even when it seems difficult.

MY ALONE TIME is as essential to my spirit as food, sleep, and exercise are to my body. I hope I am able to remember that.

❧ March 16

TEARS

I have been told that crying makes me seem soft and therefore of little consequence. As if our softness has to be the price we pay out for power, rather than simply the one that's paid most easily and most often.
—Audre Lorde

Our tears and our softness are not valued much in this society, especially in the work place. In the past, women have been led to believe that we could gain indirect, manipulative power through our tears and our gentle willingness to take care of others.

Many modern women have rejected using our tears and our gentleness to get what we want. Unfortunately, this rejection of our gentler side has resulted in our trying to appear tough and aggressive and in our losing our wholeness.

We are neither all soft nor all tough. We just are.

SHARING my tears and softness is an act of love. Sharing my strength and assertiveness is also an act of love. When I share me, I am loving.

BECOMING/ACCEPTANCE

*The great thing about getting older is that you don't
lose all the other ages you've been.*
                                    —Madeline L'Engle

Life is a process. We are a process. Everything
that has happened in our lives has happened for a
reason and is an integral part of our becoming.

One of the challenges of our lives is to integrate
the pieces of our lives as we live them. It is sometimes tempting to try to deny huge periods of our
lives or forget significant events, especially if they
have been painful. To try to erase our past is to rob
ourselves of our own hard-earned wisdom.

There is not a child or an adolescent within us.
There is the child or adolescent who has grown into
us.

When we realize that among the most important
strengths that we bring to our work are the life
experiences we have had and the ages we have been,
maybe we will not resent getting older.

MY WISDOM emerges as I accept and integrate
all that I have been and all that has happened
to me.

🖙 March 18

> *For me, it's a constant discipline to remember to go back inside to connect with my intuition.*
> —Shakti Gawain

Each of us has much more brainpower than we ever use. We have so overdeveloped the logical/rational/linear parts of our brains that we frequently have left undeveloped our awareness, intuition, and creativity. We sometimes even forget that awareness, intuition, and creativity *are* brain functions.

Yet, even without being valued and exercised, these aspects of our selves remain faithful and do not leave us. Whenever we open ourselves to our intuition, it is always there. It is important that we remember to go back inside to connect with our intuition. Trusting our intuition often saves us from disaster.

IT IS SOMETIMES frightening to trust my intuition. It is always disastrous *not* to trust it.

❧ March 19

UNREALISTIC PROMISES/DESPAIR

We workaholics make so many promises that no human being could possibly keep them. That is one of the ways we keep ourselves feeling bad about ourselves.

—Lynn

One of the problems that we workaholics and careaholics have is that we overextend ourselves and believe that we can and should be able to fulfill the promises we make. We want to be nice. We want to be members of the team. We want to be seen as competent and dependable.

We also hate to say no when someone notices us and has the confidence in us to ask us to do something. We *want* to be able to deliver.

Yet, when we do not check out with ourselves whether we can or want to fulfill our promises, we end up overcommitting ourselves and ultimately feeling bad about ourselves, which just feeds our self-esteem problems.

CHECKING to see if I can and want to fulfill a promise before I make it is good for me and good for others.

FEELINGS/CONTROL

For years I have endeavored to calm an impetuous tide—laboring to make my feelings take an orderly course—it was striving against the stream.
—Mary Wollstonecraft

We have generally been taught that feelings are bad. They aren't logical and rational. They are unruly, messy, unpredictable, and often intense. How wonderful to have such a range of expression!

Often, as children, it was not just our feelings of anger, rage, sadness, or pouting that were stifled. We were told to be quiet and equally commanded to suppress our feelings of excitement, joy, creativity, imagination, giggles, laughter, and happiness. Strangely enough, we have found that it is not possible to suppress some feelings and not others. When we push down anger, joy goes with it. When we push down rage, tenderness goes with it.

We are often told as adults that our anger must be appropriate, nonoffensive, justified, and expressed in the right way. What a joke. Trying to girdle my feelings is like trying to tie down the wind.

WHEN I ignore and suppress my feelings, they come out in frightening, sometimes destructive ways. I need to learn to honor them . . . whatever they are.

ઽ∾ March 21

FORGIVENESS

If you haven't forgiven yourself something, how can you forgive others?

—Dolores Huerta

Forgiveness has to start with the self. To forgive ourself does not mean that we condone or support everything we have done. It means that we own it. We claim it. We accept that we were in the wrong, and we move on.

Often, when we recognize that we are in the wrong, we slip into our self-centeredness, becoming so absorbed and arrogant in berating ourselves that we never quite reach a stage of forgiveness. To forgive we have to let go and move on. If we do not know how to do that with ourselves, we can never forgive others.

"TO ERR is human, to forgive divine." To forgive myself and others is divinely human.

PATIENCE/DECISIONS

*Our most important decisions are discovered, not made.
We can* make *the unimportant ones but the major
ones require us to* wait with *the discovery.*
                                    —Anne Wilson Schaef

We often push ourselves to decisions that have
not ripened and are not ready to be made. We casti-
gate ourselves for being indecisive, and others share
this opinion of us. We believe that if we were just
wise enough, intelligent enough, or clear enough we
would know what we want. We do not respect that
maybe the reason we can't make a decision is because we *don't know yet.*

For many generations, women have felt that we
had to say yes to everything. Then we learned that
it is OK to say no, so we have practiced saying no.
Unfortunately, however, it is still exceedingly difficult for us to say "I don't know" and to feel comfortable staying with our not knowing, until we do
know.

THE QUALITY of my decisions is directly proportionate to my patience with my not knowing.

HANGING IN THERE

To be somebody you must last.

—Ruth Gordon

We women who do too much know how to "hang in there." We stick with a situation that a sane person would have given up on years ago. This persistence is, indeed, often a part of our insanity. We get so fixated on hanging in that we lose perspective and fail to see that our very persistence may be exacerbating a sick situation. If we withdraw from the situation, organizations in which we are involved might have the opportunity to test their reality, or they may even be allowed to "hit bottom" and come out the other side.

We accept the virtue of perseverance but unfortunately our dedication to it has affected our judgment and our ability to discern what is really needed.

IN SOME situations it is better to leave; in some it is important to persevere, in some we simply have to wait and see. The trick is to discern which is which.

ஃ March 24

GRATITUDE

> *You love like a coward. Don't take no steps at all. Just stand around and hope for things to happen outright. Unthankful and unknowing like a hog under an acorn tree. Eating and grunting with your ears hanging over your eyes, and never even looking up to see where the acorns are coming from.*
>
> —Zora Neale Hurston

So often we go through life like hogs. We root around and munch on the goodies around us without ever once acknowledging where they come from or that we are receiving them as gifts.

The process of the universe is so generous with us that we take too much for granted. We "love like cowards." We expect everyone and everything around us to take risks, while we *take*. We become so arrogant that we convince ourselves that everything that we have is a gift from us to us. We don't stop to see that we couldn't be munching those tasty acorns unless there were some celestial oak tree dropping them.

TODAY, I have the opportunity to stop, look up, and be grateful for the many gifts that are mine.

❧ March 25

BUSYNESS

My husband and I have figured out a really good system about the housework: neither one of us does it.
—Dottie Archibald

I wonder if this would work. Have I ever had the courage and security to let my housework go for several years, to see if there was a natural limit to the amount of dirt that accumulated? Nope, and I'm not sure I want to.

Yet, how much of the constant repetitive housework I do is because of my need to keep busy and not because it actually needs to be done?

One of the characteristics of a workaholic is procrastination. Often, our busyness is a subtle form of procrastination that keeps us away from what we *really* need to be doing.

I AM GRATEFUL for the things I hear which give me the opportunity to shift my perception ever so slightly.

COURAGE/FEAR

Courage—fear that has said its prayers.
—Dorothy Bernard

I wonder if it is possible to be in touch with our true courageousness without being in touch with our spirituality? We know how to be foolhardy. We know how to take risks. We even know how to put ourselves on the line.

But do we know how to soar through the tempering fires of our fear, reach deep into our spirit, and find the courage that is there? Do we have the courage for the dailiness of life? Can we admit a mistake and not give in to the luxury of self-castigation? Do we have the courage to be honest about who we really are with those we love? Do we have the courage to return a bad piece of meat to the butcher, or do we just grumble?

When we face our fears and let ourselves know our connection to the power that is in us and beyond us, we learn courage.

MY COURAGE is everyday just like my spirituality.

ɞ‍ March 27

DISCOURAGEMENT

Only the dusty flowers, the clank of censers and tracks, leading from somewhere to nowhere.
—Anna Akhmatova

What a beautiful expression of discouragement! . . . Tracks that lead from somewhere to nowhere. We have all tried so hard to do the right things. We have gone to the right schools, followed the rules, worked long hours, skipped long showers . . . and for what? . . . tracks that lead from somewhere (with dusty flowers along the way), or perhaps even tracks that lead from nowhere to nowhere.

Relax. Of course we feel discouraged at times. Recovery is more like a spiral than a line. Our struggles offer us the opportunity to become better acquainted with the many facets of our disease.

RECOVERY doesn't have to be a straight line. As long as I am on the road, I must be going somewhere.

﹖ March 28

DESPAIR
STEP THREE

> *If God is a fly on the wall, Nanny, hand me a fly swatter.*
>
> —Gaby Brimmer

Even Jesus felt forsaken by God. We can identify with him. We have been angry with God, and we have abandoned our Higher Power because we felt abandoned. This God on whom we want to depend simply refuses to live our lives for us. We want to turn it all over to our Higher Power and lie back and relax, and old H.P. is not cooperating.

Where's the fly swatter? If my Higher Power won't do it my way, to hell with it.

Right! Enjoying ourselves, are we? Isn't this fun? A fight with God—that should keep us occupied for quite some time.

WHEN I FEEL abandoned by my Higher Power, I am the one who has gone away.

PASSION

It is the soul's duty to be loyal to its own desires. It must abandon itself to its master passion.
—Rebecca West

Many competent women have a difficult time distinguishing between passion and workaholism. When we hear the emerging concern about the lethal effects of compulsive working, we almost always ask ourselves (or justify to ourselves): "But what about being passionate with my work? Are you saying that to be passionate about my work is to be a workaholic? I don't want to give up my work."

Many of our role models for success are people who were willing to be devoured by their work. This is confusing to us.

True passion and doing what is important for us to do does not require us to destroy ourselves in the process. In fact, it is when passion gets distorted to compulsivity that it is destructive.

MY PASSION feeds me. My addictiveness devours me. There is a great difference between the two.

BECOMING

A clay pot sitting in the sun will always be a clay pot. It has to go through the white heat of the furnace to become porcelain.

—Mildred Witte Stouven

Actually, there's nothing wrong with being a clay pot. It's just that all of us have the possibility of becoming porcelain. And it isn't quite so simple as just being fired or not being fired. Some of us explode in the kiln. Some of us collapse before we ever reach the kiln, and some of us develop horrible cracks that seriously threaten our utilitarian value.

Yet probably the saddest response is to have gone through the firing and to refuse to become porcelain. All of us have furnaces in our lives. Not all of us glean the lessons from the firing.

IT IS our faith that facilitates our surrender to the firing.

PAIN/SUFFERING

Flowers grow out of dark moments.
—Corita Kent

Pain is inevitable in life. As we begin to recover, we can see that much of the suffering that we experience is directly related to our stubbornness and illusion of control. The more we hold on to issues, beliefs, or experiences that we long since have grown beyond, the harder we have to get "whacked along side the head" to get the learning. Contrary to much religious belief, suffering is not noble. It is often just plain stupid and comes out of our stubbornness and need to control.

When we are attached to our suffering, we often miss those "flowers that grow out of dark moments."

MY SUFFERING teaches me about my disease. My pain teaches me about my life.

8× April 1

GIFTS

April
Comes like an idiot, babbling, and strewing flowers.
—Edna St. Vincent Millay

One of the gifts of life is the changing of the weather and the seasons. As we relinquish some of our illusions of control, we realize that each change of the weather and each season of the year have many gifts in store for us, if we participate in them and live with them. When we fight and struggle against the weather and the seasons, we dissipate the energy that could be used for enjoyment.

April does seem to enter "like an idiot" sometimes . . . a playful, energetic, sparkling idiot that brings in riots . . . riots of flowers. Summer gives us longer days to enjoy and a time for laziness, if we accept the offers of summer. Fall gathers in, and winter cozies in. In living with the seasons, we receive many gifts.

ACCEPTING nature's gift of the seasons is like opening brightly colored packages loosely tied with crinkled ribbons.

❧ April 2

LIVING LIFE FULLY

Don't be afraid your life will end; be afraid that it will never begin.

—Grace Hansen

So often our focus upon death and the possibility of dying is an escape from our real fear . . . that of living our lives.

We have become comfortable with a way of life that is actually a slow death. Our constant working, busyness, taking care of others, and rushing around relieves us of the responsibility of being fully alive and kills us slowly, and in a socially acceptable way to boot. What more could we ask from an addiction?

Why are we so afraid of living our lives? What would our lives be like if we decided to show up for them and live them? Why is it so frightening to anticipate feeling our feelings and being present to each moment?

MY INNER PROCESS never gives me more than I can handle. I may not like handling it, and I *can* handle it. It is when I refuse to handle my life that it backs up on me.

❧ April 3

CONFUSED THINKING
STEP TWO

Any addiction is a falling into unconsciousness.
                              —Marion Woodman

Some of us want to deny what happens to our thinking processes as we become progressively addicted. It is easy for us to see how alcohol and drugs affect our thinking. We are even open to the possibility that nicotine, caffeine, and sugar affect the way we think. But overworking, rushing around, compulsively taking care of others, can these *activities* really affect the way we think? *Yes, they can and do!*

In Twelve-Step circles we often hear the words "stinkin' thinkin'" used to describe the thinking processes of the addict. We lose our ability to make judgments, we become "unconscious," we obsess, and we become "insane." We do the same thing again and again, even when it has always failed. This is *insanity.* Any, I repeat, any addiction can result in insanity, unconsciousness, and lack of judgment.

HOW can I make myself better if I am confused, unconscious, and insane? *I can't.* That is why I may be ready to see the need for a power greater than myself that can restore me to sanity.

INTEGRITY/SUCCESS
STEP FOUR

Integrity is so perishable in the summer months of success.

—Vanessa Redgrave

I wonder, have I let my integrity slip in order to succeed? Have there been times that I was willing to look the other way or take the easy way out in order to avoid conflict or to gain acceptance?

Every day we are offered opportunities to sacrifice our integrity on issues that may be of the utmost importance or on ones that appear insignificant. Without our integrity, there is no way that we can feel good about ourselves. Success and loss of integrity are not synonymous. In fact, true success requires great integrity.

These "little" incidents of integrity slippage eat away at us like termites. How important it is to stop and take a look at the decisions we have made! What a relief it is to know that our valued integrity is there deep within us and that we can reconnect with it at a moment's notice.

CHECKING for possible slips of integrity allows me to feel better about myself.

ও April 5

CONNECTEDNESS

The motions and patterns and connections of things became apparent on a gut level.
—Robyn Davidson

Each of us has magical moments in our lives when we become aware of the oneness of all things. When that happens, we see the "motions and patterns and connections." A feeling of warmth permeates our being and we heave a sigh of heartfelt relief. We can know the unknowable. We *know* the unknowable.

Yet when we try to share these experiences, we find ourselves inarticulate. In our feeble attempts to describe them, words seem like balls of cotton growing larger and larger as we try to push them out of our mouths. Often, in talking about such an experience, we lose our connection with the experience itself.

I WILL TRUST these profound pauses. And I know that I cannot have them unless I pause.

FAILURE

> *The clouds gathered together, stood still and watched the river scuttle around the forest floor, crash headlong into haunches of hills with no notion of where it was going, until exhausted, ill and grieving, it slowed to a stop just twenty leagues short of the sea.*
>
> —Toni Morrison

My, can that woman write! I read a passage like the one above, and I just want to read it over and over. It is such a beautiful description of how we sometimes bash and batter ourselves in trying to reach a goal and then end up "ill and grieving" and exhausted, not realizing that we are almost there. We, like the river, rush helter-skelter, headlong into the barriers of our being.

NONE OF US can avoid failure. We *can* avoid battering ourselves in the process.

❧ April 7

MONOTONE MINDS

Life ought to be a struggle of desire toward adventures whose nobility will fertilize the soul.
—Rebecca West

One of the side effects of doing too much is developing monotone minds. We spend so much time in our work and in work-related activities that our awarenesses and our perceptions become narrower and narrower. We reach a point where we can't talk about anything but our work and, if the truth be known, we don't *want* to talk about anything but our work.

We have become dull and uninteresting. We may even find that we're bored with ourselves. This happens to those of us who work full time at home, and it happens to those who sit at the top of a corporation.

We have taken a rainbow and compressed it into a solid, uninteresting beam of light.

THE TEARS for myself may be the prism needed to rediscover the rainbow that is me.

❧ April 8

FRIENDSHIP

She became for me an island of light, fun, wisdom where I could run with my discoveries and torments and hopes at any time of day and find welcome.
—May Sarton

We sometimes forget all the friends we have had in our lives. The negative thinking of our disease tends to focus on what is missing. But let's take today and let ourselves remember the friends who have been there for us.

For me, there was the little old lady with the beautiful flower garden who would not let my parents spank me when I tried to pick some flowers and inadvertently pulled them up by the roots. "She was only admiring their beauty," she said when my mother marched me over to apologize. And there was the friend in grade school who came forward to share the rap when I was the only one caught. There were friends who shared our tentative relationships and sexual explorations and never told. There were friends we studied with, hung out with, and grew up with—who were there for us. There were adults who served as models and mentors and judged us not. There were friends.

REMEMBERING the friends I have had in my life caresses my mind and being like a warm bath caresses my body.

❧ April 9

> *The prayer that reforms the sinner and heals the sick is an absolute faith that all things are possible to God.*
> —Mary Baker Eddy

Step Two of the Twelve-Step program states that we "came to believe that a power greater than ourselves could restore us to sanity." That's a tough one.

As we have climbed the ladder of success, we have discovered that one of the subtle requirements is the development of a certain sophisticated, scientific cynicism. We no longer want to appear or be innocent, and we believe that the only other choice is to become cynical and "scientific." Thank goodness we have the option of leaving both our innocent gullibility and our cynical sophistication behind. We can let ourselves believe that all things are possible . . . not controllable—possible.

PART of my "insanity" is not seeing that my life has become insane and not believing that I can return to sanity.

❧ April 10

DUTY

Ah, duty is an icy shadow.

—Augusta Evans

Many are the crimes that have been committed in the name of duty. Ministers neglect their children in the name of duty. People kill one another in the name of duty. We abandon ourselves and our dreams in the name of duty. We feed our addiction by overworking and then justify our behavior as our duty to our family. We batter our bodies in the name of duty. Duty becomes the excuse for much of our addictive life.

We addicts will use anything for a fix. We will take the most noble idea and turn it into a nightmare to perpetuate our addictions. We are tricky, and the disease is tricky.

When we use duty to batter ourselves and others, it has, indeed, become an "icy shadow."

I DON'T WANT to be loved out of duty. Do you?

Busyness/Rushing/Distractibility
Step One

A mark of a true workaholic is cleaning house in your underwear.

—Coleen

We workaholics can see so many unfinished projects and so many things that need to be done that we are easily distracted. Getting dressed in the morning is not always an easy process. We take our shower, and then we see something that needs to be done. We get our underwear on, and then we see something that needs to be done. It is difficult to focus on the task at hand, and when we do, we see a million other little things that we'll just tidy up before we get dressed.

Surely we have time to pick up the papers on the way to the kitchen to get our morning coffee. On the way back to the bathroom we can straighten the pillows on the couch. If we put the laundry in now, it can run while we do a quick vacuum.

Is it any wonder that we secretly see ourselves as incompetent? Even though we get a lot of little tasks done, we are so distractible that we jump from one task to another and never have a real feeling of completion. It is helpful to remember that our dis-ease is busyness and distractibility. It is only in recognizing these behaviors as part of a disease and not truly who we are that we open ourselves to the possibility of recovery.

I AM POWERLESS over these behaviors and my admission of my powerlessness is the first step toward health.

ᘒ April 12

WEEKENDS/UNSTRUCTURED TIME

I hate weekends. There's no structure. There's no compass. How will I know what to do if I don't have to do it?

—Susan

Weekends are awful for women who do too much. We miss the structure of the work week. We do not like the lack of schedule, and we feel lost without our work.

To avoid experiencing these feelings, we have developed certain insurance strategies. We bring work home. We schedule our weekend projects and activities so that we almost have the secure feeling of being at work. We panic and go into the office to "pick up some things and tie up some loose ends."

WHAT are we afraid of? . . . ourselves?

⁂

ADRENALINE/BUSYNESS

They sicken of the calm that know the storm.
—Dorothy Parker

Ah, that adrenaline rush! How we love it! We are so accustomed to dealing with crisis that we get nervous when things get calm.

Many women who are recovering from workaholism and doing too much are beginning to recognize that they have become addicted to their own adrenaline rush. We used to get a "buzz" with the excitement of a new project or an impending deadline. We functioned best under pressure (or so we believed). We got nervous and tense when our lives became too quiet. We needed the emotional arousal. We needed our fix.

Fortunately, we began to see that our adrenaline rushes were exhausting our bodies and our beings. Our addiction to our own adrenaline was as destructive to our bodies as drugs or alcohol. Recovery from adrenaline addiction has been a slow, painful process. Yet, we have the hope of a new life and the possibility of living it in a healthy body.

I HAVE DISCOVERED that what I used to call numbness may just be contentment, and contentment feels great.

❧ April 14

TAKING STOCK/GRATITUDE
STEP FOUR

Long term change requires looking honestly at our lives and realizing that it's nice to be needed, but not at the expense of our health, our happiness, and our sanity.
— Ellen Sue Stern

There is no quick fix to any addiction, and workaholism, rushaholism, busyaholism, and careaholism *are* addictions. Part of the "stinkin' thinkin'" of the addict is to want a quick fix. *There is none.* Even wanting the quick fix is part of the disease.

The twelve steps work, and it is possible for us to live serene, happy, and productive lives. But recovery takes time. There are many hills and valleys along the way, and if we keep going to meetings, calling our sponsor, and working the program, we find that we do have a connection with a power greater than ourselves, and our lives get better.

I AM so fortunate to have the support of a program that works and the company of others to travel this journey with me.

❧ April 15

ACCEPTANCE/HONESTY

With him for a sire and her for a dam,
What should I be but just what I am?
                    —Edna St. Vincent Millay

Some of us do not know the difference between putting ourselves down, thus refusing to accept our gifts and talents, and accepting who we are.

Indeed, we often bounce between being worthless and being totally arrogant. Interestingly, feeling "like a piece of shit" and feeling that we are unique and wonderful are intimately related. In both illusions, we refuse to see ourselves as we really are.

It is only when we are able to say, "I know nothing about that," or "I am really good at doing that and quite knowledgeable about that," that we are moving toward acceptance of self. Seeing our shortcomings allows us to accept them. Accepting our strengths allows us to soar. Honesty about self is the key.

TODAY I have the opportunity not to be grandiose about either my shortcomings or my capabilities. I can be me.

INDEPENDENCE

Dependency invites encroachment.
—Patricia Meyer Spacks

We women who do too much are terrified of being dependent. We clearly understand that "dependency invites encroachment." Unfortunately, our fear of dependency often results in behavior that looks like independence but is really what the psychologists call counterdependence. We are so afraid of dependency that we can't trust anyone, which means that we are still controlled by our dependency needs. Whenever we are circling around any form of dependency, whether it be dependence, independence, or interdependence, we probably are in trouble.

Another option is not to define ourselves in terms of dependency. We can learn to be self-defining. We can learn not to ask others to form our identities for us. Only then can we be truly free and bring the gift of ourselves to any relationship.

INDEPENDENCE and dependence may both be cages.

HEALING

The new space . . . has a kind of invisibility to those who have not entered it.

—Mary Daly

It is especially difficult for women who do too much to consider willingly entering the unknown. Like any addict, we like to keep everything under control, and we certainly don't want even to start a journey without an accurate road map. Unfortunately, recovery doesn't work that way. Recovery is a leap of faith.

Most of us, because we grew up in dysfunctional families, work in addictive settings, and live in an addictive society, don't have experiential knowledge of what it's like to live our process, live sobriety, or live out of our clarity. Yet many people are making that leap of faith and taking the first step on the road to recovery. We know that there has to be something better. We have a vague recollection of something. We can't quite remember what it is, and we know it is there. One of the true present-day miracles is that so many are beginning recovery when we really have no clear idea of what recovery is.

I HAVE WISHED for a miracle, and I can be one.

❧ April 18

APPRECIATION

And to all those voices of wisdom that have whispered to me along the way.

—Dhyani Ywahoo

Gratitude and appreciation are important facets of our lives. There have been so many women who have shared their wisdom and their knowledge with us. Some of that wisdom has been learned from others, and some of it has been self-taught, and all of it has been profound.

Remember the neighbor who taught us how to care for plants? Remember the mother who shared some helpful hints about staying out of the way of our children? Remember that little old lady in our place of worship who quietly seemed to live what we were being taught about spirituality? Remember that book that seemed just to appear when we needed it? There have been voices of wisdom all around us all our lives.

PERHAPS, as one of my wise friends says, "It's time to have a gratitude attack."

๛ April 19

RUSHING AND HURRYING

Sometimes I wish I had suction cups to hold me down.
—Pam

Sometimes we really do feel powerless over our need to rush around and keep busy, and we just wish there were some way to stop ourselves. Our life truly feels overwhelming and unmanageable.

We are amazed at how relieved we feel when we can actually admit that we are powerless over this crazy behavior and our lives just are not working the way we would like them to work.

We are powerful women, *and* we are powerless over our crazy lives.

What a consolation it is to know that a power greater than ourselves *can* restore us to sanity. What a relief it is to know that our admission that our lives are insane right now opens the door to sanity.

What a relief it is to sigh and know that, as we turn our lives and wills over to that power greater than ourselves, we have the path to renewed sanity before us.

SUCTION CUPS probably won't help much anyway, but turning our lives over sounds like an option with real possibilities.

❧ April 20

REALITY/INVENTORY

> *You need to claim the events of your life to make yourself yours. When you truly possess all you have been and done, which may take some time, you are fierce with reality.*
>
> —Flonda Scott Maxwell

Being "fierce with reality" requires that we break through our denial about ourselves and our lives layer by layer. At some point in our lives, we need to stop and take a thorough inventory of who we are and what we have done. This fearless and searching inventory not only focuses upon the things that we have done wrong and the things we wish we had done in some other way, it also focuses upon our strengths and the things we have done right.

So many of us forget that taking stock of ourselves also means writing down what is good about us and the things we appreciate and like about ourselves. After all, honesty is not only about the mistakes, it is also about the good, the powerful, the creative, the loving, and the gentle, compassionate aspects of ourselves.

WHEN WE STOP and truly possess all we have been, and done, we are on the path to becoming who we are.

❧ April 21

SELF-AWARENESS

> *Until the missing story of ourselves is told, nothing besides told can suffice us: we shall go on quietly craving it.*
>
> —Laura Riding

Probably the most important journey we will ever take is the journey inward. Unless we know who we are, how can we possibly offer what we have?

Each of us is a unique combination of heredity and experiences. No one else has to offer what we have to offer. Yet, if we do not have the self-awareness to undergird our uniqueness, we never make our contribution.

One of the most disastrous effects of our disease is that we never really have the time for the process of self-awareness, and then, when we do, we may be too exhausted to care.

I NEED to know my story . . . all of it.

SELF-RESPECT

When self-respect takes its rightful place in the psyche of woman, she will not allow herself to be manipulated by anyone.

—Indira Mahindra

Being a woman isn't always the easiest thing in the world, but it's what I have to work with right now. There are so many aspects of ourselves that merit self-respect. We are unbelievably competent at what we do. We are flexible and strong and can be both simultaneously. We have good ideas that are practical and creative, and we can articulate them well. We have the ability to deal with several tasks simultaneously and attend to each one. We are organizers, creators, and doers and we have a great capacity for being. We have much to contribute including a perspective on life that is different from that of the men around us. We are here to stay, and we and others need to accept that fact.

MY SELF-RESPECT is not only essential to me, it is important to the world.

❧ April 23

GUILT

> *Shit work is infinitely safe. In exchange for doing it you can extract an unconscionable return . . . the women's pound of flesh.*

—Colette Dowling

We are often experts in guilt. Certainly we have learned it from masters. We unquestionably and with great doggedness go about our assigned tasks without a grumble or a reproach.

We are armed, however, with our sighs, our clenched teeth, our pathetic looks of acceptance, and our sagging shoulders. Our favorite phrase is, "That's okay," but we really don't mean it. One of our greatest skills is suffering, and we do it so well. We get our pound of flesh, and we lose our souls in the process.

TELL ME, is it really worth it? Are we ready to give up the guilt game? It gets infinitely boring.

BEING PROJECTLESS

Out of the strain of the Doing,
Into the peace of the Done.
　　　　　　　—Julia Louise Woodruff

When most women finish a task, they heave a sigh of relief, pat themselves on the back, and give themselves a well-deserved break. Not so for women who do too much. The "peace of the Done" simply does not compute. There is no experience to which we can relate this concept.

Fortunately, as we let ourselves see that we are not just talking about doing too much, we begin to have a different perspective.

We begin to learn that completion and beginning are not the same process. We begin to see that the completion of an important project has every right to be dignified by a natural grieving process. Something that required the best of us has ended. We will miss it.

BEING PROJECTLESS and being worthless are not synonymous.

BELIEF

The experience of God, or in any case the possibility of experiencing God, is innate.

—Alice Walker

We cry to a God "out there," and our voices return like burned-out space ships that have traversed the universe. We ask authorities how to experience God and realize that they have come to worship their rituals and techniques, yet seem to know little of God. No ancient prophet lost in the wilderness felt more isolated than we do as we buzz around the wilderness of our cities and organizations. How could any God get through this steel and concrete?

Yet, when we stop, we have a glimmer of understanding of what it means to say that "the possibility of experiencing God *is innate."* We do not have to look for that possibility. It is already in us.

THE POSSIBILITY of experiencing a power greater than myself has always been there, knocking on my inner door.

BUSYNESS

The season is changeable, fitful, and maddening as I am myself these days that are cloaked with too many demands and engagements.

—May Sarton

When we do not recognize that we have become too busy and overextended, we too find ourselves being "changeable, fitful, and maddening." Our lack of awareness of our needs and our inability to attend to them sets up a situation where our only recourse is to become so obnoxious that others will leave us alone. Then we do not have to take the responsibility for stating that we need time to ourselves and taking it. Of course, this particular technique for getting alone time usually results in fences that need to be mended.

There are other ways of having what we need. We can let ourselves know that we need time to ourselves and then we can arrange to have it.

TAKING THE TIME I need for myself when I need it may be a lot less exciting than creating a crisis, and it certainly is less messy.

CHOICES/FEELING TRAPPED

I discovered I always have choices and sometimes it's only a choice of attitude.
—Judith M. Knowlton

One of the most devastating characteristics of the addictive process is that our perceptions, our judgment, and our thinking become so distorted that we come to believe that we have no choices and are completely trapped. We have the illusion that there are only two choices (usually to stay or leave) and neither looks attractive.

We do have options. We do have choices, even if the only choice available at the moment is to see that we are stuck and to accept that "stuckness." Amazingly, when we truly accept our stuckness, our situations begin to change. Often it is not the situation that is keeping us stuck but our *attitude* about our situation.

CHOICES are part of being human. When I feel I have no choices, I am probably operating out of my disease.

೪ April 28

BEAUTY

Oh, it was a glorious morning! I suppose the best kind
of spring morning is the best weather God has to offer.
It certainly helps one to believe in Him [sic].
          —Dodie Smith

How long has it been since we have allowed
ourselves to rejoice in a beautiful day? How long has
it been since we allowed ourselves to notice that it
even *is* a beautiful day?

Those of us who live and work in cities have
given ourselves obstacles that challenge us to have
to work a little harder even to notice what kind of
day it is.

For women who do too much, the beautiful day
may be noteworthy only in the absence of hassle
that rain or snow might present. A beautiful day,
then, only becomes the vehicle to get more done.
There are other options.

I LONG for the awareness to say, "Oh, it was a
glorious morning!"

Fear/Manipulation

All women hustle. Women watch faces, voices, gestures, moods. The person who has to survive through cunning.
—Marge Piercy

Most women are accomplished research scientists. We have developed skills for gathering data that would put most researchers to shame. We are constantly scanning faces, bodies, and situations for clues about what is acceptable and what we can get away with. We have, unfortunately, in many situations become people who "survive through cunning." Our hyperalertness emanates from our fear that whatever we do will not be enough—our fear that *we* are not enough no matter what we do. We have to be cunning to survive, or so we have come to believe. Some have said that this revolution of women is the only revolution where the outpost of the enemy is in our own heads.

I AM ENOUGH. We all will just have to accept what I have to give.

ISOLATION

One of the reasons our society has become such a mess is that we're isolated from each other.
—Maggie Kuhn

Isolation is one of the characteristics of addiction. Isolation is one of the characteristics of women who do too much.

We may be surrounded by people all day long but our singleminded dedication to our work isolates us. We do not like to be interrupted by friends. We would rather get our work done. We get angry when things don't fall into place and others are afraid to approach us.

We have become just as locked up and closeted with our working, our busyness, our hurrying around as any alcoholic is with her bottle. We have forgotten how to reach out, and we don't have the time for it, even if we remember how. We think if we just had more time to focus on our work we'd feel better, and instead we feel exhausted. Isolation is an energy drain.

I NEED to learn the difference between isolation and solitude.

❧ May 1

TODAY

*Normal day, let me be aware of the treasure you are.
Let me learn from you, love you, bless you before you
depart. Let me not pass you by in quest of some rare
and perfect tomorrow. Let me hold you while I may, for
it may not always be so. One day I shall dig my nails
into the earth, or bury my face in the pillow, or stretch
myself taut, or raise my hands to the sky and want,
more than all the world, your return.*

—Mary Jean Iron

This moment is right now. It is what we have.
How often we have squandered the treasure of
today and dreamed of the fortunes of the future,
only to mourn for the loss of this day. Today, we can
see the excitement in the eyes of a child over some
new discovery. Today, we can listen to an old friend
before we get on to the next task. Have we missed
today by not being present to it? Will we later weep
tears of mourning and wish for its return? How
much better to live it today.

JUST a normal day—what a gift!

COURAGE

Remember, Ginger Rogers did everything Fred Astaire did, but she did it backwards and in high heels.
—Faith Whittlesey

That's right! Ginger Rogers was amazingly good at what she did, and so are we. It takes courage for women to acknowledge how good we are at what we do. We are caught in a strange cultural expectation of having to be simultaneously competent and passive. This often results in a kind of humility that really is a denial of our expertise.

Also, women who do too much seem to vacillate between exaggerating our competence and feeling that we are worthless and totally incompetent. This vacillation between extremes is part of the addictive disease.

The real test of courage is being realistic and letting ourselves know that we really are competent at many things.

BEING GOOD at what we do isn't a curse. It's a gift that comes from ourselves *and* from a power greater than ourselves.

DESPAIR

That was a time when only the dead could smile.
—Anna Akhmatova

We have known times like these. In fact, the point where we realized that we had to admit that doing too much was no longer something that *we* did, *it did us,* and was our personal moment of hitting bottom. Before we completely admitted our powerlessness over our working too much, we despaired, fearing that nothing could change.

Yet we *have* changed. We have reached the depths of despair and lived through it. We have gone into the abyss and found that God is nothingness too.

We remember our despair, and we are also grateful to it because hitting bottom in our disease has paved the way for our recovery, and recovery is great!

I NEVER THOUGHT I would be grateful for this disease, and it has opened up a possibility of a whole new life for me.

❧ May 4

LIVING IN THE PRESENT

Yesterday is a cancelled check
Tomorrow is a promissory note
Today is cash in hand; spend it wisely.
—Anonymous

What a challenge to live in the present! We are often so busy killing the present moment with worries about tomorrow or regrets about yesterday that we kill our todays. Ironically, all we can really do is be in the present.

Living in the present means noticing—noticing when we are tired, noticing when we need to go the bathroom, noticing when we need to rest.

Living in the present means taking a walk for the sake of the walk, not just to get someplace. Living in the present means noticing and appreciating our now. Living in the present means doing our lives, not thinking about them.

IF I DO MY LIFE then I won't be undone.

‹› May 5

FEELING OVERWHELMED

The social workers have named a new syndrome. It's called "compassion fatigue". Why does it sound so familiar?

—Anne Wilson Schaef

Careaholics never quite know when it all happened. We were trained to believe that, if we just took care of people and listened and understood, they in turn would take care of us. We firmly believed that relationships are built on people taking care of each other, and if we took care first, we would certainly get the same in return. What a shock to find out that this belief is not only not held by everyone, but the more we take care of people, the more they want.

We feel drained, resentful, taken advantage of, and overwhelmed. Those seem to be normal feelings in the situation. Thank goodness we don't have to stay stuck there, however. Just recognizing the feelings helps us begin to check out our assumptions about caretaking.

LOVING isn't caretaking and caretaking isn't love. We can't buy love . . . it's a gift.

❧ May 6

GRATITUDE

*Make a prayer acknowledging yourself as a vehicle of
light, giving thanks for the good that has come that day
and an affirmation of intent to live in harmony with all
your relations.*

—Dhyani Ywahoo

As we begin to recover and get clearer, we are
often overcome with moments of gratitude. We
begin to see the possibility that we are not our disease. We have the disease of overworking and doing
too much, and that is not who we are. We begin to
see that we do have moments of clarity, and we
truly like the person we experience during those
moments. We begin to see the good that we do each
day and the good that comes to us each day. We
have times of deep, heartfelt gratitude and love for
ourselves, our family, our friends, and the world
around us. We even begin to have a glimmer of what
it would mean to live in harmony with all those
around us. We are healing.

I CAN TRULY give thanks for the good that is in
my life. I can give thanks for being me.

FEELINGS

> *What you know in your head will not sustain you in moments of crisis . . . confidence comes from body awareness, knowing what you feel in the moment.*
> —Marion Woodman

We live in a culture that worships logical, rational, linear thought processes and disdains and ignores feelings. Feelings are seen as uncontrollable, dangerous, and unnecessary.

Yet, it is our feelings that make us human. Our feelings warn us of danger. If we are out of touch with them, we may miss danger signals.

It is our feelings, not our minds, that tell us when someone is lying to us. When we are being lied to, we feel it right in our solar plexus. We need our feelings to help us deal with the world.

MY FEELINGS are a gift. I am lucky to have such a range of them.

❧ May 8

BEING PRESENT TO THE MOMENT

She would greet us pleasantly, and immediately she seemed to surround the chaotic atmosphere of morning strife with something of order, of efficient and quiet uniformity, so that one had the feeling that life was small and curiously ordered.

—Meridel LeSueur

Whew! Isn't it a relief to know that there are people in the world who are so present to the moment that when they enter a chaotic atmosphere they create calm? This calm is not born of control or manipulation. This calm is born of presence.

Only a person who is present to herself carries a feeling of serenity with her. As we work the Twelve-Step Program, we begin to experience this kind of serenity for ourselves.

ORDER that comes out of control is full of tension. Order that comes out of rigidity is full of strife. Order that comes out of serenity is peaceful.

‏❧ May 9

Busyness/Loneliness

You can get lonesome—being that busy.
                                        —Isabel Lennart

Workaholics are lonely people. Our work is like a jealous lover. It demands more and more of us. We see ourselves becoming progressively isolated from those who are important to us. We schedule lunches two weeks in advance so that we can keep up social contact with friends and then have to break or postpone these lunches because "something has come up." We get "antsy" if we are interrupted; we get irritable if someone stops by to talk because we want to get back to our work. We often don't know we are lonely because we don't stop long enough to let ourselves know what we are feeling.

IT IS GOOD to be productive, and busyness is no substitute for intimacy.

INTIMACY

So instant intimacy was too often followed by disillusion.

—May Sarton

We live in an age of instant dinners, instant success, and instant intimacy. We expect ourselves to meet someone and know immediately that we were meant for each other. After all, in our busy lives we don't have the time for long, drawn-out courtships.

Instant intimacy is one of the characteristics of addictive relationships. In fact, when recovering women experience a bit of instant intimacy, they have learned to run for the hills. This kind of instant connection usually does not wear well.

Intimacy takes time. It is a process. It needs to be fed, valued, nurtured, and allowed to grow. When we try to manipulate intimacy, we kill it. In fact, we often use instant intimacy to avoid the possibility of real intimacy.

INTIMACY takes time. If I don't have time, I probably won't have intimacy.

⧖ May 11

ANGUISH

Each woman is being made to feel it is her own cross to bear if she can't be the perfect clone of the male superman and the perfect clone of the feminine mystique.
—Betty Friedan

No wonder we sometimes find ourselves filled with anguish. There is just too much to do. Too many demands are made upon us. We are asked to be too many people—some of whom we are and some of whom we are not. Anguish is probably a normal response to such a situation.

Luckily, we do not have to stop with anguish. It is important to feel our anguish, go through it, and move on. One of the ways we stay stuck is to block our feelings and refuse to admit them. Sometimes life presents us with vises, puts us in them, and screws them tight. Then we find that as we let ourselves feel our feelings of hurt and anguish, we can move on.

A VISE is something like a girdle: We can step out of it.

❧ May 12

LOVE

I wish I'd a knowed more people. I would of loved 'em all. If I'd a knowed more, I woulda loved more.
—Toni Morrison

We all have an infinite capacity for loving. Sometimes we get confused about loving, and we start thinking that we only have so much to go around. We start thinking in zero-sum terms. We believe that we only have so much love and if we give some away, we have that much less. We start parceling out our love like we pay the bills at the end of the month. We meet all of our "love obligations," and we try to keep a little bit in savings, just in case of an emergency. Controlled love is not loving. Obligatory love is not loving. Love is something that flows out of our deep sense of loving ourselves. It is not possible to love another if we don't know and love ourselves.

When we love ourselves, there is no limit to the amount of love we can share. But loving can never be manufactured because we should, need to, or want to get something in return. Love is an energy that is shared because we have it.

LOVING the people I know allows me to know the people I love.

ᏨᏭ May 13

PARENTING

The thing about having a baby is that thereafter you have it.

—Jean Kerr

What a shock! Our children do not always fit into our fantasies. They do not always provide us with the "perfect little family." They do not always fit in with our schemes and plans. And the worst thing about them is that we simply cannot get them shaped up the way we want them and expect them to stay that way.

When we give birth to a child, we give birth to a process that continues in one form or another for the rest of our lives. Somehow, we seemed to have missed the concept that parenting is an intimate interactive process that continues.

WHEN WE STOP trying to make our children fit our fantasies of who they *should* be, we can begin to see who they are!

RESPONSIBILITY/GUILT

If you believe you are to blame for everything that goes wrong, you are going to stay until you fix it.
—Susan Forward

We women who do too much are *responsible.* That is one of our great virtues, or so we think. We are willing to take accountability and blame for *everything.* When something happens at work, it must be our fault. If our relationships fail, we must have done something wrong. If our children have difficulties, we are to blame. Guilt and blame are old familiar friends. It is inconceivable to us that we did not cause . . . whatever. This is one form of our self-centeredness. We put ourselves right squarely in the middle of any disaster. Of course, the other side of the dualism is to be totally blameless and a victim. We bounce back and forth between the two.

What a difference it is to move into respond-ability, a place where accountability and blame have no meaning and our ability to respond is the key.

MY ABILITY to respond is hampered by accountability and blame.

ANGER

I am a woman in the prime of life, with certain powers and those powers severely limited by authorities whose faces I rarely see.

—Adrienne Rich

It is time! As women we have been limited as to what we can do, say, think, and feel. Some of us hate to admit it. Yet, down deep we know that there are many forces that limit our lives, forces over which we have little power. Only a person with no feelings and no awareness would not feel the smolder of anger, even rage, deep inside at times.

It seems that we, as women, have only had two options—to go along with the authorities and thus support them, or to fight them and thus support them. Either way we lose.

Fortunately, there is a third option. We can be ourselves. We can see what is important for us and do it. In order for us to exercise this third option, we may have to go through our anger first.

WHEN WE RESPECT our anger and deal with it, **we discover doors that were not obvious before.**

ASKING FOR HELP

Advice is what we ask for when we already know the answer but wish we didn't.

—Erica Jong

Right! Usually when we ask for advice, it is because we are already aware of the answer within us, and we do not want to heed our inner knowing. Let someone else take the rap!

Also, when we ask for advice, there is a part of us just daring anyone to give it. When they do, it takes the pressure off of us, even when we know it will not work and we will secretly reject it.

Asking for help, on the other hand, is a completely different matter. Most women who do too much have great difficulty asking for help. We usually can do it ourselves, whatever "it" is, and are more comfortable doing it ourselves. We can give orders and *tell* others to do what needs to be done. We can organize and supervise. We have learned many ways of getting help without asking for it and without admitting we need it. Yet, there is something infinitely more honest in asking for help when we need it.

ASKING FOR HELP does not mean that we are weak or incompetent. It usually indicates an advanced level of honesty and intelligence.

Awareness

> *I felt like I was in a fog. I knew that I was desperately searching for something of great importance, the loss of which was life-threatening, but I couldn't see clearly.*
>
> —Judy Ness

We keep ourselves so busy and so overworked that we do not have time to see that we are in a fog and searching for something of great importance.

We look to our work, our money, or our families to fulfill us, and all these "solutions" fail miserably.

Even if we are successful, when we stop long enough we are aware of a feeling of loneliness and emptiness. We have failed to realize that nothing from outside can really fill us up and that the person we really long to find is ourselves. Not having ourselves and not being in touch with ourselves is life-threatening. When we leave ourselves, we are more vulnerable to outside influences and less aware of what we really need.

How exciting it is to begin to see the fog lift and to know that that for which we so desperately search has been there within us all the time.

WHAT I am looking for is not "out there." It is in me. It *is* me.

❧ May 18

ONE DAY AT A TIME/TRUST/CONTROL

Living is a form of not being sure, not knowing what next or how. The moment you know how, you begin to die a little. The artist never entirely knows. We guess. We may be wrong, but we take leap after leap in the dark.

—Agnes de Mille

How arrogant *and* ignorant of us to believe that we can do anything but live one day at a time! We are so deluded by our illusion of control that we really believe that we can control the future, make things happen the way we want and completely control our lives. When we do this, we cease living.

Living fully is living a life of faith. We do our footwork, make our plans, and then let go. Living fully is taking a leap of faith and, before our feet are squarely on the ground, leaping again. When we think we have things under control, we "begin to die a little."

IT TAKES a lot of faith to live one day at a time, and the alternatives don't look that inviting.

❧ May 19

UNWORTHINESS/CHOICES

The strongest lesson my mother gave me is that you are not worthwhile if you are not doing.

—Ferrand

Addiction to work is not something that crops up suddenly in mid-life. The seeds have often been sown in our childhoods, and we are only living out the rules and expectations that our parents instilled in us.

How many of our parents really believed that idleness is the devil's workshop and that if they did not keep us constantly busy, there was no telling what we would get into? How many of us are really afraid of idle, quiet time when nothing is on the schedule?

One mayor of a large midwest city publicly stated that if he looked at his calendar and Tuesday night was free, he immediately thought that his staff had goofed. He also stated that his workaholism had ruined his marriage and his health.

ISN'T IT EXCITING to know that we do not have to live out our childhood messages? As adults, we have choices.

BEING PRESENT TO THE MOMENT

Nobility of character manifests itself at loopholes when it is not provided with large doors.
—Mary Wilkins Freeman

Opportunities do not always come at the time or in the form we had hoped. Instead of blinding flashes of light, they are often still small voices that whisper to us in unexpected moments.

Our potential for greatness is linked with our ability to be present to the moment. Noticing may be one of the most important skills we have. When we are present to notice a small, obscure opportunity, we may discover that we have taken a major turn on the path of our life.

ANYBODY can walk through a wide-open door. I hope for the nobility of character to see the loophole.

CONFLICT

It's better to be a lion for a day than a sheep all your life.

—Elizabeth Henry

Conflict is inevitable in our lives. We feel conflicted over a choice we must make, and the conflict is within. We feel strongly about the way a business decision must go, and we are in conflict with our peers.

Some of us believe that there are only two options when conflict arises. We must either roar like a lion and impose our will or back off like a sheep and give in (and *subtly* try to impose our will). Neither choice has much to say for it.

Thank goodness we have another option. We can check out what is going on inside of us. We can listen to what others are saying. We can get clear with ourselves and see what we have to learn.

CONFLICT is inevitable. Fighting is a choice.

CONNECTEDNESS/CONFUSION/LONELINESS

Women who set a low value on themselves make life hard for all women.

—Nellie McClung

As women we have a special connectedness with each other. We have been raised to be competitive with other women and to see them as enemies and competitors. We have also been raised to see female as inferior and told that if we wanted to get ahead, we needed to identify with men and either become like them or be what they wanted us to be. It has all been very confusing. Frequently, we have felt alone and isolated.

A major factor in our healing has been to recognize that we are women and to seek connectedness with other women. We find ourselves reflected in their stories, and our loneliness changes to connectedness.

I AM NOT ALONE. Other women share my experiences. Healing and connectedness are the same.

CONTROL/ARROGANCE

The passion for setting people right is in itself an afflictive disease.

—Marianne Moore

Women who do too much often think that it is our job to set others right. After much gathering of information and acquisition of knowledge, we really have come to believe that we can and do know what is best for other people. Since we know what is best, we have no difficulty sharing this important information with any who will—or sometimes even will not—listen. Some of us even get *paid* for knowing what is best for others and setting them right.

Ugh, it doesn't look so good on paper, does it?

PERHAPS TODAY would be a good day to look at my arrogance. Benevolent arrogance is still arrogance.

ह~ May 24

HOPES AND DREAMS

As long as we think dugout canoes are the only possibility—all that is real or can be real—we will never see the ship, we will never feel the wind blow.
—Sonia Johnson

Women who do too much have grown afraid to dream. We know how to lust—after power, after money, after security, after relationships—but we have forgotten how to dream.

Dreaming is not limited to the unreal. Dreaming is stretching the real beyond the limits of the present. Dreaming is not being bound by the merely possible. Dreaming is not safe for our illusion of control and it is *infinitely* safe for our soul.

When we deprive ourselves of our hopes and dreams, we relegate ourselves to keeping our eyes to the ground, carefully calculating every step, and missing the pictures in the clouds and the double rainbows.

TO HOPE and dream is not to ignore the practical. It is to dress it in colors and rainbows.

Healing

The human heart does not stay away too long from that which hurt it most. There is a return journey to anguish that few of us are released from making.
—Lillian Smith

Those hurts and pains that we experience in childhood don't just magically evaporate as we grow older. They rumble around in us, and when we have reached a level of strength, maturity, insight, and awareness to handle them, they come up to be worked through. This is one of the ways our inner being is loving to us. It gives us every opportunity to heal the hurts that we need to heal, and it gives us that opportunity when we are strong enough to handle it.

Frequently, as children, we have experiences that we simply aren't strong enough to handle without a lot of support and help, and often that support is absent. So we push them down and we wait. When we are ready, they come back up. This gives us the chance to work through these old anguishes when we have what we need for this task.

WHEN I AM READY, I will have the opportunity to make these journeys to old hurts with the knowledge that I can heal them and move on.

❧ May 26

LIVING LIFE FULLY

And reach for our lives . . . for all *life . . . deep into the cosmos that is our own souls.*
—Sonia Johnson

Each of us is a cosmos unto ourselves. When we are living our lives fully, we are separate persons, and we are also one with the universe. We are ourselves with our boundaries, and we are also connected with all things.

Luckily, we are not really asked to live any one else's life. All we have to do is live our own, and that seems to be quite enough for us.

When we live life fully, we allow ourselves to taste the range of our experiences. We see what we see, feel what we feel, and know what we know. We accept every opportunity to live out of our own souls.

LUCKILY, living life fully is not a task. It is an opportunity.

AWARENESS OF PROCESS

He was teaching me something about flow, about choosing the right moment for everything, about enjoying the present.

—Robyn Davidson

Sometimes our teachers appear in the most unlikely forms. Robyn Davidson is speaking of an old Aborigine who traveled with her for a while. Although their cultures were vastly different, he taught her some elemental wisdom that needed to be acknowledged and experienced in her culture.

We all need to know about flow. Nothing gets done at once even when we demand it. Work and living flow in a series of nonlinear events.

Timing is also very important. We cannot correct and edit a report until it is written. When our boss is having a bad day, it is not a good idea to bring up an interpersonal problem that happened last week. We cannot control another's reactions by choosing "the right moment," and we can choose the time that is best for us. And we always have the choice to stop and enjoy the present.

WHEN I STAY in my present, I have the opportunity to experience the flow of my life.

ᵫ May 28

BUSYNESS/EXHAUSTION/SLEEP

I am so keyed up I can't go to sleep at night. I just can't relax. I'm lucky if I get five hours of sleep a night.
—Barbie

One of the side effects of our lives as women who do too much is that we get ourselves so keyed up that we cannot get the rest and sleep we so desperately need. We are constantly on the run. Even when our bodies are ready to drop from exhaustion, we cannot relax and let them experience the soothing regeneration of deep sleep. Sometimes, even when we try to let down, it is too painful to let go, and we find we cannot. We are deprived of the healing that occurs in the alpha phase of sleep. We travel on nerves worn ragged like socks that have not been mended by caring hands. We have deprived ourselves of the unconscious experience of pulling together the tattered and torn threads of our souls and reweaving the holes gouged out by the civility of daily skirmishes. We need our rest.

SLEEP is one of the regenerative gifts of life. I only miss it when I don't have it.

RUSHING/FRANTIC/UNWORTHY

My pattern is go, go, go . . . collapse.

—Rosie

When we are addicted to working, being busy, rushing around, and taking care of other people, the only way that we can give ourselves permission to rest is by collapsing.

It has been said that workaholism is the addiction of choice for those who feel unworthy. We are so driven to prove ourselves and to make a place for ourselves that we can never quite do enough, no matter how much we do. If we just do enough, maybe we can justify our existence. We have trouble accepting that just our being may be enough.

We all need solitude, and those of us who do too much can only justify taking it when we are near collapse.

Rushing and then collapsing is not only exhausting to me, it wears everyone around me out too.

RUSHING and collapsing is cruel and inhuman behavior. Practicing it on myself is cruel and inhuman.

ॐ May 30

SHAME

No one can make you feel inferior without your consent.
—Eleanor Roosevelt

Shame is a learned response. There is a lot of interest in shame these days in relation to addiction and recovery from addiction. When we start feeling shameful, we leave ourselves and operate much like someone on drugs or alcohol. Nothing clear can get in. Nothing clear can come out.

It is important to remember that shame is learned and that anything that is learned can be unlearned. Shame was used to control us when we were younger, and now we often use it to control others. When we start feeling ashamed, no new information can come in, we cannot process information clearly, and we cannot communicate clearly. We are in our addictive disease.

IT IS IMPORTANT to see the role shame has played in our lives. It is also important not to stay stuck in it.

ACCEPTANCE

It is in the knowledge of the genuine conditions of our lives that we must draw our strength to live and our reasons for living.

—Simone de Beauvoir

What a beautiful expression of the profundity of acceptance of our lives! Sometimes we are so busy rushing around that we do not take the time simply to accept who we are and what we have. Paradoxically, it is in that full acceptance that our lives then move on.

Our lives do have meaning . . . just as they are. It is our illusions that rob us of meaning, not our reality. When I accept my reality, I claim my strength and reasons for living.

MY LIFE is what it is. It may change, and right now it is what it is.

❧ June 1

FREEDOM

We have not owned our freedom long enough to know exactly how it should be used.
—Phyllis McGinley

As we women have struggled to become free, we have tried out various forms of freedom. We used to think we were free when we were the kind of women men wanted us to be. Then we thought we were free when we could be like men. We thought we were free when we could treat men the way we had been treated.

We thought we were free when we had access to jobs where we could reduce our life span through stress-related diseases. We thought we were free when we had made the team and were allowed to play games in which we had no interest. We thought we were free when we had money, power, and influence.

IT TAKES TIME to grow into freedom. We have time yet.

৯ June 2

BUSYNESS/HOUSEWORK

There are days when housework seems the only outlet.
—Adrienne Rich

One of the comforting qualities about housework is that it is always there. When we feel at a loss for something to feed our need for busyness, we can always plunge in to housework. For some of us that means we have to be pretty desperate. In this regard the workaholic is comparable to the alcoholic who prefers a good scotch and will settle for a beer in a pinch.

It is hard for us to admit how addicted we have become to keeping busy. Our busyness affords the same numbed-out state that others get on drugs. Some of us go for the adrenalin high just as a drug addict goes for a drug high. Let's face it: we are hooked.

WHAT A RELIEF to admit I am addicted to my busyness! Now I know recovery is possible!

❧ June 3

EXHAUSTION

> *You white people are so strange. We think it is very primitive for a child to have only two parents.*
> —Australian Aboriginal Elder

Past generations had the luxury and support of extended families. Grandparents were around and often found meaning in sharing stories about their life and times. As children sat listening, their parents felt the warm glow of recognition and familiarity and chuckled inwardly as old tales were told and retold.

But now many of us are isolated from extended family, or we don't have the time for family. We are it for our children. We have to be past, present, and guides to the future. This is exhausting.

IN HAWAII, people always take time to "talk story." We can learn something from them.

❧ June 4

GOALS

We were brought up with the value that as we sow, so shall we reap. We discarded the idea that anything we did was its own reward.

—Janet Harris

We live in a goal-oriented society. We are often so busy trying to get to the top of the mountain that we forget to notice the rocks with lichen, the alpine flowers, and even the people along the way. We are ruled by the cult of the orgasm. Foreplay is only a means to an end. Yet for many women the touching, holding, talking, stroking, and intimacy are equally if not more important that the moment of orgasm. Orgasms and goals can be fun, but not if they obliterate everything that goes before.

Setting goals can be useful and important, especially if we are willing to let them go when they become irrelevant, and if we remember that the journey itself is important.

IF I LOOK only at the top of the mountain, I may miss the fossils along the mountainside that can teach me about time and my place in the universe.

ᔓ June 5

BEING IN CHARGE

Never retract, never explain, never apologize . . . get the thing done and let them howl.
—Nellie McClery

There are so many levels on which one could respond to this quote. At one level, it sounds like advice on how to be a bulldozer and run down anyone who offers opposition. I don't recommend that.

At another level, one can zero in on the time lost in explaining, retracting, and apologizing, while the house is burning down. There is something to be said for just moving ahead.

And at another level, when we clearly feel the direction we must take and the job we must get done, there is a certain serenity that emerges when we are truly willing to "let them howl."

HOW WONDERFUL that every issue has so many levels of truth. That makes life anything but dull.

ᐒ June 6

I'll bet you when you get down on them rusty knees and get to worrying God, He goes in his privy-house and slams the door. That's what he thinks about you and your prayers.

—Zora Neale Hurston

Many of us who do too much have long since forsaken our childhood "God" and have found nothing to replace "Him." When we have called upon "Him," we were sure that he went "into his privy-house" and slammed the door. The sound of that door slamming has echoed and careened throughout our aloneness. We were on our own now. We had to do it ourselves. How dualistic we have been. If the God of our childhood didn't work, we would have no contact with any spirituality. Yet, the real loss is our loss of contact with our spiritual selves. We do need time for prayer, meditation, and reflection that is congruent with who we are. When we take that time, we find there is something there beyond ourselves.

BELIEF is not always easy for me. Most of all, my thinking gets in the way.

CAUSES/LOVE

*Those who serve a cause are not those who love that
cause. They are those who love the life which has to be
led in order to serve it . . . except in the case of the
very purest, and they are rare.*

—Simone Weil

To care about something is to bring ourselves to
it. When we give ourselves up for something,
whether it be our families, our work, our church, or
our causes, we bring an empty shell.

We have confused so much of our religious
training to mean that if we are pure, we will have no
person, no self. What most spiritual disciplines ad-
vocate is the need to let the ego go, the need to let
go of the addictive self, the need to recognize our
unique oneness with all things. When we love a
cause and bring ourselves to it, we bring the very
best we have.

LEARNING to access my true self and my oneness with all things allows me to love.

❧ June 8

CREATIVITY

Clutter is what silts up exactly like silt in a flowing stream when the current, the free flow of the mind, is held up by an obstruction.

—May Sarton

Clutter seems like a constant in our lives. Our houses are cluttered, our desks are cluttered, our minds are cluttered, and our lives are cluttered. This is the curse of women who do too much.

We can never find our creative selves unless we reduce some of the clutter in our lives. The mind must have the opportunity to flow freely if we are to be healthy.

We are such strong, powerful, beautiful, and intelligent women. The world needs what we have to offer.

RECOVERY is like a dredge clearing a silted stream.

COMPETITION/COMPARISON

*It's them that takes advantage that gets advantage i'
this world.*
　　　　　　　　　　　　　—George Eliot

Unfortunately, we have been taught that to get
ahead one has to compare, compete, and take advantage of others. And we see evidence of these
behaviors all around us.

Yet as we begin to recover from our addictions,
we begin to see that comparison and competition are
both forms of external referenting. When we compare, we become jealous, feel bad about ourselves,
find ourselves becoming resentful, and end up not
liking ourselves much. When we compete, we treat
others as objects, become ruthless, and justify our
destructive behavior. When we take advantage of
others, we lose the opportunity of relationships, we
become people we do not really like, and ultimately
we lose. Any of these behaviors threatens our serenity and our recovery.

WE CONTINUE to learn what it means to be willing to put our sobriety first. It's not always easy
and it's a matter of life.

৯ June 10

Satisfaction

Notwithstanding the poverty of my outside experience, I have always had a significance for myself, and every chance to stumble along my straight and narrow little path, and to worship at the feet of my Deity, and what more can a human soul ask for?

—Alice Jones

Satisfaction with one's life is like being anointed with warm oil. It is so peaceful to read the words of someone who is content. Often we equate contentment and satisfaction with stagnation. They are anything but that! True satisfaction with one's life is an acceptance of what is, continuing to prepare for what can be, while letting go of what we thought needed to be.

Satisfaction is an active place of quietude, a busy place of stillness. Satisfaction is a relief in living rarely felt by women who do too much. Satisfaction is the soul breathing a sigh of relief.

SOMETIMES, when I take stock, I only look at what isn't done. I also need to look at what I have, what's been done, and what's being done.

BEAUTY

Adornment is never anything except a reflection of the heart.

—Coco Chanel

Everyone pays so much attention to how women dress: "We should wear three-piece suits, look just like men, and dress for success." "Women who get raped were asking for it by the way they dressed." "Men like women who dress in a feminine fashion. It makes men feel masculine."

Is it any wonder that we sometimes feel confused about what seems right for us to wear?

What if the way we dress is simply a reflection of our hearts? What if our main criterion for beauty is what feels good on our bodies and reflects who we are? What if we wear colors because we like them and not because they are "our colors" or make us look thin? This opens up all kinds of possibilities, doesn't it?

IF I ADORNED MYSELF to reflect my heart, what would I wear?

❧ June 12

SELF-AWARENESS

Men look at themselves in mirrors. Women look for themselves.

—Elissa Melamed

"Mirror, mirror, on the wall" . . . where did I go? It seems only yesterday that when I looked in the mirror I saw someone I recognized. Those little pieces of myself that I gave away one by one seemed so insignificant at the time. What has become of me?

So many of us who do too much have the experience of disappearing before our very eyes. We did not plan it that way. It just seemed to happen over the years.

Yet, if there is still someone to look in the mirror, we have not left completely.

I NEED to look closely. The mirror could be my friend. It could help lead me back to me.

❧ June 13

LIVING LIFE FULLY/CURIOSITY

Life was meant to be lived and curiosity must be kept alive. One must never, for whatever reason, turn his [sic] back on life.

—Eleanor Roosevelt

As I look back over the significant teachers in my life, one of the characteristics that consistently stands out is their curiosity. We sometimes think that curiosity is reserved for youth and is only natural in young children.

Yet I am sure that if we think about the people we have known, those that we remember most vividly are those who remained incurably curious throughout their lives.

There is an intimate link between curiosity and aliveness. Curiosity appears to be in the gene bank of the human species. My curiosity is not dead, even though it may seem to have been slumbering for a while.

MAY I NEVER BE "cured" of my curiosity!

❧ June 14

AWARENESS OF PROCESS/WISDOM

The events in our lives happen in a sequence in time, but in their significance to ourselves, they find their own order . . . the continuous thread of revelation.
                                        —Eudora Welty

Wouldn't it be boring if our lives were completely linear? How dull to have completely worked through each experience and trauma right when it happened!

Yet we all become resentful when old skeletons that we believed were long since buried begin to rattle their bones. How inconvenient when the effects of events that happened at age five begin to erupt at age thirty-five! How disquieting when memories long hidden from consciousness signal us that they are ready to be worked through!

Can we believe that our own inner process knows when we are ready to deal with old issues? Can we trust that the very fact that they are coming up is an indication of how much we have grown and how strong we are?

THERE IS SOMETHING within me that knows more than I know. Trusting it can only result in healing.

CONFUSION/NEGATIVISM

Why is it when I don't know what I want, there is always someone waiting to tell me what it is? I'm just lucky, I guess.

—Anne Wilson Schaef

I have heard so many women say, "I have a good marriage. My husband doesn't beat me, he doesn't gamble, and he doesn't run around with other women." Or they say; "Well, my job isn't boring, it keeps me busy, and it pays the bills." Somehow, OK becomes the absence of awful. If something in our lives isn't too destructive, it must be all right.

We get so confused about what we really want and what is really good for us. We are so accustomed to doing what is expected of us that we have lost our ability to determine what we want.

UNLESS I KNOW what I want and what is right for me, there is no way I can be an honest person.

❧ June 16

CONTROL

War is the unfolding of miscalculations.
                              —Barbara Tuchman

We are so invested in the illusion of control that we rarely step back and see how pervasive and destructive this illusion is. Much of what goes on at an international level between nations is based upon the illusion of control. When we believe we can control everything or we have everything under control, we are appalled by our miscalculations. Miscalculations on a personal level can be just as devastating as miscalculations on an international level. It is not the *mis* in miscalculating that is the problem; it is the calculating. When we operate out of a belief system that says that we should be able to understand everything and that when we do we can control everything, we are in big trouble.

WARS are disastrous whether they are within me, between individuals, or between countries.

৯ June 17

SELF-AWARENESS

I want to find out who I am and give up letting everyone else define me.

—Judith

As women, we have been trained to look for our identity outside ourselves. We have been raised to be someone's daughter, someone's wife or partner, and someone's mother. What others think of us has been who we are. Even when we are successful professional women, we find ourselves looking outside for identity and validation. This habit is embedded deep in the marrow of our bones even when we look strong and self-defined.

An important part of our recovery is finding out who we *really* are—not who we have been *told* we should be, not who we *think* we should be, and not who we image ourselves to be.

Who is this person I call me? She has the potential of being one of the most interesting persons I have ever met. Yet, I hardly know her.

TODAY I have the opportunity to begin or continue an inner journey that can last the rest of my life.

LIVING IN THE PRESENT

*I know the solution. When we have a world of only
now with no shadows of yesterdays or clouds of
tomorrow, then saying what we can do will work.*
—Goldie Ivener

Imagine starting each day fresh with no "shadows of yesterdays or clouds of tomorrow." In our more negative, cynical moods, we hear such an idea and we scoff, impossible! It is not possible to let go of the past and have no concern for the future. Yet this is what every great spiritual teacher on this planet has taught in one way or another. In fact, the greatest gift our spiritual teachers have given us has often been to show us how to live in the present, how to simply be totally present to the moment.

How often we miss our life by focusing on the past or yearning for the future. We miss the look in our children's eyes today, because we are thinking about how to get them to the dentist tomorrow. We miss the interesting idea that has just now come across our desk, because we are worrying about what we said in the meeting yesterday. Stop—relax—be here!

THE PRESENT is all I have: to leave it is to kill it.

ॐ June 19

ACCEPTANCE OF SELF

Do nothing because it is righteous or praiseworthy or noble to do so; do nothing because it seems good to do so; do only that which you must do and which you cannot do in any other way.
—Ursula K. Le Guin

We are so accustomed to doing what others want us to do, or doing what is right, or doing that which earns us praise, that LeGuin's words urging us to do only that which we *must* do and cannot do in any other way seem unrealistic. We think: That's fine for her to say, she's a writer—she schedules her own time.

Yet, what truth is there for us in her words? We certainly can admit that we have done many things for the wrong reasons, and the pain of our righteousness, "nobility," or praise-seeking is often bitter in our hearts. Often when we do something because it seems good to do so, we waste everyone's time, including our own.

What a relief to believe that we are enough just as we are and that our unique way of accomplishing a task is just what is needed.

I WILL sit with these ideas. After all, who else could make my contribution!

ꝗ June 20

EXPECTATIONS

Life's under no obligation to give us what we expect.
—Margaret Mitchell

Expectations are real killers! They are setups for disappointment. Often, because of our expectations, we are completely oblivious to what is really going on in a situation. Because we are so wedded to what we think *should* be happening, or what we want to happen, we don't see what *is* happening.

Many a possible relationship has been aborted because we were too determined to turn it into *a relationship*.

Expectations also keep us in illusion. We set up our expectations for someone, we project them onto the other person, and then we start reacting to our expectations as if they were real. Expectations and the illusion of control are intimately linked.

WHEN WE are tied to our expectations we usually miss what's happening . . . life, that is.

BEAUTY/COMPARISON

I am as my Creator made me, and since He [sic] *is
satisfied, so am I.*
                                    —Minnie Smith

How beautiful and how simple it is just to accept ourselves the way we are. Women, especially, have difficulty simply seeing the beauty in who we are. We are always comparing ourselves to others: no matter what we have or who we are, it never quite seems to be enough. We are always too much or too little, too fat or too skinny, too intelligent or not intelligent enough, too aggressive or not assertive enough. Whenever we compare ourselves to others, we lose.

The very act of comparison is part of the problem. Comparison is one of the processes of addiction. In that process, we leave ourselves and lose ourselves. There are other options.

IMAGINE a day—*today* for example—of just being satisfied with who I am.

ଽ June 22

AWARENESS OF PROCESS

Life comes in clusters, clusters of solitude, then clusters when there is hardly time to breathe.
—May Sarton

We workaholics, busyaholics, and rushaholics feel much more familiar with and comfortable with times when we hardly have time to breathe. We know how to function under pressure and with deadlines hovering over us. These times are when we shine.

Unfortunately, it is the time of calm and potential solitude after the project is finished that scares us. To be without a project or a deadline strikes terror in our bones. Fortunately, we rarely have to deal with that terror because we have arranged our lives in such a way as to rarely have a "breather."

If we take time to notice, this ebb and flow in life has a reason. We need breathers. Our bodies need to rest from our constant adrenaline push, or they blow up.

As we let ourselves get healthier, we begin to experience and treasure the "clusters" of our lives and welcome them as examples of infinite wisdom.

THE OCEAN never tires of the ebb and flow of the tides. I have something to learn from the ocean.

ℰ୰ June 23

Awareness

In contemporary America people are again discovering how to drink from their own wells.
— Lynn R. Laurence

Part of our disease is looking outside ourselves for someone who will fix our lives for us. We sometimes even believe that God or a power greater than ourselves can make everything all right—that we just have to sit back and let it happen. Not so.

When we recognize that the force we believed to be outside of ourselves is indeed within us—then we begin to heal. Healing is the experience of the oneness of all things and our ability to take our place in that oneness.

As a society, our "other-directedness" has been destructive. Changing to "me-ness" and self-centeredness has not helped much either. Recognizing that we are one with all things and accepting our place in that oneness moves us into and beyond ourselves.

MY THIRST can only be quenched from my own well and my awareness that this well is mine and is shared by all.

❧ June 24

Courage

This is the art of courage: to see things as they are and still believe that the victory lies not with those who avoid the bad, but those who taste, in living awareness, every drop of the good.

—Victoria Lincoln

How aptly put! Courage is not just seeing things as they are, which is vastly important, courage is accepting reality with the ingenuity to continue to see and experience the many good things that happen to us.

I remember in graduate school I acquired the nickname "Pollyanna," because I always could see something interesting and exciting in everything that happened. I did not always like those grueling reports and seemingly sadistic examinations and yet, when I was honest with myself, I always had to admit that I had learned something when I finished. Because of the nickname and the subtle judgmentalism attached to it, I began to question myself. After some reflection, I realized that a pollyanna was someone who denied the negative and only saw the positive. I did not do that. I saw and accepted the negative and delighted in whatever positive there was. As a consequence, graduate school was not difficult for me. Working has not been hard for me either.

A SMILE, a nod in the elevator, a few minutes of quiet time—these are living every drop of the good.

UNWORTHINESS

I switched from my negative thinking to my workaholism. That's how I continue to abuse myself.
—Judy

Our feelings of unworthiness take many forms, and one of the most obvious is self-abuse. Many women are beginning to see that their addiction to self-abuse is their most basic addiction.

It is abusive to the self to work too much. It is abusive to the self to keep so busy that we have no time for ourselves. It is abusive to the self to be so busy taking care of others that we have no awareness of our needs. It is abusive to the self to be so externally referented that we have lost a sense of self.

When we abuse ourselves, it is inevitable that we will also abuse others. Both forms of abuse are destructive.

ALTHOUGH I have become inured to self-abuse, I really do not believe that it is right for me. I will try to open myself to what *is* right for me.

ও June 26

LIVING LIFE FULLY

When I speak of the erotic, then I speak of it as an assertion of the life force of women; of that creative energy empowered, the knowledge and use of which we are now reclaiming in our language, our history, our dancing, our loving, our work, our lives.

—Audre Lorde

What a wonderful opportunity today is to celebrate ourselves as women! To celebrate ourselves does not mean that we put men down or do not like men. We are only celebrating ourselves and the unique contribution that women have made, are making, and can make.

All of us have gifts that are unique to us. No one else has quite the combination of gifts that each of us has to offer and many of those gifts are not in spite of being a woman, they are *because* we are women. Not to share the fullness of our woman gifts is a form of stinginess, and no one likes to be stingy.

WHEE! I celebrate me!

ACTION

If you want a thing well done, get a couple of old broads to do it.

—Bette Davis

If there is anything we "old broads" know how to do, it is to get things done. We women are so practical. We have an uncanny ability to see what needs to be done, roll up our sleeves, and do it. We are rarely too proud, too prissy, or too elitist to do what needs to be done.

Sometimes we fail to see how important our practical everydayness is. We long for the great inspiration, the important recognition, or the big breakthrough. Yet all our lives are made up of common tasks that need to be done. When something is common and ordinary, we frequently fail to see its real importance. What we do *is* important, and we do it well. Failing to see that is a form of dishonesty. And we don't want to be dishonest, do we?

I AM a competent "old broad." At least Bette Davis appreciated me. Maybe I can appreciate myself.

❧ June 28

WHOLENESS

Don't you realize that the sea is the home of water?
All water is off on a journey unless it's in the sea, and
it's homesick, and bound to make its way home
someday.

—Zora Neale Hurston

We are all like water. We are off on a journey to return to ourselves. Some of our journeys have taken us far afield, and many of our days have been absorbed by the sandy river banks that contain us. Yet we continue to flow—heavy and swollen in the spring of our lives and often reduced to a trickle as we approach the fall of our years. "Return, return, return," we murmur, as we tumble over the stones in our paths, ever cognizant that although we may wander through new and strange lands, our destination is a return.

WATER has to return to the sea, just as I have to return to me.

ε♭ June 29

Self-Affirmation/Power

Think of yourself as an incandescent power, illuminated perhaps and forever talked to by God and his [sic] messengers.

—Brenda Ueland

As we begin to get more in touch with ourselves and accept ourselves for who we are, we begin to entertain the thought that we might, indeed, be "an incandescent power." We begin to feel our power and know it not as power over others, but as personal power, glowing within.

As we clear out the garbage of our crazy addictive behavior, we uncover a spiritual being lying dormant, not dead, within us. We have a sense of what it means to be in tune with the infinite, and life feels easy and flowing. This feeling of oneness is not an illusion; it is real. Only as we learn to affirm who we are do we move beyond ourselves.

AS WE AFFIRM who we are, we become who we are.

❧ June 30

RECOVERY
STEP ONE

> *Recovery is a process, not an event.*
> —Anne Wilson Schaef

Now that we are beginning to recognize that overworking, caretaking, rushing around, and always keeping busy are manifestations of the addictive process and are just as much a disease as chemical addictions, we want to stop this immediately. Unfortunately, it is not that easy. The very definition of an addiction or compulsive behavior is something that has us in its grip over which we are powerless. We can't "just say no." We can't just stop what we are doing. This disease is in the cells of our muscles and in the marrow of our bones.

We need to realize that recovery is a process. It took time for us to get this way, and it takes time for us to recover. Part of our disease is wanting everything to happen at once. We need patience with ourselves and support from others to progress in our recovery process.

"I HAVE to do it [recovery] myself; I don't have to do it alone," are statements often heard in recovery circles.

NICENESS

I haven't been being nice . . . I've been chicken.
—Claudia

As women we have been trained to be nice. We *do* "nice" things for people, we *say* "nice" things, and we *are* "nice." Many of us fear that if we stop being nice, we have to become nasty. Having become bored with our niceness, many of us have experimented with nasty.

For those of us trying to get clearer with ourselves and others, we have discovered that our niceness is intimately linked with our dishonesty. If we want to be more honest, we have to be willing to let go of our "niceness." In letting go of our niceness, we find ourselves becoming more honest. Getting honest about ourselves and our lives is an essential step toward health. To be more honest, we also have to give up being chicken and put ourselves out there.

OFTEN, when we say we are being nice to protect other people, the person we are really protecting is ourselves.

❧ July 2

LIVING LIFE FULLY

I have made a great discovery.
What I love belongs to me. Not the
chairs and
tables in my house, but the masterpieces of the
world.
It is only a question of loving them enough.
—Elizabeth Asquith Bibesco

We get so embroiled with possessions. We find ourselves feeling that we need to own places, persons, and things. We try to possess our lives, and we believe that we can. We need to learn from the butterfly that alights on our hand. If we watch it and admire it, as it chooses to stay for a while, we are blessed with its beauty. If we try to hold onto it, we will kill it. It is in the not trying to possess that we have.

Imagine what it really means that we can have all the treasures of the world—not to own, but to appreciate, to enjoy . . . to live with.

AM I capable of loving so much that I am able to appreciate that which I do not possess? I hope so.

❧ July 3

HUMOR

Yo' ole black hide don't look lak nothin' tuh me, but uh passel uh wrinkled up rubber, wid yo' big ole yeahs flappin' on each side lak uh paih uh buzzard wings.
—Zora Neale Hurston

I love the writing of Zora Neale Hurston. She has a way of cutting right through to the meat of things, and she does it with humor and clarity. How often have we had thoughts similar to those quoted above, and we haven't let ourselves enjoy the tickle and the giggle in our own minds? We make life so *serious* and everything so *important* that we don't dare laugh—it might offend. We might offend.

In order not to offend, we render ourselves and our lives humorless. How dull.

I THINK it might be helpful to remember that our humor adds color to a world gone grey with inattention.

๕ July 4

SELF-ESTEEM

People call me a feminist whenever I express sentiments that differentiate me from a doormat or a prostitute.
—Rebecca West

When a woman believes that she is equal, she is called uppity. When we stand up for what we know and for what we believe, we are called aggressive and unfeminine. When we state that women are wonderful and that we are proud to be a woman, we are told that we are antimale.

When we put forth our perceptions, we are told that we don't understand reality. When we put forth our values, we are told that we are crazy and we just don't understand the way the world works. Is it any wonder that we sometimes have trouble with self-esteem?

BATTERING comes in many forms. My self-esteem is constantly assailed, yet it's really mine when I get right down to it.

❧ July 5

ISOLATION

I create my own prisons. No one else is putting these walls around me.

—Michelle

Rarely do we recognize the construction of our enclosures until they are already built. We are fooled by their illusionary appearance: they look like security, prestige, power, influence, money, and acceptance. It is only when the construction is completed that we realize that we are enclosed in splendid isolation. When did it happen? We looked down at our work or our lives for only a second, and then looked up to find that our illusions of security have become a benevolent prison. Prisons have room for fantasies, but prisons have little room for dreams.

We have misjudged our priorities. We do not want the isolation of success at any cost. Somehow, we thought we could "have it all" and now all of it has us.

MY ISOLATION has been of my making, so my reaching out for help can also be of my doing.

ತ July 6

FORGIVENESS/AMENDS

*Her breasts and arms ached with the beauty of her own
forgiveness.*

—Meridel Le Sueur

To ache with my own forgiveness is to be
wholly accepting of myself. None of us is without
need of forgiveness. In our disease, we have all done
injury to those closest to us. This is one of the most
painful aspects of addictive diseases: we hurt those
we love the most. We hurt ourselves when we hurt
those we love. When we are preparing to make
amends to others, we must first make amends to
ourselves and forgive ourselves for the wrongs we
have done. Only then can we be truly ready to make
our amends to others.

There is, indeed, a beauty in our forgiveness of
ourselves. We can be simple, direct, and without
fanfare in our forgiveness of ourselves.

I AM in need of forgiveness. I am in need of
forgiveness of myself.

❧ July 7

FRIENDS

From the first time I met the little girl until her death recently, a period of a little over seventy years, we were friends.

—Mrs. Mary E. Ackley

"We were friends"—such a simple yet powerful statement: "We were friends." How many of us can truly say that we are a friend?

One of the devastating realities of busyness and doing too much is that we progressively have less and less time for friends.

We have to make appointments for friendship. Hanging out with a friend seems a luxury or even an inconvenience. Or we assume that we are friends and never do anything to nurture the relationship. We treat our friends like we treat ourselves, and that's not very nice.

IT IS NOT POSSIBLE to live a rich, full life without friends. I have to be one to have one.

ಶ July 8

GROWTH

My favorite thing is to go where I've never been.
—Diane Arbus

To go where we have never been, whether internally or externally, is always exciting. This excitement may be covered over by fear and trepidation. Yet I have always found that somewhere deep inside of us we are excited when we have the opportunity to explore the unknown.

Men are not the only explorers. We women are explorers too. Our explorations may take different forms: we love to try out a new recipe; we love to try out a new idea or ideology; we love to visit new places and learn from different cultures. We are especially adept at courageously launching into hidden and unknown areas in ourselves and others. In spite of our fears, there is a deep quest for our truth in each of us.

I PREFER a road map on my journeys, and I am willing to go without one if I must.

ENTHUSIASM

One needs something to believe in, something for which one can have whole-hearted enthusiasm. One needs to feel that one's life has meaning, that one is needed in this world.

—Hannah Senesh

Several years ago, I made a drastic decision for myself. I decided that I would do only work that I was enthusiastic about. I was a psychotherapist, speaker, and workshop leader then. This decision was very frightening for me, since I was a single parent and had many financial responsibilities.

I decided not to accept any clients about whom I wasn't enthusiastic. I would not do any speeches or workshops just because of the money, or prestige, or ego. I would do only what seemed *right* for me to do. I would do only things that intuitively seemed related to the meaning and purpose of my life. I feared I would end up a derelict, a bag lady, and starve, yet, I have had more money since that decision than I ever had before. I still live my life based on that decision.

I'M NOT SAYING this will work for everybody, *and* it worked for me.

EXHAUSTION

You came as a solemn army to bring a new life to man [sic]. You tore that life you knew nothing about out of their guts—and you told them what it had to be. You took their every hour, every minute, every nerve, every thought in the farthest corners of their souls—and you told them what it had to be. You came and you forbade life to the living.

—Ayn Rand

It sounds here as if Ayn Rand is talking about this addictive, white-male system in which we live, a system that is innately foreign to women, and one which we have come to believe that we have to learn and participate in to survive. This is not reality—it is a system, and as a system holds no more truth than any other system. Unfortunately we have been taught that it is reality, although at some level all of us know it isn't. Also, unfortunately, this system thrives on addictions and requires them in order for us to tolerate it. Fortunately, we do have other options.

I'M TIRED of trying to be something I'm not

३॰ July 11

GOALS

It is good to have an end to journey towards; but it is the journey that matters in the end.
—Ursula K. Le Guin

When we remember that life is a process, it helps us put our goal-setting in perspective. The purpose of setting goals is to give us a temporary structure in which to operate. Unfortunately, when we begin to believe that the structure is solid and real, we lose touch with the process of getting there. This is why we often feel so depressed and let down when we reach our goals. We have not let ourselves enjoy the experience of the journey, and when we reach the end, we have missed the journey.

Being in the present allows us to experience the journey and to respond to the process of the journey. When we operate this way, we see that all goals are just temporary ideas that change as we draw near to them.

EACH DAY is a journey. Each day is a process.

GUILT/ALONE TIME

I wanted to drive up here alone and several people asked if they could drive up here with me. I can't tell you how hard it was just to come by myself.

—Mary

Often we feel guilty when we do something for ourselves. We have so accepted the mandate to be aware of others' feelings, take care of them, and put ourselves last that we often feel uncomfortable if we even *have* needs. How selfish it seems to refuse a ride to someone who needs it when we are going that way anyway. Surely we could put ourselves out a little. Even if we do refuse the request and get our time alone, are we going to be so overcome with guilt that we won't enjoy the time anyway? What a lose-lose situation!

Maybe we can use that time alone to explore our gift of guilt and learn from it. Even having time to explore our guilt requires alone time. We may need that exploration desperately.

WHEN I SAY no to a request for my time, I am not going away from that person, I am going to myself.

৯ July 13

BEING IN CHARGE

I'm not going to limit myself just because people won't accept the fact that I can do something else.
—Dolly Parton

There is a vast difference between trying to control our lives and taking charge of our lives. Trying to control our lives puts us in a position of failure before we start and causes endless, unnecessary pain and suffering.

Taking charge of our lives means owning our lives and having a respond-ability to our lives and then letting it go. Taking charge of our lives means that we do not spin our wheels with impression-management and try to be what others want us to be. It also means that we do not accept their evaluation of what we cannot be and stop there.

WHEN I LET GO of my need to control, I am in a better position to be in charge and to receive information from my power greater than myself.

BEING TORN

At work, you think of the children you have left at home. At home, you think of the work you've left unfinished. Such a struggle is unleashed within yourself. Your heart is rent.

—Golda Meir

Being torn seems to be an accepted given for women who run a home and also have other work. Many of us have tried to be superwomen and have almost pulled it off. Yet even when it appears that we are "making it" and successful in both arenas, we are aware that internally we feel torn and guilty in relation to our family. Frequently, this results in our taking our frustration out on our children, which results in more guilt. We feel like a violin string pulled taut and about to break.

Perhaps it is time to sit down with our families and tell them how we feel. They probably need to hear that we really *want* to be with them and that we do not know how to balance our lives. They may even feel relieved to know that our lives feel overwhelming (which everyone but us has admitted!).

JUST PLAIN HONESTY works for so many things. Perhaps I really shouldn't just save it for special occasions.

CREATIVITY
STEP ELEVEN

> *I feel a recipe is only a theme, which an intelligent cook can play each time with a variation.*
>
> —Madame Benoit

It sounds so simple for creativity to find its way.

We need quiet—the word sounds familiar. We can dimly remember times of quiet. Or was it when we were sleeping?

And we need time—just for ourselves with no agenda, no deadlines, no needs of others impinging upon us.

We long for quiet and time for our themes to emerge. Recovery is not possible without both. Contact with our Higher Power is not possible without both.

NO ONE ELSE will arrange any quiet time for me. I have to see to it myself.

❧ July 16

BALANCE

Creative minds have always been known to survive any kind of bad training.

—Anna Freud

Even though her father believed that our lives are determined in our first five years, Anna Freud seems to have moved beyond him. Although we are affected by our past and our training, each of us has within us the possibility of moving beyond them.

Unfortunately, when we try *not* to be like our parents, we get caught in the same trap as when we feel that we *have* to be like them. Either way we are determined by our past and controlled by our reaction to our past. Some of us spend our entire lives vacillating between these two positions.

We do have another choice. That choice is to acknowledge our past and be ourselves.

THE THIRD option is to be me. That is where my creativity lies.

❧ July 17

CONTROL

With the only certainty in our daily existence being change, and a rate of change growing always faster in a kind of technological leapfrog game, speed helps people think they are keeping up.

—Gail Sheehy

Our illusion of control dies very slowly. The more changing and uncertain our lives are, the more we fall back on our favorite illusion that if we can just get in charge we can control everything. We have forgotten that there is a difference between control and facilitating good work. Robert Blake and Jane Mouton, management consultants, developed the concept of a back-up style for managers. Regardless of how much management training people have, or how intelligent or educated they are, under stress they resort to a back-up style, and that back-up style often is one of trying to *control* the situation. Unfortunately, control never works. It isn't even possible. That's one reason we feel like such failures.

TURNING a situation over to a Higher Power is not easy under stress, although that is probably when I most need to do so.

POWERLESSNESS

*I found out that I can cut my working time to fifteen
hours a week and I can still do that workaholically.*
—Michelle

For those of us who are workaholics, rushaholics, and busyaholics, it is almost impossible to admit
that we are powerless over our disease. Slowly and
often painfully we become aware that we simply
can't stop, even when we would like to. If we are not
busy doing something, we feel anxious and unworthy. We have arranged our lives around our
work, and we simply cannot stop. This is powerlessness. We become progressively aware that our busyness and our working are interfering with our lives.
Our lives are becoming unmanageable. There is just
too much to do.

It is difficult for us to admit powerlessness, because we can do more than others and we pride
ourselves in having things under control. As we
become aware that our control is out of control, we
may be ready to start on a path of recovering our
lives.

ONLY in acknowledging my powerlessness
over my working and busyness can I begin to
heal.

৯ July 19

ALONE TIME/BEING RESPONSIBLE

*For every five well-adjusted and smoothly functioning
Americans, there are two who never had the chance to
discover themselves. It may well be because they have
never been alone with themselves.*
— Marya Mannes

Superwomen can always be heard to say, "I
know that having time to oneself is important. It's
just not possible for me. I just have too many responsibilities."

One always wonders how women who seem so
powerful and so much on top of their lives can
become so helpless in determining what they do
with their time. Our helplessness seems to be situa-
tional and often emerges only in relation to *our*
needs.

As successful women, we are often least successful in caring for ourselves. We need skill training in self-help.

THE CHOICES I make about what I do with my
time are *my* choices (even when they don't appear
to be!).

INTIMACY/EXCUSES
STEP ONE

> *Because of his need to concentrate absolutely on his*
> *work, George Sarton had developed extreme resistance to*
> *anything that might prove disturbing, such as my*
> *mother's health or lack of it.*
>
> —May Sarton

How easy it is to become so self-centered in our work that we cannot even see the needs of those closest to us! Often, our work is used as an excuse to avoid intimacy with ourselves and others. No matter what the work is, if it is "work," it is justified.

Often we ask those we love to make tremendous sacrifices in the name of our work, and we become unfeeling and uncaring in the process. It is the work that matters. Women who are addicted to their housework are just as demonic as those who are addicted to their businesses. Both can be escapes from intimacy.

Recovery offers us the possibility of intimacy with ourselves and others. However, to experience the joy of recovery we have first to admit what we are doing.

INTIMACY is like a drink of fresh water to a work-worn soul. Even a taste can bring forth desert flowers.

ठ July 21

AWARENESS OF PROCESS/FEAR

Now some people when they sit down to write and nothing special comes, no good ideas, are so frightened that they drink a lot of strong coffee to hurry them up, or smoke packages of cigarettes, or take drugs or get drunk. They do not know that ideas come slowly, and that the more clear, tranquil and unstimulated you are, the slower the ideas come, but the better they are.

—Brenda Ueland

One of the side effects of our addictive doing too much is that we begin to use chemicals and other addictive substances to keep us going. Then our addiction to doing too much becomes compounded with a complex array of other addictions.

Another side effect of being women who do too much is that we find ourselves progressively out of touch with our creativity and our productivity.

Brenda Ueland uses the focus of becoming a writer to call us back to ourselves. Yet, the truth in what she is saying applies not only to writers, it applies to all of us. Our creativity and productivity always suffer when we use addictive substances to try to force them.

I DON'T NEED to *do* something for my creativity to emerge. I probably need to *stop* doing some things.

ᨔ July 22

SUCCESS

Life is a succession of moments. To live each one is to succeed.

—Corita Kent

Perhaps it is not the concept of success that is the problem, it is the way we define success. If we define success as lots of money, getting to the top of the organizational ladder, two BMWs in our garage, and a designer house, success may be dangerous to our health.

If we define success as living each successive moment to its fullest, we may have money, prestige, and possessions, and this success may *not* be disastrous to our health. The difference is in the attitude and in the beliefs behind that attitude.

In fact, it is often easier to gather the accouterments of success than it is to live a successful life. Living a successful life demands our presence, our presence in each moment.

SUCCESS gets confusing. Is it what I have or what has me? Probably neither.

ACCEPTANCE/SELF-CONFIDENCE

One startling finding, given that these women had an average IQ of one hundred forty three, was their lack of confidence in their abilities and the belief that their intellectual selves were ephemeral or were not developed.
—Carol Tomlinson-Keasey

People have said that the women's movement is the only revolution where the outpost of the enemy is in our own minds (not that we need to think in terms of enemies). We like to think that women have overcome their negative programming and that we really do feel good about ourselves. Then we read a study like the one done by Carol Tomlinson-Keasey, and we feel a lingering sadness for a group of intelligent women who do not believe in themselves or their abilities.

We are aware that these women who mistrust themselves and their intellect are, down deep, not so different from us.

We may put up a good front, and yet we know there are still those little hidden niggling fears that maybe we just are not good enough.

I AM SAD when women do not value themselves. I am sad when I do not value myself. I will let myself feel that sadness.

❧ July 24

ACCEPTANCE/HUMILITY

But if you go and ask the sea itself, what does it say? Grumble, grumble, swish, swish. It is too busy being the sea to say anything about itself.
— Ursula K. Le Guin

No one who has ever sat beside the sea and experienced her eternal power and gentleness can have any question that the sea knows that she is just that, the sea. Nature has such an ability to be exactly what she is, with no pretense . . . and she does not even have to stop and think about it.

When we have to stop and think who we are, we are not being who we are. When we are trying to be someone we believe we should be, we are not being who we are. When we are trying to be what someone else has told us we should be, we are not being ourselves. To be myself, I have to *be*.

NATURE teaches great lessons in humility. In order to learn from her, I have to be in her.

ಕ July 25

WONDER

> *I take a sun bath and listen to the hours, formulating, and disintegrating under the pines, and smell the resiny hardi-hood of the high noon hours. The world is lost in a blue haze of distances, and the immediate sleeps in a thin and finite sun.*
> —Zelda Fitzgerald

I read the above passage, and I feel lost in wonder—wonder at the beauty of the words and phrases. I read it and I remember the wonder of a spontaneous sunbath in a light-speckled woods where the sun on my skin enhanced the mixed scent of forest musk and pungent pine, as the smells permeated my body. I can remember listening to the hours as they initially crashed around me, then gradually smoothed into a murmur as my body relaxed into the earth and into myself. The world seemed far away, and there was no need to bring it closer.

WONDER is a gift of living. Living is a gift of wonder.

TRUST

Nature has created us with the capacity to know God, to experience God.

—Alice Walker

We often think that we have to work to know God and that we have to have experts to teach us how to know our Higher Power.

What a wonderful surprise it is suddenly to discover that the capacity to know God and be connected with our Higher Power dwells within us and to discover that instead of working at this connection, we have only to admit that it is already there. We may have lost our awareness of our relationship with our Higher Power, and the connection has never stopped. It is only that our awareness of it has dimmed and become obscure.

I HAVE all I need within me to know and experience my Higher Power. All I have to do is step out of my way.

PERFECTIONISM/LONELINESS

> *"She happens to belong to a type [of American woman]*
> *I frequently met . . . it goes to lectures. And entertains*
> *afterwards . . . , amazing, their energy," he went on.*
> *"They're perfectly capable of having three or four*
> *children, running a house, keeping abreast of art,*
> *literature and music—superficially of course, but good*
> *Lord, that's something—and holding down a job into*
> *the bargain. Some of them get through two or three*
> *husbands as well, just to avoid stagnation."*
> —Dodie Smith

It sort of grates to see ourselves described on paper. We have learned to cope. We have learned to be superwomen. So what if we don't go very deeply into anything. How can we? We just don't have the time. Our biggest fear is not knowing enough or not being enough. We feel that we are inadequate if we cannot talk intelligently about almost everything and do almost anything. We would like to have more intimate relationships, but we just do not have the time—we are perfect women.

WE ARE perfect women, and being perfect is boring to ourselves and others.

ã» July 28

Reality/Denial

We flood our minds with words! They mesmerize and manipulate us, masking the truth even when it's set down squarely in front of us. To discover the underlying reality, I've learned to listen only to the action.
—Judith M. Knowlton

Letting go of our ability to discern reality is one of the characteristics of addiction. As well-known psychotherapist Marion Woodman says, "In addiction you create a fantasy and try and live there." So often we women who do too much are gullible on a very deep level. We *want* to believe what others tell us, and we do not want to have to be on our toes all the time. As a result, we often feel resentful and sad because we find ourselves dealing with illusion and not reality. It's not that we don't perceive reality. We do. We just don't want to have to deal with it. We would rather complain and be hurt. We can always see reality when we take off our filters. And reality is always easier to deal with than fantasy in the long run.

ACTIONS do speak louder than words, and when I believe what others *do* and do not listen so much to what they *say*, I feel saner.

ॐ July 29

INTEGRITY

> Tell me
> > Mother
> > > What has taken your soul
> > > > away
> > > > > so cruelly?
> > > > > > —Chungmi Kim

One of the effects of an addictive disease is that it destroys our integrity. We see ourselves doing things at work that compromise our value system, and we say nothing. We are reprimanded for something for which we were not responsible, and we say nothing. We act in ways that are not in keeping with our own personal morality.

The addiction to doing too much is just like any other addiction in that it puts us in a position where we are willing to do anything to get our "adrenalin buzz"; to get our "fix." We see ourselves participating in decisions that are wrong for us, we neglect ourselves, and we neglect our families. We have lost our integrity.

WHEN I lose my integrity, I, like Chungmi Kim's Mother, have lost (or at least misplaced) my soul.

ैं July 30

CONTRADICTIONS

If I could see what's going on with myself as well as I see what's going on with others, I'd be "fixed" by now.
                                                    —Pat

So much of our lives are glaring contradictions. We swear that we will never be like our mothers, then find ourselves screeching on the same note. We know we would never manipulate others the way our boss manipulates us, and then we catch ourselves doing it.

We seem to see so clearly "out there," while "in here" is a muddle. Relax, it's all part of this addictive disease process. It's called denial. Breaking through the denial about what is really going on in our lives is the first step in recovery.

MAYBE what we notice "out there" is what we need to see "in here." I'll check that out.

❧ July 31

HAPPINESS/DEPRESSION

When a small child . . . I thought that success spelled happiness. I was wrong, happiness is like a butterfly which appears and delights us for one brief moment, but soon flits away.

—Anna Pavlova

There is no difference between happiness and depression. They both have the same process. It is just the content that is not the same. Both will come and go. The major difference between them is what we *do* with them.

We are always seeking happiness. When we see it coming we say, "Ah, come here, I see you. Stay with me always." Happiness laughs and says, "Oh, she's seen me, I can leave now." And it does.

With depression, we see it coming, and we say: "Go away, I don't want you. Not me." And depression sighs and says, "Here we go again, I'm going to have to get bigger and bigger for her to hear me and learn what I have to teach." So it taps us on the shoulder and says, "Over here, over here!" until it gets our attention. Then it leaves.

Both happiness and depression have something to teach us. Both will come and go. Both will return. It is our response and openness to learn from both that makes the difference.

MY HAPPINESS is a gift. My depression is a gift. Both are like butterflies in my life.

❧ August 1

JOYFULNESS

*Not all songs are religious, but there is scarcely a task,
light or grave, scarcely an event, great or small, but it
has its fitting song.*

—Natalie Curtis

How long has it been since we let ourselves
savor the pure joy of listening to music? I am not
talking about the songs on the radio that we crowd
in as we speed along the freeway. I am talking about
the sheer joy of bathing ourselves in the music we
like the most.

Likewise, how long has it been since we have let
ourselves hear the song of the task we are doing?
When we do too much, we lose our joy in the doing
and see only the labor and the deadlines. Even when
we do not see the song in our work, it is still there.
We have but to listen.

TODAY I have the opportunity to open myself
joyfully to the music around me.

&~ August 2

HOLIDAYS/VACATIONS

Travel not only stirs the blood . . . It also gives strength to the spirit.

—Florence Prag Kahn

Part of the destructiveness of being women who do too much is that we don't take the time for those things that "stir the blood" and "give strength to the spirit." We simply do not take time for vacations and trips with those we love. And even when we do, we frequently do them like we do the rest of our life—rushing, pressured, and frantic.

Vacations mean a change of pace, a gentleness with ourselves, a time of rest and renewal, and a time to stretch ourselves and encounter new people, new lands, new ways, and new options. The very newness opens the possibility of expanding our spirits and flushing out the stagnant particles in our blood.

WE OWE it to ourselves and those around us to take vacations.

ࢬ August 3

Freedom

*Would you sell the colors of your sunset and the
fragrance
Of your flowers, and the passionate wonder of your
forest
For a creed that will not let you dance?*

—Helene Johnson

Would you? Have you? What kind of creed
have we accepted that tells us that we are of no
value unless we are working ourselves to death?
What kind of creed have we adhered to that tells us
that *doing* is superior to *being*? What belief have we
accepted that suggests that, if we are not rushing
and hurrying, we have no meaning?

We don't have time for sunsets, fragrances of
flowers, or the "passionate wonder of our forests."
We don't even see sunsets, flowers, or forests. Do
they still exist?

Dancing surely must be for pagans who don't
have to make money. We used to dance before we
became so important.

WHEN a creed is not articulated as a creed and
is assumed to be reality, we don't have much freedom of choice.

❧ August 4

WORK/TRUTH

I was brought up to believe that the only thing worth doing was to add to the sum of accurate information in the world.

—Margaret Mead

We live in a time of intense information exchange so rapid that it boggles the mind. We are constantly bombarded with news items, new scientific information, new ideas, and new possibilities. Where do we fit? What is our place in all this?

As women, we often discount our knowledge and try to skew our information or our perceptions so that they are acceptable to others. In so doing, we rob the world of our accumulated knowledge. Accurate information is important to the world. Accurate information from a variety of perspectives is *essential.*

I DO have a place and my information *is* important.

❧ August 5

AMBITION

Why do you climb philosophical hills? Because they are worth climbing . . . There are no hills to go down unless you start from the top.
—Margaret Thatcher

One of the marks of an intelligent person is to be able to distinguish what is worth doing and what isn't and to be able to set priorities. The significance of the climb may not be in reaching the top. One can go down a hill from halfway up or from three-quarters of the way up. Or it may be more interesting and intriguing to walk around the hill.

To have the opportunity to explore the philosophical hill, we must step on to it. From then on it is in the process of the walking and noticing the rocks, plants, and strangers along the way that wisdom comes.

GETTING to the top isn't bad, and it is probably best done as an afterthought.

৯৮ August 6

GRATITUDE

> *Big Blue Mountain Spirit,*
> *The home made of blue clouds . . .*
> *I am grateful for that mode of goodness there.*
> —Apache chant

It is impossible to come into contact with Native American spirituality and not be struck with the immensity of the gratitude expressed. Theirs is a gentle, quiet, flowing form of gratitude that runs as deep as the still lakes and soars as high as the peaked mountains. The Native American form of gratitude is peaceful. This peacefulness permeates all their legends and stories.

Sometimes we feel that if everything isn't perfect, we cannot be grateful for anything. We easily fall into all-or-nothing thinking. When we do, we miss the sunrise and the other forms of goodness that surround us.

I AM GRATEFUL. Perhaps that is enough. I am grateful.

GROWTH

Character building begins in our infancy and continues until death.

—Eleanor Roosevelt

Somehow, we always have the secret hope that we can get ourselves together, work out all our issues, discover all our talents, accept our life's work, and then relax and get on with it.

What a shock it is when we finally recognize that "character building" and growth are life-long processes and continue throughout our lives. Just when we think we are clear about the direction of our lives, and we settle into that security (stagnation), something shakes our complacency. How much easier it is to recognize in the first place that life is a process and to open ourselves to the cycles of growth in ourselves.

TO GROW and develop is the normal state for the human organism. . . . I am a human organism. It would be logical, therefore, to assume that growth and development are normal for me.

❧ August 8

ENTHUSIASM

Whenever I have to choose between two evils, I always like to try the one I haven't tried before.
—Mae West

Mae West was a rough-and-tumble lady (no pun intended) who always exhibited enthusiasm and lust for life. Whenever we see one of her movies or an interview with her, we are always impressed with her brash vitality. She is a good role model in some ways.

We don't have to be brash and we can learn something about our enthusiasm. Enthusiasm is not rounded. It has pointed corners and it is sometimes irritating to those who don't share it. Many of us have tried to curb our enthusiasm so as not to be offensive. We may even have equated getting rid of it with maturity. What a waste! Another piece of ourselves whacked off.

MY ENTHUSIASM and my aliveness are intimately connected. And it's just fine for me to have both of them.

৯ August 9

Being Present to the Moment

Dying is a wild night and a new road.
                                        —Emily Dickinson

Emily Dickinson was present to the process of her dying when she said these words. She seemed to be fully with herself and, at the same time, open to what would come. When we think of our own death, most of us hope that we can be open to the moment.

For most addicts, the idea of dying and the experience of slowly killing ourselves through overwork is something with which we are comfortable. It is the living of our lives at each moment that terrifies us and that we seek to avoid.

Luckily, we can get through this terror and come to know that we have all the caring support we need to live our lives.

THIS is my moment. I will live each moment. Then death will be a culmination, not an end.

৯৯ August 10

GOALS

To have realized your dream makes you feel lost.
—Oriana Fallaci

Several years ago one of my friends called me in a panic. "Anne," she said, "You have to do something immediately! There are some women really hurting out there and nobody knows!"

She had been interviewing women who had been in top executive positions for seven to ten years. She said it was as if they had made the team, and every day they got suited up, got on the bus, and went to the game, but . . . they never got off the bench. At first they were hopeful, but after a few years they had become resigned to the reality that they would never quite belong.

She said that she found more alcoholism, clinical depression, and anorexia-bulimia in this group of women than she had ever seen.

IT IS NOT the realization of our dreams that makes us feel lost. It is what happens to us when our dreams become nightmares.

Busyness

> *We are always doing something . . . talking, reading,
> listening to the radio, planning what next. The mind is
> kept naggingly busy on some easy, unimportant,
> external thing all day.*
>
> —Brenda Ueland

What lengths we go to keep away from ourselves! We have such an inability to relax. There are always just a few more tasks we can get done. Sometimes it almost seems that we are afraid of what might happen if we let our minds be idle for even a moment. We fill in every crack and crevice with activity. Sometimes, we even try to crowd two or more activities in at once, like making out a list of things that need to be done while we watch the news, or directing the activities of the kids while we are working on a report.

We have become addicted to busyness, and if we are not busy we feel worthless, at a loss, and even frightened.

NOTICING how busy I keep myself is the first step. Realizing that I am powerless over this busyness is the second. Recognizing that my busyness is adversely affecting my life is next.

❧ August 12

DEFENSIVENESS

I'm defensive even when what's going on has nothing to do with me. I just know I must be wrong somehow.
—Elizabeth

Being on the defensive is part of this cunning, baffling, powerful, and patient disease. If somebody offers some advice or constructive criticism, we immediately feel we are being attacked and need to defend ourselves. Or we feel we must always apologize when *anything goes wrong.* If it is going wrong, it must be our fault. Sometimes we almost seem to be apologizing for our very existence. It is as if we don't have a right to exist.

Our defensiveness, like our other character defects, will lessen as we progress in our recovery. We have but to follow the Twelve-Step program and do our work.

REMEMBER, my defensiveness is not who I am, it is what I do when I am operating out of my addictive disease. It is a red flag for me.

✌ August 13

CONTROL

People that keep stiff upper lips find that it's damn hard to smile.

—Judith Guest

We women who do too much sure do enjoy our illusion of control. In fact, it is one of our favorite illusions. Whatever it is, we can just "guts it through." We cannot afford to relax, because we might lose our tenuous hold on the reins.

We try to control everything. We believe that we can trick our bodies into more work and prevent burnout by participating in the appropriate stress management seminars and exercising regularly. We eat the right foods so we can continue to overwork our bodies. We do all the right things to "keep our lives under control." And then we read the statistics that say that death by heart attack is rising for professional women and that the age level is dropping. Surely, if we just do enough we can control . . . our bodies, our lives, and the lives of others.

NO WONDER we don't smile much!

❧ August 14

EXPECTATION/SUCCESS

My expectations—which I extended whenever I came close to accomplishing my goals—made it impossible ever to feel satisfied with my success.
—Ellen Sue Stern

A lot is never enough for women who do too much. Whenever it looks like we may have the experience of successfully completing a project, we add on other contingencies and set up the possibility of doing even more than we originally had thought possible.

Sometimes we even make tasks more complicated than they need be so we can keep busy. We feel safer when we are working. We get panicked with slack time. We feel it is almost impossible to let ourselves savor our successes. And, if we would be truthful, we have many of them.

IT'S ALL RIGHT to have successes. It's even all right to be successful.

🐾 August 15

BUSYNESS

I'm a workaholic. If I'm not working I exercise. If I'm not exercising, I eat. I don't ever stop from morning to night.

—Terry

Some of us have modeled our lives after the roadrunner cartoon character: jump out of bed—beep, beep. Throw in a load of laundry so it can wash while we do our exercises and shower—beep, beep. Nine minutes for make-up and hair—beep, beep. Seven minutes for starting the coffee, getting dressed, and popping in the toast. Five minutes for eating breakfast and making out a list of things that must be done today—beep, beep. Throw laundry into the dryer, grab coat, purse, and briefcase, and burst through the front door—beep, beep.

By the time we have finished our morning routine, most people would be exhausted, and we have just begun—beeep . . . beeep . . .

PERHAPS it is important to remember that I was not created to be a roadrunner, even if we have some features in common.

ASKING FOR HELP/REALITY

However, one cannot put a quart in a pint cup.
—Charlotte Perkins Gilman

There is a Zen story about a college professor who came to a Zen master seeking knowledge. The old Zen master looked over the professor carefully and then asked a student to go fetch her a pot of tea and two cups. She then placed a cup in front of the professor and began to pour. The tea filled the cup and spilled out over the table. Seeing this, the professor shouted, "Stop, can't you see the cup is full? It can hold no more!" The old Zen master smiled and said, "And so it is with you. Your mind, too, is full of too many things. Only when you empty it will there be room for more knowledge to come in."

Asking for help is a way of "emptying" our lives. Stopping and seeing that our lives have become too full may well be the beginning of a process that can empty us and make way for new ways of being.

MY CUP runneth over may in some contexts be a declaration of disaster. Emptying is fully as important as filling.

ஃ August 17

AWE

But what will never, never change is the wonder, the indescribable wonder to me of seeing Earth lying in space as in the hollow of God's hand.
—Zenna Henderson

Awe is a feeling that is rare in our busy lives. Awe means stopping and noticing. Awe is, at least momentarily, letting ourselves remember and experience the vastness of the universe or the amazingly intricate design in the petal of a tiny flower.

One of my friends from Germany came bearing gifts when she visited. The most intriguing was a tiny one-inch-square magnifying glass which unfolded such that the distance between the end of the stand and the magnifying glass was a little over an inch, exactly the distance needed to see clearly the tiniest veins in a leaf, the detail on the back of a bug, or the center of a minute flower. This little device opened up an entire universe to my awareness. What she had really given me was a gift of awe.

LIFE without awe is like food without herbs or spices. I have only to look around me to remember the feeling of awe.

ᘒ August 18

LONELINESS

> *The thing that makes you exceptional if you are at all,*
> *is inevitably that which must also make you lonely.*
> —Lorraine Hansberry

We are so afraid of experiencing our loneliness that we keep ourselves overscheduled and constantly busy. Often it is our fear of loneliness that is much more disabling than loneliness itself. We are so afraid of being alone that we make sure we never are.

Yet experiencing our loneliness and going through it is often the door to those parts of our being which are creative and exceptional.

I was recently given a tee shirt from a woman's bookstore that said, "Flaunt your uniqueness." We fear that if we really let people see who we are, we will be isolated. We fail to see that isolation and loneliness are different from being alone.

I WILL remember that to be lonely is not to die. My loneliness is mine. I may even learn something from it.

EXHAUSTION

I use food and caffeine addictions to keep going when I
am too tired to get the job done or meet deadlines.
                                                —Anonymous

No one has just one addiction. Addictions come in clusters. Frequently we use one addiction to support another or to mask another. When our body is just too tired from working too much we use chemicals or food to keep us going. When we are too buzzed up to let down after we have met a deadline, we use food, alcohol, or prescription drugs to slow us down.

We have even used positive activities to support our busyness and our workaholism. Exercise is good for us. Unfortunately, when we do it in a frantic way or when we use it to make our bodies healthier so we can work more, something good has become part of the problem. We can use anything to "protect our supply" and allow us to stay in our addiction.

IT IS NOT *what* I do, it is the *way* I do it, that will get me in the end.

?• August 20

SADNESS/MOVING ON

*If ever I had a good mind, it has been lost in the
shuffle. I seem to have stagnated, and I am aware that I
am not using any capacity I have to the fullest.*
—Anonymous

Resignation . . . despair . . . a sadness in lost
possibilities. It's time to take stock and realign our
priorities. We seem to have wandered off our path.
Perhaps we have even forgotten what our path was.

Maybe it is time to feel the grief of lost opportunities and stagnating minds. Life often teaches us
through our wrong turns and missed possibilities.
This feeling of sadness may well be the door to a
new beginning. But we will never go through the
new door if we do not let ourselves go through the
grief and sadness.

As we let ourselves feel our grief and pain, we
will truly have the opportunity to step onto a new
path and to explore our lives.

MY GRIEF and pain are mine. I have earned
them. They are part of me. Only in feeling them
do I open myself to the lessons they can teach.

DUTY

Duty should be a byproduct.

—Brenda Ueland

Addictive thinking usually results in putting the cart before the donkey. One of the fascinating skills of addiction is that it allows us to take something relatively neutral or even good and twist it ever so slightly, so that it becomes horrendous.

There's nothing wrong with duty. We just should not let duty override our clear feelings and intuitions. Duty cannot come before our own internal clarity. When it does, it is a tyrant. Duty needs to follow our clarity, just as doing things for our loved ones needs to be an expression of love, rather than ritualized behavior. Duty needs to be a byproduct of who we truly are, and what we value, and what is important to us.

RITUALIZED duty is a sham!

❧ August 22

WONDER

If a child is to keep alive his inborn sense of wonder without any such gift from the fairies, he needs the companionship of at least one adult who can share it, rediscovering with him the joy, excitement, and mystery of the world we live in.

—Rachel Carson

How fortunate if we get to be that adult who has the opportunity to be a companion to a child and support that child's sense of wonder! We are lucky because that child can offer us the opportunity to rekindle our own awareness that wonder continues to dwell in us. That child can remind us that we still have the capacity to look at cloud formations with new eyes and to giggle in excitement with a new discovery. How long has it been since we really had a belly laugh, especially at ourselves? How long has it been since we saw a rainbow in a drop of rain? How long since we studied the progress of a red and black ladybug on our hand?

I WONDER where our wonder is?

❧ August 23

STRUGGLE

You wear yourself out in the pursuit of wealth or love or freedom, you do everything to gain some right, and once it's gained, you take no pleasure in it.
— Oriana Fallaci

Sometimes we forget what's important. We struggle so long to establish ourselves that we become addicted to the struggle. We begin to think that if we are not struggling we are not alive. In fact, the excitement and intensity of the struggle become our complete focus, so that we forget our original goal.

There is no doubt that we as women have had to struggle individually and as a group. Yet, if we become like those against whom we struggle, we may find that we have lost ourselves in the process.

SOMETIMES we have to struggle . . . sometimes not. The issue is not the romance of the struggle; the issue is who we are as we engage in it.

❧ August 24

SECRETS

As awareness increases, the need for personal secrecy almost proportionately decreases.
—Charlotte Painter

As Isak Dinesen says, "a secret is an ugly thing." In the Twelve-Step program of Alcoholics Anonymous, we often hear the phrase, "you are as sick as the secrets you keep."

Often we fail to recognize the effect that secrets have on our lives. They are like a quiet cancer that eats away at our souls and devours our relationships. When we enter into a contract of secrecy with someone, we give a little piece of ourselves away. If we give away too many pieces of ourselves, we are devoured, very much like the heroine in Margaret Atwood's novel, *Edible Woman.*

An important part of recovery from the addictive process is to give up secret-keeping. It is only when we live our life in the open, accept responsibility for the decisions that we have made, and own our behavior that we begin to know health.

AS THE FRENCH say, "Nothing is so burdensome as a secret."

๏ August 25

HAPPINESS/CONTROL

They seemed to come suddenly upon happiness as if they had surprised a butterfly in the winter woods.
—Edith Wharton

Happiness, like most of the other important processes of life, cannot be planned. We often come to believe that if we just had an important job, plenty of money, the right relationship, attractive and intelligent kids, and a lovely home, we would be happy. When we attain these goals and still secretly feel depressed, or not quite fulfilled, we immediately ask ourselves, "What's wrong with me?"

We have done all the things that are supposed to bring us happiness, and we don't feel any better. Where have we gone wrong? We always question ourselves and believe that there is something innately wrong with us. It takes us a long time to stop and question the system that taught us that accumulation and control are the vehicles to happiness.

HAPPINESS is a gift. It comes like "a butterfly in the winter woods." Let it sit with us a while.

PARENTING

*So learning (making, coming to) rather than
accomplishment is the issue in parenthood.*
                                    —Polly Berrien Berends

How confused we get about parenting! So often,
we are stuck in the amazing belief that it is our
responsibility to *teach* our children. We forget that it
is equally as important to *learn* from them. Some of
our children don't take their responsibility to teach
us seriously, but then again parents are notoriously
slow learners.

It is difficult for us to learn something when we
believe that all teaching should go in one direction.
How much we miss in that arrogance.

PERHAPS one of the reasons my child chose me
as her parent was because there was so much I
needed to learn.

LONELINESS

Because they are cut off from their internal power source, they really feel alone and lost.
—Shakti Gawain

When we think about what is missing from our lives, we may come to the conclusion that *we are!* Oh, of course, we function well. We do the things that need to get done. We are even efficient and imaginative at times, and yet so often we feel like zombies carrying out an old routine in well-worn ruts. We have lost touch with ourselves, and there is nothing lonelier than not being in touch with ourselves.

When we have lost ourselves, no amount of externals will help. Spouses, friends, work—none can supply what is missing when we are cut off from our "internal power source." *We* are missing, and the only way to remedy this problem is to find ourselves again. Finding ourselves takes time. It is hard work *and* it is worth doing.

I WAS looking all over for what was missing in my life, and then I discovered *I* was.

ಎ August 28

HUMOR/RELATIONSHIPS

When you see what some girls marry, you realize how they must hate to work for a living.
                                                            —Helen Rowland

What a joke. Some of us thought if we just married the right man, or found the right partner, we wouldn't have to work. Did we ever consider how much work it is to be married to someone so we won't have to work? Did we ever consider how much work it is *not* to do *our work?* Did we ever consider that our work is not work but *our work?*

How tempting it is to sell our souls for what we think will be the prize! We women have been too willing to objectify . . . to make ourselves sex objects and make men (or other women) marriage objects. In so doing we have lost the possibilities of relationships. It is not possible to relate to an object.

REMEMBER, one has to *perform* to get the prize. One has to *be* to relate.

ও August 29

Impression Management

Women's virtue is man's greatest invention.
—Cornelia Otis Skinner

How much we distort ourselves in trying to please others. Women have historically been controlled by the demands and expectations of others. We have been so willing to let others define us and so eager to fit that definition that we have lost all track of who we are.

As we come more in contact with ourselves, we realize that many of the definitions of who women "naturally are" are generated to take care of others. For example, it has been an accepted truth of psychology that women are "natural nesters." Yet, in recent times, when women have been getting divorced, it appears that it is the men who quickly find another woman to make a nest for them, while women become the wanderers. So many of our definitions of who we are have been invented for us by others, to please them and meet their needs—and we have desperately tried to fit their images of what is acceptable.

A VIRTUOUS woman is someone who is herself.

ও August 30

INTERRUPTIONS

It is distraction, not meditation, that becomes habitual;
interruption, not continuity; spasmodic, not constant toil.
—Tillie Olsen

How we hate interruptions, especially when we are working on something important. In fact, when we are working on something important, everything is an interruption. As Tillie Olsen says, distraction, interruption, and the spasmodic seem to be our lot sometimes.

How difficult it is to mesh the process of our life and the process of our work. Yet, how sweet it is when that happens!

One of the reasons that "meditation," "continuity," and "constant toil" have not been possible is because we have not believed that we deserve the time for ourselves to do our own work. Just as the addict who is into her self-centeredness is out of touch with herself, the workaholic who is into her workaholism is out of touch with her work.

WHEN I trust my process, I trust the process of my work.

❧ August 31

ALONE TIME

*So you see, imagination needs moodling,—long,
inefficient, happy idling, dawdling and puttering.*
                                        —Brenda Ueland

What wonderful words: moodling, dawdling, and puttering! I have a friend who says that she likes to "frither." The word sounds just like what it is: putzing—really doing nothing.

I used to have a big dog named Bubber who was one of my most important teachers. He used to sit out on our deck up in the mountains and just look. It was difficult for me to imagine what he was looking at all the time, so one day I just went out and sat beside him and "looked." I sat with him for a long time and experienced just sitting and just looking. I learned to take time just to sit and look. One sees so much when one just sits and *looks.* Doing nothing else . . . just looking.

Bubber has since died, and his great wisdom in having taught me to sit and look lives on.

NOT ALL of us can have Bubbers, *and* all of us can develop the skill to sit and look.

❧ September 1

HONESTY

I give myself sometimes admirable advice, but I am incapable of taking it.
—Mary Wortley Montagu

How refreshing when we can be honest, even humorously honest, about ourselves! Often we are so busy protecting ourselves that we don't dare risk letting others know that we aren't perfect. Of course usually we are the only ones fooled by our masquerades, but we make ourselves believe that others are fooled, too.

When we can be honest with ourselves, we usually know very clearly what we need and what is destructive to us. The trick is, can we listen to ourselves? Are we capable of following our own good advice? Can we let ourselves see our foibles and laugh about them? After all, no one knows us as well as we know ourselves. So, naturally, we are the persons who are most capable of seeing ourselves clearly. Are we courageous enough to let ourselves see ourselves and be honest about what we see?

ADVICE is difficult, even when it comes from ourselves. Even if we can't put our advice into action, we don't need to beat ourselves up about it.

ε• September 2

JOYFULNESS/CONTROL

In search of my mother's garden I found my own.
—Alice Walker

One of the greatest joys in life is to be in search of one thing and to discover another.

Before we started our recovery, we were so controlling that surprises struck terror in our heart even when they were wonderful. We just didn't want anything coming at us that wasn't planned, structured, and under control. We now realize that trying to control everything has been one of the ways that we have robbed ourselves of the joy of living.

No wonder life has seemed dull at times—we have made it that way. It's not that the potential for joy wasn't there. We just were too busy and controlling to notice it.

THE PURE joyfulness of the unexpected can be a source of wonder to me.

❧ September 3

In Touch with
a Power Greater than Oneself

Those who lose dreaming are lost.
—Australian Aboriginal proverb

If we are to have any hope of being in touch with the process of the universe or with a power greater than ourselves, we must learn to move beyond our rational, logical minds and to let ourselves "dream."

That does not mean that there is anything wrong with our rational, logical minds, but we can have trouble connecting with a force greater than ourselves when we *lead* with our rational minds.

There are so many things in this universe that affect us and with which we are connected. Sometimes the only way we can be aware of that connection is to let ourselves dream beyond our knowing. We have so much to learn from everything around us, if we just open ourselves to that which may be.

I ADMIT I don't know it all yet. Learning comes in many forms.

◈ September 4

LEARNING

Patterns of the past echo in the present and resound through the future.

—Dhyani Ywahoo

We are a process, and the key to living that process is learning. Mistakes are not proof that we are bad; they are doors for learning and moving on. It is often said of addicts that they don't learn from their past because they have no memory. If we have no past, we have no present and we have no future.

Everything in our lives is an opportunity for learning. Often, our most painful experiences open doors that must be opened before we can take our next steps. That doesn't mean that we don't sometimes have to walk over what seem like beds of hot coals to reach the door. Yet once we reach the other side the learning is there.

Kurt Vonnegut talks about "wrang-wrangs" in our lives, great teachers who are placed in our path. The lessons they teach us are vastly important, and they are taught through struggle, pain, trial, and tribulation. Still, they are important teachers.

THE NEXT TIME a "wrang-wrang" drops into my life, I have the option of recognizing that person as a teacher.

ঌ September 5

AWARENESS/CONTROL

Discoveries have reverberations. A new idea about oneself or some aspect of one's relations to others unsettles all one's other ideas, even the superficially related ones. No matter how slightly, it shifts one's entire orientation. And somewhere along the line of consequences, it changes one's behavior.
—Patricia McLaughlin

How amazing we human beings are! One little change in any aspect of our life affects so many other facets of our being in as yet unimagined or undreamed of ways that we never really quite know where anything will lead. We say no to something at work that for many months we have wanted to say no to and instead of the backlash we expected, we experience some subtle indication of respect. We certainly respect ourselves more.

We break our necks to earn respect and admiration, only to discover that we really have no control over how others perceive us. Our letting go of our illusion of control in even the smallest way reverberates throughout our lives.

I KNOW that gradually, ever so gradually, I am growing and changing. My life is much more like a mobile than a ladder. Each new discovery affects every aspect of my being.

ઙ September 6

COMPETITIVENESS/OPTIONS

The only way we got any attention from our father was if we made straight A's, he would give us three dollars. You can bet I worked my tail off. It wasn't the money either. Sooo, the seeds of my workaholism were planted early.

—Mary

How subtly we are given the message that we are what we produce! Acceptance and approval were very important to us as children, and we could get them by "working our tails off." Unfortunately, no matter what we did or how well we did it, it never seemed to be enough. At least, it did not really take care of that longing inside that is sometimes so intense it hurts.

Getting rewards and recognition can take away the growing internal pain momentarily, but it always comes back. We can get our three-dollar award as children, or we can get impressive salaries and positions as adults, and somehow the emptiness inside just goes underground. It does not disappear.

The seeds of our workaholism and busyness were indeed sown early. We must, however, remember that anything that has been learned can be unlearned. We were not created to work ourselves to death. We have *learned* to work ourselves to death.

I HAVE OPTIONS for my life, and one option is to see options.

❧ September 7

DEMANDING TOO MUCH OF ONESELF

I believe that IQ's change, and mine dropped considerably. I'm no longer very competent in any area. My children all turned out well not due to me, but rather to a strict father who allowed no nonsense.
—Anonymous

What has happened to this woman? Where did she go? As we read what she says about herself, we have the feeling that she is disappearing before our very eyes. Many of us have had the experience of being devoured by our families, our houses, our jobs, and our lives. I once knew a woman who used to keep looking back for footprints on the sidewalk, because she had the strange feeling that her soul was seeping out through the soles of her feet and she would see the evidence on the sidewalk.

I can remember feeling as if I did not exist as a separate person when I used to work at the kitchen counter and my children would stand on my feet to make themselves just a little higher. I also felt myself disappearing when, as toddlers, they wanted to get from one end of the couch to the other and they just walked over me as if I were not there. Life can, at times, invite us to disappear.

We feel ourselves disappearing. Yet, how arrogant it is for the woman quoted above to accept that her children turned out well and to believe that she had nothing to do with it! What a dedication to self abnegation!

TODAY, I will be willing to look at the possibility that my self-battering is an arrogant and self-centered activity that is not useful to me or anyone else.

AMBITION

*Sometimes you wonder how you got on this mountain.
But sometimes you wonder, "How will I get off?"*
—Joan Manley

Ambition has been important to many of us. When we were little girls, we realized that it was important that we work hard and become somebody. We wanted to get ahead, and we were willing to go to any lengths to be competent and important. In the last few years women have had many more options for our lives, and we wanted to take advantage of these opportunities.

When did things change? When did we cross over the line from having ambition, which was good, to being had by our ambition, which is killing us?

Often, with addictions, the very skills which kept us alive when we were younger (like dishonesty, control, and manipulation) are now lethal and are draining the life from us. This may be true about our ambition. If it now is running our lives, it may be time to take another look.

WHAT WAS GOOD for us at one stage of our lives may be lethal now. We need to take stock and see where we are with our lives.

ɞ September 9

WISDOM

> *Women have always been the guardians of wisdom and humanity which makes them natural, but usually secret, rulers. The time has come for them to rule openly, but together with and not against men.*
> —Charlotte Wolf

It is time to listen—to listen to myself and to listen to the ancient wisdom that is all around me.

Women are such masters of practical wisdom and we live in a world that is dying for lack of practicality. What good is the best invention in the world if it doesn't *work?* What good are the best ideas in the world if we cannot use them?

If we are indeed the guardians of wisdom, it behooves us to share that wisdom.

AS MERIDEL LE SUEUR says, "The rites of ancient ripening / Make my flesh plume."

࣌ September 10

STARTING OVER

The two important things I did learn were that you are as powerful and strong as you allow yourself to be, and that the most difficult part of any endeavor is taking the first step, making the first decision.
—Robyn Davidson

These words were written by a woman who learned to handle camels and traveled alone with them across the Australian Outback. Somehow the intensity of the circumstances under which she gathered these learnings makes them even more profound. What if each of us believed that we are "as powerful and strong" as we allow ourselves to be? What if we quit trying to be accepted by everyone and gave up trying not to alienate anyone and just let ourselves be as strong and powerful as we are? Nothing extraordinary, mind you, just as wonderfully powerful as we naturally are.

And, what if we let ourself take that first step toward what we really want? Nothing big . . . no fanfares . . . just do it!

REMEMBER today really *is* the first day of the rest of my life.

ᕪ September 11

SERENITY

The silence of a shut park does not sound like country silence; it is tense and confined.
—Elizabeth Bowen

When we are not really dealing with our disease of doing too much, we are often silent and not serene. We have only shut up for awhile and are still "tense and confined," like a city park shut off from activity.

Serenity is more like having a "country silence" within. Serenity is an acceptance of who we are and a *being* of who we are. Serenity is an awareness of our place in the universe and a oneness with all things.

Serenity is active. It is a gentle and firm participation with trust. Serenity is the relaxation of our cells into who we are and a quiet celebration of that relaxation.

LONGINGLY, way back somewhere, I remember what it is like to have a "country silence" within. I can be grateful for that sense of knowing.

❧ September 12

REACHING OUR LIMITS

I have had enough.

—Golda Meir

What beautiful words, and how rarely are they spoken by women who do too much. Part of our craziness is not recognizing that we have limits and not knowing when we reach them. In fact, many of us may see having limits as an indicator of inadequacy. We cannot forgive ourselves for not being able to carry on when we are exhausted or for not being able to keep going regardless of the circumstances.

Recognizing that we are approaching our limits and accepting those limits may be the beginning of recovery.

EVERY human being has limits, and I am a human being.

❧ September 13

LIVING LIFE FULLY

She wants to live for once. But doesn't know quite what that means. Wonders if she has ever done it. If she ever will.

—Alice Walker

Most of us would like to live life fully. Yet when it comes to putting those words into practice, we are not quite sure how. We wonder if we know what living life fully really means, or if we have ever known.

Our temptation is to rush out and stock up on "how to" books. If we can just find the right book, we will know what to do. We have read enough so that we are pretty good at following directions. Or we start going to lectures and workshops. We try meditation, drumming, chanting, special diets, special exercises, and special therapies. Always looking outside ourselves for the formula and answers.

At some point we realize that in spite of how good all these approaches are, we have to come back to the realization that only *we* know how to live *our lives* fully. We can accept guideposts, and ultimately, living our lives is up to us.

EVEN IF we have never done it, the knowledge of how to live our lives fully lies deep within us.

FEELING OVERWHELMED

Feeling overwhelmed isn't surprising. Being surprised about it is.

Anne Wilson Schaef

Is it any wonder we often feel overwhelmed? Just the bills for all the "necessities" of life seem more than we can handle sometimes. And then there are federal income taxes, state taxes, changing deductions, investments, sales, best buys, 10,000-mile checkups on our cars, teeth cleaning, pap smears, travel arrangements, and planning family vacations, if we dare to take one.

Recent estimates on the rate of information processing tell us that every few minutes we process more information than was processed in a lifetime by those living in the Middle Ages.

Feeling overwhelmed feels like a normal reaction.

SOMETIMES it helps to know that I just can't do it all. One step at a time is all that's possible— even when those steps are taken on the run.

৯ September 15

FEELINGS

Sorrow is tranquility remembered in emotion.
—Dorothy Parker

How lovely! All feelings are equally as lovely.

We have done ourselves such a disservice by talking about "negative" and "positive" feelings. Feelings are just feelings, and like every other aspect of our being are gifts from which we can learn.

Sorrow and grieving are feelings that we try to avoid. They take time and are not easy. Yet we make them worse by avoiding them. We feel sad when some promotion doesn't come through. We feel sorrow when we lose those we love. How beautiful to think of it as "tranquility remembered in emotion."

Grief is real, and it is human. We grieve our losses, whatever they are. Grief is an unfolding process that has many levels. It is important for us to accept our passage through the levels of grief. It is even normal to feel grief when we finish an interesting project, or when our company or family restructures.

IT IS FIGHTING our feelings that causes our suffering, not our feelings.

❧ September 16

Being Obsessed

> *I feel when people say "bigger and better" they should say "bigger and badder."*
> —Marie Elizabeth Kane
> (13 years old)

Women who do too much have embraced the cultural expectation of more, more, more. We want more money, more power, more recognition, more acceptance, more. . . . We become obsessed with getting whatever it is we feel that we must get. As our addictions progress, our values regress.

It is easy to see how an alcoholic or drug addict will do anything for a fix. But workaholics and careaholics can become just as deadly when their supply is threatened. The cornerstone of any addictive behavior is a loss of touch with our own morality and spirituality. We become "spiritually bankrupt." We get "bigger and badder."

IT IS a relief to know that recovery from any addiction is guaranteed if I just do the work I need to do. I really don't want to be one of the bad guys.

❧ September 17

GIFTS/WORRYING

I think these difficult times have helped me to understand better than before how infinitely rich and beautiful life is in every way and that so many things that one goes around worrying about are of no importance whatsoever.

—Isak Dinesen

It's not that we need to seek pain and suffering to glean the rich learnings of life. When they happen, however, we learn so much more if we can see these situations as rich opportunities for learning. We spend so much time worrying, and worrying is nothing more than an attempt at remote control. Often what we worry about never comes to pass. Unfortunately, we may be so preoccupied with worry that we miss the gifts our life is presenting to us at the moment.

When will we realize that the unfolding process of our lives is so much richer and varied than we ever could have planned? The unplanned and uncontrollable gifts we receive add color to the tapestry of living.

I NEVER KNOW in advance what will be an important gift for me. Hence it behooves me to be open to possibilities.

ᶓᵂ September 18

GUILT

I even feel guilty about feeling guilty.

—Nicole

Women are the first in line to stand up for a good cause. We can mobilize an army of volunteers to save a faltering school system, a crumbling church, or a sagging corporation. We are willing and able to put our weight behind any cause that is politically correct. We genuinely care about the homeless, the starving, the brutalized, and the forgotten, and we do a great deal of good. Who knows how much of our causes are motivated by guilt? Only we can know that, as we look inside.

The one cause that we have difficulty supporting is that of women. We are covered with guilt if we take a stand on our own behalf. We believe we should always be putting our energies "out there" for those who need it more. Women are notorious for not recognizing and standing up for our own needs and, on those rare occasions when we do, we are quickly immobilized when anyone calls us selfish.

GIVING OUT of guilt is like sharing an apple full of worms. We have to take care of ourselves before we can clearly and cleanly give to others.

❧ September 19

BEING PRESENT TO THE MOMENT

What they took for inattentiveness was a miracle of concentration.

—Toni Morrison

Have you ever watched a cat stalk a bird? Every muscle, every tendon, every heartbeat is focused on the prey.

Have you ever watched a cat stretch after a nap? Every muscle, every tendon, every heartbeat is totally involved in the stretch.

Sometimes when we are totally concentrating on a task we may seem rude and inattentive. Yet we are wholly present. We are present to our moment of focus.

These moments of complete focus are magical moments and frequently are times when we experience the oneness with our Higher Power and the process of the universe. We are totally within ourselves, and we are totally beyond ourselves.

I REJOICE for the moments of total oneness. I am truly myself when within and beyond myself.

ঙ় September 20

CONTROL/COURAGE

Even cowards can endure hardship; only the brave can endure suspense.

—Mignon McLaughlin

Before we started our recovery program, we never thought that we could tolerate the suspense of living. We believed that if we could just control everything—how people see us, how our children turn out, how a client progresses—then we would be safe.

As we have begun to let go of our illusion of control, we find that life is indeed scary sometimes (of course it was before, too, but we just didn't let ourselves feel our feelings). We also find that it holds the potential of undreamed-of surprises and suspenseful moments that we handle well and from which we grow.

I ALWAYS thought it true courage to suffer. Now I see that being alive is a special kind of bravery.

৯ September 21

CLARITY

Women know a lot of things they don't read in the newspapers. It's pretty funny sometimes, how women know a lot of things and nobody can figure out how they know them.

—Meridel Le Sueur

What a struggle it has been for us to repress our knowing for all these years . . . for all these centuries. Our addiction to doing too much enables us to ignore our own wisdom, so that we fit more easily into an addictive society.

How often have we kept our mouths shut at board meetings and staff meetings because sharing our knowledge would arouse a great hue and cry, or be completely ignored?

We have tried so hard to fit into a society that we did not create and to become acceptable to that society that we have become the amazing shrinking women. Yet, we know and we know we know.

THE WORLD needs our knowledge and our wisdom. Our companies need our clarity. Our families need our clarity. We need our clarity.

❧ September 22

CONFUSION

I seem to have an awful lot of people inside me.
—Dame Edith Evans

Frequently it is the people that we carry around inside us who encourage our workaholism, our busyness and our careaholism.

We have little voices in our minds that tell us, "You are expendable. Employers can get rid of people who are not high producers. You are what you do. If you aren't doing something, you are nothing. No one will ever want you just for who you are. You have to make yourself indispensable, and then you can feel secure. You aren't intelligent *enough*. You're *too* intelligent." Voices, voices, voices.

No wonder we often feel confused. We have a chorus on twenty-four-hour duty.

GROWING UP and claiming our own lives is partially a process of listening to our own voices and distinguishing them from the crowd inside us, especially when the internal committee is a group of addicts.

Confusion/Doing It All

Being a "good mother" does not call for the same qualities as being a "good" housewife, and the pressure to be both at the same time may be an insupportable burden.

—Ann Oakley

Trying to be all things to all people is characteristic of women who do too much. We accept a number of roles, many of which are contradictory in their demands on us and the skills they require. We find that the skills we need to communicate in the world of business are disastrous when used with our children. And the skills we need to be good mothers are not valued in the workplace. Is it any wonder that we feel confused?

Thank goodness recovery gives us a model for operating out of ourselves and not trying to fit ourselves into roles and become those roles.

WHEN I bring myself to a situation, that is the best I have to offer.

❧ September 24

BALANCE

There is a time for work. And a time for love. That leaves no other time.

—Coco Chanel

Well, at least Coco Chanel recognized that one has to do something besides work! How many of us have ruled out love and living from our lives and seen them as expendable? Even if we are married, we act as if love is a luxury that we can ill afford. Our disease of doing too much has isolated us more and more from ourselves and others.

Just as nature needs balance, people need balance. We need time to be whole persons, and this means balance. We are constantly being drained. Therefore, we need to be fed, and we need time to digest the nourishment. Work and love are better than just work alone and . . . there is more.

A HUMAN BEING is multidimensional. A human doing may be more like a drawn line than a faceted gem.

ৰ September 25

Confused Thinking

Every time you don't follow your inner guidance, you feel a loss of energy, loss of power, a sense of spiritual deadness.

—Shakti Gawain

Sometimes we just think too much. We have a problem to solve, and we believe that if we just can figure it out we will be all right. The more we figure, the more confused we become, until we have ourselves in a complete muddle. Then we use this occasion to beat ourselves up for being so dumb and stupid that we can't figure out the solution—and the downward spiral continues. We are in our disease of addiction. We are operating out of the addictive process. We are indeed experiencing a loss of energy, a loss of power, a sense of spiritual deadness.

stop!! It's time to wait with our "inner guidance." It's always there. We have just covered it over with the compacted concentration of mental masturbation.

ॐ September 26

AMENDS/PARENTING/
CONTROL/SELF-CENTEREDNESS
STEPS EIGHT AND NINE

> *I treated my children like projects, efficiently managing and orchestrating their lives, often at the expense of their feelings.*
>
> —Ellen Sue Stern

As we begin to look at the effects of trying to control everything and "efficiently manage and orchestrate" our lives and the lives of those around us, we realize that, just like the alcoholic, our disease has seriously damaged those we love the most. They are victims of our disease as much as the family of an alcoholic or a drug addict is a victim of the disease.

We begin to see that in our confused, diseased way of thinking, what we thought was good for our children and those we love was really a self-centered way of trying to stay in control.

Seeing what we have been doing is the first step toward recovery. We need to admit what we, perhaps unwittingly, have done to others, and, where possible, without harming them, make amends.

AS I LOOK BACK on my enmeshment in my work, I am not always proud of what I have done. I hope, however, that I have another chance with those I love.

❧ September 27

Honoring Self/Panic/ Choices/Support

The place where I work is supposed to be a place that heals people, and it violates the people who work there.
—Rosie

We have been hearing more and more about unhealthy buildings and their effect upon our lives. However, as many of us begin our recovery and start to take better care of ourselves, we discover that our workplaces not only do not support our quest to become healthier, they actively interfere with it.

We find ourselves feeling frightened and over-whelmed. Are we going to have to give up our jobs to be healthy? Are we going to have to give up our journey into health in order to maintain our jobs? Neither option is too attractive.

Luckily, we do not have to make either of these choices today. We *do* need to get support for our journey toward health, however. Hopefully, there are possibilities for this support within and outside of the work setting. Support is crucial for becoming more whole.

I WILL look around and open myself to as yet undiscovered sources of support wherever they are available.

❧ September 28

Indispensable

> *But my family* needs *me.*
> —Anonymous housewife

There is nothing as secure as being needed . . . or is there?

There is nothing as draining as being needed. We have often made ourselves indispensable at work and at home so that we would feel secure and wanted. Down deep it was inconceivable that people in our lives could love us for who we are. Even if they might, could we afford to take the risk and let their love come to us?

Of course our children need us, but often much less than we wish. Unfortunately, trying to make ourselves indispensable is not relegated to the home and women who work in the home. Often we equate being indispensable with being secure. In fact, we confuse the two.

WHEN I AM trying to make myself indispensable, I know that I need to look inside to see what I am feeling.

ॐ September 29

BUSYNESS/FRIENDSHIP

What a new idea! I had this friend who came to visit and it dawned on me . . . I didn't have to do anything.
—Mary

We busyaholics cannot even imagine the possibility of not having to *do* something. When a friend comes to visit, that gives us the opportunity to indulge in our disease—rushing around, getting things in order, arranging, and preparing so they will feel welcome and have a good time.

We are so busy *before* they arrive that we are exhausted *when* they arrive. Or we keep ourselves so busy making them comfortable that we do not get to sit and be with them.

Somewhere in our busy little beings it is inconceivable that they can care for themselves and they just wanted to be with *us*.

TODAY I have the possibility to be open to the possibility that someone who reaches out just wants to be with *me*.

❧ September 30

FEAR/WORK

Know that it is good to work. Work with love and think of liking it when you do it. It is easy and interesting. It is a privilege. There is nothing hard about it but your anxious vanity and fear of failure.
—Brenda Ueland

Our work and the ability to do our work are gifts we have. Doing our work is so simple. We just do it. Our work is not difficult, confounding, or complicated. We make it that way sometimes. When we are able to focus on our work and just get down to it and do it one step at a time, it gets done and it usually gets done well. When we overwhelm ourselves by seeing only the totality of it looming before us and do not break it down into its smaller components, we begin to feel inadequate and incapable of completing the task. We then procrastinate as our anxiety and fears click into gear.

WHEN I take my work one step at a time it is easy. Luckily, I can only do one step at a time anyway.

ࣈ❧ October 1

AWARENESS OF PROCESS/COMMITMENT
STEP THREE

To believe in something not yet proved and to
underwrite it with our lives: it is the only way we can
leave the future open.
                                    —Lillian Smith

There once was a woman who said that she experienced the idea of Living in Process as akin to
jumping off a cliff. Sometime after making that
statement she related a dream in which she had
come to the edge of a cliff and was aware of being
very fearful of something coming up behind her. In
the dream, she felt that she had only one positive
choice—to jump off the cliff, which she did with
great terror. Suddenly she was aware of a wonderful
floating feeling. She opened her eyes and realized
that her skirt had become a parachute: she was safe
and floating comfortably.

"Leaving the future open" may be one of the
most important commitments we make with our
lives. Believing in something not yet proved may
just be believing in ourselves.

WE NEVER know what will make good parachutes. When one is leaving the future open, it
helps to know that there are parachutes not of our
making in our lives.

❧ October 2

BECOMING/GETTING OLDER

We grow neither better or worse as we get old, but more like ourselves.
—Mary Lamberton Becker

I once met a woman in her sixties who shared what a marvelous revelation it was to her to become completely gray. "I can just put my ideas out the way I want to," she said, "and I don't get all of that strange sexual energy from men coming at me like I did when I was younger."

Another woman in her fifties confided that one of the best-kept secrets in this culture was what she called "post-menopausal zest." "I thought I was a whiz before menopause," she whispered conspiratorially, "and you should see me now."

These were obviously women who had chosen to let process of aging facilitate their becoming more fully themselves.

AS THE DEMANDS to falsify ourselves lessen, we can more easily concentrate on being the person we have always been.

ಕ October 3

FEELING CRAZY

You were once wild here. Don't let them tame you!
— Isadora Duncan

We feel so overwhelmed by our feelings some-times that we just feel like screaming. Women (and men!) do scream. We scream at our children, we scream at our spouses, we scream at our friends, and we scream at our employees. Often we and they attribute this behavior to the "time of the month" and write it off as crazy hormonal behavior. Down deep we feel ashamed, guilty, crazy, and unclean about this show of emotions.

Sometimes screaming is normal and necessary. We need to cry. We need to scream. It is part of our process and a normal response to living in a high-pressure, addictive society. However, we need *not* to scream at others. We need to have our safe places where we can let our feelings out: have a good cry or have a good scream. This processing is normal for the human organism. We just believed that we were the only ones who needed it.

WHEN I let my feelings out on others, I feel bad. When I just let my feelings out in a safe place, I feel good.

❧ October 4

FREEDOM

Sisterhood, like female friendship, has at its core the affirmation of freedom.

—Mary Daly

For women to be truly friends, we have to shed the suspicious competitiveness toward one another that we have been trained into. We have to move beyond seeing other women as competitors for the "goodies" (males and male validation and attention). We have to be open to the possibility that *because* we are women we have mutual concerns and experiences that we need to share. To do this, we have to be willing to move beyond our training and education for separateness, to leap the chasm and become free to be ourselves with one another.

Once we have made the leap, we find a richness and depth in our female friendships that simply is not possible with men. We find ourselves saying again and again, "I know," "I know." It is in "affirming our freedom" from old brainwashing that we move into friendship and sisterhood.

THOUGH I have been told otherwise, I need friends who are women.

ও October 5

EMPTINESS

When one is a stranger to oneself, then one is estranged from others too.
—Anne Wilson Schaef

Whenever we stop long enough, we are aware of an inner feeling of emptiness. This feeling is so terrifying that we immediately get busy and try to block it out. We head for the refrigerator and attempt to bury it with food. We try to drown it with drink. We get very active with new projects or activities. We watch television.

If we just knew what we need to do to make this feeling go away, we would do it. We are competent women, and we can handle almost anything *when we know what it is.* All we really experience is the absence of something. We have a vague recollection that we once knew what it was, and we can't remember it now.

MAYBE what I'm missing is myself and my connection with my Higher Power.

ತಿ October 6

BEING OBSESSED

Why Women Who Do Too Much Housework Should Neglect It for Their Writing.
—Brenda Ueland

This quotation is a chapter heading in Brenda Ueland's book *If You Want to Write.* It sums up the issue of being obsessed with our work. Yet she goes on to devote an entire chapter to it.

Why is it that the first things we give up and neglect are ourselves and the things that mean the most to us, like our creativity, our health, our children, and our loves? How sad it is that we often neglect our treasures for activities of far less value.

Well, that's what the insanity of addiction is about isn't it? We cast our pearls into the pig pen, and we scrub the colors off the kitchen tiles.

LET's get clear here about what needs to be neglected.

ट० October 7

BEING PRESENT TO THE MOMENT

Miracles are unexpected joys, surprising coincidences,
unexplainable experiences, astonishing beauties . . .
absolutely anything that happens in the course of my
day, except that at this *moment I'm able to recognize*
its special value.

—Judith M. Knowlton

Miracles are constantly occurring around us. Serendipities abound in daily life.

The issue is not that these miracles are absent. The issue is that often *we* are absent. We are standing on a hill of diamonds, and we are looking for the gold mine beyond the next ridge.

As we reclaim ourselves, we begin to notice the extraordinariness of the ordinary. We quit *thinking* about being present and we start doing it.

THANK GOODNESS I have walked in circles long enough to wear the soles of my shoes so thin that the diamonds on which I stand can now get my attention.

ᘒ October 8

INDISPENSABLE/CONTROL

A few years ago, had someone called me an Indispensable Woman, I would have said, "Thank you." I would have considered it a compliment. Today, I know better.

—Ellen Sue Stern

As women who are caretakers and overworkers, we have often believed that we are indispensable. We have even made ourselves indispensable and then felt exhausted but secure. We believed that if the company, our children, our spouses, and our friends could not get along without us that there would always be a place for us in their lives. Our little hearts glowed when someone said, "What would I do without you?"

Thank goodness it *is* possible to teach an old dog new tricks! Many of us have seen that our indispensability not only was destructive to us, it was destroying all our relationships. We began to notice an undertone of resentment in those around us. People always resent those on whom they are dependent and those who try to control their lives.

I AM so relieved that I discovered that being indispensable was killing me and my relationships. Now I have options!

DESPAIR

A vacuum can only exist, I imagine, by the things that enclose it.

—Zelda Fitzgerald

A vacuum isn't just emptiness. It is the absence of something, and if it were not encased in its walls, a vacuum would not be possible.

We are familiar with the feeling of emptiness. There have been many times when we have felt that there just wasn't a drop of energy left in us. These periods are the "dark night of the soul." We will do anything to avoid feeling them; we even become addicted to whatever helps us not feel.

We have been trapped by the very lives we have designed. Our architectural wonders have become prefabricated horrors. Our enclosures are of our own making, and only we can dismantle them.

JUST REMEMBER, when a vacuum is opened up, many interesting possibilities rush in.

❧ October 10

CONFUSION

She's half-notes scattered without rhythm.
— Ntozake Shange

We know that our lives have the potential of being a unique melody, and often they feel like "half-notes scattered without rhythm." When did the melody of our life go sour? Was it when we began to schedule more than we could handle? Was it when we began having difficulty relaxing? Was it when we began to feel resentful about the tasks we had agreed to do?

Sometime, probably gradually, our lives moved from concerto to crisis. The more we slip into this disease of doing too much, the more confused we become.

It is comforting to know that this confusion *is* part of the disease and recovery promises us the possibility of clarity.

WHEN I see my confusion as part of a progressive, fatal disease, I am not so hard on myself.

❧ October 11

Monotone Mind

I don't want to get to the end of my life and find that I just lived the length of it. I want to have lived the width of it as well.

—Diane Ackerman

When we become overly focused on our work, our children, our homes, or our relationships, we become one-dimensional women. Throughout history, and more recently with the women's movement, we have been painfully aware that women have often been limited to the more mindless tasks of the society.

Unfortunately, as more of us break in to the ranks of the privileged (as we have viewed them), we again find that we have the opportunity to become dull and narrow . . . just in a different way. The content has changed. The process remains the same.

In order to reclaim our souls, we need to recognize that width is as important as length in the living of our days.

WIDTH adds a dimension to length. Depth adds a dimension to length and width. The world is at least three-dimensional.

❧ October 12

CONFUSED THINKING/JUDGMENTALISM

I realize what a lot of negativity there is in the world and all around us, and how easy it is to become part of that negativity and to be sucked into it and become part of the chaos and confusion if one isn't very careful.
—Eileen Caddy

Negativity is one aspect of the typical confused thinking of the addict. The addictive disease feeds on these thinking processes. In our work lives, we are rewarded for analyzing, comparing, criticizing, and being negative. It is easy to see how we become sucked into negativity and the focus upon what's wrong. The key here is judgmentalism.

It's important to see what's wrong in any situation and what needs to be changed. When judgmentalism enters in, however, the observation takes on a tone of negativity, and that negativity is very seductive.

LEARNING to see clearly and not get sucked into confusion and negativity is one of the challenges of my recovery.

CONTROL

When nothing is sure, everything is possible.
— Margaret Drabble

These words strike terror in the heart of the woman who does too much. Even the prospect of admitting that nothing is sure stimulates our minds to get very busy listing the things in our lives that we are sure about. When we are honest, the list is very small: death is perhaps the only really *sure* thing. Everything else is merely possible.

One of the exciting wonders of recognizing our need for control and beginning to let it go is the weightlessness of the anticipation that everything is possible. When we realize we don't know, we are open to what we don't know.

LIVING by faith is flying by the seat of my pants. I'm really living that way anyway, but I have denied it as long as I could.

❧ October 14

Feeling Overwhelmed

I feel like I'm fighting a battle when I didn't start a war.

—Dolly Parton

Sometimes we feel overwhelmed with forces outside ourselves. We find ourselves embroiled in family or organizational wars and infighting that we do not believe we started and that we certainly do not want to participate in. Yet once in them we feel as if we have to fight, or at least try to stop them.

Both behaviors feed such battles. The one thing we have the power to decide about is our participation. We have the power to decide *not* to participate. It is amazing how battles dissipate when no one participates. When we feel overwhelmed by the battle, we cannot see or we forgot that we have the power of nonparticipation.

WARMONGERING is common in an addictive workplace. I have a choice about my warmongering.

BEAUTY

Because the best way to know the truth or beauty is to try to express it. And what is the purpose of existence here or yonder but to discover truth and beauty and express it, i.e., share it with others?
—Brenda Ueland

If the purpose of existence is to discover truth and beauty and share our discovery with others, some of us may have been on the wrong track.

In our need to achieve and move ahead, we have become stingy. As addicts, we believe that there is a limited amount of power and success and that if we give anything away, we will have less. So we develop the wonderful character defect of stinginess.

We have begun to think that if we share ideas or awareness, others will steal them. We censor, copyright, and choke our knowledge, and . . . we lose.

GREAT IDEAS belong to everyone. It is only the small ones that have to be counted.

ॐ October 16

BECOMING/CONTROL

I also know that when I'm trusting and being myself as fully as possible, everything in my life reflects this by falling into place easily, often miraculously.
—Shakti Gawain

We have been taught by the control system in which we work and live that we have to fight, control, and struggle to succeed. Consequently, we often end up exhausted and bloody from our efforts.

We are convinced that just being ourselves cannot possibly be enough. Yet as we get to know others who are further along than we are in their recovery, we see women who seem to do quite well by trusting and being themselves. Their lives just seem to unfold.

THE UNFOLDING of my life is not an issue of competence or control. It is an issue of faith.

BEAUTY/ONENESS/AWE

Since you are like no other being ever created since the beginning of time, you are incomparable.
                                                    —Brenda Ueland

When I read those words of Brenda Ueland, I take a deep breath and let it out very slowly. I am incomparable. Just letting myself truly know that elicits a feeling of awe and reverence . . . reverence for myself.

In Twelve-Step circles there is a concept of "terminal uniqueness." One is terminally unique when one believes that no one else has had it so bad and that we are the center of the universe. When we insist in defining the world from our own perspective, we are operating out of terminal uniqueness. Terminal uniqueness erodes the soul.

When we accept and celebrate our uniqueness, we take our place in the universe.

THERE ARE many things of beauty, and I am one of them!

ઠ• October 18

AWARENESS

There are no new truths, but only truths that have been recognized by those who have perceived them without noticing.

—Mary McCarthy

Our greatest learnings often come when we are unaware that we are learning something. We can study a technique or focus upon a project for days, and the truth or the essence of it just does not seem to click. Then something happens. The fog clears and we notice that we have moved to a new level of truth without ever knowing how we got there. It was not our straining or trying that brought us to this new level. It was our willingness to be aware of what had already taken place that opened new doors.

We do not control all the processes of our being. Sometimes we have but to notice. That is all.

TODAY has the potential of being a day in which I can recognize the truths working within me.

❧ October 19

JUSTIFICATION

I use other addictions (eating, sex, drinking, spending) to reward my workaholism.

—Barb

"If I just get this project finished on time, I will take us to that expensive new restaurant, and we will order whatever we want on the whole menu."

"When I work so hard, I feel I deserve a drink or two in the evening to relax me. After all, I have put in a high-stress, productive day. I deserve to relax!"

"Sex is a good release. It gets too complicated if I put extra baggage on it like love, communication, and connectedness. Sometimes a woman just needs a release. This isn't using my partner. Partners have their needs, too. Using each other for a release of tension isn't *really* using each other."

I DO, after all, have a right to my addictions. It's my life, isn't it?
Yes, it is!

ಠ October 20

Awareness of Process/Control

Time is a dressmaker specializing in alterations.
        —Faith Baldwin

We often think that we are "just about to get it together" when life gives us another opportunity for learning. Many of us have tried to treat our lives like our houses. We have believed that we could get our houses fixed up just the way we wanted them and then they would stay that way forever. We have felt personally attacked when slip covers wear out, when a room needs to be repainted, or when an appliance breaks down. We have set up our lives based upon a static notion of the universe. We have believed that once fixed things should stay fixed, whether they be our houses, our jobs, or ourselves. In trying to make ourselves and our universe static, we have set ourselves up for intense moments of frustration and failure. Our attempts to control the normal processes of life have taken their toll on ourselves and those around us.

I AM a process. Life is a process. Alterations are part of the process.

FEAR

While we wait in silence for that final luxury of
fearlessness, the weight of that silence will choke us.
—Audre Lorde

Our silence about the issues that matter most to us thunders in our heads and bodies like a galloping herd of buffalo. The canyons of our inner beings resound with our unspoken ideas and perceptions.

Our fear confines our souls in the daily holocausts of silent existence. Our fear is real. It is palpable. We can feel it. We must learn to honor it and move through it. We cannot deny it, and we cannot "wait for that final luxury of fearlessness." To become fixated in our fear is to creep in to that choking silence that devours our soul. No woman must speak when she is not ready. We must respect one another in our silence. When we face our fears, we may hear our voices.

MY FEAR is real. I will honor it. And I do not need to be controlled by it.

ॐ October 22

AMENDS

I have refrained from speaking the truth and have just gone along with a lot of things.
—Marion Cohen

One of the most important steps in our recovery from our addiction to work, caretaking, rushing, and busyness is the amends process. First we need to make a list of those whom we have wronged. Then we need to make amends for our wrongs when it would not be harmful to do so.

It is important to remember that we make amends for ourselves. We do not make amends to get forgiveness. We do not make amends to make others like us. We do not make amends to control or manipulate.

We make amends because we need to do so in order to maintain our clarity and our sobriety. We make amends because it clears our soul to admit our wrongs, say we are sorry, and turn them over to a power greater than ourselves.

AMENDS-MAKING is a way of vacuuming my soul. The result is, I feel clean.

ACCEPTANCE/LIVING IN THE NOW

The opportunity of life is very precious and it moves very quickly.

—Ilyani Ywahoo

This is it! The life that is ours is the one we are living today. There is no other. The more we try to hold onto our illusions of what we *think* it is or what we think it *should* be, the less time and energy we have to live it.

How many times have we heard about people who worked hard and longed for the day when retirement would come, only to drop dead just before or just after they retired? How fast it all went!

Our lives are so precious. Each moment has the possibility of a new discovery. Yet when it passes, that moment never returns.

ONLY AS I AM aware of the present will I have the opportunity to be fully alive.

ছ় October 24

PARENTING

If we try to control and hold onto our children, we lose them. When we let them go, they have the option of returning to us more fully.

—Anne Wilson Schaef

Few of us have a Ph.D. in parenting. If we did, we would probably be worse than we are now. How much energy we put into trying to mold and control our children, not for their sakes, but so they will reflect better on us.

We are unable to see them as separate and important beings who are here to share a time with us so that we can learn from each other. We think we *need* them to validate our lives and our choices in life. When we do that, we use them as objects, which is totally disrespectful of them and of ourselves.

TO LOVE our children is to see them, respect them, share life with them . . . and always to let go.

HOPES AND DREAMS

"Hope" is the thing with feathers
That perches in the soul . . .
And sings the tune without words
And never stops . . . at all
                              —Emily Dickinson

It is nice to remember that we have a little feathered being deep in us that sings unceasingly.

So often, we believe that we have come to a place that is void of hope and void of possibilities, only to find that it is the very hopelessness that allows us to hit bottom, give up our illusion of control, turn it over, and ask for help. Out of the ashes of our hopelessness comes the fire of our hope.

To be without hopes and dreams is a place of loss . . . loss of our birthright as a human being. Hope does spring and sing eternal, even when we have wax in our ears.

BY RECOGNIZING **and affirming my feelings of hopelessness, I open the possibility of something else.**

❧ October 26

IMPRESSION MANAGEMENT

*"The purpose of these workshops is to share . . .
everything we have learned from the dying patient who
has been our teacher . . . things that regrettably no one
helped them accomplish earlier so that they would have
been able to say, 'I have truly lived'."*
—Elizabeth Kübler-Ross

From many years of helping the terminally ill to
resolve their unfinished business in this life, Dr.
Küber-Ross knows better than most how many
things get in the way of our experiencing fully what
it means to live. One major block we often use is
impression management.

Trying to be what others want us to be is a form
of slow torture and certain spiritual death. It is not
possible to get all our definitions from outside and
maintain our spiritual integrity. We cannot look to
others to tell us who we are, give us our validity,
give us our meaning, and still have any idea of who
we are. When we look to others for our identity, we
spend most of our time and energy trying to be who
they want us to be. And we are so fearful of being
found out. We truly believe that it is possible to
make others see what we want them to see, and we
exhaust ourselves in the process.

**IMPRESSION MANAGEMENT is a form of the illu-
sion of control and I know that my illusion of
control will kill me.**

CREATIVITY

> *It is the creative potential itself in human beings that is the image of God.*
>
> —Mary Daly

What a beautiful way to think of our creativity! If we do not express our creativity, we are blocking the potential of the flowing energy of the image of God.

For most women who do too much, creativity has a very low place in our list of priorities. We don't have time to be creative. We will be creative later (and later . . and later). We don't really believe in *our* creativity. Only special women have real creativity, and we are so terrified that we may not be one of these women that we won't even try to see what *our* creativity is. After all, "If you can't do something outstanding, it's better not to do anything at all."

WHEN I THINK of my creative potential as the "image of God" within me, I feel awe.

COMMUNICATION

The only listening that counts is that of the talker who alternately absorbs and expresses ideas.
—Agnes Repplier

Women have historically been good listeners. We have been trained to listen carefully and even to "listen with the third ear." Caretakers need to listen, often not saying what they think they need to say.

As we have become women who do too much, we find our listening skills on the wane. We cut people off in the middle of sentences. We assume we know what an employee is going to say, and we act on that assumption. We even become enamored with the sound of our own voice.

We must remember that communication is more than a monologue. Good communication is a balance of speaking and sharing, listening carefully, and absorbing before we speak again.

We as women often limit ourselves to listening or talking. Thus we miss the meaning of communication.

TODAY I have the opportunity to observe if I practice all three aspects of communication.

ONENESS

To the Indian mind, the life of the universe has not been analyzed, classified, and a great synthesis formed of the parts. To him [sic] the varied forms are equally important and varied.

—Alice C. Fletcher

Recently, I heard a woman discussing why she enjoyed spending part of her time with an elderly woman friend in a household of women. "Everything gets done so easily," she said. "All the jobs have equal status. Washing the clothes or cooking a meal has just as much status as the work we do in our offices as physicians. It all just flows."

I was reminded of how much we analyze our universe, assign random values, and chop up our lives. That process not only makes our lives more difficult, it alienates us from the experience of oneness with all things, and without that experience, we don't know that we belong.

WHEN I diminish other's belongingness in the universe, *my* belongingness becomes uncertain.

❧ October 30

BEING OBSESSED/NEEDING OTHERS

She who rides a tiger is afraid to dismount.
—Proverb

Being obsessed with our work is often thought to be a requirement for success. Yet, when was it that the tail started wagging the dog? Where was the point at which we stopped doing our work, and it began doing us?

It is a lot harder to get off the roller coaster in the middle than it was to get on it. This is why we need the companionship of others who are struggling with the same issues: they support our process of getting unhooked from our obsessive doing.

It is only with the support of others and the renewed connection with a power greater than ourselves that we can hope to recover and become whole.

I SUPPOSE I can dismount if I have a few people holding the tiger.

❧ October 31

BEING PROJECTLESS

How beautiful it is to do nothing, and then rest afterward.

—Spanish proverb

For many of us the thought of doing nothing is terrifying. We cannot imagine what life would be like if we were not slaving away at our projects. Not to have our projects waiting for us is like trying to live with parts missing. We have become so dependent upon the security of the next project that they are no longer *our* projects. We are owned by them.

Workaholics often experience some depression when they complete a task. Instead of dealing with the natural feeling of letdown, we overlap completion with a new beginning. Hence, like the relationship addict, we never have to deal with separation or beginnings and endings. In fact, we never have to deal with anything.

PERHAPS TODAY I could experiment with doing nothing, and resting afterward.

❧ November 1

WORK/CAUSES

Beware of people carrying ideas. Beware of ideas carrying people.
— Barbara Grizzuti Harrison

Ideas can be so seductive, and we are so easily seduced. We forget that ideas are just that, abstractions that have been thought up.

We often lose ourselves in ideas and become so caught up in them that we cannot distinguish between ourselves and the idea. When we reach this level of enmeshment with our ideas, we experience any attack on our ideas as an attack on our being.

Being so attached to our ideas often results in a widening gap between what we are espousing and what we actually do. How often we kill in the name of love. We talk about cooperation and we try to force it on others. We get an idea for high productivity and we interfere with productivity by demanding an adherence to our idea. We start out carrying an idea and soon it is carrying us.

I WILL NOT let what I think destroy what I believe.

GUILT

Who I am is what I have to give. Quite simply, I must remember that's enough.

Anne Wilson Schaef

Often, when we look in our inner recesses, we feel that we are lacking. We have been a disappointment to others. We couldn't "be there" when we should have been, and we didn't have all the information we should have had. Somehow, though it may be just a vague feeling, we have failed.

It appears that feeling guilty is a sex-linked gene. There seems to be an infinitely close connection between feeling guilty and being female.

When we feel guilty, we try to make up for what we have or have not done. We feel we need to "make something special," to make things all right. We need to make up for a "transgression" even if we don't know what it was. Unfortunately, our technique for making up is usually addictive and not good for us or the person to whom we give it.

I CANNOT make up for something I think I haven't done or have done wrong by trying to make others or myself feel guilty.

&~ November 3

CRISIS ORIENTATION

> *The Physician says I have "Nervous*
> *prostration."*
> *Possibly I have—I do not know the names of*
> *sickness. The crisis*
> *of the sorrow of so many years is all that*
> *tires me.*
>
> —Emily Dickinson

Physicians have invented many erudite and confounding names for women who work themselves to a complete frazzle. We spend our lives moving from one crisis to another. As a matter of fact, we have become so competent at handling crisis that we feel most at home in the middle of one. If the truth were known, we women who do too much often create a crisis when things are going smoothly. When things are quiet, we keep waiting for the other shoe to fall and we feel relieved when we have a crisis to be managed. We know how to do that.

SERIAL CRISES are exciting, *and* they are exhausting. I don't want crises to be the origin of yet another medical label. Recovery offers another option.

ঙ November 4

CONTROL/RECOVERY

You know you're recovering when you can go to a family reunion and you don't have to teach, preach, or leave literature.

—Karen

A big part of our disease is believing that we not only have the right answers for ourselves but for other people as well. Our investment in this belief is such that we truly believe that we can make other people think and behave as we want. And we actually believe that it is right to do so, since we know best.

How arrogant we have become in our illusion of control! How disrespectful of others to try to control their lives and convince them of what is best for them! How much easier it is to work *with* people instead of trying to overpower them with the righteousness of our rightness. Control is deadly for everyone.

I WILL REMEMBER that my illusion of control is just that . . . an illusion.

❧ November 5

FINANCIAL SECURITY

It seems that the rewards of an affluent society turn bitter as gall in the mouth.

—Natalie Shaeness

An affluent society often functions as a giant tranquilizer. In the pursuit of the rewards of affluence, we have to tune out our awareness so completely that we become destructive to our bodies and our psyches. We have to develop our addictions to shut off our awareness of what is *really* important to us. We operate out of denial and are threatened by anyone wanting to challenge our denial.

When we see the sole purpose of our work as the pursuit of affluence, we have lost track of ourselves and what is meaningful work for us. Our spiritual selves have become an abstraction, if they exist at all.

GALL is useful for digesting fats and reducing the risk of heart attack. It is useless in the mouth.

❧ November 6

DEADLINES/PROCRASTINATION

The shortest answer is doing.
—English proverb

Although we women who do too much do over-work and overextend ourselves, we also struggle with procrastination. Just let a deadline approach, and we slip in to the sloughs of lethargy. We just can't get ourselves going. Working at a steady pace is not our style. We work in spurts: intense crisis-mode operating and then nothing. Just thinking about deadlines exhausts us. Meeting them wipes us out.

Deadlines are a threat to the sobriety of the recovering workaholic. They offer us an opportunity to slip back into our old patterns. Remember, relapse is just as dangerous for a workaholic as it is for an alcoholic. We both have a progressive, fatal disease.

Deadlines offer us the opportunity to reach out and ask for support. Talking with our sponsor is a necessary facet of our recovery.

THIS DEADLINE is a gift to help me see how much progress I have made and how I can function differently.

ఠ November 7

COURAGE

> *What I am actually saying is that we each need to let our intuition guide us, and then be willing to follow that guidance directly and fearlessly.*
> —Shakti Gawain

One of the most frightening things in the world is to trust our intuition and follow that trusting. It is hard for us to believe that what the Quakers call our "inner light" is really the way our power greater than ourselves speaks most clearly to us.

When we are one with ourselves and our process, we are truly one with the process of the universe. When we are one with ourselves, our lives seem to fall into place effortlessly. All of us know the feeling of moments of effortless living. When we have the courage to trust our intuition, life begins to live itself.

MY INTUITION connects me with the voice I need to hear.

ACTION

There is really nothing more to say—except why. But since why is difficult to handle, one must take refuge in how.

—Toni Morrison

There are often events in our lives that just do not make sense. In spite of our best efforts, projects fail. It is important to take stock of the situation and accept our part in the failure and then move on.

When we get stuck on the why, we can stay stuck for a long time. We so want to understand, and it is so difficult to admit that some things just make no sense. In Twelve-Step circles, people say, "Whying is dying."

Faith in living does not ask why. Faith in living asks how and does it.

THE EVENT may not be the problem. Our need to understand it may be the problem.

೪ November 9

HANGING IN/STUBBORNNESS

It is not true that life is one damn thing after another
. . . it's the same damn thing over and over again.
                    —Edna St. Vincent Millay

Our inner process gives us every opportunity to learn what we need to learn. Our inner being is very conservation minded—it continues to recycle our shit, and recycles our shit, and recycles our shit. If we don't get the lesson the first time around, we get another chance . . . and another . . . and another. Life gives us every opportunity to work through whatever we need to work through.

Unfortunately, every time an opportunity for learning recycles, it comes with a greater and greater force. The intensity of the force with which we have to be hit is directly related to our denial, stubbornness, and illusion of control. Life will cycle the same damn thing over and over again, until we get it.

I'M GLAD my inner process hangs in with me. Sometimes I'm a slow learner.

Letting Go/Control

The true secret of giving advice is, after you have honestly given it, to be perfectly indifferent whether it is taken or not and never persist in trying to set people right.

—Hannah Whitall Smith

Actually, we probably should never give advice, even when someone asks for it. However, it is often helpful to give information and then *let it go.* Too often we get invested in our information and are so sure of our rightness that we have to make certain the other person *accepts* it. Somehow, deep inside of us their acceptance of our information is directly tied to our self-worth. If they don't accept our advice and act on it, we are somehow not liked, respected, valued, and a whole string of other adjectives.

As we get healthier and begin to give up some of our addictive behaviors, we find that our need to control others is lessening. We are learning to give and let go.

I HAVE good information to share. It is more likely to be heard when I give it and let it go.

๛ November 11

Busyness/Causes/Awareness

> *Why is it that when people have no capacity for private usefulness they should be so anxious to serve the public?*
> —Sara Jeanette Duncan

How many of us use our causes and our projects as a front for our addiction to our busyness? Do we impose ourselves and our views on others as a way of not having to look inside?

Causes look so noble, and serving the public seems so pure. Are nobility and purity really what we are about? Is our need for power and recognition related to our feelings of unworthiness? I wonder how honest we are with ourselves about the real motivation behind our causes and our service. We may only be developing subtle, more socially acceptable ways of practicing our disease. We do have options, however.

AWARENESS is the key. When I know what I am doing, I have the option to change.

CREATIVITY

*As soon as I began painting what was in my head the
people around me were shocked.*

—Leonor Fini

Our creativity, once unleashed, knows no time
or space. It is like a passionate lover that demands
to be heard. No wonder we are so afraid of it. It can
turn our world topsy-turvy. And maybe our worlds
need to be turned topsy-turvy.

When our creativity shows itself, it is now. The
ideas we are having now are a result of who we are
now, our life situations now, and what is going on
inside us now. We will not be the same women
fifteen years from now.

Expressing our creativity now in whatever form
it takes is a way of enriching our lives, making us
more interesting women, and releasing the tension
of not creating.

**I OWE IT to myself to find time for my creative
self.**

ã€œ November 13

DEMANDING TOO MUCH

If you knew how often I say to myself: to hell with everything, to hell with everybody, I've done my share, let the others do theirs now, enough, enough, enough.
—Golda Meir

Before we began to get healthier, we always were the first to go the extra mile. We were sure we were indispensable and if we didn't handle each situation, no one would.

Now we have a different perspective. When we get to a point where we feel like saying "to hell with everything," we know that the issue is not "out there," it is "in here" and that we have not been taking care of ourselves. When we take care of ourselves, we quit before we are forced to our knees. Working our recovery program has taught us to be alert to the signs of self-neglect.

I'M NOT there yet. As I pay attention to the signals I give myself, I'm getting better and better.

CONTROL

> *I was torn by two different time concepts. I knew which
> one made sense, but the other one was fighting hard for
> survival. [Structure, regimentation, orderedness. Which
> had absolutely nothing to do with anything.]*
> —Robyn Davidson

One of the ways we practice our illusion of control and protect our disease is to surround ourselves with people like ourselves who do the same things we do. When we are surrounded by women who also rush around, are always busy, work too much, and take care of everyone, we seem normal. Our addictions seem normal. We avoid putting ourselves in situations where our control skills are not shared and valued, because then in that situation we might notice that we do not like controlling at all. Structure, regimentation, and orderedness are the way things have to be, or so we believe. That is why when we do allow ourselves to travel, we stay in American hotels with well-known names, if possible.

OUR ILLUSION of control is more cunning than a cat, and it has more than nine lives.

Acceptance/Control/Serenity Prayer

Now I think my point is that I have learned to live with it all . . . with being old . . . whatever happens . . . all of it.

—Edelgard

How wonderful that we not only have the opportunity to live our lives, we have the opportunity to *accept* them! We have spent so much time and energy foolishly fighting things that we cannot change and butting our heads up against steel-reinforced brick walls that we have not stopped to ask ourselves if this is the hill we want to die on.

Part of learning to live our lives is developing the ability to accept what cannot be changed and learn to live creatively with those situations. Also, we need to discover what can be challenged and to move forward with courage when necessary. Acceptance is not resignation. Acceptance is serenity embracing life.

TODAY my life is enough just the way it is, *and it is mine.*

❧ November 16

FEELING CRAZY
STEPS ONE, TWO, AND THREE

> *Crazy and coping are interactive. They go together and are mutually supportive. When I'm crazy, I believe I have to cope and whem I am trying to cope, I get crazy.*
> —Karen M.

The crazier we feel, the more we feel we should be able to cope. That's part of the progression of this disease: we lose our ability to make clear and sane judgments about ourselves and the situations in which we find ourselves. We find ourselves trying to accomplish feats that no sane person would even attempt and fully expecting that we should be able to accomplish them with great ease. In fact, our progressively taking on more and more is directly related to our creeping closer to the brink. It is difficult to tell which is the chicken and which is the egg—probably neither. They are interactive. Our taking on more and more drives us closer and closer to the brink and getting closer and closer to the brink results in our taking on more and more.

INERTIA is the force that keeps an object at rest when at rest or in motion when in motion, unless acted upon by an external force.

We have an inertia problem. We need an outside force. We can't do this by ourselves.

SELF-AWARENESS

There's a period of life when we swallow a knowledge of ourselves and it becomes either good or sour inside.
—Pearl Bailey

Self-knowledge is always a good thing. No one else possesses the capacity to know us as well as we can know ourselves.

It is in the awareness of ourselves that our strength lies. And awareness of every aspect of ourselves allows us to become who we are.

Often our rejection of various aspects of ourselves keeps us stuck. Some of us quite readily see those aspects of our personalities that we perceive as negative and just as readily beat ourselves up for those characteristics. Others go to the other extreme and sugar-coat our self-perceptions, putting all blame and responsibility for who we have become on anyone and anything outside of ourselves. Neither approach is helpful or growth-producing.

OWNING ourselves is probably the richest gold mine any of us will ever possess.

❧ November 18

ACCEPTANCE/AMBITION

I long to accomplish a great and noble task, but it is my chief duty to accomplish small tasks as if they were great and noble.

—Helen Keller

Such amazing words from a person whose life in itself was such "a great and noble task"! In Helen Keller's words we sense such deep acceptance of her life. We have a glimmer of insight into the paradox that if we just take one step at a time and do each task as it presents itself, we may discover we have done great and noble things. If we are *trying* to do great and noble tasks, we may well find that we have missed those magic opportunities just to do what we need to do.

As the author Brenda Ueland says, "Try to discover your true, honest, untheoretical self." Our theoretical self often interferes with our real self.

MY ILLUSION of myself may not be who I am. My illusion of my work may not be what it is.

❧ November 19

TIME MANAGEMENT

I'm working so hard on my time management that I don't get anything done.

—Anonymous

We can get so involved in a new technique that the technique itself becomes another monster in our lives, and we become slaves to it.

Time management can be a good thing. It can help us look at how we spend our time. It can help us become more efficient in getting a job done and can help us learn new ways of doing old things. None of us is as efficient as we could be, and efficiency is useful.

However, when we use any technique to support our disease of workaholism, that technique becomes part of the problem. Unfortunately, addicts are good at using anything to support the disease.

When we are recovering, we have a better perspective for evaluating our use of such tools to make our lives more serene and healthy.

I WILL BE OPEN to tools for recovery, recognizing that the Twelve Steps of Workaholics Anonymous are some of the best tools available.

❧ November 20

APPRECIATION

You must not think that I feel, in spite of it having ended in such defeat, that my "life has been wasted" here, or that I would exchange it with that of anyone I know.

—Isak Dinesen

One of the most important aspects of our lives is that they are *our* lives. No one else could live them exactly the way we are living them. Everything that happens in our lives is an opportunity for learning. Those moments of frustration often turn into moments of joy and creativity.

What an extraordinary experience it is to look back and truly feel that we can celebrate our lives—all of them.

Being in recovery and returning to our spiritual selves provides a path to appreciation.

I HAVE the opportunity to walk the path of appreciation today.

ༀ November 21

ALONE TIME

Women's normal occupations in general run counter to creative life or contemplative life or saintly life.
—Anne Morrow Lindbergh

There is not much in our lives that supports our creativity. Work in the home and work outside the home are generally not conducive to the kind of nurturing that every human being needs. As we buy into the workaholism, competitiveness, and stress of the dominant society, we find ourselves changing and losing many of the qualities that were most precious to us.

We have rebelled against women's work, and we have raced headlong into men's work. Now we not only get to do women's work, we get to do both and work twice as hard.

We find our moments of creative time or contemplative time, or even saintly time are few and far between. Yet, we need these times and we deserve these times for ourselves.

I WILL TRY to remember that when I take time for myself, I have much more to offer to myself, my work, and those around me.

৯৶ November 22

WHOLENESS

Women's work is always toward wholeness.
—May Sarton

When we women do *our* work, we move toward wholeness. The world is in need of wholeness. The world is in need of women's way of working.

Too long we have doubted ourselves and tried to fit comfortably into a male modality. To have wholeness, we need to make our contribution too. To have wholeness, we need to know our values and value our knowing.

We have reneged on our responsibility to this society and this planet. It is time that we courageously put our thoughts, ideas, and values out there and let them stand for themselves.

WHEN I DO my work, my work is wholeness.

❧ November 23

TURNING IT OVER

*I need to take an emotional breath, step back, and
remind myself who's actually in charge of my life.*
— Judith M. Knowlton

How often we want to stop, turn around angrily,
and shout, *"who's in charge here?"* We have tried to be
in charge of our lives and have learned again and
again that our being in charge has not quite worked.
Sooooo . . . if we aren't, who is?

It seems too nebulous for a practical, professional woman just to step back and turn her life over
to some vague power that may exist out there. Isn't
religion for weaklings? Aren't those who want to
depend upon a power greater than themselves just
being dependent and not taking responsibility for
themselves? Perhaps. Yet, when we think dualisti-
cally like that, when we grab the power or we give
it up, we miss the point.

Life is a process of cooperating with the forces
in our lives and living out that partnership.

WE ARE in charge together. Not as controllers
. . . as a living process.

Solitude

Like water which can clearly mirror the sky and the trees only so long as its surface is undisturbed, the mind can only reflect the true image of the Self when it is tranquil and wholly relaxed.

—Indra Devi

How often are our minds "tranquil and wholly relaxed?" Do we recognize that time for solitude is just as important to our work as keeping informed, preparing reports, or planning? As author Brenda Ueland says, "Presently your soul gets frightfully sterile and dry because you are so quick, snappy and efficient about doing one thing after another that you have no time for your own ideas to come in and develop and gently shine."

We have to give ourselves time. We have to give our ideas time. If we don't neither we nor they can gently shine, and we cannot hear the voice of our inner process speaking to us.

SOLITUDE is not a luxury. It is a right and a necessity.

ꙮ November 25

PERFECTIONISM

Don't try to be such a perfect girl, darling. Do the best you can without too much anxiety or strain.
—Jesse Barnard

How many of us have longed for words from our mothers like the ones Jesse Barnard wrote to her daughter. Perhaps, if our parents hadn't needed us to be perfect, *we* wouldn't need to be perfect. Unfortunately, even when others do not demand perfection of us, we who do too much demand it of ourselves.

We forget that when push comes to shove the only standard of perfection we have to meet is to be perfectly ourselves. Whenever we set up abstract, external standards and try to force ourselves to meet them, we destroy ourselves.

DOING THE BEST I can without too much anxiety or strain sounds like a relaxing way to live.

REACHING OUT
STEP TWELVE

May our Mayness become All-embracing. May we see in one another the All that was once All-one rebecome One.

—Laura Riding

Part of the beauty of recovering from doing too much is realizing that our lives are changing and that we seem to be taking on a more spiritual quality despite ourselves.

Also, as we stop working ourselves to death, we find that we have more time to reach out to others and that the very act of reaching out seems to be good for us and, surprisingly, seems to facilitate our growth and recovery.

We grow beyond wanting to fix others. We realize that sharing our journey toward recovery with others is one of the ways we remember our stories, remember where we have been, remember who we are, and progress in our recovery.

WHEN WE REACH OUT to another, we have the possibility of remembering that we are one, we are the same.

HAPPINESS

If you haven't been happy very young, you still can be happy later on, but it's much harder, you need more luck.

—Simone de Beauvoir

We all carry influences and experiences from our childhood into our adult lives. Dysfunctional families are the norm for this society and probably the question is not do we have something that needs to be worked out from our childhood? The appropriate question probably is, what do we have to work on from the experiences of our childhood?

The amazing thing about the human adventure is that no matter how horrendously awful our childhood was, as we work through it, we always find some memories of moments of happiness that had long since been forgotten. And no matter how perfect our family seemed on the surface, we always have some painful experiences to work through.

TRUE HAPPINESS does not come from a perfect childhood. Happiness comes from claiming our unique childhood and working through the lessons it holds for us.

ಶ November 28

In Touch with
a Power Greater than Ourselves

*It is not primarily abstract ideas which affect our
spirituality, that is, our experience of and with God.*
— Sandra M. Schneiders

We cannot approach God or the process of the
universe through ideas. Theology is trying to think
out God and often asking us to deny our *experience* of
a power greater than ourselves.

When we learn to trust our own perceptions and
experience, we discover that we begin to have a
relationship with the process of the universe. In fact,
as we do our recovery work, we discover that when
we are living out of our own process, we are one
with the universe. We are the holomovement.

This living process that is us is, at the same time,
greater than ourselves. When we are truly ourselves,
we are more than ourselves. We do not have to look
for spirituality. We *are* spirituality.

MY EXPERIENCE of the infinite cannot begin
with my head.

LAUGHTER

One loses many laughs by not laughing at oneself.
—Sara Jeannette Duncan

Well said! Part of the recovery process is to be able to see how really funny we are in our disease. We take ourselves so seriously.

One of my better moments was when I was invited to be the guest speaker at an important luncheon for one of the Fortune Five Hundred corporations. I had been out camping just prior to this speaking engagement, so I felt a little seedy. In order to make the right impression, I had brought a conservative business suit, silk blouse, high heeled boots, and panty hose. After being in the wilderness for some time, I wasn't even sure I knew how to get into this garb. Just before it was time to speak, I went to the bathroom to "pee my anxieties down the toilet" as we say in clinical circles. I came out of the bathroom feeling a little cocky and ready to go. Just as I reached the door to the auditorium, I was aware of a breeze and realized that my skirt was caught up in my panty hose and my rear was "exposed to the rockies." I had an instant opportunity for humility. Of course it made a great opener for my speech.

WHEN WE SEE how funny we are, we see how dear we are.

GUILT

> *Women keep a special corner of their hearts for sins they have never committed.*
> —Cornelia Otis Skinner

We are so ready to take responsibility for everything that we are constantly feeling guilty.

If our spouse is feeling down or depressed it must be something we have done. If our children aren't doing well, it must be our fault. If the deadline isn't met, we should have put in more time. Women are so ready to take on the guilt of the world. It makes no difference whether we have committed these transgressions. If they exist, we must be responsible. Unfortunately, there are plenty of people around us who are happy to support us in these illusions of guilt.

We have never really stopped to see how self-centered it is to take on the responsibility for everything that happens, whether we are involved or not. When we take on the guilt for everything that happens around us, we make ourselves the center of everything.

THERE MUST be an easier way to be included.

ટ✦ December 1

FINANCIAL SECURITY

Actually we are slaves to the cost of living.
—Carolina Marin deJesus

All of us have to cope with the cost of living. Existing gets more and more expensive, and living seems sometimes as if it is only for the wealthy.

We have lost track of the difference between what we want and what we need. Everything has become a need. If we don't have what we think we need, it lowers our self-esteem and our feelings of worth. We can hardly remember what is important anymore.

We are important. Our children are important. Our relationships are important. The planet is important. Our lives are important.

LEST WE FORGET what we are all about, let's stop today and remember.

ஃ December 2

INTERESTS/OVEREXTENDED

I am involved in so many things—both purely practical and also where my feelings, my life itself are concerned—possibly by my own fault or perhaps quite by chance, that it is going to take all my strength if I am going to get through them or over them.

—Isak Dinesen

Sometimes women who do too much get confused between healthy excitement about our work, a passion for our work, and workaholism. Passion moves to workaholism when it becomes destructive to the self and others. Workaholism isn't pursuing our interests. Workaholism doesn't give us time for our interests.

We often may overextend ourselves in the pursuit of our interests and the workaholic doesn't know when to stop. She just piles on more and more. The woman who has a healthy relationship with her interests is able to give her interests the time they deserve and savor them.

MY INTERESTS add richness to my life, but not when I go after them compulsively.

❧ December 3

Freedom

*We must get in touch with our own liberating
ludicrousness and practice being harmlessly deviant.*
— Sarah J. McCarthy

Freedom for me means being who I am. Professional women are supposed to have short, neat hair. I have long hair which has a mind of its own. It's harmless . . . and it's me. It is, indeed, liberating to be "ludicrous" and harmlessly deviant.

I once was a speaker at a university and while on campus was invited to attend a luncheon for the women faculty and staff on campus. During my luncheon speech, I asked if there was a dress code. I was quickly assured that the students could wear whatever they wanted. I told them I was asking about the women who worked on campus. They were all dressed exactly alike—suits, shirts, and some form of little tie. The only deviant was one woman who had a ruffle on her shirt!

FREEDOM is choosing the clothing that fits our personalities and feels good on us. This is one way we express who we are.

ટ~ December 4

GIFTS

"We cannot find peace if we are afraid of the windstorms of life."
—Elizabeth Kübler-Ross

Our lives don't always go smoothly. In fact, many of us have had many traumas and struggles. When we are in the midst of a difficult time, it is hard to see it as a gift. Nevertheless, at some mega level, every experience is an opportunity for learning.

When we spend our energy blaming and complaining, we are handing over our power to those whom we blame. Our time and energy is well spent when we stop and say, "What is my part in this situation, and what do I have to learn from it?" In doing this, we are not blaming ourselves. We are not blaming at all. We are opening ourselves to glean whatever learnings are there for us. It is in this process that we become whole.

I MAY NOT always like the gift wrapping, and it's the gift that is important.

೭☙ December 5

BEING IN CHARGE

Our strength is often composed of the weakness we're damned if we're going to show.
                                        —Mignon McLaughlin

How in the world did I get to be in charge? There must be some mistake. I don't know what to do with this contract. I don't know how to raise these kids. I must have misrepresented myself for "them" to believe that I knew what I was doing. I am secretly at my best when someone else has the ultimate responsibility. Who has made this terrible mistake?

Often we truly believe that there must be someone who really has it all together and knows just what to do in every situation. Where is that person anyway? Maybe we can ask the right questions and get the right information, and then no one will suspect our charade.

YOU'RE IT, HONEY. Go for it.

๖๏ December 6

COURAGE/OPENNESS/FEAR

To appreciate openness, we must have experienced encouragement to try the new, to seek alternatives, to view fresh possibilities.
— Sister Mary Luke Tobin

Courage and openness go hand in hand. Our courage helps us to take the risk to "try the new." When we are fearful, we only see one way, our way. Courage opens the way for new possibilities.

As we face our fears, we find that we are endowed with a level of courage that we never knew existed. Fortunately, we do not have to be a hero to demonstrate courage. We have many possibilities every day to act courageously. It takes courage to germinate and put forth new ideas. It takes courage to stand up for what we know in our hearts is right. Sometimes it even takes courage to take a nap.

EVERYDAY COURAGE is all I ask.

CLIMBING THE LADDER

The best careers advice to give the young is, find out what you like doing best and get someone to pay you for doing it.

—Katherine Whilehaen

What we love doing often has no connection with our career choice. We live in a culture that teaches us to orient ourselves to what will sell. We have learned to ignore what we love and turn ourselves into a commodity. Commodities can be bought and sold, and we fear that we can be bought and sold. We don't feel that we have the luxury to see what it is we really want to be doing.

We forget one very central and essential factor: if we are doing what we love, we will probably do it exceedingly well.

IF WE FOCUS on success, we will probably forget about living. If we focus on living and doing what we love, we have a good chance of being successful.

SHARING
STEP TWELVE

> *When one's own problems are unsolvable and all best efforts are frustrated, it is lifesaving to listen to other people's problems.*
>
> —Suzanne Massie

Sometimes we just reach an impasse in our lives. In spite of our intelligence, competence, and tenacity, we just do not seem to be able to pull our lives together. Often times, this is where the wisdom of the twelfth Step in the Twelve-Step program of Alcoholics Anonymous comes into play in our lives.

Because we have begun to be in touch with our spirituality and because we have begun to experience the healing of the Twelve-Step program, we are ready to share our strength and hope with others. Yet, when we do this, we are not reaching out in a self-centered way and we must simultaneously realize that when we reach out we often receive great benefit.

WHEN I AM at an impasse in my life, I do not feel very strong. That may be just the time when reaching out to another is just what I need.

ફ* December 9

CONFUSION/BUSYNESS

*As a workaholic, I have learned that I have even
worked the Twelve Steps of Alcoholics Anonymous
workaholically: Yeah!! Yeah!! Fix those addictions!!
Work those steps!! Rah! Rah!*

—Michelle

Part of the subtlety of this disease is taking
something that is good for us and doing it in such
a way that it is destructive and perpetuates the
problem.

Work is good. But if we do it compulsively and
batter ourselves and those we love with it, it
becomes destructive. Exercise is good. But if we use
it to destroy our bodies, avoid intimacy, and keep
out of touch with ourselves, it can have the same
effect as heavy drinking.

At some deeper level in our lives, *how* we do
things is just as important as *what* we do.

WHEN I destroy or punish myself with *good*
things, I am still destroying or punishing myself.

৯০ **December 10**

FEELING TRAPPED

Women are the slave class that maintains the species in order to free the other half for the business of the world.
—Shulamith Firestone

We wanted to become professional women partly because we wanted to remove ourselves from being the "slave class that maintains the species." Yet, it is difficult fully to escape that trap. We find that any job can become a trap, whether we are full-time homemakers, volunteers, support personnel, or executive-level managers. Our society is set up in such a way that it takes a great many to support the work of a few. And even if we are part of the few, we are not always free.

We need to recognize that all of us, regardless of what we do, are part of the "business of the world," and the world needs all of us.

ACCEPTING who I am and what I have to offer is empowering to me and the society.

❧ December 11

EXPECTATIONS

Know that if you have a kind of cultured know-it-all in yourself who takes pleasure in pointing out what is not good, in discriminating, reasoning, and comparing, you are bound under a knave. I wish you could be delivered.
—Brenda Ueland

We don't need anyone else to criticize us. We have so many superhuman expectations of ourselves that the expectations of others pale into insignificance. We really believe that we should be able to handle everything. We really believe we should know everything. We really believe that we should be on top of everything. When we are caught unprepared, instead of just admitting it, we either get defensive or feel guilty (or both). It rarely occurs to us just to admit we are unprepared. We feel we should always be prepared for anything. (No control issues here!)

OUR EXPECTATIONS keep us from crying "uncle" (or for any other relative help, for that matter).

🍃 December 12

RESPONSIBILITY

Take your life in your own hands, and what happens?
A terrible thing: no one to blame.

—Erica Jong

Women have been reluctant to take responsibility for our lives because we have been taught that responsibility means to be held accountable for what has happened to us and therefore to be blamed. Unfortunately, in reacting against this idea of responsibility we have missed the opportunity to own and claim our lives and thus have left ourselves without roots, ties, and understanding. We need to own our lives. We need to claim our experiences, all of them, and integrate them into our existence and decisions. We need to claim who we are and be who we are. That does not mean that we are to blame for our experiences. It means that we have before us the option of living our lives and not leaving that pleasure up to someone else.

WHEN I take responsibility for my life, I have the ability to respond to all of it.

❧ December 13

BECOMING

One is not born a woman, one becomes one.
                    —Simone de Beauvoir

We live in a society that puts so much emphasis upon youth, looks, and attractiveness that we have very few models for womanliness.

Without knowing how to get there, we are suddenly expected to be women and to have the wisdom and stature of a woman.

In a society that knows little about process, there is an assumption that one is a little girl and then suddenly one is a woman. In our sexualized culture, becoming a woman almost always is linked to our sexuality. Womanhood is much more than being sexual and producing babies. Womanhood is the progressive process of bringing all we have to offer as persons to ourselves and those around us.

I AM being a woman. That is a process, not a state.

ใ December 14

STRENGTH

From a timid, shy girl I had become a woman of resolute character, who could no longer be frightened by the struggle with troubles.

—Anna Dostoevsky

Finding and accepting our strength is a very important aspect of knowing ourselves as women. Adolescents do not usually know their own strength, but women do. When we deny our strength, we give up pieces of who *we* are. When we use our strength for power over others, we deny who *they* are. Either way, we lose.

Much of our strength comes from knowing and accepting ourselves and accepting that we are not the center of the universe. As we accept ourselves, we come to realize that our strength is directly connected with and one with a power greater than ourselves. When we tap into that power, we know that we have all the strength we need for whatever comes.

AS THE OLD Ethiopian proverb states, "When spider webs unite, they can tie up a lion."

❧ December 15

SELF-CONFIDENCE

Class is an aura of confidence that is being sure without being cocky. Class has nothing to do with money. Class never runs scared. It is self-discipline and self-knowledge. It's the sure-footedness that comes with having proved you can meet life.

—Ann Landers

Self-confidence is so relaxing. There is no strain or stress when one is self-confident. Our lack of self-confidence mostly comes from trying to be someone we aren't. No wonder we do not feel confident when we are living a lie. When we realize that the best we have to bring to any situation is being just who we are, we relax. People who are cocky often show an alarming lack of self-confidence. They don't know what they have to offer. When we know what we have to offer and we bring it to each situation, that's all we need to do.

I LIKE being a classy woman. No show . . . no blow . . . just the facts.

HOLIDAYS/FRANTIC

Holidays and frantic aren't necessarily synonymous.
— Anne Wilson Schaef

We see the holiday season coming and we immediately feel exhausted and overwhelmed. We have to maintain our usual workday and in addition, shop for gifts, decorate the house, do the extra holiday baking, attend additional social functions, and look great. For some of us, "the season to be jolly," becomes the season to wipe ourselves out. As women who do too much, we have come to dread the holiday season.

This is a good year for us to stop, take stock, and see what is really important for us this season. Perhaps we love the traditions. Which ones can we continue and be healthy? Perhaps we can try asking for help and stop trying to do everything ourselves. This season we have the opportunity to let ourselves feel the meaning of peace—peace within and peace with the world.

DOING THE HOLIDAY SEASON sanely is part of my healing process. I have that opportunity this season. Ho ho ho.

❧ December 17

HEALING

I will tell you what I have learned myself. For me, a long five- or six-mile walk helps. And one must go alone and every day.

—Brenda Ueland

Healing takes time. Healing is an every day affair. Some traumatic events in our lives require physical, emotional, and/or spiritual healing, and sometimes we just need to let the nicks, chips, and dents from everyday living heal. Doing the work we do and holding things together the way we do takes its toll.

When we need these healing times, there is nothing better than a good long walk. It is amazing how the rhythmic movements of the feet and legs are so intimately attached to cobweb cleaners in the brain. And we must take a *long* walk, because at first we think about our problems. These thoughts dissipate over time, thus allowing the healing to begin and we are less focused on our thinking.

WHEN MY HEELS touch the earth, I am healing my wounds.

LOVE

We can only learn to love by loving.
—Doris Murdock

Many women who do too much believe that there are tricks to loving. If we can just look sexy enough, we can make others love us. Or if we just take care of others and make ourselves indispensable, they will love us. We don't learn to love by loving, we try to control love by manipulation. Unfortunately, these methods do not teach us much about loving.

Loving is a risk. It is letting go of expectations and just allowing. Some of us doubt our capacity to love because we have been raised in dysfunctional families and never really have had much experience of clear loving. Loving always had strings attached or demands that we had to meet. Hence we have practiced loving as we learned it in our families.

Fortunately, we are capable of new learning. And it starts right inside of us. When we experience loving ourselves, we begin to learn by loving.

AS I LOVE MYSELF, it is only a short step to the loving of others.

❧ December 19

COMMUNICATION

If you have anything to tell me of importance, for God's sake begin at the end.
—Sarah Jeanette Duncan

Women have always believed that the goal of communication is to bridge, connect, clarify, and facilitate understanding. We have often developed this skill and been good communicators.

Then we find that in our worklives, communication is used in quite different ways than we had realized. Communication is used to manipulate, control, confuse, and intimidate—to create barriers rather than to bridge them. Success is intimately linked with this confusing and confounding form of communication. We are told that we have to play the game.

Later we find that the people we admire often are very direct and refuse to play the game. We have been tempted to abandon our communication skills, and we sorely need them.

BEGINNING at the end may be a good start. At least it's more direct.

ɞ December 20

JOYFULNESS

Surely the strange beauty of the world must somewhere rest on pure joy!

—Louise Bogan

Indeed, the world is so beautiful . . . and so imaginative. Who would have thought to design a tree such that its limbs, when they become too heavy, send down another trunk, so that a single tree repeating this process many times over can eventually cover an area the size of an entire block? Imagine a tree that is so tall that we can't really see the top—a tree and that has developed at least three methods of reproducing itself so as not to become extinct? Indeed, "the strange beauty of the world must somewhere rest on pure joy." We have the opportunity to experience that joy. When we notice, the strange beauty of the earth is all around us.

IT PROBABLY WON'T HURT to give thanks that the design and creation of the world was not left in our hands.

ॐ December 21

INSPIRATION

Inspiration comes very slowly and quietly.
—Brenda Ueland

Sometimes we forget that to do our work well, whatever it is, we must have inspiration. This is true for any work, no matter how menial it may seem. Inspiration is the gentle listening to the wisdom of our inner being.

Brenda Ueland said that it comes slowly and quietly. I might also add that it comes when it wishes and not on demand. Like any process, we cannot force it. We must wait with it.

How sad that we have relegated inspiration to poets, artists, and writers! How sad that we cannot see that good child-rearing requires inspiration, that good management requires inspiration, regardless of the task. When we take away the possibility of our own inspiration, we relegate ourselves to a tedious existence. Inspiration adds spice and zest to our lives and allows them to be lives, not existences.

WHEN I WAIT with inspiration, my time is not wasted.

࿊ December 22

CHOICES/FEAR/CHANGE

Change really becomes a necessity when we try not to do it.

—Anne Wilson Schaef

Risk and fear—we will do anything to avoid them both. Where did we get the idea that it is bad to feel fear and that we cannot handle our fear? We will do anything to avoid the fear of making a choice. We have another baby, or take on more work, or get busy with a new project around the house—anything.

We have so much fear of facing ourselves and confronting the choices we need to make that we are willing to wreck our lives and the lives of those around us in order not to have to make a choice.

We always resent it when others make decisions for us, *and* we do not want to be responsible for our choices. If we can manage to get someone else to make a choice for us, then we do not have to own the consequences.

I SAY I want to be my own person, and sometimes that scares me to death. . . . That's OK.

❧ December 23

FEAR/CONTROL

Fear has a smell, as love does.
—Margaret Atwood

The tightening of the stomach, the sweaty palms, the increasing inability to focus, the tingling in our arms and hands, and the anxiety about looking good or having the right answer—we all know about fear.

Unfortunately, the life of the woman who does too much is controlled by fear. What if we're not good enough? What if we're not on time? What if nobody likes us? By the time we have worked ourselves up into a lather, we are incapable of producing anything good. Fear and our illusion of control are intimately related. It is when we believe that we can control the outcome and the responses of others that we get fearful. Our worrying is a form of pre-control.

AS I ACKNOWLEDGE my fear and turn it over to a power beyond myself, I can get the job done and done well.

∂• December 24

Causes/Dualism

The main dangers in this life are the people who want to change everything . . . or nothing.
—Lady Astor

How aptly put! Lady Astor put her finger on the meaning of dualism and the horror of being caught in a dualism. Those who want to change everything often become ruthless in their laser focus upon what they know is right.

Those who want to change nothing have become so enured to themselves and other beings that they only pass through life not looking to the right or to the left. Neither group does much for itself or anyone else. Actually, both groups operate out of the same self-centered focus.

What is the third option? The third option is to be present to ourselves and others, accepting those things which we cannot change, changing the things we can, and knowing the difference.

WHEN I get caught up in a "cause," I become the problem. When I do nothing about the world in which I live, I am the problem.

ঙ্গ December 25

CONNECTEDNESS

God knows no distance.
—Charleszetta Waddles

How far away we seem at times from any Higher Power. We simply cannot connect with a power greater than ourselves, and we lose faith in its existence.

It is important to remember that the distance is within *us*. We are the ones who have moved away from that power and that connectedness. It has not moved away from us.

Our rushing around, our busyness, our constant caretaking and compulsive working leave little or no time or energy for anyone or anything to enter. Yet when we stop and notice, the connection with this power greater than ourselves is always there. It has never left us. *We* have left us.

THE DISTANCE is mine. The potential for connectedness is mine, also.

GROWTH

> *Lying, walking, sitting in this room, she felt herself*
> *ripening and coloring.*
>
> —Meridel Le Sueur

We have such a cult of youth in this society that, for a woman, growing older is a terrifying experience. Meridel Le Sueur's usage of the words "ripening" and "coloring" are very soothing. If I see myself ripening and becoming richer as I grow older, if I see myself developing a more intricate patina, my process of growth takes on a different tone.

We have two big dogs in our household, a seven-year-old Great Dane queen (seven is old for a Great Dane!) and a happy tramp-like German shepherd about two years old. Although she is busy being a queen, and he is busy growing up, they have the most beautiful, devoted, and caring relationship. He does not seem to mind that she is an "old lady" and has some grey hair. As I watch them, I realize that human beings are probably the only species that worship youth and disdain maturity. Among animals, it just doesn't seem to matter.

I COULD NOT KNOW what I know today if I weren't the age I am. I have the continual opportunity to grow.

PROCRASTINATION
STEP ONE

When I keep putting something off, it may not be
procrastination, but a decision I've already made and
not yet admitted to myself.
—Judith M. Knowlton

Contrary to popular belief, we workaholics are
not women who are constantly doing something.
We are often too busy and overworked, so that
many times we just collapse into a morass of procrastination. We know that we have things that
need to be done, and the more we think about them,
the more leaden we feel. Sometimes it seems that we
just cannot get our bodies out of bed, lift our arms,
or hold a pen. We just cannot *make* ourselves do any
more. Of course, when this lethargy takes over, we
can sink into black periods of self-castigation.

At such times, it is important to remember that
procrastinating is part of our disease and that we are
powerless over this disease. It is only when we
admit this powerlessness, acknowledge that we
become insane with our procrastination, see that a
power greater than ourselves can restore us to sanity, and turn our life and will over to that power,
that we may, indeed, see that we have made a decision and can admit this decision to ourselves.

I CERTAINLY DO make my life complicated
sometimes. Fortunately, there is another way.

❧ December 28

CLARITY/CHANGES/GROWTH

Then I began to realize that I had to take another step in my evolution and growth.

—Eileen Caddy

We sometimes avoid getting clear because we intuitively know that when we get clear we will have to make some changes in our lives. We are so accustomed to doing what is expected of us that it is difficult to know what we want or need. We can so easily give in to the demands of others, especially if they are in positions of authority, that we find ourselves confused and lacking clarity.

In spite of our confusion, our inner process continues to push us toward our evolution and growth. Something in us struggles for clarity.

GROWTH and evolution are like breathing and eating . . . natural and intimately part of being human.

ॐ December 29

AWARENESS OF PROCESS

Fate keeps happening.

—Anita Loos

Our lives are not set in stone. Lives, like flowers, continue to unfold. We have options and we have choices all along the way.

Certainly we have been influenced by our past and the many forces that have impinged upon us in our formative years. Yet we do have the ability to alter our present and our future.

Fate is a process that continues to emerge. As we accept who we are, we have the possibility of becoming someone else. That is the paradox of life and of living.

When I can let life happen, I feel better. When I can participate in the happening of my life, I soar.

LIFE IS in the living. The process of life keeps happening.

COMPASSION/LOVING

Nobody has ever measured, even poets, how much the heart can hold.

—Zelda Fitzgerald

Some of us have become estranged from our feelings of compassion and love. We have believed that we had to become so tough and that we had to keep so busy that love and compassion became luxuries we could ill afford. Surely we could maintain our humanness with a few tax-deductible checks to the proper charities at the end of the year!

Yet, we know down deep that we are loving, compassionate women. When we give ourselves time, we care about people, and there are many things we love about our lives. Our hearts have a limitless capacity for caring and compassion.

TO LET MY HEART swell with feelings of love and compassion is better than any combination of vitamins and exercise I could ever devise.

BEAUTY

> *Happily may I walk.*
> *May it be beautiful before me.*
> *May it be beautiful behind me.*
> *May it be beautiful below me.*
> *May it be beautiful above me.*
> *May it be beautiful all around me.*
> *In beauty it is finished.*

—Navajo prayer

If one reads this prayer very slowly, one feels its immensely profound simplicity. Imagine ourselves surrounded by beauty! When we think of being surrounded by beauty, we think of some island paradise or Shangri-la.

Yet, when we read this poem slowly, we begin to realize that we *are* surrounded by beauty! We see that this prayer is not only a request, it is simultaneously a statement of fact.

My life does have elements of beauty before, behind, below, and above me. I am surrounded by beauty.

WHEW! Beauty *is* in the eye of the beholder!

❧ Alternate Meditation 1

CREATIVITY/ALONE TIME

I can always be distracted by love, but eventually I get horny for my creativity.

—Gilda Radner

Nothing can replace creativity in our lives—not work, not love, not children, nothing. We may be creative in all these areas, Yet our creative impulses must find their own avenue for expression.

Regardless of how interesting and challenging our work is and how creative we are with our work, we need times of quiet reflection to tap into the deep recesses of our being and see what is perking there. There is no substitute for our creativity, which is usually tapped when we are alone.

I LIKE the way Gilda Radner puts it: "eventually I get horny for my creativity."

❧ Alternate Meditation 2

CONFUSION

> *It was an immense betrayal—the more terrible because he [she] could not grasp what had been betrayed.*
> —Ayn Rand

One of the primary characteristics of the addictive process is confusion. We are told that we should be logical and rational, and so we try to be. Yet so many of the things that happen to us just don't make any sense. We become confused and frustrated, and we try harder to understand. We believe that if we can just understand what is happening we will feel better and we can then handle the situation.

In our recovery we have learned that when any person or group is functioning addictively, nothing makes sense. We can't understand what is going on because it's insane. It's not understandable.

WHEN something is not understandable, it is best to turn it over to a Higher Power and move on.

❧ Alternate Meditation 3

PERFECTIONISM/PROCRASTINATION

I know if I do it just one more time, I can get it right.
—Anonymous

And one more time, and one more time, and one more time. Perfectionism is a difficult and impossible task master. Also, perfectionism is a way of defining the task and ourselves from outside and may have nothing to do with what the task really is or who we really are.

In fact, we may use perfectionism to keep ourselves from getting anything done. If it has to be done perfectly, why even start? Perfectionism and procrastination go hand in hand, and accomplish nothing.

We need to remember that we are doing the task at hand and therefore what we have to bring to the task is ourselves, our accumulated knowledge and experience, and our creativity. Who could ask for anything more?

LET ME NOT ASK for anything more today than to bring what I have to each task at hand.

ᨠ Alternate Meditation 4

HONESTY

But I don't let the cold feeling stay there because, just the same . . . I know that what I say is true, because it is true to me and therefore I say it freely and you must have it.

—Brenda Ueland

If something is true for us, we must trust that truth. We live in a society that is built on dishonesty and ambiguity. In some business and political circles, the "good communicator" is the one who can intimidate, confuse, confound, and *win.* The art of clear, honest communication sometimes seems to have disappeared with the age of innocence.

But somewhere down deep inside each of us is a longing to be honest, to say what is true for us and speak it freely, letting others have it. We live in a society that is shriveling up from the lack of honesty. We are shriveling up from the lack of honesty. Our honesty is essential for our recovery.

WE HAVE BEEN TAUGHT to be afraid of our honesty. Yet it is the key to breaking down denial and the door to healing.

❧ Alternate Meditation 5

TRUST

Believing in our hearts that who we are is enough is the key to a more satisfying and balanced life.
—Ellen Sue Stern

I am enough! I have always been afraid of being too much or too little. What a relief I feel when I just sit with the possibility that I am enough. Can it really be true that I am not what I do or what I produce or what I accomplish? What if I am enough and I accomplish what I want to do? Would that truly be enough? Probably!

I would like a "satisfying and balanced" life. I would like more time and energy for my work, myself, and those I love. When I recognize that *I am enough,* I will have what I want and need.

I WILL SIT with this feeling of being enough and let it be with me today.

❧ Alternate Meditation 6

Relationships

Girls must be encouraged to go on [after college], to make a life plan. It has been shown that girls with this kind of commitment are less eager to rush into early marriage . . . Most of them marry, of course, but on a much more mature basis. Their marriages then are not an escape but a commitment shared by two people that become part of their commitment to themselves and society.

—Betty Friedan

We don't know much about healthy relationships in this society. Most of our models for relationships are of addictive relationships, and we do those well. Too often we look to relationships as an external fix. We expect them to give us our identity and make our lives all right. When we do this, we bring no one to the relationship. We are like jello, and we ask our partners to give us form by means of a relationship. Without the external mold of a relationship, the jello dissolves into a puddle. Who wants to or even can relate to a puddle of jello?

IF I WANT to be in a relationship, I have to bring someone to it . . . me.

❧ Alternate Meditation 7

BEING TORN/GUILT

No woman should be shamefaced in attempting, through her work, to give back to the world a portion of its heart.

—Louise Bogan

It is difficult for women to do our own work. Women artists are frequently expected to keep house, run a family, do the carpool, cook all the meals, do the cleaning, and be able to spend their "spare" moments in their (usually makeshift) studio with their work. Life is never easy for an artist in this culture. Life is almost impossible for a woman artist in this culture.

But women artists are not alone in this struggle. Any woman who does too much cannot help but see the effect of her addiction on her family. Even when we firmly believe that our work should come first, we feel terrible pangs of guilt when our spouses and children have to make appointments with us to see us at all.

A WORKING WOMAN is one of the best balancing acts in this three-ring circus we call life. At least we are not alone in struggling with this issue.

ॐ Alternate Meditation 8

CREATIVITY

They say the moon is feminine. What will happen to me if I bathe myself in the creative feminine?
—Michelle

I like the image of the moonlight acting as an activator to help the emergence of what is already there within me!

If I bathe myself in moonlight, what miraculous and surprising images might emerge?

I suppose the real issue is not the magic of the moonlight, but whether I am willing to slow down enough to let any form of nature have an opportunity to bathe me.

Ancient peoples knew that connecting with nature released curative and creative energies. I, too, need nature in my life.

GETTING in nature may not be easy and even cities have moonlight.

ಶಿ Alternate Meditation 9

GIFTS/CONTROL/RIGIDITY/STUBBORNNESS

We don't make mistakes. We just have learnings.
                    —Anne Wilson Schaef

When we look at how our fear of making mistakes has deprived us of many of the most important issues of our lives, we give thanks that we no longer have to be so fearful of doing something wrong.

Life gives us many opportunities to learn the lessons we need to learn. Our inner beings are very conservation minded—they recycle our experience until we learn the lesson we need to learn.

The cost of the personal tuition that we have to pay is directly proportionate to our stubbornness and rigidity. The more stubborn and rigid we are, the harder we have to get hit along side the head in order to learn. If we do not learn from our mistakes the first time, we'll get another chance . . . and another . . . and another.

I GIVE THANKS for my opportunities to learn, even if they don't always look like gifts at the time.

❧ Alternate Meditation 10

CREATIVITY

Why should we all use our creative power . . . ?
Because there is nothing that makes people so generous,
joyful, lively, bold and compassionate, so indifferent to
fighting and the accumulation of objects and money.
—Brenda Ueland

So much of our frustration and irritability is a reaction to not using our creative powers. All of us have areas of creativity, and each of us has a unique creativity that is especially related to our talents and personality. Whenever we look at others and think, "I can't paint like that," or "I don't have the talent she does," we move a step further away from realizing what *we* have.

When we block our creativity, we lose touch with our joy and our liveliness. Is it any wonder that we become cantankerous and try to fill up the loneliness for our creative selves with money and things—which never quite do the job.

WHAT I REALLY search for is me, and I am by nature creative.

᎒᙭ Alternate Meditation 11

HOUSEWORK

*Cleaning your house while your kids are still growing
is like shoveling the walk before it stops snowing.*
                                        —Phyllis Diller

I never understand why housework is not added
to the list of inevitables like taxes and death. No
matter what we are trying to get done or how much
we need a rest, etc., housework is always calling to
us like the siren's song: "Come do me . . . come do
me." I have thought of inventing a birth control
spray that prevents the housework from reproducing itself while we sleep. When we get up in the
morning there always seems to be more housework
than when we went to bed.

The nice thing about housework, of course, is
that it doesn't go away. We can go ahead and do
some of our creative work or soak in the tub, and it
will be there waiting when we come back to it.

SINCE HOUSEWORK is always there waiting for
me, I might as well go ahead and do what I want.

❧ Alternate Meditation 12

ACTION/CONTROL

I have always had a dread of becoming a passenger in life.
                            —Princess Margrethe of Denmark

As women, we have been raised to expect someone to take care of us. Most professional women prize our independence. Yet down deep we often have a secret wish that someone else would take responsibility for our lives. Frequently we vacillate between wishing to be passengers in life and asserting that we can handle things ourselves. Sometimes we get stuck between these two polarities. We believe that we must either resign ourselves to going along for the ride or we must be in the engine running the train. We do not see the third option—take responsibility for our lives and simultaneously turn them over to a power greater than ourselves.

To participate in our lives does not mean that we control our lives. Not to control our lives does not mean that we are passive.

I DO NOT NEED to choose between being a passenger or being an engineer. I can live my process.

❧ Alternate Meditation 13

HONESTY/HONORING ONESELF

How many are silenced, how many women never "find their vioce" because in order to get to their art they would have to scream?

—Ann Clark

Some of us find the words "obligations to myself" foreign. We have been raised to believe that we should sacrifice ourselves in order to be good. Then others of us have reacted to the female cult of self-sacrifice and decided that we needed to be selfish and to focus upon ourselves. Often we bounce back and forth between these two choices. Unfortunately (or fortunately, as the case may be), neither is satisfactory. Either way, we feel lonely, at loose ends, and unfulfilled.

The third option is to *honor* ourselves. When we honor ourselves and give out of that honoring, our giving is very clean. If we are not honoring ourselves, our giving has strings attached and is uncomfortable for the giver and the receiver.

WHEN I HONOR myself, I discover the magic of my voice and my productions.

ᙖ Alternate Meditation 14

IMPRESSION MANAGEMENT

> *We will discover the nature of our particular genius when we stop trying to conform to our own or to other people's models, learn to be ourselves, and allow our natural channel to open.*
>
> —Shakti Gawain

Impression management is trying to control how others see us. It is a subtle form of control and comes out of our feelings of insecurity, fear, and vulnerability. Impression management is exhausting and time-consuming. Impression management keeps us so busy trying to please and trying to keep ourselves safe that it completely keeps us away from the nature of our "own genius."

Impression management has become a way of life for the contemporary professional woman. And she is not the only woman who specializes in impression management. Any woman who is out of touch with herself believes she has to control the perceptions of others. Therefore, she never really takes the risk of being known.

WHEN WE TRY to manage, we try to control. When we are ourselves, we can genuinely be *with* others.

๛ Alternate Meditation 15

DEMANDING TOO MUCH

To dream of the person you would like to be is to waste the person you are.

—Anonymous

We had so many dreams about the person we wanted to be that we never had the time to be the women we were. It is exciting to look back at our growth and see that there is an intimate relationship between our no longer trying to be someone and our beginning to be who we are. We used to demand so much of ourselves. We have, in the past, tried to mold ourselves into persons who had nothing in common with our real selves, because we were fearful that our true selves would never be enough.

Our Twelve-Step work has helped us to see that demanding too much of ourselves is part of the disease and will dissipate as we work on our recovery.

ENOUGH OR NOT—I'm all I've got—if you include my Higher Power.

৯ Alternate Meditation 16

FREEDOM

Freedom means choosing your burden.
—Hephzibah Menuhin

No one has complete freedom. Complete freedom is a myth that is terrifying to most and a dream-filled illusion for others. While we are wrestling with our terror of complete freedom or fighting the constrictions in our lives, we forget the freedoms we already have. We have the freedom to choose our burdens.

Women who have no children have chosen the burden of full-time work *without* the freedom that relating to children brings. Women who have chosen to have children have chosen the burden of rearing children (and often full-time work out of the home also!). Whatever our choices, we have made them. They are ours. We have the freedom to live with them.

I HAVE CHOSEN my burdens. Sometimes I don't see the freedom in that.

❧ Index

Thai

phrase book

Berlitz Publishing Company, Inc.

Princeton   Mexico City   Dublin   Eschborn   Singapore

How best to use this phrase book

● We suggest that you start with the **Guide to pronunciation** (pp. 6-9), then go on to **Some basic expressions** (pp. 10-16). This gives you not only a minimum vocabulary, but also helps you get used to pronouncing the language. The phonetic transcription throughout the book enables you to pronounce every word correctly.

● Consult the **Contents** pages (3-5) for the section you need. In each chapter you'll find travel facts, hints and useful information. Simple phrases are followed by a list of words applicable to the situation.

● Separate, detailed contents lists are included at the beginning of the extensive **Eating out** and **Shopping guide** sections (Menus, p. 39, Shops and services, p. 97).

● If you want to find out how to say something in Thai, your fastest look-up is via the **Dictionary** section (pp. 164-189). This not only gives you the word and phonetic transcription, but is also cross-referenced to its use in a phrase on a specific page.

● If you wish to learn more about constructing sentences, check the **Basic grammar** (pp. 160-163).

● Note the **colour margins** are indexed in Thai and English to help both listener and speaker. And, in addition, there is also an index in Thai for the use of your listener.

● Throughout the book, this symbol ☛ suggests phrases your listener can use to answer you. If you still can't understand, hand this phrase book to the Thai-speaker to encourage pointing to an appropriate answer. The English translation for you is just alongside the Thai.

Cover Photo: R.M. Arakaki/International Stock
Seventh printing - June 2000

ISBN 2-8315-7739-X
Printed in Spain

Contents

4

Travelling around 65

Sightseeing 80

Relaxing 86

Making friends 92

Shopping guide 97

Acknowledgements
We are particularly grateful to Wasant Paileeklee and Rachel
Harrison for their help in the preparation of this book.

Guide to Pronunciation

This chapter is intended to make you familiar with the phonetic transcription we have devised and to help you get used to the sounds of Thai. If you follow carefully the indications supplied below, you will have no difficulty in making yourself understood.

The Thai Script

The Thai script dates back to stone inscriptions of the 13th century and is written from left to right, as in English. The marked difference, however, is the absence of spaces between words, so that words are joined together in one long phrase.

There are 44 consonants in the Thai script and 48 different vowels producing sounds not usually found in Western languages. Vowels take one of four possible positions in relation to the consonant; they can appear to its right, its left, above it or below it. Some of the more complex "vowel clusters" are made up of two or three components surrounding the vowel on two or three sides. There are no punctuation marks in the Thai script, although spaces are left between the end of one sentence and the beginning of the next. There are no capital letters either.

Tones

Thai is a tonal language and the script has five different tones represented by four different tone marks. In the phonetic transcriptions devised in this phrase book, the tonal system is represented by the following tone marks above the first vowel of each syllable:

Tone	Pitch	Symbol
Mid tone:	normal speaking with the voice at a steady pitch	no mark
High tone	pitched slightly higher than normal	´
Low tone	pitched slightly lower than normal	`
Falling tone	pitched high and falling sharply	^
Rising tone	pitched low and rising sharply	ˇ

Every syllable in Thai has a definite tone, and therefore tones play an integral part in the meaning of words. The syllable *kar* provides a good example of this:

kar	mid tone	to dangle
kàr	low tone	galanga (a spice used in cooking)
kár	high tone	to trade
kâr	falling tone	to kill
kǎr	rising tone	a leg

Consonants

Consonants are considerably easier to pronounce in Thai than vowels since all but a few have English equivalents. The sounds you will find as **intial consonants** of syllables are as follows:

Aspirated sounds—consonants with a "huh" sound in them

b	like **b** as in banana	**k**	like **k** as in kiss
ch	like **ch** as in cheese	**p**	like **p** as in pinch
d	like **d** as in door	**s**	like **s** as in sit
f	like **f** as in free	**t**	like **t** as in take
h	like **h** as in happy		

It is important to recognize the above sounds as aspirates, because some Thai letters also have an unaspirated version, which is not the case in English. These are:

(b)p	pronounced like a sharp **p** with the "uh" sound removed.
(d)t	pronounced like sharp **t** with the "uh" sound removed
g	like **g** as in gas
j	like **j** as in jump
l	like **l** in letter
n	like **n** in new
ng	like **ng** as in sing it
r	like **r** in red
w	like **w** in win
y	like **y** in yellow

The range of consonant sounds **at the end** of Thai syllables are much fewer than the group above. They are the unaspirated sounds **p**, **t**, and **k** which should ideally be pronounced **(b)p**, **(d)t** and **g** but have not been written as such for simplicity sake.

Also **y**, **n**, **r**, **w** and **ng** occur as final consonant sounds, as do long and·short vowels.

Vowels

Many Thai vowels have a long and a short version. For example:

aih/air	a/ar
euh/eur	i/ee
eh/ey	u/oo
oh/oe	o/or

There are a very large number of vowel sounds in Thai. You will need to persevere with pronunciation practice here, using the full list of vowel sounds below:

a	like **a** in t**a**n
ar	like **ar** in c**ar**t, without pronouncing the **r**
ai	like **y** in tr**y**
i	like **i** in sp**i**t
ee	like **ee** in fr**ee**
eh	like a short, sharp exclamation "**eh**?"
er	like **er** in p**er**k, without pronouncing the **r**
ey	a long version of the above, as in pr**ey**
o	like **o** in sp**o**t
oe	like **oe** in t**oe**
oo	like **oo** in sh**oo**t
or	like **or** in w**or**n, without pronouncing the **r**
u	like **u** in p**u**t

Diphthongs

Other vowel sounds are made by combining two vowels. For example:

	i + a gives **ia**, written here as **ear**
	u + a gives **ua**, written here as **ua**
	eur + a gives **eura**, written here as **eua**
air	like **air** in f**air**, without pronouncing the **r**
aih	a shortened version of **air** above
ear	like **ear** in d**ear**, without pronouncing the **r**

eua	no comparable sound in English except "**Eugha**! How horrible."
euh	as we might say in English "**uh**? What's that? I didn't hear"
eur	the closest sound in English is an exclamation of revulsion: "**Eugh**? What's that horrible thing?'
ia	a shortened version of **ear** above
oey	like **oeil** in the French "trompe l'**oeil**"
ow	like **ow** in c**ow**
ua	like **ure** in mat**ure**

Thai alphabet

The full Thai alphabet in order is given below:

Consonants

ก	g	ฑ	t	ฟ	f
ข	k	ณ	n	ภ	p
ค	k	ด	d	ย	y
ฆ	k	ต	(d)t	ร	r
ง	ng	ถ	t	ฤ	ri
จ	j	ธ	t	ล	l
ฉ	ch	น	t	ว	w
ช	ch	บ	n	ษ	s
ซ	s	ป	b	ส	s
ญ	y	ผ	(b)p	ห	h
ฎ	(d)t	ฝ	p	ฬ	l
ฏ	t	พ	f	อ	h
ฐ	t	ฟ	p		

Vowels*

◌ั	an	◌ึ	eur	เ◌ีย	ear
◌ะ	a	◌ิ	u	เ◌ียะ	ia
◌ัว	ua	◌ู	oo	เ◌ือ	eua
◌อ	or	เ◌ย	ey	แ◌	air
ไ◌	ai	เ◌ะ	eh	แ◌ะ	aih
◌า	ar	เ◌ย	oey	โ◌	oe
◌ำ	am	เ◌อ	er	โ◌ะ	oh
◌ิ	i	เ◌อะ	erh	ใ◌	ai
◌ี	ee	เ◌า	ow		
◌ึ	euh	เ◌าะ	o		

---

* – indicates the position of the consonant in relation to the vowel or vowel cluster.

Some basic expressions

Yes*.	ครับ (ค่ะ)	kráp (kâ)
No.	ไม่	mâi
Please.	กรุณา	ga run ar
Thank you.	ขอบคุณ	kòrp kun
Thank you very much.	ขอบคุณมาก	kòrp kun mârk
That's all right/ You're welcome.	ไม่เป็นไร	mâi pehn rai

Greetings สวัสดี

Good morning/ afternoon.	สวัสดี	sa wàt dee
Good evening.	สวัสดี	sa wàt dee
Good night.	ราตรีสวัสดิ์	rar tree sa wàt
Goodbye.	สวัสดี	sa wàt dee
See you later.	แล้วเจอกัน	láiw jer gan
Hello/Hi!	สวัสดี	sa wàt dee
This is Mr./Mrs./ Miss...	นี่คุณ...	nêe kun
How do you do? (Pleased to meet you.)	ยินดีที่รู้จัก	yin dee têe róo jàk
How are you?	เป็นยังไง?	pehn yang ngai
Very well, thanks. And you?	สบายดี ขอบคุณ แล้วคุณละ?	sa bai dee kòrp kun. láiw kun lâ
How's life?	เป็นไง?	(b)pehn ngai
Fine.	สบายดี	sa bai dee
I beg your pardon?	อะไรนะ?	arai ná
Excuse me. (May I get past?)	ขอโทษ	kŏr tôet
Sorry!	ขอโทษ	kŏr tôet

---

* In Thai there is no exact word meaning yes and no. Instead, to affirm something the polite word is used; a man would say **kráp** and a woman **kâ**. For more information see the GRAMMAR section.

Questions   คำถาม

Where?	ที่ไหน?	têe nǎi
How?	ยังไง?	yang ngai
When?	เมื่อไหร่?	mêua rài
What?	อะไร?	arai
Why?	ทำไม?	tam mai
Who?	ใคร?	krai
Which?	อันไหน?	an nǎi
Where is/are...?	...อยู่ที่ไหน?	... yòo têe nǎi
Where can I find/ get...?*	ผม(ดิฉัน)จะหา ...ได้ที่ไหน?	pǒm (dì chán) ja hǎr...dâi têe nǎi
How far?	ไกลไหม?	glai mǎi
How long?	นานไหม?	narn mǎi
How much/ How many?	เท่าไหร่?	tôw rài
How much does this cost?	อันนี้เท่าไหร่?	an née tôw rài
When does... open/ close?	....เปิด/ปิดเมื่อไหร่?	...(b)pèrt/(b)pìt mêua rài
What do you call this/that in Thai?	...นี่/นั่นภาษาไทย เรียกว่าอะไร?	nêe/nân par sǎr tai rêarg wâr arai
What does this/that mean?	นี่/นั่นมีความหมาย ว่ายังไง?	nêe/nân mee kwarm mǎi wâr yang ngai

Do you speak...?   คุณพูด...ได้ไหม?

Do you speak English?	คุณพูดภาษา อังกฤษได้ไหม?	kun pôot par sǎr ang grìt dâi mǎi
Does anyone here speak English?	ที่นี่มีใครพูดภาษา อังกฤษได้บ้าง?	têe nêe mee krai pôot par sǎr ang grìt dâi bârng
I don't speak (much) Thai.	ผม(ดิฉัน)พูดภาษาไทย ได้นิดหน่อย	pǒm (dì chán) pôot par sǎr tai dâi nít nòy
Could you speak more slowly?	พูดช้าลงหน่อยได้ไหม?	pôot chár long nòy dâi mǎi

---

* The man would refer to himself as **pǒm**, a female speaker would say **dì chan**.

Could you repeat that?	พูดอีกทีได้ไหม?	pôot èek tee dâi mǎi
Could you spell it?	ช่วยสะกดให้ดูหน่อย?	chûay sa gòt hâi doo nòy
How do you pronounce this?	อันนี้ออกเสียงยังไง?	an née oìk sěarng yang ngai
Could you write it down, please?	เขียนให้ดูหน่อย?	kěarn hâi doo nòy
Can you translate this for me?	ช่วยแปลอันนี้ให้ ผม(ดิฉัน)หน่อย?	chûay (b)plair an née hâi pǒm (di chán) nòy
Can you translate this for us?	ช่วยแปลอันนี้ ให้เราหน่อย?	chûay (b)plair an née hâi row nòy
Could you point to the... in the book, please?	ช่วยชี้...นั้นในหนังสือ ให้คุณหน่อย?	chûay chée... nân nai náng sěur hâi doo nòy
word	คำ	kam
phrase	วลี	wa lee
sentence	ประโยค	(b)pra yôek
Just a moment.	สักครู่	sàk krôo
I'll see if I can find it in this book.	ผม(ดิฉัน)จะลองดูว่าจะ หามันเจอไหมในหนังสือ เล่มนี้	pǒm (di chán) ja lorng doo wâr ja hǎr man jer mǎi nai náng sěur lêhm née
I understand.	ผม(ดิฉัน)เข้าใจ	pǒm (di chán) kôw jai
I don't understand.	ผม(ดิฉัน)ไม่เข้าใจ	pǒm (di chán) mâi kôw jai
Do you understand?	คุณเข้าใจไหม?	kun kôw jai mǎi

Can/May...? ขอ/ช่วย...?

Can I have...?	ขอ...ได้ไหม?	kǒr...dâi mǎi
Can we have...?	ขอ...ได้ไหม?	kǒr...dâi mǎi
Can you show me...?	ช่วยบอกผม (ดิฉัน)หน่อย...?	chûay bòrk pom (di chán) nòy
I can't...	ผม...ไม่ได้	pǒm...mâi dâi
Can you tell me...?	ช่วยบอกผม (ดิฉัน)หน่อย...?	chûay doo pǒm (di chán) nòy
Can you help me?	ช่วยผม(ดิฉัน) หน่อยได้ไหม?	chûay pǒm (di chán) nòy dâi mǎi

| Can I help you? | มีอะไรให้ช่วยไหม? | mee arai hâi chûay măi |
| Can you direct me to...? | ช่วยบอกทางไป... ให้ผม(ดิฉัน)หน่อย? | chûay bòrk tarng pai...hâi pŏm (di chán) nòy |

Do you want...? *คุณอยาก...ไหม?*

I'd like...	ผมอยาก...	pŏm yàrk
We'd like...	เราอยาก...	row yàrk
What do you want?	คุณต้องการอะไร?	kun (d)tông garn arai
Could you give me...?	ให้...ผม(ดิฉัน)ได้ไหม?	hâi...pŏm (di chán) dâi măi
Could you bring me...?	เอา...มาให้ผม(ดิฉัน) หน่อยได้ไหม?	ow...mar hâi pŏm (di chán) nòy dâi măi
Could you show me...?	ช่วยบอกผม (ดิฉัน)หน่อย...?	chûay bòrk pŏm (di chán) nòy
I'm looking for...	ผม(ดิฉัน)กำลังหา...	pŏm (di chán) gam lang hăr
I'm searching for...	ผม(ดิฉัน)กำลังค้นหา...	pŏm (di chán) gam lang kón hăr
I'm hungry.	ผม(ดิฉัน)หิว	pŏm (di chán) hĭw
I'm thirsty.	ผม(ดิฉัน)หิวน้ำ	pŏm (di chán) hĭw nárm
I'm tired.	ผม(ดิฉัน)เหนื่อย	pŏm (di chán) nèuay
I'm lost.	ผม(ดิฉัน)หลงทาง	pŏm (di chán) lŏng tarng
It's important.	มันสำคัญ	man săm kan
It's urgent.	มันด่วนมาก	man dùan mârk

It is/There is... *มัน/มี...*

It is...	มัน(คือ/เป็น)...	man (keur/pehn)
Is it...?	มัน...ไหม?	man...măi
It isn't...	มันไม่...	man mâi
Here it is.	นี่อยู่ที่นี่	nêe yòo têe nêe
Here they are.	นี่อยู่ที่นี่	nêe yòo têe nêe
There it is.	นั่นไงอยู่ที่นั่น	nân ngai yòo têe nân

| There they are. | นั่นไงอยู่ที่นั่น | nân ngai yòo têe nân |

There is/There are ...	มี...	mee
Is there/Are there ...?	มี...	mee
There isn't/aren't ...	ไม่มี...	mâi mee
There isn't/aren't any.	ไม่มี	mâi mee

It's ... มัน...

beautiful/ugly	สวย/น่าเกลียด	sŭay/nâr glèart
better/worse	ดีกว่า/เลวกว่า	dee gwàr/leyw gwàr
big/small	ใหญ่/เล็ก	yài/léhk
cheap/expensive	ถูก/แพง	tòok/pairng
early/late	เช้า/สาย	chów/sǎi
easy/difficult	ง่าย/ยาก	ngâi/yârk
free (vacant)/ occupied	ว่าง/ไม่ว่าง	wârng/mâi wârng
full/empty	เต็ม/ว่าง	(d)tehm/wârng
good/bad	ดี/เลว	dee/lehw
heavy/light	หนัก/เบา	nàk/bow
here/there	ที่นี่/ที่นั่น	têe nêe/têe nân
hot/cold	ร้อน/เย็น	rórn/yehn
near/far	ใกล้/ไกล	glâi/glai
next/last	หน้า/ที่แล้ว	nâr/têe láiw
old/new	เก่า/ใหม่	gòw/mài
old/young	แก่/เด็ก	kàir/dèhk
open/shut	เปิด/ปิด	(b)pèrt/(b)pìt
quick/slow	เร็ว/ช้า	rehw/chár
right/wrong	ถูก/ผิด	tòot/pìt

Quantities ปริมาณ

a little/a lot	น้อย/มาก	nóy/mârk
few/a few	น้อย/ไม่กี่	nóy/mâi gèe
much	มาก	mârk
many	หลาย	lăi

| more/less than | มากกว่า/น้อยกว่า | mârk gwàr/nóy gwàr |

| enough/too | พอ/เกินไป | por/gern (b)pai |
| some/any | บาง/ใด | barng/dai |

A few more useful words คำที่เป็นประโยชน์อีกจำนวนหนึ่ง

above	บน	bon
after	หลังจาก	lăng jàrk
and	และ	láih
at	ที่	têe
before (time)	ก่อน	gòrn
behind	หลัง	lăng
below	ต่ำกว่า/ใต้	(d)tàm gwàr/(d)tâi
between	ระหว่าง	ra wàrng
but	แต่	tàir
down	ลง	long
downstairs	ชั้นล่าง	chán lârng
during	ระหว่าง	ra wàrng
for	เพื่อ/สำหรับ	pêua/săm ràp
from	จาก	jàrk
in	ใน	nai
inside	ข้างใน	kârng nai
near	ใกล้	glâi
never	ไม่เคย	mâi koey
next to	ติดกับ	(d)tìt gàp
none	ไม่เลย	mâi loey
not	ไม่	mâi
nothing	ไม่มีอะไร	mâi mee arai
now	ตอนนี้	(d)torn née
on	บน	bon
only	เท่านั้น	tôw nán
or	หรือ	rĕua
outside	ข้างนอก	kârng nôrk
perhaps	บางที	barng tee
since	ตั้งแต่	(d)tâng (d)tàir
soon	ในไม่ช้า	nai mâi chár
then	แล้วก็	láiw gò
through	ผ่าน	pàrn
to	ถึง	tĕuhng
too (also)	เหมือนกัน	mĕuan gan
towards	ตรงไปที่	(d)trong (b)pai têe
under	ใต้	(d)tâi
until	กระทั่ง	gra tâng
up	ขึ้น	kêuhn
upstairs	ชั้นบน	chán bon
very	มาก	mârk
with	กับ/ด้วย	gàp/dûay
without	ไม่มี	mâi mee
yet	ยัง	yang

Arrival

Passport Control *ที่ตรวจหนังสือเดินทาง*

Before arrival you will be asked to fill out an immigration card and a customs declaration form asking for details of valuables, electrical equipment and amounts of money in excess of $10,000 being taken into the country. When you leave Thailand you may be asked to prove that you are taking with you the items you have listed.

For most foreign nationals a visa is not required to enter Thailand for a stay of under 15 days. Transit visas are valid for 30 days, tourist visas for 60 and non-immigrant visas for 90 days.

Visitors may be asked to prove their solvency by producing the equivalent of 10,000 baht (per person) or 20,000 baht (per family) in currency, traveller's cheques or credit cards.

You may be asked to show a vaccination certificate if you are travelling from an area infected with yellow fever. Vaccinations against cholera are no longer required but those for typhoid fever and hepatitis A are strongly recommended.

Here's my passport.	นี่หนังสือ เดินทางของผม(ดิฉัน)	née náng sěur dern tarng kŏrng pŏm (di chán)
I'll be staying...	ผม(ดิฉัน)จะอยู่...	pŏm (di chán) ja yòo
a few days	สองสามวัน,	sŏrng sǎrm wan
a week	หนึ่งอาทิตย์	nèuhng ar tìt
2 weeks	สองอาทิตย์	sŏrng ar tit
a month	หนึ่งเดือน	nèuhng deuan
I don't know yet.	ผม(ดิฉัน)ยังไม่รู้	pŏm (di chán) yang mâi róo
I'm here on holiday.	ผม(ดิฉัน)มาเที่ยว	pŏm (di chán) mar têaw
I'm here on business.	ผม(ดิฉัน)มาธุระ	pŏm (di chán) mar tu rá
I'm just passing through.	ผม(ดิฉัน)แค่แวะ ผ่านเท่านั้น	pŏm (di chán) kâir wáih pàrn tôw nán

If things become difficult:

I'm sorry, I don't understand.	ขอโทษ ผม (ดิฉัน)ไม่เข้าใจ	kŏr tôet pŏm (dì chán) mâi kôw jai
Does anyone here speak English?	ที่นี่ มีใครพูดภาษา อังกฤษได้ไหม?	têe nêe mee krai pôot pa sǎr ang krìt dâi mǎi

ศุลกากร
CUSTOMS

After collecting your baggage at the airport you have a choice: use the green exit if you have nothing to declare. Or leave via the red exit if you have items to declare (in excess of those allowed).

มีรายการสิ่งของต้องแสดง
goods to declare

ไม่มีรายการสิ่งของต้องแสดง
nothing to declare

The chart below shows what you can bring in duty-free

	Cigarettes	Cigars	Tobacco	Spirits (Liquor)	Wine
Into Thailand:	200	or 200	or 250g.	1 l. or 1 l.	

I have nothing to declare.	ผม(ดิฉัน) ไม่มีรายการสิ่งของ ต้องแสดง	pŏm (dì chán) mâi mee rai garn sìng kŏrng (d)tôrng sa dairng
I have ...	ผม(ดิฉัน)มี...	pŏm (dì chán) mee
a carton of cigarettes	บุหรี่หอหนึ่ง	bu rèe hòr nèuhng
a bottle of whisky	วิสกี้ขวดหนึ่ง	wít sa gêe kùat nèuhng
It's for my personal use.	อันนี้สำหรับใช้ส่วนตัว	an née sǎm ràp chái sùan (d)tua
It's a gift.	อันนี้เป็นของฝาก	an née (b)pehn kŏrng fàrk

ขอดูหนังสือ เดินทาง (พาสปอรต)หนอย		Your passport, please.
คุณมีรายการสิงของตองแสดงไหม?		Do you have anything to declare?
ชวยเปิดถุงใบนี้หนอย		Please open this bag.
คุณจะ ตองจายคาภาษีสำหรับสิงนี้		You'll have to pay duty on this.
คุณมีกระเปาอีกไหม?		Do you have any more luggage?

Baggage—Porter *กระเปา คนยกกระเปา*

Porters are readily available in the airport arrival hall, as well as at the mainline railway station and coach terminals.

Porter!	คนยกกระเปา	kon yók gra (b)pǒw
Please take (this/my)...	ชวยยก...	chûay yók
luggage	กระเปา	gra (b)pǒw
suitcase	กระเปา	gra (b)pǒw
(travelling) bag	กระเปา(เดินทาง)	gra (b)pǒw (dern tarng)
Take this luggage...	ยกกระเปา ใบนี้...ใหหนอย	yók gra (b)pǒw bai née...hâi nòy
to the bus	ไปที่รถบัส	(b)pai têe rót bàt
to the luggage lockers	ไปที่ฝากกระเปา	(b)pai têe fàrk gra (b)pǒw
to the taxi	ไปที่รถแท็กซี่	(b)pai têe rót táihk sêe
How much is that?	เทาไหร?	tôw rài
There's one piece missing.	มีของหายไปชิ้นหนึ่ง	mee kŏrng hǎi (b)pai chín nèuhng
Where are the luggage trolleys (carts)?	รถเข็นกระเปาอยู่ที่ไหน?	rót kĕhn gra (b)pǒw yòo têe nǎi

Changing money *แลกเงิน*

Banks are open between 8.30am and 3.30pm, Monday to Friday. In tourist areas most banks operate a foreign exchange service until 8pm or later, seven days a week, including public holidays.

BANK—CURRENCY, see page 129

Where's the nearest currency exchange office?	กเงินที่ใกล้ ที่สุดอยู่ที่ไหน?	têe lâirk ngern têe glai têe sùt yòo têe nǎi
Can you change these traveller's cheques (checks)?	รับแลกเช็คเดินทางไหม?	ráp lâirk chéhk dern tarng mǎi
I want to change some dollars/pounds.	ผม(ดิฉัน)อยาก แลกเงินดอลลาร์/ ปอนด์หน่อย	pǒm (di chán) yàrk lâirk ngern dorn lar/(b)porn nòy
Can you change this into baht?	ขอแลกอันนี้ เป็นเงินบาทได้ไหม?	kǒr lâirk an née (b)pehn ngern bàrt dâi mǎi
What's the exchange rate?	อัตราแลกเปลี่ยนเป็น ยังไง?	a (d)trar lâirk (b)plèarn/ (b)pehn yang ngai

Where is...? ...อยู่ที่ไหน?

Where is the...?	...อยู่ที่ไหน?	...yòo têe nǎi
booking office	ที่จองตั๋ว	têe jorng (d)tǔa
duty (tax)-free shop	ร้านขายของปลอดภาษี	rárn kǎi kǒrng (b)plòrt par sěe
newsstand	ร้านขายหนังสือพิมพ์	rárn kǎi nǎng sěur pim
How do I get to...?	จะไป...ไปยังไง?	ja (b)pai...(b)pai yang ngai
Is there a bus into town?	มีรถบัสเข้าไปในเมืองไหม?	mee rót bàt kôw (b)pai nai meuang mǎi
Where can I get a taxi?	ผม(ดิฉัน)จะ เรียกแท็กซี่ได้ที่ไหน?	pǒm (di chán) ja rêark táihk sêe dâi têe nǎi
Where can I hire (rent) a car?	ผม(ดิฉัน)จะ เช่ารถได้ที่ไหน?	pǒm (di chán) ja chôw rót dâi têe nǎi

Hotel reservation จองโรงแรม

Do you have a hotel guide (directory)?	คุณมีสมุดรายชื่อ โรงแรมไหม?	kun mee sa mùt rai chêur roeng rairm mǎi
Could you reserve a room for me?	ช่วยจองห้องพักให้ผม (ดิฉัน)ห้องหนึ่งได้ไหม?	chûay jorng hôrng pák hâi pǒm (di chán) hôrng nèuhng dâi mǎi
in the centre	ที่ใจกลางเมือง	têe jai glarng meuang
near the railway station	ใกล้กับสถานีรถไฟ	glai gàp sa tǎr nee rót fai
a single room	ห้องเดี่ยว	hôrng dèaw
a double room	ห้องคู่	hôrng kôo
not too expensive	ไม่แพงนัก	mâi pairng nák

HOTEL/ACCOMMODATION, see page 22

| Where is the hotel/ guesthouse? | โรงแรม/ เกสเคเฮ้าสอยู่ที่ไหน? | roeng rairm/gèyt hôwt yòo têe nǎi |
| Do you have a street map? | คุณมีแผนที่ถนนไหม? | kun mee pǎirn têe ta nǒn mǎi |

Car hire (rental) รถเช่า

To rent a car you must be over 21 and hold a valid International Driving Licence. You may be asked to pay a deposit equal to the estimated cost of the rental. Larger companies, however, waive this deposit for credit-card holders.

I'd like to hire (rent) a car.	ผม(ดิฉัน)อยากเชารถ สักคัน	pǒm (di chán) yàrk chôw rót sàk kan
small	เล็ก	léhk
medium-sized	ขนาดกลาง	ka nàrt glarng
large	ใหญ	yài
automatic	อัคโนมัติ	àt a noe mát
I'd like it for a day/ a week.	ผมอยากเช่าวันหนึ่ง/ อาทิตย์หนึ่ง	pǒm yàrk chôw wan nèuhng/ar tìt nèuhng
Do you have any special rates?	มีราคาพิเศษไหม?	mee rar kar pi sèyt mǎi
What's the charge per day/week?	ค่าเช่าเท่าไหร่ต่อวัน/ อาทิตย์?	kâr chôw tôw rài (d)tòr wan/ar tìt
Is mileage included?	บวกระยะทางแล้วยัง?	bùak rá yá tarng láiw yang
What's the charge per kilometre?	คิดค่าเช่าต่อ กิโลเมตรเท่าไหร่?	kít kâr chôw (d)tòr gi loe mét tôw rài
I'd like to leave the car in . . .	ผม(ดิฉัน) ต้องการทิ้งรถไว้ที่...	pǒm (di chán) (d)tôrng garn tíng rót wái têe
I'd like full insurance.	ผม(ดิฉัน)อยากได้ที่มี ประกันเต็มที่	pǒm (di chán) yàrk dâi têe mee (b)pra gan (d)tehm têe
How much is the deposit?	ค่ามัดจำเท่าไหร่?	kâr mát jam tôw rài
I have a credit card.	ผม(ดิฉัน)มีบัตรเครดิต	pǒm (di chán) mee bàt krey dìt
Here's my driving licence.	นี่ใบขับขี่ของผม(ดิฉัน)	née bai kàp kèe kǒrng pǒm (di chán)

CAR, see page 75

Taxi แท็กซี่

You shouldn't have any difficulty finding a taxi as every time you venture outside you will probably be hailed by a number of over-enthusiastic taxi drivers. Only those with the official yellow registration plates and signs on the roof should be used. Although a small number of Bangkok taxis have meters, the majority do not and a price must be agreed with the driver before the journey begins. In addition to taxis there are three-wheeled tuk tuks which are slightly cheaper. Outside Bangkok, their equivalent is the pedal-powered *samlor* or rickshaw.

Where can I get a taxi/tuk tuk?	ผม(ดิฉัน)จะเรียกแท็กซี่/ ตุ๊กตุ๊กได้ที่ไหน?	pŏm (di chán) ja rêark táihk sêe/(d)túk (d)túk dâi têe nǎi
Where is the taxi rank (stand)?	ที่จอดรถแท็กซี่อยู่ที่ไหน?	têe jòrt rót táihk sêe yòo têe nǎi
Could you get me a taxi?	เรียกแท็กซี่ให้ผม(ดิฉัน) คันหนึ่งได้ไหม?	rêark táihk sêe hâi pŏm (di chán) kan nèuhng dâi mǎi
What's the fare to ...?	ไป...คิดเท่าไหร่?	(b)pai...kit tôw rài
That's too expensive. How about ... baht?	แพงไป ...บาทได้ไหม	pairng (b)pai...bàrt dâi mái
How far is it to ...?	ไป...ไกลไหม?	(b)pai...glai mǎi
Take me to ...	พาผม(ดิฉัน) ไปส่งที่...ด้วย	par pŏm (di chán) (b)pai sòng têe...dûay
this address	ที่อยู่นี้	têe yòo née
the airport	สนามบิน	sa nǎrm bin
the town centre	ใจกลางเมือง	jai glarng meuang
the... Hotel	โรงแรม...	roeng rairm
the railway station	สถานีรถไฟ	sa tǎr nee rót fai
Turn... at the next corner.	เลี้ยว...ที่หัวมุมข้างหน้า	léaw...têe hǔa mum kârng nâr
left/right	ซ้าย/ ขวา	sái/kwǎr
Go straight ahead.	ตรงไป	(d)trong (b)pai
Please stop here.	จอดที่นี่	jòrt têe nêe
Could you wait for me?	รอเดี๋ยวนะ?	ror děaw ná
I'll be back in 10 minutes.	ผม(ดิฉัน)จะกลับมา ในอีกสิบนาที	pŏm (di chán) ja glàp mar nai èek sìp nar tee

TIPPING, see inside back-cover

Hotel—Other accommodation

Information on some of the larger hotels can be obtained from international branches of the Tourism Authority of Thailand (TAT) and booking made direct. A booking service is also available at the Thai Hotels Association desk in the arrival hall of Bangkok airport. Most large provincial towns in Thailand have TAT branches which can provide names and addresses of hotels in the area.

Most large hotels add 11% government tax and 8-10% service charges to the bill.

โรงแรม
(roeng rairm)

Hotel. It is a good idea to book a hotel in Bangkok before you arrive as the majority of its 30,000 rooms are often full. Prices vary from the very cheapest guest houses in the Khao Sarn Road (ta nŏn kòw sărn) to some of the most luxurious first class hotels in the world. Among the middle range hotels, many offer a choice of air conditioning or a simple ceiling fan. The latter are cheaper. Most hotels have a swimming pool.

Outside Bangkok, hotel accommodation may be more basic but prices are cheap.

โรงแรมม่านรูด
(roeng rairm mârn rôot)

Motels are known in Thai as "hotels with curtains" (the curtains are to hide the car so the guests retain their anonymity) and are usually rented out by the hour. While people can stay for several days at a time this would probably not be the best type of tourist accommodation.

บังกาโล
(bang ga loe)

Beach resorts not only have a full range of hotel accommodation but also offer bamboo bungalows built on the beach which are clean, simple and very good value for money.

บ้านพักชายทะเล
(bârn pák chai ta ley)

A beach bungalow is a complex of huts on the beach, with a central bungalow which acts as a reception area and restaurant.

กระท่อม
(gra tôm)

In jungle and hill resorts (in Kanchanaburi and Northern Thailand) cottages that are part of a larger complex are also available.

แพ (pair)	For the adventurous, there are rafts on the River Kwai (*mâir nárm kwair*).	
Can you recommend a hotel/guest house?	ช่วยแนะนำโรงแรม/ เกสต์เฮาส์ให้หม (ดิฉัน)หน่อย?	chûay náih nam roeng rairm/gèyt hòwt hâi pŏm (di chán) nòy
Are there any self-catering flats (apartments) vacant?	มีแฟลต/ อพาร์ตเม้นท์ที่ทำอาหาร กินเองได้ว่างไหม?	mee fláiht/ar pàrt méyn têe tam ar hărn gin eyng dâi wârng măi

Checking in—Reception เช็คอิน แผนกต้อนรับ

My name is...	ผม(ดิฉัน)ชื่อ...	pŏm (di chán) chêur
I have a reservation.	ผม(ดิฉัน)ของห้องไว้	pŏm (di chán) jorng hôrng wái
We've reserved 2 rooms/ an apartment.	เราของห้องเอาไว้สองห้อง /อพาร์ตเม้นท์เอาไว้ หลังหนึ่ง	row jorng hôrng ow wái sŏrng hôrng/ar pàrt méyn ow wái lăng nèuhng
Here's the confirmation.	นี่คือคำยืนยัน	nêe keur kam yeurn yan
Do you have any vacancies?	คุณมีห้องว่างไหม?	kun mee hôrng wârng măi
I'd like a...	ผม(ดิฉัน)อยากได้...	pŏm (di chán) yàrk dâi
single room	ห้องเดี่ยว	hôrng dèaw
double room	ห้องคู่	hôrng kôo
We'd like a room...	เราอยากได้ห้องๆหนึ่ง...	row yàrk dâi hôrng hôrng nèuhng
with twin beds	ที่มีเตียงเดี่ยวสองเตียง	têe mee (d)teang dèaw sŏrng (d)teang
with a double bed	ที่มีเตียงคู่	têe mee (d)teang kòo
with a bath	ที่มีห้องน้ำด้วย	têe mee hôrng nárm dûay
with a shower	ที่มีฝักบัว	têe mee fàk bua
with a balcony	ที่มีระเบียง	têe mee ra beang
with a view	ที่มีวิวทางนอก	têe mee wiw kârng nôrk
at the front	ด้านหน้า	dârn nâr
at the back	ด้านหลัง	dârn lăng
It must be quiet.	มันจะต้องเงียบ	man ja (d)tôrng ngêarp
Is there...?	มี...ไหม?	mee...măi
air conditioning	แอร์	air
a conference room	ห้องประชุม	hôrng (b)pra chum

CHECKING OUT, see page 31

24

a laundry service	บริการซักรีด	bo ri garn sák rêet
a private toilet	ห้องน้ำส่วนตัว	hông nárm sùan (d)tua
a radio/television in the room	วิทยุ/โทรทัศน์ในห้อง	wít a yú/to ra tát nai hông
a swimming pool	สระว่ายน้ำ	sà wâi nárm
hot water	น้ำร้อน	nárm rórn
room service	บริการรูมเซอร์วิส	bo ri garn room ser wít
running water	น้ำประปา	nárm (b)pra (b)par
Could you put an extra bed/a cot in the room?	ช่วยใส่เตียงอีกเตียง/อุ่นนอนเข้าไปในห้องด้วย?	chûay sài (d)tearng èek (d)teang/òo norn kôw (b)pai nai hông dûay

How much? เท่าไหร่?

What's the price...?	...เท่าไหร่?	...tôw rài
per day	วันละ	wan lá
per week	อาทิตย์ละ	ar tìt lá
for bed and breakfast	ค่าที่พักและอาหารเช้า	kâr têe pák láih ar hårn chów
excluding meals	ไม่รวมอาหาร	mâi ruam ar hårn
for full board (A.P.)	รวมอาหารทุกมื้อ	ruam ar hårn túk méur
Does that include...?	นั่นรวม...ด้วยไหม?	nân ruam...dûay mǎi
breakfast	อาหารเช้า	ar hårn chów
service	ค่าบริการ	kâr bo ri garn
Is there any reduction for children?	มีส่วนลดสำหรับเด็กไหม?	mee sùan lót sǎm ràp dèhk mǎi
Do you charge for the baby?	คิดค่าเด็กอ่อนด้วยหรือเปล่า?	kít kâr dèhk òrn dûay rěua (b)plŏw
That's too expensive.	แพงเกินไป	pairng gern (b)pai
Do you have anything cheaper?	มีอะไรที่ถูกกว่านั้นไหม?	mee arai têe tòok gwàr nán mǎi
Is electricity included in the rental?	ค่าไฟฟ้ารวมอยู่ในค่าเช่าด้วยหรือเปล่า?	kâr fai fár ruam yòo nai kâr chôw dûay rěua (b)plow

How long? นานไหม?

We'll be staying...	เราจะอยู่...	row ja yòo
overnight only	แค่คืนเดียว	kâir keurn deaw
a few days	สองสามวัน	sǒrng sǎrm wan
a week (at least)	(อย่างน้อย)อาทิตย์หนึ่ง	(yàrng nói) ar tìt nèuhng

NUMBERS, see page 147

I don't know yet.	ผม(ดิฉัน)ยังไม่รู้เลย	pŏm (di chán) yang mâi róo loey

Decision คัดสินใจ

May I see the room?	ขอดูห้องก่อนได้ไหม?	kŏr doo hôrng gòrn dâi mǎi
That's fine. I'll take it.	ตกลง ผม(ดิฉัน)เอาห้องนี้	(d)tòk long. pŏm (di chán) ow hôrng née
No. I don't like it.	ไม่ ผม(ดิฉัน)ไม่ชอบห้องนี้	mâi. pŏm (di chán) mâi chôrp hôrng née
It's too...	มัน...เกินไป	man...gern (b)pai
cold/hot	หนาว/ร้อน	nǒw/rórn
dark/small	มืด/เล็ก	mêurt/léhk
noisy	เสียงดัง	sǎrng dang
I asked for a room with a bath.	ผม(ดิฉัน)ขอห้อง ที่มีอ่างอาบน้ำ	pŏm (di chán) kŏr hôrng têe mee àrng àrp nárm
Do you have anything...?	คุณมีอะไร...ไหม?	kun mee arai...mǎi
better	ดีกว่านั้น	dee gwàr nán
bigger	ใหญ่กว่านั้น	yài gwàr nán
cheaper	ถูกกว่านั้น	tòok gwàr nán
quieter	เงียบกว่านั้น	ngêab gwàr nán
Do you have a room with a better view?	คุณมีห้องที่มีวิว ดีกว่านี้ไหม?	kun mee hôrng têe mee wiw dee gwàr née mǎi

Registration ลงทะเบียน

Upon arrival at a hotel or guesthouse you may be asked to fill in a registration form (ใบลงทะเบียน —*bai long ta biarn*).

นามสกุล/ ชื่อ	Name/First name
เมือง/ ถนน/ เลขที่	Home town/Street/Number
สัญชาติ/ อาชีพ	Nationality/Occupation
วัน/ สถานที่เกิด	Date/Place of birth
มาจาก/ จะไปที่	Coming from.../ Going to...
เลขที่หนังสือเดินทาง	Passport number
สถานที่/ วันที่	Place/Date
ลายมือชื่อ	Signature

| What does this mean? | อันนี้มีความหมายยังไง? | an née mee kwarm măi yang ngai |

ขอดูหนังสือเดินทาง (พาสปอร์ต)หน่อย?	May I see your passport, please?
ช่วยกรอกแบบฟอร์ม ลงทะเบียนนี้ด้วย?	Would you mind filling in this registration form?
ช่วยเซ็นชื่อตรงนี้ด้วย	Please sign here.
จะอยู่ที่นี่นานไหม?	How long will you be staying?

| What's my room number? | ห้องผม(ดิฉัน) หมายเลขเท่าไหร่? | hôrng pŏm (di chán) măi lêyg tôw rài |

| Will you have our luggage sent up? | ช่วยขนกระเป๋าของเรา ขึ้นไปให้ด้วย? | chûay kŏn gra (b)pŏw kŏrng row kêuhn (b)pai hâi dûay |

| Where can I park my car? | ผม(ดิฉัน)จะ จอดรถได้ที่ไหน? | pŏm (di chán) ja jòrt rót dâi têe năi |

| Does the hotel have a garage? | ที่โรงแรมมีโรงรถไหม? | têe roeng rairm mee roeng rót măi |

| I'd like to leave this in the hotel safe. | ผม(ดิฉัน)อยากจะฝาก อันนี้เอาไว้ในตู้เซฟของ โรงแรม | pŏm (di chán) yàrk ja fàrk an née ow wái nai (d)tôo seyf kŏrng roeng rairm |

Hotel staff พนักงานโรงแรม

hall porter	พนักงานยกกระเป๋า	pa nák ngarn yók gra (b)pŏw
maid	พนักงานดูแลห้อง	sŏw chái
manager	ผู้จัดการ	pôo jàt garn
porter	คนยกกระเป๋า	kon yók gra (b)pŏw
receptionist	พนักงานต้อนรับ	pa nák ngarn (d)tôrn ráp
switchboard operator	พนักงานรับโทรศัพท์/ โอเปอเรเตอร์	pa nák ngarn ráp toe ra sàp/oer (b)per rey (d)têr
waiter	พนักงานเสิร์ฟ/บ๋อย	pa nák ngarn sèrp/bŏy
waitress	พนักงานเสิร์ฟ	pa nák ngarn sèrp

Hotel staff may be addressed as *kun kráp* if you are a male speaker or *kun kâ* if you are female.

TELLING THE TIME, see page 153

General requirements ความต้องการทั่วไป

The key to room..., please.	ขอกุญแจห้อง...ด้วย	kŏr gun jair hôrng...dûay
Could you wake me at... please?	ช่วยปลุกผม(ดิฉัน) เวลา...ด้วย?	chûay (b)plùk pŏm (di chán) wey lar...dûay
When is breakfast/ lunch/dinner served?	อาหารเช้า/เที่ยง/ เย็นเสิร์ฟตอนกี่โมง?	ar hărn chów/têang/yehn sèrp (d)torn gèe moeng
May we have breakfast in our room, please?	ขออาหารเช้าที่ห้องได้ไหม?	kŏr ar hărn chów têe hôrng dâi mái
Is there a bath on this floor?	ชั้นนี้มีอ่างอาบน้ำไหม?	chán née mee àrng àrp nárm măi
What's the voltage?	ที่นี่ใช้ไฟฟ้ากี่โวลท์?	têe nêe chái fai fár gèe woel
Where's the shaver socket (outlet)?	ปลั๊กเสียบเครื่อง โกนหนวดไฟฟ้า อยู่ที่ไหน?	(b)plák sèarp krèuang goen nùat fai fár yòo têe năi
Can you find me a...?	ช่วยหา...ให้ผม (ดิฉัน)หน่อย?	chûay hăr...hâi pŏm (di chán) nòy
babysitter	คนเลี้ยงเด็ก	kon léarng dhèk
secretary	เลขานุการ	ley kăr nú garn
typewriter	เครื่องพิมพ์ดีด	krèuang pim dèet
May I have a/an/ some...?	ขอ...หน่อย?	kŏr...nòy
ashtray	ที่เขี่ยบุหรี่	têe kèar bu rèe
bath towel	ผ้าขนหนู	pâr kŏn nŏo
(extra) blanket	ผ้าห่ม(อีกผืน)	pâr hòm (èek pěurn)
envelopes	ซองจดหมาย	sorng jòt măi
(more) hangers	ไม้แขวนเสื้อ(อีกหน่อย)	mái kwăirn sêua (èek nòy)
hot-water bottle	ถุงน้ำร้อน	tŭng nárm rórn
ice cubes	น้ำแข็ง	nárm kăihng
needle and thread	เข็มกับด้าย	kěhm gàp dâi
(extra) pillow	หมอน(เพิ่ม)	mŏrn (pêrm)
reading lamp	โคมไฟหัวเตียง	kŏem fai hŭa (d)teang
soap	สบู่	sa bòo
Where's the...?	...อยู่ที่ไหน?	yòo têe năi
bathroom	ห้องอาบน้ำ	hôrng àrp nárm
dining-room	ห้องทานอาหาร	hôrng tarn ar hărn
emergency exit	ทางออกฉุกเฉิน	tarng òrk chùk chĕrn
lift (elevator)	ลิฟท์	líf
Where are the toilets?	ห้องน้ำอยู่ที่ไหน?	hôrng nárm yòo têe năi

BREAKFAST, see page 40

Telephone—Post (mail) *โทรศัพท์ ไปรษณีย์*

Can you get me Pattaya 123-45-67?	ช่วยต่อทางไกลไป พัทยา หมายเลข ๑๒๓-๔๕-๖๗?	chûay (d)tòr tarng glai (b)pai pát a yar mâi lêyk nèung sŏrng sărm-sèe hâr-hòk jèht
Do you have any stamps?	มีแสตมป์ไหม?	mee sa (d)tàirm mǎi
Would you post this for me, please?	ช่วยส่งอันนี้ทาง ไปรษณีย์ให้ควย?	chûay sòng an née tarng (b)prai sa nee hâi dûay
Are there any letters for me?	มีจดหมายมาถึงผม (ดิฉัน)บ้างไหม?	mee jòt mǎi mar tĕuhng pǒm (di chán) bârng mǎi
Are there any messages for me?	มีใครฝากขอความอะไรถึ งผม(ดิฉัน)บ้างไหม?	mee krai fàrk kôr kwarm arai tĕuhng pǒm (di chán) bârng mǎi
How much is my telephone bill?	ค่าโทรศัพท์ของผม (ดิฉัน)เท่าไหร่?	kâr toe ra sàp kǒrng pǒm (di chán) tôw rài

Difficulties *ปัญหายุ่งยาก*

The . . . doesn't work.	. . .ไม่ทำงาน	. . . mâi tam ngarn
air conditioning	แอร์	air
fan	พัดลม	pát lom
heating	เครื่องทำความร้อน	krêuang tam kwarm rórn
light	ไฟฟ้า	fai fár
radio	วิทยุ	wít ta yú
television	โทรทัศน์	to ra tát
The tap (faucet) is dripping.	ก๊อกน้ำหยด	gòk nárm yòt
There's no hot water.	ไม่มีน้ำร้อน	mâi mee nárm rórn
The washbasin is blocked.	อ่างล้างหน้าอุดตัน	àrng lárng nâr ùt (d)tan
The window is jammed.	หน้าต่างเปิดไม่ได้	nâr (d)tàrng (b)pèrt mâi dâi
The mesh screen is broken.	มุ้งลวดขาด	múng lûat kàrt
The curtains are stuck.	ผ้าม่านเลื่อนไม่ได้	pâr mârn lêuan mâi dâi
The bulb is burned out.	หลอดไฟขาด	lòrt fai kàrt
My bed hasn't been made up.	เตียงของผม(ดิฉัน) ยังไม่มีคนปูให้เรียบร้อย	(d)teang kǒrng pǒm (di chán) yang mâi mee kon (b)poo hâi rêarp róy

POST OFFICE AND TELEPHONE, see page 132

The... is broken.	...เสีย/ชำรุด	... sĕar/cham rút
blind	มู่ลี่	môo lêe
lamp	หลอดไฟ	lòrt fai
plug	ปลั๊กไฟ	plák fai
shutter	หน้าต่างบานเกล็ด	nâr (d)tàrng barn glèht
switch	สวิทช์ไฟ	sa wìt fai
Can you get it repaired?	ช่วยซ่อมให้หน่อยได้ไหม?	chûay sôrm hâi nòy dâi mǎi
Can you spray the room, please?	ช่วยฉีดยากันยุง ในห้องให้ด้วย	chûay chèet yar gan yung nai hôrng hâi dûay

Laundry—Dry cleaner's ซักรีด ซักแห้ง

Thais are scrupulous about cleanliness and most hotels and guest houses have a laundry service. Although dry cleaning is rare in Thailand facilities are available in large hotels, department stores and tourist areas.

I'd like these clothes...	ช่วยเอาเสื้อผ้าพวกนี้ไป... ให้ด้วย	chûay ow sêua pâr pûak née (b)pai...hâi dûay
cleaned	ซักแห้ง	sák hâirng
ironed	รีด	rêet
washed	ซัก	sák
When will they be ready?	จะเสร็จเมื่อไหร่?	ja sèht mêua rài
I need them...	ผม(ดิฉัน)อยากได้...	pǒm (di chán) yàrk dâi
today	วันนี้	wan née
tonight	คืนนี้	keurn née
tomorrow	พรุ่งนี้	prûng née
before Friday	ก่อนวันศุกร์	gòrn wan sùk
Can you... this?	ช่วย...ตัวนี้หน่อยได้ไหม?	chûay...(d)tua née nòy dâi mǎi
mend	ซ่อม	sôrm
patch	ปะ	(b)pà
stitch	สอย	sǒy
Can you sew on this button?	ช่วยเย็บตรงกระดุม นี้หน่อยได้ไหม?	chûay yéhp (d)trong gra dum née nòy dâi mǎi
Can you get this stain out?	ช่วยจัดการกับ รอยคราบนี้ด้วย?	chûay jàt garn gàp roy krârp née dûay
Is my laundry ready?	เสื้อผ้าที่ผม(ดิฉัน)เอามา ซักเสร็จหรือยัง?	sêua pâr têe pǒm (di chán) ow mar sák sèht rěua yang

| There's something missing. | มีอะไรหายไปบางอย่าง | mee arai hăi (b)pai barng yàrng |
| There's a hole in this. | อันนี้เป็นรู | an née (b)pehn roo |

Hairdresser—Barber *ร้านเสริมสวย ร้านตัดผม*

Is there a hairdresser/ beauty salon in the hotel?	ในโรงแรมนี้มีร้าน เสริมสวยไหม?	nai roeng rairm née mee rárn sěrm sŭay măi
Can I make an appointment for Thursday?	ขอนัดวันพฤหัสฯไหม?	kôr nát wan pa ru hàt dâi măi
I'd like a cut and blow dry.	อยากให้ตัดและเป่า	yàrk hâi (d)tàt láih (b)pòw
I'd like a haircut, please.	ผม(ดิฉัน)อยากตัดผม	pŏm (di chán) yàrk (d)tàt pŏm

bleach	กัดสีผม	gàt sěe pŏm
blow-dry	เป่า	(b)pòw
colour rinse	ทำสีผม	tam sěe pŏm
dye	ย้อม	yórm
face pack	ฟอกหน้า	fôrk nâr
hair gel	เยลใส่ผม	yeyl sài pŏm
manicure	แต่งเล็บ	(d)tàirng léhp
permanent wave	ดัดถาวร	dàt tăr won
setting lotion	น้ำยาเซ็ทผม	nárm yar séht pŏm
shampoo and set	สระเซ็ท	sà séht
with a fringe (bangs)	ไว้ผมด้านหน้า(ผมม้า)	wái pŏm dârn nâr (pom már)

I'd like a shampoo for... hair.	อยากได้แชมพู สำหรับผม...	yàrk dâi chairm poo săm ràp pŏm
normal/dry/ greasy (oily)	ธรรมดา/ แห้ง/ มัน	ta ma dar/hâirng/man
Do you have a colour chart?	มีตารางสีไหม?	mee (d)tar rarng sěe măi
Don't cut it too short.	อย่าตัดสั้นเกินไปนะ	yàr (d)tàt sân gern (b)pai ná

A little more off the...	เอา...ออกอีกนิด	ow...òrk èek nít
back	ด้านหลัง	dârn lăng
neck	แถวคอ	tăiw kor
sides	ด้านข้าง	dârn kârng
top	ข้างบน	kârng bon
I don't want any hairspray.	ไม่ต้องฉีดสเปรย์ให้นะ	mâi (d)tôrng chèet sa (b)prey hâi ná
I'd like a shave.	ช่วยโกนหนวดให้ด้วย	chûay goen nùat hâi dûay

DAYS OF THE WEEK, see page 151

Would you trim my..., please?	ช่วยเล็ม...ให้ด้วย?	chûay lehm...hâi dûay
beard	เครา	krow
moustache	หนวด	nùat
sideboards (sideburns)	จอน	jorn

Checking out เช็คเอ้าท์

May I have my bill, please?	ขอใบเสร็จด้วย?	kŏr bai sèht dûay
I'm leaving early in the morning.	ผม(ดิฉัน)จะ ออกจากนี่ตอนเช้า	pŏm (di chán) ja òrk jàrk nêe (d)torn chów
Please have my bill ready.	ช่วยเตรียมใบเสร็จให้ เรียบร้อยด้วย	chûay (d)trearm bai sèht hâi rêarp róy dûay
We'll be checking out around noon.	เราจะเช็คเอ้าท์ราวๆเที่ยง	row ja chéhk ôw row row têarng
Is everything included?	รวมทุกอย่างแล้วหรือยัง?	ruam túk yàrng láiw rĕua yang
Can I pay by credit card?	จ่ายด้วย บัตรเครดิตได้ไหม?	jài dûay bàt krey dìt dâi măi
I think there's a mistake in the bill.	คิดว่ามีอะไรผิด ในใบเสร็จนี้	kìt wâr mee arai (b)pìt nai bai sèht née
Can you get us a taxi?	ช่วยเรียกแท็กซี่ให้หน่อย ได้ไหม?	chûay rèark táihk sêe hâi nòy dâi măi
Could you have our luggage brought down?	ช่วยขนกระเป๋าลงไป ข้างล่างให้ด้วย?	chûay kŏn gra (b)pŏw long (b)pai kârng lârng hâi dûay
Here's the forwarding address.	นี่คือที่อยู่ที่สามารถติดต่อ ผม(ดิฉัน)ได้หลังจากนี้	nêe keur têe yòo têe sărmârt (d)tìt tòr pŏm (di chán) dâi lăng jàrk née
You have my home address.	คุณมีที่อยู่ของผม(ดิฉัน) แล้ว	kun mee têe yòo kŏrng pŏm (di chán) láiw
It's been a very enjoyable stay.	อยู่ที่นี่สนุกมาก	yòo têe nêe sa nùk mârk

TIPPING, see inside back-cover

Camping แค้มปิ้ง

Several National Parks offer camping facilities, and tents can be hired out on a number of the islands. However, camping sites are not common in Thailand and camping out in the wilds is not recommended.

Is there a camp site near here?	แถวนี้มีที่ตั้งแค้มป์ไหม?	tǎiw née mee têe (d)tâng káirm mǎi
Can we camp here?	เราตั้งแค้มป์พักที่นี่ได้ไหม?	row (d)tâng kâirm pák têe nêe dâi mǎi
Do you have room for a tent/caravan (trailer)?	คุณมีที่สำหรับกางเต็นท์/จอดรถนอนไหม?	kun mee têe sǎm ràp garng (d)têyn/jòrt rót norn mǎi
What's the charge...?	คิดเท่าไหร่...?	kít tôw rài
per day	ต่อวัน	(d)tòr wan
per person	ต่อคน	(d)tòr kon
for a car	ต่อคัน	(d)tòr kan
for a tent	ต่อเต็นท์	(d)tòr têyn
Is tourist tax included?	รวมภาษีนักท่องเที่ยวด้วยหรือเปล่า?	ruam par sěe nák tôrng têaw dûay rěua plôw
Is there/Are there (a)...?	มี...ไหม?	mee...mǎi
drinking water	น้ำดื่ม	nárm dèurm
electricity	ไฟฟ้า	fai fár
playground	สนามวิ่งเล่น	sa nǎrm wîng lêhn
restaurant	ร้านอาหาร	rárn ar hǎrn
shopping facilities	ที่ชอปปิ้ง/ร้านขายของ	têe chórp (b)pîng/rárn kǎi kǒrng
swimming pool	สระว่ายน้ำ	sà wâi nárm
Where are the showers/toilets?	ที่อาบน้ำฝักบัว/ห้องน้ำอยู่ที่ไหน?	têe àrp nárm fàk bua/hôrng nárm yòo têe nǎi
Where can I get butane gas?	ผม(ดิฉัน)จะหาก๊าซบิวเทนได้ที่ไหน?	pǒm (di chán) ja hǎr gárt biw teyn dâi têe nǎi
Is there a youth hostel near here?	แถวนี้มีที่พักเยาวชนไหม?	tǎiw née mee têe pák sǎm ràp yow wa chon mǎi

CAMPING EQUIPMENT, see page 106

Eating out

Thai cuisine combines Indian and Chinese influences with its own distinctive blend of flavours and aromas: lemongrass and coconut milk, galangal and garlic, fresh coriander and sweet basil, lime leaves and fish paste. Thai food will normally use fresh ingredients, speedily cooked, with a healthy combination of firm vegetables, steamed rice and lean, trimmed meats, beautifully served in an array of colour and texture.

Thais are fond of eating out and dining is a social activity. You'll find numerous foodstalls, coffee shops, restaurants and bars. Pavements are often teeming with vendors selling snacks and appetizers from mobile trolleys or from a pair of wicker baskets carried on a pole over the shoulder. Both savoury and sweet foods are on offer.

You will also see mobile vendors with cabinets of fresh fruit, ready-peeled and sliced. This is sold in polythene bags, complete with wooden skewers and an explosive mixture of sugar, salt and chilli powder (*prík gà gleua*) which Thais use as a dip. Some vendors wheel barrows of dried squid pegged to rails and grill them to order. You may also see people deep frying locusts.

แผงลอย
(pǎirng loy)

The cheapest places to eat are roadside stalls selling noodles or rice dishes from a barrow surrounded by stools. Here you can eat fresh food, prepared while you wait: a skewer of spicy satay, rice with tasty fried chicken or pork in a rich coconut sauce, with a sweet pancake topped with fresh coconut to finish.

ศูนย์อาหาร
(sǒon arhǎrn)

These food plazas, often found in department stores, offer a full range of simple meals such as noodle soup, boiled chicken on rice, fried rice, curry or mussel omelettes. Most operate on a coupon system where coupons are bought from a central cash point and then used as currency at individual stalls. One of the busiest and best known food halls is in the Mahboonkhrong Centre in Bangkok's Siam Square, but there are many others.

ร้านข้าวแกง
(rárn kôw gairng)

These curry and rice bar restaurants have a display cabinet in the doorways with trays of different curries and soups. You can have one or two of these served on rice or served separately as a side dish with rice.

ร้านอาหาร ร้านอาหาร
(rárn ar hǎrn)

Cheap range roadside restaurants sell a variety of fried rice and noodle dishes which are ideal for lunch. These tend not to be air-conditioned and are largely open for day-time trade, closing in the early evening.

ภัตตาคาร ภัตตาคาร
(pát ta karn)

Grander establishments serve full Thai meals comprising numerous succulent dishes accompanied by rice. Most *pát ta karn* are air-conditioned, although some may have an open-air section. Look for the *Thai Shell Good Food Guide* signs: a rice-bowl with blue letter-ing signifying that the establishment serves the very best of authentic Thai food.

สวนอาหาร
(sǔan ar hǎrn)

Some restaurants are large, open-air com-plexes known as food gardens. While the atmosphere is relaxing and refreshing, the food tends to be similar to that in the *pát ta karn*. The biggest restaurant in the world is the Tamnak Thai (*(d)tàm nàk tai*) food garden complex on Bangkok's Ratchadapisek Road. It is divided into four different sectors, cor-responding to the four different regions of Thailand, and serves the appropriate regional cuisine in each sector. The restaurant is so vast that waiters deliver food on roller skates.

ร้านอาหารทะเล
(rárn ar hǎrn ta ley)

These restaurants, usually open-air, special-ize in seafood which is often on display pre-cooked, or which can be chosen and cooked to order. These are particularly popular at coastal resorts, where you will find a dazzling array of the day's catch: crabs and lobsters, squid, clams and giant prawns, and a tempt-ing variety of fresh fish. Inland seafood res-taurants can also be found in Bangkok and Chiang Mai.

ผับ
(pàp)

Western-style pubs have become popular in Bangkok and many provincial capitals, and they sell a wide range of foods. As an accom-paniment to alcohol, Thais like to eat snacks called *gàp glâihm*.

Meal times *เวลาอาหาร*

Thai food is meant for sharing and Thais eat their main meal of the day in groups, each with their own individual plate of boiled rice and dipping into the shared savoury dishes that accompany it. The emphasis is on balance and variety, with hot and sour flavours soothed by rich and sweet, steamed dishes and fried, tender and crispy textures.

Thais eat rice at all times of the day, though for breakfast and lunch they may opt for noodles instead.

Breakfast (*ar hărn chów* or *kôw chów*) usually consists of a bowl of thick rice soup, flavoured with ground pork, chicken or prawns, pepper, garlic, fresh coriander and sometimes an egg.

Lunch (*ar hărn glarng wan* or *kôw têang*) is usually taken between 11.30am and 1pm and tends to consist of a single plate of food, either rice based or noodle based. A typical Thai lunch would involve both a "wet" and a "dry" noodle dish.

Dinner (*ar hărn kâm* or *kôw yehn*) can be long and protracted. Evening meals comprise two main parts, rice (*kôw*) and savoury dishes served with rice (*gàp kôw*).

Thai cuisine *อาหารไทย*

Thai food is heavily influenced by Chinese and Indian cuisine. The Chinese influence is mainly in the eating of noodles and the techniques of stir-frying and steaming, while the Indian influence is felt in the delicious blends of hot and aromatic spices. Others, such as Japanese, Malaysian, Arabian and Portuguese, have also added some of their flavours, varying according to the region. Nevertheless, Thai food retains its own distinctive character.

Chinese restaurants are quite common throughout the country. Western and Japanese restaurants are also present in big hotels as well as in tourist areas. Other foreign restaurants such as Vietnamese and Indian can also be found in tourist areas.

รับอะไร?	What would you like?
อันนี้น่าทาน	I recommend this.
ดื่มอะไร?	What would you like to drink?
ที่นี่ไม่มี...	We don't have...
คุณจะรับ...ไหมครับ?	Would you like...?

Hungry? หิวไหม?

I'm hungry/I'm thirsty.	ผม(ดิฉัน)หิว/ หิวน้ำ	pŏm (di chán) hĭw/hĭw nárm
Can you recommend a good restaurant?	ช่วยแนะนำภัตตาคารดีๆ ไหหนอยได้ไหม?	chûay néh nam pát tar karn dee dee hâi nòy dâi măi
Are there any inexpensive restaurants around here?	แถวนี้มีภัตตาคาร ที่ไม่แพงไหม?	tăirw née mee pát tar karn têe mâi pairng măi

If you want to be sure of getting a table in a well-known restaurant, it may be better to book in advance.

I'd like to reserve a table for 4.	ขอจองโต๊ะสำหรับสี่ค น	kŏr jorng (d)tóh săm ràp sèe kon
We'll come at 8.	เราจะไปถึงนั่นตอนส องทุ่ม	row ja (b)pai tĕuhng nân (d)torn sŏrng tûm
Could we have a table...?	ขอโต๊ะ...ได้ไหม?	kŏr (d)tóh...dâi măi
in the corner	ที่มุมห้อง	têe mum hôrng
by the window	ติดหน้าต่าง	(d)tit nâr (d)tàrng
outside	ด้านนอก	dârn nôrk
on the terrace	ที่ระเบียง	têe rá beang
in a non-smoking area	ในบริเวณห้ามสูบบุหรี่	nai boh ri weyn hârm sòop bu rèe

Asking and ordering ซักถามและสั่ง

Waiter/Waitress!	บ๋อย/ คุณ	bŏy/kun
I'd like something to eat/drink.	ผม(ดิฉัน)อยากได้ อะไรมาทาน/ ดื่ม	pŏm (di chán) yàrk dâi arai mar tarn/ dèurm

May I have the menu, please?	ขอดูรายการอาหารหน่อย ได้ไหม?	kŏr doo rai garn ar hărn nòy dâi măi
Do you have a set menu*/local dishes?	มีอาหารชุด/ พื้นบ้านไหม?	mee ar hărn chút/péurn bârn măi
What do you recommend?	มีอะไรน่าทานบ้าง?	mee arai nâr tarn bârng
I like hot and spicy food.	ผม(ดิฉัน)ชอบอาหารรสจัด	pŏm (dì chán) chôrp ar hărn rót jàt
Nothing too spicy, please.	ไม่เอารสจัดนะครับ(คะ)	mâi ow rót jàt ná kráp (kâ)
Do you have anything ready quickly?	มีอะไรที่เสร็จเร็วๆบ้าง?	mee arai têe sèht rehw rehw bârng
I'm in a hurry.	ผม(ดิฉัน)ต้องรีบไป	pŏm (dì chán) (d)tông rêep (b)pai
I'd like...	ผม(ดิฉัน)อยากได้...	pŏm (dì chán) yàrk dâi
Could we have a/ an..., please?	ขอ...ได้ไหม?	kŏr...dâi măi
ashtray	ที่เขี่ยบุหรี่	têe kèar bu rèe
chopsticks	ตะเกียบ	(d)ta gèap
cup	ถ้วยกินน้ำ	tûay gin nárm
fork	ส้อม	sôrm
glass	แก้ว	gâiw
knife	มีด	mêet
napkin (serviette)	กระดาษเช็ดปาก	gra dàrt chét (b)pàak
plate	จาน	jarn
spoon	ช้อน	chórn
toothpicks	ไม้จิ้มฟัน	mái jîm făn
May I have some...?	ขอ...หน่อยได้ไหม?	kŏr...nòy dâi măi
bread	ขนมปัง	ka nŏm (b)pang
butter	เนย	noey
lemon	มะนาว	ma now
oil	น้ำมัน(มะกอก)	nám man (ma gòrk)
pepper	พริกไทย	prík tai
salt	เกลือ	gleua
seasoning	เครื่องปรุง	krêuang (b)prung
sugar	น้ำตาล	nárm (d)tarn
vinegar	น้ำส้มสายชู	nárm sôm săi choo

---

* A set menu is a number of pre-chosen courses, usually cheaper than à la carte.

Special diet *อาหารพิเศษ*

Some useful expressions for those with special requirements:

I'm on a diet.	ผม(ดิฉัน)กำลังลด ความอ้วน	pŏm (di chán) gam lang lód kwarm ûan
I'm vegetarian.	ผม(ดิฉัน)เป็นมังสวิรัติ	pŏm (di chán) (b)pehn mang sawi rát
I don't drink alcohol.	ผม(ดิฉัน)ไม่ดื่มอัลกอฮอล์	pŏm (di chán) mâi dèurm al gor horl
I don't eat meat.	ผม(ดิฉัน)ไม่ทานเนื้อ	pŏm (di chán) mâi tarn néua
I mustn't eat food containing...	ผม(ดิฉัน)จะ ต้องไม่ทานอาหารที่มี...	pŏm (di chán) ja (d)tông mâi tarn ar hărn têe mee
flour/fat	แป้ง/ไขมัน	(b)pâirng/kăi man
salt/sugar	เกลือ/น้ำตาล	kleua/nárm (d)tarn
Do you have ... for diabetics?	ที่นี่มี...สำหรับ คนที่เป็นเบาหวานไหม?	têe nêe mee...săm ràp kon (b)pehn bow wărn măi
cakes	ขนมเค้ก	ka nŏm kéyk
fruit juice	น้ำผลไม้	nárm pŏn la mái
a special menu	รายการอาหารพิเศษ	rai garn ar hărn pi sèyt
Do you have any vegetarian dishes?	ที่นี่มีอาหารมังสวิรัติ บางไหม?	têe nêe mee ar hărn mang sawi rát bârng măi
Could I have cheese/ fruit instead of dessert?	ขอเนยแข็ง/ ผลไม้ แทนของหวานได้ไหม?	kŏr noey kăihng/pŏn la mái tairn kŏrng wărn dâi măi
Can I have an artificial sweetener?	ขอน้ำตาลเทียม หน่อยได้ไหม?	kŏr nárm (d)tarn team nòy dâi măi

And ...

I'd like some more.	ขอสั่งเพิ่ม	kŏr sàng pêrm
Can I have more ..., please?	ขอ...เพิ่มได้ไหม?	kŏr...pêrm dâi măi
Just a small portion.	ขอที่เล็กๆก็พอ	kŏr têe léhk léhk gôh por
Nothing more, thanks.	ไม่รับอะไรแล้ว ขอบคุณ	mâi ráp arai láiw kòrp kun
Where are the toilets?	ห้องน้ำไปทางไหน?	hôrng nárm (b)pai tarng năi

What's on the menu? *รายการอาหารมีอะไรบ้าง?*

Menus are not usually displayed outside restaurants. Most restaurants in Bangkok and other large cities and tourist areas have menus in English. Look out for local specialities of the region: tiny spare-ribs with coriander root and peppercorns in the South; pork and ginger curry with sticky rice and chunky chilli dip with raw vegetables in the North; freshwater fish cooked with lemongrass in banana leaves in the North-East; and crab and prawns cooked with garlic in a clay pot on the Gulf Coast.

Under the headings below, you'll find alphabetical lists of dishes that might be offered on a Thai menu with their English equivalent. You can simply show the book to the waiter. If you want some fruit, for instance, let *him* point to what's available on the appropriate list. Use pages 36 and 37 for ordering in general.

Reading the menu   *ดูรายการอาหาร*

อาหารเรียกน้ำย่อย	ar hărn rêark nárm yôy	appetizers
เบียร์	bear	beer
เครื่องดื่ม	krêuang dèurm	beverages
เบอร์เกอร์	ber ger	burgers
ไก่	gài	chicken
ของหวาน	kŏrng wărn	desserts
อาหารประเภทไข่	ar hărn (b)pra pèyt kài	egg dishes
อาหารจานหลัก	ar hărn jarn làk	entrées
ปลา	(b)plar	fish
ผลไม้	pŏn la mài	fruit
ไอศครีม	ai sa kreem	ice cream
ก๋วยเตี๋ยว	gwáy tĕaw	noodles
เป็ดไก่	(b)pèt gài	poultry
ข้าว	kôw	salads
สลัด/ ยำ	sa làt/yam	rice
อาหารทะเล	ar hărn ta ley	seafood
อาหารว่าง	ar hărn ra wârng	snacks
ซุป	súp	soups
ผัก	pàk	vegetables
เหล้าไวน์	lôw wai	wine

Breakfast   *อาหารเช้า*

Breakfast—*ar hărn chów* or *kôw chów*—literally means morning food, or morning rice. For Thais this is usually a bowl of rice soup, either flavoured with ground pork, chicken or prawns, or served plain with separate condiments such as salted fish, salted egg and pickled vegetables.

Most hotels and many restaurants in tourist areas serve Western style breakfasts of toast, butter and marmalade with orange juice and coffee. Breakfast cereals are much more difficult to come by. Ordering boiled eggs can also be a shock since the nearest Thai equivalent (*kài lûak*) really means scalded eggs. Two eggs are momentarily scalded with boiling water, then cracked into a glass and topped with pepper and soy sauce. Fried eggs are a safer bet!

| I'd like breakfast, please. | ผม(ดิฉัน) อยากได้อาหารเช้า | pŏm (di chán) yàrk dâi ar hărn chów |

I'll have a/an/ some...	ขอ...	kŏr
bacon and eggs	เบคอนกับไข่	bey korn gàp kài
boiled egg	ไข่ต้ม	kài (d)tôm
soft/hard	ไม่สุกมาก/เอาสุกๆ	mâi sùk mârk/ow sùk sùk
cereal	ซีเรียล	see re arl
eggs	ไข่	kài
fried eggs	ไข่ดาว	kài dow
scrambled eggs	ไข่คน	kài kon
scalded eggs	ไข่ลวกๆ	kài lûak
fruit juice	น้ำผลไม้	nárm pŏn la mái
orange	น้ำส้ม	nárm sôm
ham and eggs	แฮมกับไข่ดาว	hairm gàp kài dow
jam	แยม	yairm
marmalade	แยมเปลือกส้ม	yairm (b)plèuak sôm
rice soup	โจ๊ก	jóek
with pork	โจ๊กหมู	jóek mǒo
with chicken	โจ๊กไก่	jóek gài
with prawns	โจ๊กกุ้ง	jóek gûng
with egg	โจ๊กใส่ไข่	jóek sài kài
toast	ขนมปังปิ้ง	ka nǒm (b)pang (b)pîng
yoghurt	โยเกิร์ต	yoe gèrt

May I have some...?	ขอ...หน่อยได้ไหม?	kŏr... nòy dâi mǎi
bread	ขนมปัง	ka nǒm (b)pang
butter	เนย	noey
(hot) chocolate	ช็อคโกแล็ต(ร้อน)	chók goe láiht (rórn)
coffee	กาแฟ	gar fair
decaffeinated	ชนิดไม่มีคาเฟอีน	cha nít mâi mee kar fey een
black/with milk	ดำ/ใส่นม	dam/sài nom
honey	น้ำผึ้ง	nárm pêuhng
milk	นม	nom
cold/hot	เย็น/ร้อน	yen/rórn
pepper	พริกไทย	prík tai
rolls	ขนมปังก้อน	ka nǒm (b)pang gôrn
salt	เกลือ	gleua
tea	ชา	char
with milk	ใส่นม	sài nom
with lemon	มะนาว	ma now
(hot) water	น้ำ(ร้อน)	nárm (rórn)

Starters (Appetizers) อาหารเรียกน้ำย่อย

Thai people don't usually have starters at meal time since every dish is served at the same time. However, it has become quite common, especially in the smart restaurants, to have starters. Thai pre-dinner snacks can include such tasty dishes as spicy sausage, nibbled with tiny cubes of fresh ginger, and grated raw papaya in a spicy dressing of fish sauce with fresh green chillies.

I'd like an appetizer.	ผม(ดิฉัน)อยากได้อาหารเรียกน้ำย่อย	pŏm (di chán) yàrk dâi ar hărn rêark nárm yôy
What would you recommend?	มีอะไรน่าทานบ้าง?	mee arai nâr tarn bârng
ปีกไก่ยัดไส้	(b)pèek gài yát sâi	stuffed chicken wings
เกี๊ยวกรอบ	géaw gròrp	deep-fried, crispy wan ton
แหนมสด	năirm sòt	fresh sausage
ไส้กรอกอีสาน	sâi gròrk ee sărn	spicy North-Eastern sausage
ข้าวเกรียบกุ้ง	kôw grèarp gûng	rice cakes with prawn dip
ปลาหมึกย่าง	(b)pla mèuhk yârng	grilled squid

ปอเปี๊ยะ
((b)por (b)pía)
Thai spring rolls. Often served with a sweet sauce, these are more delicate and compact than Chinese spring rolls and are mildly flavoured.

กระทงทอง
(gra tong torng)
Deep-fried batter cups filled with minced pork and spices.

ถุงเงินยวง
(tŭng ngern yuang)
Delicate little cups of batter, filled with lightly curry-spiced pork.

สะเต๊ะหมู/เนื้อ
(sa téh mŏo/néua)
Pork or beef satay. Originally introduced to Thailand through the southern region from Malaysia, satay is a delicious blend of spicy barbecued meat and hot peanut sauce.

ทอดมันปลา
(tôrt man (b)plar)
Deep-fried, spicy fishcakes made from fresh fish fillets, flavoured with a spicy combination of chillies, coriander, galangal and lime.

ขนมปังหน้าหมู/กุ้ง

(ka nŏm (b)pang nâr mŏo/gûng)

Fried bread topped with minced pork or prawn; accompanied by a cucumber pickle dip, made with fresh chillies, these light but spicy toasts make a delicious starter.

Soups and curries ซุปและแกง

A typical selection of savoury dishes usually includes a soup and/or a curry. Thais always have their soup and curry at the same time as other savoury dishes, as soup was traditionally served as a beverage with the meal.

ต้มยำเห็ด	(d)tôm yam hèht	clear, hot and sour soup with mushroom
แกงจืดลูกชิ้นปลา	gairng jèurt lôok chín (b)plar	clear soup with fish balls
แกงจืดเกี้ยมฉ่าย	gairng jèurt gêarm chài	clear soup with pickled vegetables
แกงจืดสาหร่ายทะเล	gairng jèurt săr rài ta ley	clear soup with seaweed
แกงจืดรวมมิตร	gairng jèurt ruam mít	clear soup with a mixture of ingredients
ต้มจับฉ่าย	(d)tôm jàp chài	clear soup with pork ribs and mixed vegetables
แกงเลียง	gairng leang	clear soup with fresh vegetables, prawns and black pepper
ต้มโคล้ง	(d)tôm klóeng	hot and sour curry with dried fish and spices
ต้มเค็ม	(d)tôm kehm	salty soup

ต้มยำกุ้ง/ไก่

((d)tôm yam gûng/gài)

Clear, hot and sour soup with prawn or chicken. This soup, from the central region of Thailand, forms the perfect centrepiece of a typical Thai meal. It should be eaten with lots of rice, as it is flavoured with roasted chilli paste and lemongrass and is extremely hot!

ต้มข่าไก่
((d)tôm kàr gài)

Chicken and coconut milk soup flavoured with galanga. One of the most famous Thai dishes, this soup is rich with coconut milk, but sharp with the flavours of lemongrass, wild lime leaves and galanga, which is a citrus-scented member of the ginger family.

แกงจืดวุ้นเส้น
(gairng jèurt wún sêhn)

Clear soup with Chinese glass noodles, minced pork and vegetables. The delicate, silvery noodles are made from mung beans, and add a subtle texture to this mildly flavoured soup.

แกงจืดเต้าหู้
(gairng jèurt (d)tôw hôo)

Clear soup with tofu. Its name means "mildly flavoured", flavoured simply with fish sauce and spinach. This soup is traditionally served to soothe the effects of other dishes.

แกงส้มผักกระเฉด
(gairng sôm pàk gra chèyt)

Hot and sour curry with fish and pungent green vegetables. Unlike other Thai curries, made with sweet coconut milk, this one from the south of Thailand is based on the sharp, sour flavours of tamarind and lime.

Egg Dishes *อาหารประเภทไข่*

ไข่ดาว	kài dow	fried egg
ไข่เจียว	kài jeaw	deep-fried omelette
ไข่ลวก	kào lûak	soft boiled eggs
ยำไข่เค็ม	yam kài kèhm	salty egg salad

ไข่เจียวยัดไส้
(kài jeaw yát sâi)

Although called an omelette, this dish is more like a filled crêpe, with a sweetly flavoured stuffing of peppers, tomato and pork.

ไข่ลูกเขย
(kài lôok kŏei)

"Son-in-law" eggs. A popular Thai wedding dish, served as an accompaniment. Traditionally made from hard-boiled duck eggs, deep-fried with a coating of ground chillies, and eaten dripping with tamarind sauce.

Fish and seafood ปลาและอาหารทะเล

There are a large number of freshwater fish and seafood dishes in Thai cuisine, although the highland areas of the North and North-East might have a smaller selection compared to Bangkok and the coastal provinces of the South and the East.

I'd like some fish.	ผม(ดิฉัน)อยากทานปลา	pŏm (di chán) yàrk tarn (b)plar
What kind of seafood do you have?	มีอาหารทะเลอะไรบ้าง?	mee ar hărn ta ley arai bârng
ปลาทู	(b)plar too	mackerel
ปลาจาระเม็ด	(b)plar jar ra mèht	pomfret
ปลากระพง	(b)plar gra pong	sea bass
ปลาหมึก	(b)plar mèuhk	squid
ปลาไหล	(b)plar lăi	eel
ปลาช่อน	(b)plar chôn	serpent-headed fish
ปลาดุก	(b)plar dùk	catfish
ปลาสำลี	(b)plar săm lee	*samlee* fish
ปลากราย	(b)plar grai	*grai* fish
ปลาสลิด	(b)plar sa lìt	gouramy
กุ้ง	gûng	prawn
ล็อบสเต้อร์	lóp sa (d)têr	lobster
ปูทะเล	(b)poo ta ley	crab
หอยลาย	hŏy lai	scallops
หอยแมลงภู่	hŏy mairng pòo	mussels
หอยนางรม	hŏy nang rom	oyster

You may want to try one of these dishes:

ปลาสลิดทอดกรอบ	(b)plar sa lìt tôrt gròrp	crispy, deep-fried gouramy
ยำปลาสลิด	yam (b)plar sa lìt	spicy gouramy salad
ยำปลาดุกฟู	yam (b)plar dùk foo	spicy catfish salad
ผัดเผ็ดปลาดุก	pàt pèht (b)plar dùk	spicy stir-fried catfish
ปลาดุกย่าง	(b)plar dùk yârng	grilled catfish
ปลาเปรี้ยวหวาน	(b)plar (b)prêaw wărn	sweet and sour fish
ปลาช่อนแป๊ะซะ	(b)plar chôn (b)pàih sá	serpent-headed fish steamed with herbs
แกงส้มปลาช่อน	gairng sôm (b)plar chôrn	hot and sour fish curry with mixed vegetables
ห่อหมกปลา	hòr mòk (b)plar	steamed fish curry

ห่อหมกทะเล	hòr mòk ta ley	steamed seafood curry
ทอดมันปลา	tôrt man (b)plar	deep-fried spicy fishcakes
ปลาทูทอด	(b)plar too tôrt	deep-fried sardines
ปลาจาระเม็ดนึ่งเกี้ยมบ๊วย	(b)plar jar ra méht nêuhng gêarm búay	steamed pomfret with sour plums
ปลาหมึกย่าง	(b)plar mèuhk yârng	grilled squid
กุ้งเผา	gûng pŏw	roasted prawns
หอยลายผัดผงกะหรี่	hŏy lai pàt pŏng ga rèe	scallops fried with curry powder
หอยลายผัดน้ำพริกเผา	hŏy lai pàt nám prík pŏw	scallops fried with roasted chilli paste

ปลาสำลีเผา
((b)plar săm lee pŏw)
Roasted *samlee* fish. A simple but delicious country dish, traditionally cooked in banana leaves on an open charcoal oven, flavoured with coriander and garlic.

กุ้งอบหม้อดิน
(gûng òp môr din)
Roasted prawns in a clay pot with soy sauce and pepper. This dish is Chinese in origin, combining soy and oyster sauces, sesame oil and ginger, but has been given a Thai flavour with the classic mix of coriander, peppercorns, garlic and fish sauce.

ปูผัดผงกะหรี่
((b)poo pàt pŏng ga rèe)
Crab fried with curry powder. Despite its name, this dish is not particularly hot, but rather gently spiced with curry and without the usual heat of chillies.

ปูอบหม้อดิน
((b)poo òp môr din)
Crab roasted in a clay pot with soy sauce and pepper.

ปลาราดพริก
((b)plar rârt prík)
Fish topped with chillies. Called "three-flavoured fish", this dish is typical of Thai cuisine, combining the three elements of sweet, sour and hot.

baked	อบ	òp
boiled	ต้ม	(d)tôm
curried	แกง	gairng
fried	ผัด	pàt
deep-fried	ทอด	tôrt
grilled	ปิ้ง/ ย่าง	(b)pîng/ yârng
scalded	ลวก	lûak
smoked	รมควัน	rom kwan
steamed	นึ่ง	nêuhng

Meat เนื้อ

Pork and beef are common in Thai cuisines, while lamb is relatively rare. Meats are usually sliced or cut into small, lean pieces for ease of consumption and speed of cooking.

I'd like some...	ผม(ดิฉัน)อยากได้...	pŏm (di chán) yàrk dâi
beef	เนื้อวัว	néua wua
lamb	เนื้อลูกแกะ	néua lôok gàih
pork	เนื้อหมู	néua mŏo
veal	เนื้อลูกวัวอ่อน	néua lôok wua òrn

เบคอน	bey korn	bacon
เครื่องใน/ไส้	krêuang nai/sâi	chitterlings
เนื้อสัน	néua săn	fillet
หมูแฮมรมควัน	mŏo hairm rom kwan	(smoked) ham
ไต	(d)tai	kidneys
ขา(ลูกแกะ)	kăr (lôok) gàih	leg (of lamb)
ลูกชิ้นเนื้อ	lôok chín néua	meatballs
เนื้อแกะ	néua gàih	mutton
หางวัว	hăerng wua	oxtail
หัวหมู/ขาหมู	hŭa mŏo/kăr mŏo	pig's head/trotters
ไส้กรอก	sâi gròrk	sausage
ขาช่วงล่าง	kăr chûang lârng	shank
เนื้อสันนอก	néua săn nôrk	sirloin
หมูหัน	mŏo hăn	suckling pig
ตับอ่อน	(d)tàp òrn	sweetbreads
เนื้อสันใน	néua săn nai	tenderloin
ลิ้น	lín	tongue

baked	อบ	òp
barbecued	ปิ้ง/ย่าง	(b)pîng/yârng
boiled	ต้ม	(d)tôm
fried	ผัด/ทอด	pàt/tôrt
grilled	ปิ้ง/ย่าง	(b)pîng/yârng
roast	อบ	òp
sautéed	ผัด	pàt
stewed	ตุ๋น	(d)tŭn
very rare	ไม่เอาสุก	mâi ow sùk
underdone (rare)	เอาไม่ค่อยสุก	ow mâi kôy sùk
medium	สุกปานกลาง	sùk (b)parn glarng
well-done	เอาสุกๆ	ow sùk sùk

Some meat specialities อาหารจานพิเศษประเภทเนื้อ

เนื้อผัดพริก	néua pàt prík	beef fried with chillies
เนื้อผัดน้ำมันหอย	néua pàt nám man hŏy	beef fried with oyster sauce
เนื้ออบ	néua òp	roast beef
เนื้อตุ๋น	néua (d)tŭn	stewed beef
พะแนงเนื้อ/ หมู	pa nairng néua /mŏo	mild beef or pork curry
เนื้อทอด	néua tôrt	deep-fried beef
หมูย่าง	mŏo yârng	grilled pork
หมูทอดกระเทียม	mŏo tôrt gra team	pork fried with garlic
ผัดคะน้าหมูกรอบ	pàt ka ná mŏo gròrp	spinach fried with crispy pork
ขาหมูพะโล้	kăr mŏo pá lóe	leg of pork in cinnamon and star anise sauce
หมูกรอบ	mŏo gròrp	crispy roast pork
หมูแดง	mŏo dairng	red roast pork
หมูสะเต๊ะ	mŏo sa (d)téh	pork satay

เนื้อผัดกะเพรา
(néua pàt ga prow)

Beef fried with basil leaves. Sweet basil is deep-fried with strips of lean beef until crisp and glossy, giving this dish a lovely texture.

แกงมัสมั่นเนื้อ
(gairng ma sa mân néua)

Indian-style curry with beef or pork. Traditionally a special-occasion curry, this dish gets its name from "Muslim", and its Indian origins can be tasted in the sweet, rich blend of cinnamon, cloves, cardamom and nutmeg over a background of hot red chillies.

แกงเขียวหวานเนื้อ/ หมู
(gairng kĕaw wărn néua/mŏo)

Fragrant green curry with beef or pork. An aromatic mixture of tastes: with hot green chillies, lemongrass and lime, sweetened with coconut milk, this curry is typically Thai.

ยำเนื้อย่าง
(yam néua yârng)

Spicy grilled beef salad. This dish is from the North-Eastern region of Thailand, where roasted rice powder adds texture and fragrance to a hearty salad tossed in chilli and lime dressing.

หมูผัดขิง
(mŏo pàt kĭng)

Pork fried with ginger. A dish frequently found in market and roadside foodstalls, where customers are tempted with strips of fragrant ginger, tender black mushrooms, and slabs of fresh pork.

Poultry เป็ดไก่

Chicken features heavily in Thai cuisine. Duck is also quite common. As with other meats, they are usually sliced or cut into small pieces, and fried swiftly to be crisp or tender.

ไก่ตอน	gài (d)torn	capon
ไก่	gài	chicken
หน้าอก/ขา/ปีก	nâr òk/kǎr/(b)pèek	breast/leg/wing
ไก่ย่าง	gài yârng	barbecued chicken
เป็ด	(b)pèht	duck
ลูกเป็ด	lôok (b)pèht	duckling
ห่าน	hàrn	goose
ไก่ป่า	gài (b)pàr	grouse
ไก่ตอก	gài (d)tók	guinea fowl
นกกระทา	nók gra tar	partridge
นกพิราบ	nók pì rârp	pigeon
นกเป็ดน้ำ	nók (b)pèht nárm	teal
ไก่งวง	gài nguang	turkey
หมูป่า	mǒo (b)pàr	wild boar

Specialities อาหารจานพิเศษประเภท

ไก่ย่าง	gài yârng	grilled chicken
ไก่ทอด	gài tôrt	deep-fried chicken
ผัดกะเพราไก่	pàt ga prow gài	chicken fried with basil leaves
ไก่ผัดเม็ดมะม่วงหิมพานต์	gài pàt méht ma mûang hǐm ma parn	chicken fried with cashew nuts
ไก่ผัดขิง	gài pàt kǐng	chicken fried with ginger
ลาบไก่	lârp gài	spicy salad with minced chicken
พะแนงไก่	pa nairng gài	mild chicken curry
ต้มยำไก่	(d)tôm yam gài	hot and sour chicken soup
ต้มข่าไก่	(d)tôm kàr gài	chicken in coconut milk flavoured with galanga
เป็ดย่าง	(b)pèht yârng	grilled duck
เป็ดตุ๋น	(b)pèht (d)tǔn	stewed duck
ลาบเป็ด	lârp (b)pèht	spicy salad with minced duck

แกงเขียวหวานไก่
(gairng kĕaw wǎrn gài)
: Fragrant green curry with chicken. In Thai markets, this green curry, which is based on pungent, hot *kii noo* chillies, will often be served with tiny nests of white rice noodles.

แกงเผ็ดไก่
(gairng pèht gài)
: Spicy red chicken curry. Flavoured with red chillies and Thai spices, this dish is topped with tiny, pea-sized green aubergines.

ไก่ห่อใบเตย
(gài hòr bai (d)toey)
: Chicken cooked in pandan leaves. Fresh pandan leaves are wrapped around tender pieces of chicken, and are then steamed and fried, imparting a delicate fragrance to the meat.

แกงเผ็ดเป็ดย่าง
(gairng pèht (b)pèht yârng)
: Hot red curry with grilled duck, combining Chinese and Thai flavours. Order lots of rice with this dish, as it takes its name from hot red chillies!

Rice and noodles ข้าวและก๋วยเตี๋ยว

Thais eat rice at all times of the day, though for breakfast and lunch they may opt for noodles. The boiled or steamed rice served in most ordinary restaurants and eating establishments is called *kow plow* or *kôw sŭay*. More exclusive restaurants may serve jasmine-scented rice (*kôw hŏrm ma lí*) which has a toasty and somewhat nutty flavour.

Fried rice is usually eaten as a complete meal rather than as an accompaniment to savoury dishes. Traditionally using left-over rice from the previous evening, it is fried up with pineapple, prawns and chillies, or spiced slivers of chicken.

In the North-East of Thailand, glutinous or sticky rice is steamed and served in baskets. Sticky rice (*kôw nĕaw*) is eaten with the fingers, rolled into balls and dipped into the spicy sauces of accompanying savoury dishes.

Noodles come in several different breadths and varieties, based either on rice or soya flour. While the type of noodle used for stir-fried dishes is traditionally set, you will be asked to make a choice for soup.

The most famous noodle dish of all is *pat tai*, which has some claim to be the national dish. Thais will adjust the flavour of their own *pat tai*, in a serious ritual, using an array of seasonings (*kruang prung*), including fish paste, crushed chillies, and chilli vinegar.

ก๋วยเตี๋ยวเส้นหมี่	gúay tĕaw sêhn mèe	fine thread noodles
กวยเตี๋ยวเส้นเล็ก	gúay tĕaw sêhn léhk	medium thread noodles
ก๋วยเตี๋ยวเส้นใหญ่	gŭay tĕaw sêhn yài	large thread noodles
กวยเตี๋ยวเชียงใฮ	gŭay tĕaw sĕang hái	short, clear noodles
วุ้นเส้น	wún sêhn	Chinese glass noodles
เส้นกวยจับ	sêhn gŭay jáp	short, clear noodles
บะหมี่	ba mèe	egg noodles
เส้นขนมจีน	sêhn ka nŏm jeen	fermented rice noodles

Why not sample some of these popular rice-based dishes?

ข้าวผัดกุ้ง/ปู/หมู	kôw pàt gûng/(b)poo/mŏo	fried rice with prawn/crab/pork
ข้าวผัดอเมริกัน	kôw pàt a mey ri gan	American fried rice
ขาวคลุกกะปิ	kôw klúk ga (b)pì	fried rice mixed with fermented shrimp paste
ข้าวหมูแดง	kôw mŏo dairng	boiled rice with roast pork
ข้าวหน้าเป็ด	kôw nâr (b)pèht	boiled rice with roast duck
ข้าวมันไก่	kôw man gài	boiled rice with steamed chicken
ข้าวขาหมู	kôw kăr mŏo	boiled rice with stewed leg of pork
ข้าวแกง	kôw gairng	boiled rice topped with curry
แกงมัสมั่น	gairng ma sa mân	Indian style curry
แกงพะแนง	gairng pá nairng	mild curry
ขาวแกงเขียวหวาน	kôw gairng kĕaw wărn	boiled rice with fragrant green curry
แกงเผ็ด	gairng pèht	hot red curry
ขาวผัดพริกเนื้อ/หมู/ไก่	kôw pàt prík néua/mŏo/gài	spicy fried rice with beef/pork/chicken
ข้าวผัดพริกกระเพรา เนื้อ/หมู/ไก่	kôw pàt prík gra prow néua/mŏo/gài	fried rice with basil leaves and beef/pork/chicken

And here are some noodle-based dishes to try.

ก๋วยเตี๋ยวราดหน้า	gúay těaw rârt nâr	fried noodles in thickened sauce
ก๋วยเตี๋ยวผัดซีอิ๊ว	gúay těaw pàt see íw	noodles fried with soy sauce
ก๋วยเตี๋ยวน้ำ/แห้ง	gúay těaw nárm/hâirng	rice noodle soup/dry boiled rice noodles
บะหมี่น้ำ/แห้ง	ba mèe nárn/hâirng	egg noodle soup/dry boiled egg noodles
ก๋วยเตี๋ยวเรือ	gúay těaw reua	beef noodle soup
ก๋วยเตี๋ยวเนื้อ/หมู/เป็ด/ไก่	gúay těaw néua/mǒo/(b)pèht/gài	rice noodle soup with beef/pork/duck/chicken
โกยซีหมี่	goey see mèe	fried noodles with chicken
ขนมจีนน้ำยา/น้ำพริก	ka nǒm jeen nám yar/nám prík	fermented rice noodles with sauce/curry

ก๋วยเตี๋ยวผัดไทย
(gúay těaw pàt tai)

Noodles fried with dried prawns and peanuts. A popular, classic Thai dish, found in all regions. Slender rice noodles are fried with a combination of sweet, sour and salty ingredients to give a piquant Thai flavour.

ข้าวซอย
(kôw soy)

Spicy noodle soup with chicken or beef. *Kow soy* is a Thai/Burmese dish, common in open-air restaurants, combining a curry and coconut soup with crispy fried noodles.

Sauces ซ้อส/น้ำจิ้ม

Most Thai sauces are spicy and a small quantity is sufficient. The most common sauce is chilli fish and shrimp sauce (น้ำปลาพริก —*nám (b)plar prík*), a real taste of Thailand around which a whole meal can be based, acting as a dip for raw vegetables and deep-fried fish. There are a number of spicy sauces, accompanied by raw vegetables, which become dishes in their own right. These include น้ำพริกอ่อง —*nám prík ong*, น้ำพริกหนุ่ม —*nám prík nùm* and น้ำพริกกะปิ —*nám prík ga pì*.

Vegetables and salads ผักและสลัด

It is not easy to find vegetarian food in Thailand, although large towns and cities, particularly those with substantial tourist populations, will have some vegetarian restaurants. Most ordinary restaurants will be prepared to cook vegetable and egg dishes without meat if asked.

หน่อไม้ฝรั่ง	nòr mái fa ràng	asparagus (tips)
มะเขือยาว	ma kĕua yow	aubergine (eggplant)
ถั่ว	tùa	beans
ถั่วฝักยาว	tùa fàk yow	long beans
มะระ	má rá	bitter gourd
บร็อคโครี่	bròk koe rêe	broccoli
กระหล่ำ	gra làm	cabbage
แคร็อต	kair rôt	carrots
กระหล่ำดอก	gra làm dòrk	cauliflower
คื่นช่ายฝรั่ง	kêuhn châi fa ràng	celery
พริก	prík	chilli
ผักกาดขาว	pàk gàrt kŏw	Chinese leave
ผักชี	pàk chee	coriander
ข้าวโพด	kôw pôet	corn
แตงกวา	(d)tairng gwar	cucumber
ถั่วแขก	tùa kàirk	lentils
ผักสลัด	pàk sa làt	lettuce
ผักรวมมิตร	pàk ruam mít	mixed vegetables
เห็ด	hèht	mushrooms
กระเจี๊ยบมอญ	gra jíap morn	okra
หอมหัวใหญ่	hŏrm hŭa yài	onions
พริกหยวก	prík yûak	(sweet) peppers
เขียว/แดง	kĕaw/dairng	green/red
มันฝรั่ง	man fa ràng	potatoes
ฟักทอง	fák torng	pumpkin
ผักขม	pàk kŏm	spinach
ข้าวโพด	kôw pôet	sweetcorn
มันหวาน	man wărn	sweet potatoes
มะเขือเทศ	ma kĕua téyt	tomatoes
แฟง	fairng	vegetable marrow

Vegetables may be served...

boiled	ต้ม	(d)tôm
stewed	ตุ๋น	(d)tŭn
stir-fried	ผัด	pàt
stuffed	ยัดไส้	yát sâi

Here are some common vegetable dishes.

ซุปเห็ด	súp hèht	mushroom soup
ซุปผัก	súp pàk	vegetable soup
ซุปข้าวโพด	súp kôw pôet	sweetcorn soup
จับฉ่าย	jàp chài	clear mixed vegetable soup
ต้มยำเห็ด	(d)tôm yam hèht	hot and sour mushroom soup
ต้มข่าเห็ด	(d)tôm kàr hèht	mushrooms cooked in coconut milk and galanga
แกงเขียวหวานเจ	gairng kěaw wǎrn jey	fragrant green vegetable curry
แกงเผ็ดเจ	gairng pèht jey	hot red vegetable curry
แกงเลียงเจ	gairng leang jey	clear, spicy vegetable soup with pepper
แกงจืดรวมมิตรเจ	gairng jèurt ruam mít jey	clear mixed vegetable soup
ผัดเปรี้ยวหวานเจ	pàt (b)preaw wǎrn jey	sweet and sour fried vegetables
ผัดผักรวมมิตรเจ	pàt pàk ruam mít jey	mixed fried vegetables
ผัดถั่วลันเตา ข้าวโพดอ่อนเจ	pàt tùa lan (d)tow kôw pôet òrn jey	mangetout peas fried with baby sweetcorn
ผัดซีอิ๊วเจ	pàt see íw jey	noodles stir fried with soy sauce
สลัดแขก	sa làt kàirk	fresh salad with peanut sauce
ลาบเห็ด	lârp hèht	spicy salad of minced mushrooms
ยำวุ้นเส้นเจ	yam wún sêhn jey	spicy Chinese glass noodle salad
ผักชุบแป้งทอด	pàk chúp (b)pâirng tôrt	deep-fried, battered vegetables
ปอเปี๊ยะเจ	(b)por (b)pía jey	vegetarian spring rolls
ไข่เจียว	kài jeaw	omelette
เต้าหู้ทอด	(d)tôw hôo tôrt	deep-fried bean curd

ผัดผักบุ้ง
(pàt pàk bûng)

Stir-fried water spinach. A delicious deep green vegetable with hollow stems and arrow-head shaped leaves, fried with garlic and peppercorns.

ผัดกะเพราเห็ดกับ
ข้าวโพด
(pàt ga prow hèht gàp kôw pôet)

Mushrooms fried with basil leaves and baby sweetcorn.

ผัดไทยเจ
(pàt tai jey)

Fried noodles with peanuts. This is perhaps the most commonly found vegetarian dish, which can include chunks of crispy bean curd and pickled white radish.

ยำถั่วพูเจ
(yam tùa poo jey)

Spicy green bean salad with coconut sauce. The strongly flavoured sauce, with a rich, creamy coconut base, is complemented perfectly by the spicy beans.

Herbs and spices *สมุนไพรและเครื่องเทศ*

โป๊ยกั๊ก	(b)póey gák	aniseed
กระชาย	gra chai	aromatic ginger
โหระพา	hŏe ra par	basil
ใบกระวาน	bai gra warn	bay leaf
ยี่หรา	yêe ràr	caraway
พริก	prík	chillies
อบเชย	òp choey	cinnamon
กานพลู	garn ploo	clove
พริกไทยอ่อน	prík tai òrn	fresh peppercorns
ข่า	kàr	galanga
กระเทียม	gra team	garlic
ขิง	kĭng	ginger
ตะไคร้	(d)ta krái	lemongrass
มะนาว	ma now	lime
ใบมะกรูด	bai ma gròot	lime leaf
สะระแหน่	sa ra nàir	mint
มัสตาร์ด	ma sa (d)tàrt	mustard
ลูกจันทร์	lôok jan	nutmeg
พริกชี้ฟ้า	prík chée fár	paprika
ผักชีฝรั่ง	pàk chee fa ràng	parsley
พริกไทย	prík tai	pepper
หญ้าฝรั่น	yâr fa ràn	saffron
เกลือ	gleua	salt
งา	ngar	sesame
หอมเล็ก/ หอมแดง	hŏrm léhk/ hŏrm dairng	shallot
ต้นหอม	(d)tôn hŏrm	spring onions
ใบกระเพรา	bai gra prow	sweet basil
สมซ่า	sôm sâr	sweet lime
มะขาม	ma kărm	tamarind
ขมิ้นผง	ka mîn pŏng	turmeric powder
วานิลา	war ni lar	vanilla

Fruit and nuts ผลไม้และลูกนัท

Fresh fruit, often exquisitely carved, is the favoured end-of-meal sweet in Thailand. Watch out for durian—this fruit smells like a sewer on a hot day, but if you can fight back the nausea, you will be rewarded with its delicious custardy sweet flesh.

Do you have any fresh fruit?	มีผลไม้สดไหม?	mee pŏn la mái sòt măi
I'd like a (fresh) fruit cocktail.	ผม(ดิฉัน)อยากได้ค็อกเทล ผลไม้(สด)	pŏm (di chán) yàrk dâi kôk teyn pŏn la mái (sòt)

อัลมอนด์	a la morn	almonds
แอปเปิ้ล	áihp (b)pêrn	apple
กล้วยหอม	glûay hŏrm	banana
เม็ดมะม่วงหิมพานต์	méht ma mûang him má parn	cashew nuts
เชอรี่	cher rêe	cherries
เกาลัด	gow lát	chestnuts
มะพร้าว	ma prów	coconut
อินทผาลัม	in tá pǎr lam	dates
ผลไม้แห้ง	pŏn la mái hâirng	dried fruit
มะเดื่อ	ma dèua	figs
องุ่น	a ngùn	grapes
ฝรั่ง	faràng	guava
มะนาวเหลือง	ma now lĕuang	lemon
มะนาว	ma now	lime
ลิ้นจี่	lín jèe	lychee
มะม่วง	ma mûang	mango
แตงไทย	(d)tairng tai	melon
ส้ม	sôm	orange
ถั่วลิสง	tùa li sŏng	peanuts
ลูกแพร	lôok pair	pear
สับปะรด	sàp (b)pa rót	pineapple
ลูกพลัม	lôok plam	plums
ลูกพรุน	lôok prun	prunes
ลูกเกด	lôok gèyt	raisins
สตรอเบอรี่	sa (d)tror ber rêe	strawberries
ส้มจีน	sôm jeen	tangerine
แตงโม	(d)tairng moe	water melon

These are some of the more exotic fruit you may encounter at market stalls:

น้อยหน่า (nóy nàr)	custard apple: the green skin is easily peeled when ripe to reveal a sweet white flesh.

ทุเรียน (tú rearn)	durian: this huge, spiky green fruit with a soft, yellow flesh is only for the strong of stomach!	
ขนุน (ka nŭn)	jackfruit: a large green fruit with a leathery, sweetish flavour.	
ลองกอง (lorng gorng)	longan; a small round fruit with a brittle skin, and white flesh around a black stone.	
มังคุด (mang kút)	mangosteen: considered the Queen of fruit. A hard, dark purple shell encloses delicious segmented, creamy-white flesh.	
มะละกอ (ma lá gor)	papaya: a long, yellowy green fruit with a soft orange flesh.	
ส้มโอ (sôm or)	pomelo: a tropical cousin of the grapefruit, served in sections.	
เงาะ (ngóh)	rambutan: a sort of hairy lychee, with sweet opalescent flesh.	
มะขาม (ma kǎrm)	tamarind: with a sour, fruity taste, this fruit is often sold as pulp for use in cooking.	

Desserts—Pastries ของหวาน

Traditional Thai sweetmeats tend to be eaten as snacks rather than as desserts at the end of a meal. The ideal Thai meal will include two desserts—one dry, a cake-like sweet such as *méht kanoon*, made with egg, mung beans and sugar, and one liquid, such as bananas in fragrant coconut milk. Many restaurants also serve ice cream, referred to either as *ai sa kreem* or simply *ai tim*. Traditional ice creams are made from coconut milk (*ai tim ga tí*), but manufacturers now produce a wide range of Thai and Western flavours.

I'd like a dessert, please.	ผม(ดิฉัน) อยากได้ของหวาน	pŏm (di chán) yàrk dâi kŏrng wǎrn
What do you recommend?	มีอะไรน่าทานบ้าง?	mee arai nâr tarn bârng
Something light, please.	เอาอะไรที่ไม่หนักท้อง	ow arai têe mâi nàk tórng
Just a small portion.	ขอที่เล็กๆก็พอ	kŏr têe léhk léhk gôh por
ขนมหม้อแกง	ka nŏm môr gairng	steamed coconut cream sweet

ทองหยิบ	torng yìp	sweet made from deep-fried egg yolk
เม็ดขนุน	méht ka nŭn	sweet made from taro
ฝอยทอง	fŏy torng	sweet made from deep-fried egg
วุ้นกะทิ	wún ga tí	threads of scented sweet rice noodle
ขนมชั้น	ka nŏm chán	layers of sweet jellied coconut milk
ลอดช่องน้ำกะทิ	lôrt chôrng nárm ga tí	tapioca noodles in sweet coconut milk
บวชเผือก	bùat pèuak	taro stewed in fragrant, sweetened coconut milk
บัวลอยไข่หวาน	bua loy kài wărn	sour paste balls in sweet egg syrup
ข้าวต้มมัด	kôw (d)tôm mát	steamed sticky rice with banana or taro
สาคูถั่วดำ	săr koo tùa dam	black beans in sweetened coconut milk
ถั่วแป๊บ	tùa (b)pàihp	candied mung bean paste rolled in sesame seeds
ซ่าหริ่ม	sâr rìm	jellied noodles in sweet coconut milk
ทับทิมกรอบ	táp tim gròrp	jellied water chestnuts in coconut milk
ผลไม้รวม	pŏn la mái ruam	mixed fresh fruit

สังขยา
(săng ka yăr)
Steamed egg and coconut milk custard, made with duck eggs, palm sugar and coconut, so rich it will normally be served spooned over a mound of sticky rice.

กล้วยบวชชี
(glûay bùat chee)
Bananas stewed in fragrant, sweetened coconut milk. Its charming name means "bananas ordained as nuns", as this dessert has a creamy whiteness and delicate flavour.

กล้วยเชื่อม
(glûay chêuam)
Caramelized bananas. There are many varieties of Thai banana; the type usually used in this dessert is short, stubby and very sweet, made even sweeter with a syrupy sauce.

ข้าวเหนียวเปียก
(kôw nĕaw (b)pèark)
Boiled sticky rice in sweetened coconut milk, usually accompanied by mangoes. The still-warm sticky rice is left to soak in sweetened and salted coconut milk.

Drinks *เครื่องดื่ม*

The Thais' staple drink is plain water. You should not drink tap water in Thailand; bottled, filtered water is readily available. Ice is not always very clean, especially shaved ice, and should be avoided if you wish to be very careful.

Soft, carbonated drinks are also popular, though if you can, try to find the superb Thai soft drinks such as iced lemongrass, or *glûay bâhn*, a smooth banana drink sold by street vendors.

Beer *เบียร์*

Thai beer has a distinctive taste and makes a good accompaniment to an evening meal. There are two local beers (lager) generally available at most restaurants. Singha Beer is stronger and has a sweeter taste compared to its rival Kloster Beer. A number of exported beers are also available in big hotels and western restaurants. Beer is sold by the bottle and there are no restrictions on licensing hours.

What would you like to drink?	จะดื่มอะไร?	ja dèurm arai
I'd like a beer, please.	ขอเบียร์หน่อย	kŏr bear nòy
Have a beer!	เบียร์ที่หนึ่ง	bear têe nèuhng
A bottle of lager, please.	ขอเบียร์ขวดหนึ่ง	kŏr bear kùat nèuhng
A bottle of Singha beer, please.	ขอเบียร์สิงห์ขวดหนึ่ง	kŏr bear sing kùat nèuhng
A bottle of Kloster beer, please.	ขอเบียร์คลอสเตอร์ขวดหนึ่ง	kŏr bear klor sa (d)ter kùat nèuhng

Wine *เหล้าไวน์/เหล้าผลไม้*

In Thailand wine is much less common than whisky and beer, and in fact is not the ideal accompaniment to Thai cuisine, with its strong hot flavours. Imported wine is only available in the big hotels and western restaurants.

May I have the wine list?	ขอดูรายการเหล้าไวน์หน่อยได้ไหม?	kŏr doo rai garn lôw wai nòy dâi măi
I'd like a ... of red wine/white wine.	ขอเหล้าไวน์แดง/ไวน์ขาว...	kŏr lôw wai dairng/ wai kŏw

a bottle	ขวดหนึ่ง	kùat nèuhng
half a bottle	ครึ่งขวด	krêuhng kùat
a carafe	คาราฟ	kar rârf
a glass	แก้ว	gâiw
How much is a bottle of champagne?	แชมเปญขวดละเท่าไหร่?	chairm (b)peyn kùat lá tôw rài
Bring me another bottle/glass of..., please.	ขอ...อีกขวด/แก้ว	kŏr...èek kùat/gâiw

red	แดง	dairng
white	ขาว	kŏw
rosé	โรเซ่	roe sêy
sweet	สวีท	sa wèet
dry	ดราย	da rai
sparkling	สปาร์กลิ้ง	sa (b)park gîng
chilled	เย็นๆ	yehn yehn
at room temperature	ที่อุณหภูมิห้อง	têe una ha poom hôrng

Other alcoholic drinks เครื่องดื่มที่มีอัลกอฮอล์อื่นๆ

Thai whisky (เหล้าวิสกี้ —*lôw wí sa gêe*), is taken primarily as a drink in its own right, served with snacks and appetizers, and is usually much diluted.

| I'd like a/an... | ผม(ดิฉัน)อยากได้... | pŏm (di chán) yàrk dâi |

cognac	คอนยัค	korn yák
gin	จิน	jin
liqueur	เหล้าชนิดหวาน	lôw cha nít wǎrn
rum	เหล้ารัม	lôw ram
vermouth	เวอมัธ	wer mát
vodka	ว้อดก้า	wôd gâr
whisky	วิสกี้	wí sa gêe
neat (straight)	เพียว	peaw
on the rocks	ออนเดอะร็อค	orn der rók
with a little water	ใส่น้ำนิดหนึ่ง	sài nám nít neuhng
Give me a large gin and tonic, please.	ขอเหล้าจินกับ, โทนิคแก้วใหญ่	kŏr lôw jin gàp toe ník gâiw yài
Just a dash of soda, please.	ขอโซดานิดหนึ่ง	kŏr soe dar nít neuhng

Nonalcoholic drinks เครื่องดื่มที่ไม่มีอัลกอฮอล์

apple juice	น้ำแอ๊ปเปิ้ล	nàrm áihp (b)pêrn
boiled water	น้ำต้ม	nárm (d)tôm
iced coffee	กาแฟเย็น	garfair yehn
fruit juice	น้ำผลไม้	nárm pòn la mái
lemonade	น้ำมะนาว	lehm ma néyt
lime juice	เล็มมะเนด	nárm ma now
milk	นม	nom
milkshake	มิลค์เชค	milk chék
mineral water	น้ำแร่	nárm râir
fizzy (carbonated)	ชนิดมีก๊าซ	cha nít mee gàrt
still	ชนิดไม่มีก๊าซ	cha nít mâi mee gàt
plain water	น้ำเปล่า	nárm (b)plòw
orange juice	น้ำส้ม	nárm sôm
tomato juice	น้ำมะเขือเทศ	nárm ma kěua téyt
tonic water	โทนิค	toe ník

Hot beverages เครื่องดื่มร้อน

Thais do not tend to drink coffee or tea with their food, unless it is Chinese tea. Nevertheless, coffee has become increasingly popular in urban areas as a morning drink and both coffee and tea are readily available in most parts of the country. Far more common is iced coffee served with evaporated milk. Iced tea is also delicious and refreshing, commonly flavoured with star anise, cinnamon and vanilla.

I'd like a/an...	ขอ...ที่หนึ่ง	kòr... tée nèuhng
(hot) chocolate	ช็อคโกแล็ค(ร้อน)	chôrk goe lâiht (rórn)
camomile tea	น้ำเก๊กฮวย	nàrm géhk huay
coffee	กาแฟ	gar fair
with cream	ใส่ครีม	sài kreem
with milk	ใส่นม	sài nom
black/decaffeinated coffee	ดำ/ชนิดไม่มีคาเฟอีน	dam/cha nít mâi mee kar fey fon
espresso coffee	กาแฟเอสเพรสโซ่	gar fair eyt sa prèyt sôe
mokka	ม็อคกา	mók gâr
herb tea	ชาสมุนไพร	char sa mǔn prai
rosehip tea	น้ำกระเจี๊ยบ	nàrm gra jéarp
tea	ชา	char
Chinese tea	ชาจีน	char jeen
cup of tea	น้ำชาถ้วยหนึ่ง	nárm char tûay nèuhng
with milk/lemon	ใส่นม/ใส่มะนาว	sài nom/sài ma now

Complaints ต่อว่า

There's a plate/glass missing.	ขอจาน/ แก้วอีกที่หนึ่ง	kŏr jarn/gâiw èek tée nèuhng
I don't have a knife/fork/spoon.	ขอมีด/ ส้อม/ ช้อนอันหนึ่ง	kŏr mêet/ sôrm/ chórn an nèuhng
That's not what I ordered.	อันนี้ผม(ดิฉัน)ไม่ได้สั่ง	an née pŏm (di chán) mâi dâi sàng
I asked for...	ผมสั่ง...	pŏm sàng
There must be some mistake.	คงมีอะไรผิดพลาด	kong mee arai pìt plârt
May I change this?	ขอเปลี่ยนอันนี้ได้ไหม?	kŏr (b)plèarn an née dâi mǎi
I asked for a small portion (for the child).	ผม(ดิฉัน)ขอที่เล็กๆ (สำหรับเด็ก)	pŏm (di chán) kŏr tée léhk léhk (sǎm ràp dèhk)
The meat is...	เนื้อนี้...	néua nêe
overdone	สุกเกินไป	sùk gern (b)pai
underdone	สุกไม่พอ	sùk mâi por
too rare	ดิบเกินไป	dìp gern (b)pai
too tough	เหนียวเกินไป	nĕaw gern (b)pai
This is too...	อันนี้...เกินไป	an nêe... gern (b)pai
bitter/salty/sweet	ขม/ เค็ม/ หวาน	kŏm/kehm/wǎrn
I don't like this.	ผม(ดิฉัน)ไม่ชอบอันนี้เลย	pŏm (di chán) mâi chôrp an née loey
The food is cold.	อาหารเย็นชืดแล้ว	ar hǎrn yehn chêut láiw
This isn't fresh.	อันนี้ไม่สดเลย	an nêe mâi sòt loey
What's taking you so long?	ทำไมนานจังเลย?	tam mai narn jang loey
Have you forgotten our drinks?	เราสั่งเครื่องดื่มไป นานแล้วนะ	row sàng krêuang dèurm (b)pai narn láiw ná
The wine doesn't taste right.	เหล้าไวน์รสชาดไม่เข้าที่	lôw wai rót chârt mâi kôw tée
This isn't clean.	มันไม่สะอาด	man mâi sa àrt
Would you ask the head waiter to come over?	ช่วยเรียกหัวหน้าบ๋อย มานี่หน่อยได้ไหม?	chùay rêak hǔa nâr bǒy mar nêe nòy dâi mǎi

The bill (check) เช็คบิล

In cheaper establishments your bill will be calculated by counting the plates you have on the table in front of you at the end of the meal and will be given to you verbally. In the more expensive restaurants, however, you will be given a slip of paper. It is appropriate to tip 10–20 baht.

I'd like to pay.	เก็บเงินด้วย	gèhp ngern dûay
We'd like to pay separately.	คิดเงินแยกกันนะ	kít ngern yâirk gan ná
I think there's a mistake in this bill.	ผม(ดิฉัน)คิดว่าบิล ใบนี้มีอะไรผิดอยู่อย่าง	pŏm (di chán) kít wâr bin bai née mee arai pìt yòo yàrng
What's this amount for?	อันนี้ค่าอะไรบ้าง?	an nèe kâr arai bârng
Is service included?	รวมค่าบริการแล้ว หรือยัง?	ruam kâr boe ri garn láiw rĕur yang
Is the cover charge included?	รวมค่าบริการต่อหัว ต่อคนแล้วหรือยัง?	ruam kâr boe ri garn (d)tòr hŭa (d)tòr kon láiw rĕur yang
Is everything included?	รวมทุกอย่างแล้วใช่ไหม?	ruam túk yàrng láiw châi măi
Do you accept traveller's cheques?	จ่ายเป็นเช็คเดินทาง ได้ไหม?	jài (b)pehn chéhk dern tarng dâi măi
Can I pay with this credit card?	จ่ายด้วยบัตร เครดิตได้ไหม?	jài dûay bàt krey dít dâi măi
Please round it up to...	รวมทั้งหมดแล้วเก็บที่...	ruam táng mòt láiw gèhp têe
Keep the change.	เก็บเงินทอนเอาไว้	gèhp ngern torn ow wái
That was delicious.	อร่อยมาก	a ròy mârk
We enjoyed it, thank you.	อร่อยมาก ขอบคุณ	a ròy mârk kòrp kun

---

รวมค่าบริการแล้ว
SERVICE INCLUDED

TIPPING, see inside back-cover

TIPPING, see inside back-cover

64

Snacks—Picnic *อาหารว่าง ปิ๊กนิค*

Give me two of these and one of those.	ขออันนี้สองอันและอันนั้นอันหนึ่ง	kŏr an née sŏrng an láih an née an nèuhng
to the left/right	ด้านซ้าย/ด้านขวา	dârn sái/ dârn kŵar
above/below	ข้างบน/ข้างล่าง	kârng bon/kârn lârng
It's to take away.	ใส่ห่อไปกินที่บ้าน	sài hòr (b)pai gin têe bârn
I'd like a piece of cake.	ขอขนมเค้กชิ้นหนึ่ง	kŏr ka nŏm kéhk chín nèuhng
omelette	ไข่เจียว	kài jeaw
open sandwich	แซนด์วิชไม่ต้องห่อ	sairn wít mâi (d)tôrng hòr
with ham	ใส่แฮม	sài hairm
with cheese	ใส่ซีส (เนยแข็ง)	sài chêet (noey kăihng)
sandwich	แซนด์วิช	sairn wít
I'd like a/an/ some . . .	ผม(ดิฉัน)อยากได้...	pŏm (di chán) yàrk dâi

apples	แอ๊ปเปิ้ล	áihp (b)pêrn
bananas	กล้วยหอม	glûay hŏrm
biscuits (Br.)	ขนมปังกรอบ	ka nŏm (b)pang gròrp
beer	เบียร์	bia
bread	ขนมปัง	ka nŏm (b)pang
butter	เนย	noey
cheese	เนยแข็ง	noey kăihng
chips (Br.)	มันทอด	man tôrt
coffee	กาแฟ	gar fair
cookies	คุกกี้	kúk gêe
eggs	ไข่	kài
grapes	องุ่น	a ngùn
ice cream	ไอศครีม	ai sa kreem
milk	นม	nom
mustard	มัสตาร์ด	mát sa tàrt
oranges	ส้ม	sôm
pepper	พริกไทย	prík tai
roll	ขนมปังก้อน	ka nŏm (b)pang gôn
salt	เกลือ	gleua
sausage	ไส้กรอก	sâi gròrk
sugar	น้ำตาล	nárm (d)tarn
tea bags	ชาชนิดถุง	char cha nít tŭng
yoghurt	โยเกิร์ต	yoe gèrt

Travelling around

Plane เครื่องบิน

Most internal flights are operated by Thai Airways International (การบินไทย — *garn bin tai*) which flies to the major cities
of each region of the country. Tickets can be purchased through
travel agents or at the domestic terminal of Don Muang (*dorn
meuang*) airport. The smaller airline company, Bangkok Airways, flies between Bangkok and Hua Hin and Koh Samui.

Is there a flight to Chiang Mai?	มีเที่ยวบินไปเชียงรายไหม?	mee têaw bin (b)pai cheang mài mǎi
Is it a direct flight?	เป็นเที่ยวบินตรง หรือเปล่า?	(b)pehn têaw bin (d)trong rĕua (b)plòw
When's the next flight to Chiang Mai?	เที่ยวบินไปเชียงใหม่เที่ยว ต่อไปออกกี่โมง?	têaw bin (b)pai chearng mài têaw (d)tòr (b)pai òrk gèe moeng
Is there a connection to Lampang?	มีเครื่องบินต่อไปที่ ลำปางหรือเปล่า?	mee krêuang bin (d)tòr (b)pai têe lam parng rĕua (b)plòw
I'd like to book a ticket to Phuket.	ผม(ดิฉัน)ต้องการ จองตั๋วไปภูเก็ต	pŏm (di chán) tôrng garn jorng tŭa (b)pai poo gèht
single (one-way)	เที่ยวเดียว	têaw deaw
return (round trip)	ไปกลับ	(b)pai glàp
business class	ชั้นสำหรับนักธุรกิจ	chán sǎm ràp nák tu rá gìt
aisle seat	ที่นั่งติดทางเดิน	têe nâng (d)tìt tarng dern
window seat	ที่นั่งติดหน้าต่าง	têe nâng (d)tìt nâr tàrng
What time do we take off?	เครื่องบินจะออกกี่โมง?	krêuang bin ja òrk gèe moeng
What time should I check in?	จะต้องเช็คอินตอนกี่โมง?	ja tôrng chehk in (d)torn gèe moeng
Is there a bus to the airport?	มีรถประจำทาง ไปสนามบินไหม?	mee rót pra jam tarng (b)pai sa nǎrm bin mǎi
What's the flight number?	เที่ยวบินที่เท่าไหร่?	têaw bin têe tôw rài
What time do we arrive?	เราจะไปถึงนั่นตอนกี่โมง?	row ja (b)pai tĕuhng nân (d)torn gèe moeng

I'd like to... my reservation.	ผม(ดิฉัน)อยากจะ... การจองตั๋ว	pŏm(di chán) yàrk ja... garn jorng tŭa
cancel	ยกเลิก	yók lêrk
change	เปลี่ยนแปลง	plèarn plairng
confirm	ยืนยัน	yeurn yan

| ขาเข้า ARRIVAL | ขาออก DEPARTURE |

Train รถไฟ

Several trains run each day between Bangkok's main line Hualampong (*hŭa lam poeng*) railway station and the North, South and North-East regions of the country. Most of the trains depart between late afternoon and early evening in order to arrive at their final destination early the following morning. In addition to this some trains to the south operate from the much smaller station of Bangkok Noi. This is also the station used for trains to Kanchanaburi. Trains to Eastern Thailand run from Makkasan (*mák ga săn*) station.

Thai trains are classified either as:

รถธรรมดา (rót tam ma dar)	Ordinary train; a painfully slow service stopping at local stations. Provides third class facilities only.
รถเร็ว (rót rehw)	Rapid train; but only relatively faster than the "ordinary" train. Tends to offer only second and third class seats.
รถด่วน (rót dùan)	Long distance express with first and second class facilities, stopping at major stations only.

Whilst third class train travel is exceptionally cheap it is not advised for long journeys because of the very hard seats. Second class offer reclining seats with a fan or sleepers with either fan or air-conditioning.

Second and first class tickets should be booked in advance either through a travel agent or direct from the station itself. Third class tickets can be bought immediately prior to departure.

Visit Thailand Rail Passes (เรวพาส —*rew pars*) can be bought by overseas visitors to Thailand. Blue Passes are valid for second or third class travel for 20 days excluding supplementary charges. Red Passes do include supplementary charges.

ตู้นอน ((d)tôo norn)	Second class sleepers are good value and comfortable. The seats convert into a lower and an upper bunk, and the top one is slightly cheaper than the lower. First class accommodation is in private cabins have air conditioning and an optional fan and seats which convert into sleeping berths.
รถดีเซลราง (rót dee sehn rarng)	Air conditioned diesel "sprinters" operate on some lines, providing a faster and efficient service. The price of the ticket also includes a meal and refreshments.

Train travel is cheap in Thailand, but small supplements are charged for express and rapid trains. Children are charged under a a range of reduced prices calculated by age and height. There are measuring boards at all railway stations and on the trains themselves.

To the railway station ไปสถานีรถไฟ

Where's the railway station?	สถานีรถไฟอยู่ที่ไหน?	sa tăr nee rót fai yòo têe năi
Taxi!	แท็กซี่	táihk sêe
Take me to the...	ไปส่งผม(ดิฉัน)ที่...หน่อย	(b)pai sòng pŏm (dì chán) têe.... nòy
main railway station	สถานีรถไฟ	sa tăr nee rót fai
What's the fare?	เท่าไหร่?	tôw rài

ทางเข้า	ENTRANCE
ทางออก	EXIT
ชานชลา	TO THE PLATFORMS
ประชาสัมพันธ์	INFORMATION

Where's the...? ...อยู่ที่ไหน?

Where is/are (the)...?	...อยู่ที่ไหน?	... yòo têe nǎi
bar	บาร์	bar
booking office	ที่จองตั๋ว	têe jorng tǔa
currency exchange office	ที่แลกเงิน	têe lâirk ngern
left-luggage office (baggage check)	ที่ฝากกระเป๋าและ สัมภาระ	têe fàrk gra pǒw láih sǎm par rá
lost property (lost and found) office	แผนกของหาย	pa nàirk kŏrng hǎi
luggage lockers	ตู้เก็บสัมภาระ	(d)tôo gèhp sǎm par rá
newsstand	แผงขายหนังสือพิมพ์	pǎirng kǎi náng sěur pim
platform 7	ชานชาลาที่ ๗	charn cha lar têe jèht
reservations office	แผนกสำรองที่นั่งล่วงหน้า	pa nàirk sǎm rorng têe nâng lûang nâr
restaurant	ร้านอาหาร	rárn ar hǎrn
ticket office	แผนกจำหน่ายตั๋ว	pa nàirk jam nài tǔa
waiting room	ห้องพักผู้โดยสาร	hórng pák pôo doey sǎrn
Where are the toilets?	ห้องน้ำอยู่ที่ไหน?	hórng nárm yòo têe nǎi

Inquiries สอบถาม

When is the... train to Nongkhai?	รถไฟไปหนองคายคัน ...ออกเมื่อไหร่?	rót fai (b)pai nŏrng kai kan... òrk mêua rài
first/last/next	แรก/สุดท้าย/ต่อไป	râirk/sùt tái/(d)tòr (b)pai
What time does the train to Kanchanaburi leave?	รถไฟไปกาญจนบุรี ออกกี่โมง?	rót fai (b)pai garn ja na bu ree òrk gèe moeng
What's the fare to Ayutthaya?	ค่ารถไฟไปอยุธยาเท่าไหร่?	kâr rót fai (b)pai a yú ta yar tôw rài
Is it a through train?	ไม่ต้องเปลี่ยน รถใช่ไหม?	mâi tôrng (b)plèarn rót fai cháy mǎi
Do I have to change trains?	ผม(ดิฉัน)จะต้องเปลี่ยน รถหรือเปล่า?	pŏm (di chán) ja tôrng (b)plèarn rót rěua (b)plòw
Is the train running on time?	รถไฟวิ่งตรงเวลาไหม?	rót fai wîng (d)trong wey lar mǎi

TAXI, see page 21

What time does the train arrive in Phitsanulok?	รถไฟจะไปถึงพิษณุโลกตอนกี่โมง?	rót fai ja (b)pai těuhng pít san nú lôek (d)torn gêe moeng
Is there a dining car/ sleeping car on the train?	มีรถเสบียง/รถนอนในขบวนนี้หรือเปล่า?	mee rót sabeang/rót norn nai kabuan née rěua (b)plòw
Does the train stop in Khon Kaen?	รถไฟหยุดที่ขอนแก่นหรือเปล่า?	rót fai yùt têe kŏrn kàihn rěua (b)plòw
Which platform does the train to Nongkhai leave from?	รถไฟไปหนองคายออกจากชานชาลาไหน?	rót fai (b)pai nŏrng kai òrk jark charn cha lar nǎi
Which platform does the train from Chiang Mai arrive at?	รถไฟจากเชียงใหม่จะเขาจอดชานชาลาไหน?	rót fai jark cheang mài ja kòw jort charn cha lar nǎi
I'd like a time-table.	ขอตารางเดินรถหน่อย	kǒr (d)tar rarng dern rót nòy

---

คุณจะต้องเปลี่ยนรถที่...	You have to change at...
ชานชาลาที่ ๗...	Platform 7 is...
อยู่ที่โน่น	over there
อยู่ดานซ้ายมือ/อยู่ดานขวามือ	on the left/on the right
มีรถไฟไป...ตอน...	There's a train to... at...
รถไฟคุณจะออกจากชานชาลาที่ ๘	Your train will leave from platform 8.
รถไฟจะช้า...นาที	There will be a delay of... minutes.
ชั้นหนึ่งอยู่หัวขบวน/ตรงกลาง/ท้ายขบวน	First class at the front/in the middle/at the rear.

Tickets ตั๋ว

I'd like a ticket to Lop Buri.	ขอตั๋วไปลพบุรีใบหนึ่ง	kǒr (d)tǔa (b)pai lóp buree bai nèuhng
single (one-way)	เที่ยวเดียว	têaw deaw
return (round trip)	ไปกลับ	(b)pai glap
first/second class	ชั้นหนึ่ง/ ชั้นสอง	chán nèuhng/chán sǒrng
half price	ครึ่งราคา	krêuhng rar kar

Reservation สำรองที่นั่ง

I'd like to reserve a...	ผม(ดิฉัน) ต้องการสำรอง...	pŏm (di chán) (d)tôrng garn sǎm rorng
seat (by the window)	ที่นั่ง(ติดหน้าต่าง)	têe nâng ((d)tìt nâr (d)tàrng)
berth	เตียงนอน	teang norn
upper	ชั้นบน	chán bon
lower	ชั้นล่าง	chán lârng
berth in the sleeping car	เตียงนอนในตู้นอน	teang norn nai tôo norn

All aboard บนรถไฟ

Is this the right platform for the train to Hat Yai?	ชานชลานี้ไปหาดใหญ่ ใช่ไหม?	charn cha lar nêe (b)pai hàrt yài châi mǎi
Is this the right train to Phetchaburi?	รถไฟขบวนนี้ไปเพชรบุรี ใช่ไหม?	rót fai kabuan née (b)pai pét buree châi mǎi
Excuse me. Could I get past?	ขอโทษ ขอผ่านไปหน่อย?	kǒr tôet kǒr pàrn (b)pai nòy
Is this seat taken?	ตรงนี้มีคนนั่งไหม?	(d)trong née mee kon nâng mǎi

สูบบุหรี่ได้	ห้ามสูบบุหรี่
SMOKER	**NONSMOKER**

I think that's my seat.	นั่นเป็นที่นั่งของผม(ดิฉัน)	nân (b)pehn têe nâng kǒrng pŏm(dì chán)
Would you let me know before we get to Surin?	ช่วยบอกก่อนที่จะถึง สุรินทร์หน่อยได้ไหม?	chûay bòrk gòrn têe ja tĕuhng su rin nòy dâi mǎi
What station is this?	สถานีอะไรนี่?	sa tǎr nee arai née
How long does the train stop here?	รถไฟจะ จอดที่นี่นานแค่ไหน?	rót fai ja jòrt têe née narn kàir nǎi
When do we arrive in Lampang?	เราจะถึงลำปาง ตอนกี่โมง?	row ja tĕuhng lam (b)parng (d)torn gèe moeng

Sleeping การนอน

| Are there any free compartments in the sleeping car? | มีที่ว่างในรถนอน หรือเปล่า? | mee têe wârng nai rót norn rĕua (b)plòw |

Where's the sleeping car?	รถนอนอยู่ที่ไหน? เตียงนอนผม	rót norn yòo têe nǎi
Where's my berth?	(ดิฉัน)อยู่ที่ไหน?	teang norn pǒm (di chán) yòo têe nǎi
I'd like a lower berth.	ผม(ดิฉัน)อยากได้ เตียงนอนชั้นล่าง	pǒm (di chán) yàrk dâi teang norn chán lârng
Would you wake me at 7 o'clock?	ช่วยปลุกตอน เจ็ดโมงได้ไหม?	chûay (b)plùk (d)torn jèht moeng dâi mǎi

Eating การกิน

Long distance trains have a buffet car where you can go and sit to have a meal. Alternatively you can order from your seat and have your meal brought to you. Buffet staff will also pass through the train with plates of ready-prepared food such as fried rice (ข้าวผัด —kôw pàt).

On local trains running shorter distances vendors board the trains at each stop and pass through the carriage with bags of steamed sticky rice, cured beef, grilled chicken, fried rice and other snacks.

| Where's the dining-car? | รถเสเบียงอยู่ที่ไหน? | rót sa bearng yòo têe nǎi |

Baggage—Porters กระเป๋า คนยกกระเป๋า

Porter!	คนยกกระเป๋า	kon yók gra (b)pǒw
Can you help me with my luggage?	ช่วยจัดการกับกระเป๋า ผม(ดิฉัน)หน่อยได้ไหม?	chûay jat garn gàp gra (b)pǒw pǒm (di chán) nòi dâi mǎi
Where are the luggage trolleys (carts)?	รถเข็นอยู่ที่ไหน?	rót kěhn yòo têe nǎi
Where are the luggage lockers?	ตู้เก็บของอยู่ที่ไหน?	(d)tôo gèhp kǒrng yòo têe nǎi
Where's the left-luggage office (baggage check)?	ที่ฝากกระเป๋าและ สัมภาระอยู่ที่ไหน?	têe fàrk gra (b)pǒw láih sǎm par rá yòo tèe nǎi
I'd like to leave my luggage, please.	ผม(ดิฉัน)อยากฝาก กระเป๋าหน่อย	pǒm (di chán) yàrk fàrk gra (b)pǒw nòy

การลงทะเบียน กระเป๋า
REGISTERING (CHECKING) BAGGAGE

PORTERS, see also page 18

Coach (long-distance bus) รถทัวร์

Coaches are a popular method of long-distance travel for Thais and are much faster than the trains. The three major coach stations in Bangkok operate services to all regions of the country with air-conditioned tour buses. The tour buses classed as VIP (วีไอพี —*wee ai pee*) have fully reclining seats. A hostess is available to serve refreshments and long-distance journeys include a stop off at a restaurant en route.

In addition to coach and tour bus service, ordinary buses (รถบขส —*rót bor kŏr sŏr*) also travel to all provinces in the country. They are usually bright orange in colour, are not air-conditioned and are tightly packed with seating designed for small-framed Thais so they can be rather cramped. They are very cheap but not recommended for long-distance travel.

When's the next coach to…?	รถคันหน้าที่จะ ไป...ออกกี่โมง?	rót kan nâr têe ja (b)pai…òrk gèe moeng
Does this coach stop at…?	รถคันนี้จะ จอดที่...หรือเปล่า?	rót kan née ja jòrt têe…rĕua (b)plòw
How long does the journey (trip) take?	ใช้เวลาเดินทางเท่าไหร่?	châi wey lar dern tarng tôw rài

Bus รถเมล์/รถประจำทาง

Bangkok has the largest bus service of any Thai city and buses run very frequently. In recent years longer red and cream buses have begun to replace the older blue and cream ones, and are safer in that they have doors which close while the bus is moving. The fare varies accordingly, and is collected by a conductor or conductress with a long, steel tube-shaped receptacle in which tickets and change are kept.

In the provinces bus services are usually converted lorries or pick-up trucks called *sŏng tăiw*, which literally means "two rows" referring to the two benches on either side of the vehicle. The *sŏng tăiw* may or may not have route numbers on the sides.

Which bus goes to the town centre?	รถเมล์สายไหน ไปในเมืองบาง?	rót mey săi năi (b)pai nai meuang bârng

Where can I get a bus to the Grand Palace?	ไปวัดพระแก้วไปรถเมล์สายไหนได้บาง?	(b)pai wát pfa gâiw (b)pai rót mey săi năi dâi bârng
Which bus do I take to Siam Square?	ไปสยามสแควร์ไป รถเมล์สายไหนได้บาง?	(b)pai sa yàrm sa kwair (b)pai rót mey săi năi dâi bârng
Where's the bus stop?	ป้ายรถเมล์อยู่ที่ไหน?	(b)pâi rót mey yòo têe năi
When is the...bus to Rangsit?	รถเมล์ไปรังสิต ...ออกกี่โมง?	rót mey (b)pai rang sìt...òrk gèe moeng
first/last/next	คันแรก/คันสุดท้าย/	kan râirk/kan sùt tái/kan (d)tòr (b)pai
How much is the fare to...?	คันต่อไป คารถไป...เท่าไหร่?	kâr rót (b)pai...tôw rài
Do I have to change buses?	ผม(ดิฉัน)จะต้องต่อ รถเมล์หรือเปล่า?	pŏm (di chán) ja (d)tôrng (d)tòr rót mey rĕua (b)plòw
How many bus stops are there to...?	ไป...ประมาณกี่ป้าย?	(b)pai...(b)pra marn gèe (b)pâi
Will you tell me when to get off?	ช่วยบอกให้ผม(ดิฉัน) ลงด้วย?	chûay bòrk hâi pŏm (di chán) long dûay
I want to get off at Banglamphu.	ผม(ดิฉัน)จะลงที่บางลำภู	pŏm (di chán) ja long têe barng lam poo

ป้ายรถเมล์
BUS STOP

Boat service   บริการทางเรือ

Once known as the Venice of the East, the majority of Bangkok's canals have now been filled in. But long-tail boats do still travel along the remaining canal of the city and speedboats operate along the main Chao Praya (*jôw pfa yar*) River. The Express boat (เรือด่วน   —*reua dùan*) can be picked up from the pier at the Oriental Hotel and passes the Grand Palace on its way up river to the market at Nontaburi (*non tá bu ree*), just north of Bangkok. Like a bus, tickets are purchased on board. River trips are also available in the North of Thailand.

When does the next boat for... leave?	เรือไป...ลำต่อไป ออกกี่โมง?	reua (b)pai...lam (d)tòr (b)pai òrk gèe moeng
Where's the embarkation point?	ลงเรือได้ที่ไหน?	long reua dâi têe nǎi
How long does the crossing take?	ใช้เวลาข้ามไปนานไหม?	chái wey lar kârm (b)pai narn mǎi
Which port(s) do we stop at?	เราจะจอดที่ท่าไหนบ้าง?	row ja jòrt têe târ nǎi bârng
I'd like to take a cruise/ tour of the harbour.	ผม(ดิฉัน)อยากจะล่อง เรือเที่ยวแถวทางจอดเรือ	pǒm (di chán) yàrk ja lông reua têaw tǎiw târ jòrt reua

boat	เรือ	reua
cabin	ห้องนอนในเรือ	hôrng norn nai reua
single/double	,ห้องเดี่ยว/ ห้องคู่	hôrng dèaw/hôrng kôo
canal trip	ล่องแม่น้ำ	lông mâir nárm
deck	ดาดฟ้าเรือ	dàrt fár reua
ferry	เรือข้ามฟาก	reua kârm fârk
hydrofoil	เรือไฮโดรฟ่อย	reua hǎi droe foi
life belt/boat	เข็มขัดนิรภัย/ เรือชูชีพ	kěhm kàt ni rá pay/reua choo chêep
port	ท่าเรือ	târ reua
reclining seat	ที่นั่งเอนหลัง	têe nâng eyn lǎng
river cruise	ล่องแม่น้ำ	lông mâir nárm
ship	เรือกำปั้น/ เรือทะเล	reua gam (b)pàn/reua ta ley
steamer	เรือกลไฟ	reua gon fai

Bicycle hire เช่ารถจักรยาน

It is too dangerous to ride a bicycle amidst Bangkok's jostling traffic but bicycle hire is available from guest houses and shops catering for tourists in the provinces. Remember that the sun is extremely strong and cycling without the shade of a hat and sun block is an efficient way to get burned.

I'd like to hire a... bicycle.	ผม(ดิฉัน)อยากเช่า จักรยานสักคัน...	pǒm (di chán) yàrk chôw jàk ra yarn sàk kan
5-gear	(แบบ)ห้าเกียร์	(bàirp) hâr gear
mountain	(แบบ)เมาเทนไบค์	(bàirp) mow têyn bai

Other means of transport *การเดินทางวิธีอื่นๆ*

| helicopter | เฮลิคอปเตอร์ | hey li kôrp ter |
| motorbike/scooter | จักรยานยนต์/
รถสกุตเตอร์ | jàk ra yarn yon/rót sa gôot
têr |

Or perhaps you prefer:

| to hitchhike | โบกรถ | bòek rót |
| to walk | เดิน | dern |

Car *รถยนต์*

Driving in Thailand is on the left. While most major highways are in a reasonable state of repair, road safety is not uppermost in the Thai mind; many Thais drive with the fatalistic philosophy of good and bad karma—that when the day of your death is due even a toothpick will kill you. As a result road accidents are the cause of a large number of fatalities each year. Insurance, like the wearing of seat belts, is currently not compulsory, though this may soon change.

The official speed limit is 60 kph in towns and 80kph on highways, but rules are liberally interpreted. Driving along the middle of the road or using the verge to overtake is common practice.

Fuel and oil are readily available in both regular and super, dispensed by the litre.

Where's the nearest filling station?	ปั้มน้ำมันใกล้ ที่สุดอยู่ไหน?	(b)pâm nám man glâi têe sùt yòo nǎi
Fill it up, please.	เติมเต็มถัง	(d)term (d)tehm tǎng
Give me... litres of petrol (gasoline).	เติมเบนซิน...ลิตร	(d)term behn sin...lít
super (premium)/ regular/unleaded/ diesel	ซุปเปอร์/ธรรมดา/ ไร้สารตะกั่ว/ดีเซล	sup per/tam ma dar/rái sǎrn (d)ta gùa/dee seyn
Please check the...	ช่วยดู...ให้ด้วย	chûay doo... hâi dûay
battery	แบตเตอรี่	bàirt ter rêe
brake fluid	น้ำมันเบรก	nám man brèyk
oil/water	น้ำมันเครื่อง/หม้อน้ำ	nám man krêuang/môr nárm

CAR HIRE, see page 20

Would you check the tyre pressure?	ช่วยดูลมยางรถ ให้ด้วยได้ไหม?	chûay doo lom yarng rót hâi dûay dâi măi
1.6 front, 1.8 rear.	ด้านหน้า๑.๖ หลัง๑.๘	dârn nâr nèung jùt hòk lăng nèung jùt (b)pàirt
Please check the spare tyre, too.	ช่วยดูยางสำรองให้ด้วย	chûay doo yarng săm rorng hâi dûay
Can you mend this puncture (fix this flat)?	ช่วยปะยางที่รั่ว ให้ด้วยได้ไหม?	chûay (b)pà yarng têe rûa hâi dûay dây măi
Would you change the ... please?	ช่วยเปลี่ยน... ให้ด้วยได้ไหม?	chûay plèarn... hâi dûay dây măi
bulb	หลอดไฟ	lòrt fai
fan belt	สายพานพัดลม	săi parn pát lom
spark(ing) plugs	หัวเทียน	hŭa tearn
tyre	ยาง	yarng
wipers	ที่ปัดน้ำฝน	têe (b)pàt nárm fŏn
Would you clean the windscreen (windshield)?	ช่วยทำความสะอาด กระจกหน้ารถยนต์ ให้หน่อยได้ไหม?	chûay tam kwarm sa àrt gra jòk nâr rót yon hâi nòy dâi măi

Asking the way—Street directions ถามทาง ทิศทางตามถนน

Can you tell me the way to ...?	ช่วยบอกทางไป...ให้ หน่อยได้ไหม?	chûay bòrk tarng (b)pai...hâi nòy dâi măi
In which direction is ...?	...ไปทางไหน?	... (b)pai tarng năi
How do I get to ...?	ผม(ดิฉัน)จะไปที่... ไปยังไง?	pŏm (di chán) ja (b)pai· têe...(b)pai yang ngai
Are we on the right road for ...?	เราอยู่บนถนนสายที่ถูก หรือเปล่าที่จะไป...?	row yòo bon ta nŏn săy têe tòok rĕua (b)plòw têe ja (b)pai
How far is the next village?	หมู่บ้านข้างหน้าอยู่อีกไกล ไหม?	mòo bârn kârng nâr yòo èek glai măi
How far is it to ... from here?	จากนี้ไป...ไกลไหม?	jàrk née (b)pai...glai măi
Is there a motorway (expressway)?	มีทางด่วนหรือเปล่า?	mee tarng dùan rĕua (b)plòw

How long does it take by car/on foot?	ใช้เวลาเดินทาง เท่าไหร่ถ้าไปโดยรถยนต์/ ถ้าเดินไป?	châi wey lar dern tarng tôw rài târ (b)pai rót yon/ târ dern (b)pai
Is traffic allowed in the town centre?	ที่ใจกลางเมือง รถวิ่งได้ไหม?	têe jai glarng meuang rót wîng dâi măi
Can you tell me where... is?	ช่วยบอกผม(ดิฉัน) หน่อยว่า...อยู่ที่ไหน?	chûay bòrk pŏm (di chán) nòi wâr...yòo têe năi
How can I find this place/address?	ผม(ดิฉัน)จะหาสถานที่/ ที่อยู่โดยยังไง?	pŏm (di chán) ja hăr sa tărn têe/têe yòo nêe dâi yang ngai
Where's this?	นี่ที่ไหน?	née têe năi
Can you show me on the map where I am?	ช่วยชี้บนแผนที่ให้ดูหน่อย ว่าตอนนี้ผม(ดิฉัน) อยู่ที่ไหน?	chûay chée nai păirn têe hâi doo nòy wâr (d)torn nêe pŏm (di chán) yòo têe năi
Where are the nearest public toilets?	ห้องน้ำสาธารณะที่ใกล้ ที่สุดอยู่ที่ไหน?	hôrng nárm să tar ra ná têe glâi têe sùt yòo têe năi

คุณมาผิดถนนแล้ว	You're on the wrong road.
ตรงไป	Go straight ahead.
มันอยู่ที่นั่นด้านซ้ายมือ/ ขวามือ	It's down there on the left/ right.
ด้านตรงข้าม/ด้านหลัง	opposite/behind...
ติดกับ/เลย...ไป	next to/after...
ทิศเหนือ/ทิศใต้	north/south
ทิศตะวันออก/ทิศตะวันตก	east/west
ไปถึงสี่แยกแรก/ที่สอง	Go to the first/second crossroads (intersection).
เลี้ยวซ้ายที่แยกไฟแดง	Turn left at the traffic lights.
เลี้ยวขวาที่หัวมุมข้างหน้า	Turn right at the next corner.
ไปถนน...	Take the... road.
มันเป็นถนนวันเวย์	It's a one-way street.
คุณจะต้องย้อนกลับไปที่...	You have to go back to...
ไปตามป้ายบอกทางไปชลบุรี	Follow signs for Chon Buri.

Parking การจอดรถ

Is there a car park nearby?	มีที่จอดรถใกล้ ๆแถวนี้ไหม?	mee têe jòrt rót glâi glâi tăiw née măi
May I park here?	ผม(ดิฉัน)จอดรถ ตรงนี้ได้ไหม?	pŏm (di chán) jòrt rót (d)trong née dâi măi
How long can I park here?	ผม(ดิฉัน) สามารถจอดรถที่นี่ได้ นานแค่ไหน?	pŏm (di chán) săr mârt jòrt têe nêe dâi narn kâir năi
What's the charge per hour?	ค่าจอดเท่าไหร่ต่อชั่วโมง?	kâr jòrt tôw rài (d)tòr chûa moeng

Breakdown—Road assistance รถเสีย ความช่วยเหลือบนถนน

You can either call the firm from which you hired the car or the Highway Police Patrol Centre (*gorng bang káp garn (d)tam rûat tarng lûang*).

Where's the nearest garage?	อู่รถที่ใกล้ที่สุดอยู่ที่ไหน?	òo rót têe glâi têe sùt yòo têe năi
My car has broken down.	รถผม(ดิฉัน)เสีย	rót pŏm (di chán) sĕar
Where can I make a phone call?	ผม(ดิฉัน)จะไปโทรศัพท์ ได้ที่ไหน?	pŏm (di chán) ja (b)pai toe ra sàp dâi têe năi
I've had a break-down at...	รถผม(ดิฉัน)เสียที่...	rót pŏm (di chán) sĕar têe
Can you send a mechanic?	คุณช่วยส่งช่าง มาดูได้ไหม?	kun chûay sòng chârng mar doo dâi măi
My car won't start.	รถผม(ดิฉัน)สตาร์ทไม่ติด	rót pŏm (di chán) sa târt mâi (d)tìt
The battery is dead.	แบตเตอรี่หมด	bàiht ter rèe mòt
I've run out of petrol (gasoline).	รถผม(ดิฉัน)น้ำมันหมด	rót pŏm (di chán) nárm man mòt
I have a flat tyre.	รถผม(ดิฉัน)ยางแบน	rót pŏm (di chán) yarng bairn
The engine is over-heating.	เครื่องยนต์ร้อนเกินไป	krêuang yon rórn gern (b)pai
There's something wrong with the...	มีอะไรผิดปกติที่...	mee arai pìt (b)pòk a tì têe
brakes	เบรก	brèyk
carburettor	คาร์บิวเรเตอร์	kar biw rey ter

exhaust pipe	ท่อไอเสีย	tôr ai sĕar
wheel	ล้อรถ	lór rót
Can you send a break-down van (tow truck)?	คุณช่วยส่งรถลาก มาช่วยหน่อยได้ไหม?	kun chûay sòng rót lârk mar chûay nòy dâi măi
How long will you be?	อีกนานไหมถึงจะมาได้?	èek narn măi tĕung ja mar dâi
Can you give me an estimate?	บอกคร่าวๆ, ได้ไหมว่าเท่าไหร่?	bòrk krôw krôw dâi măi wâr tôw rài

Accident—Police อุบัติเหตุ ตำรวจ

Please call the police.	ช่วยเรียกตำรวจด้วย	chûay rêark tam rùat dûay
There's been an accident. It's about 2 km from . . .	มีอุบัติเหตุ ห่างจาก...ประมาณ ๒กิโลเมตร	mee u ba tì hèyt hàrng jàrk. . .(b)pra marn sŏrng gi loe méht
Where's there a telephone?	แถวนี้มีโทรศัพท์ที่ไหน?	tăiw née mee toe ra sàp têe năi
Call a doctor/an ambulance quickly.	เรียกหมอ/รถพยาบาล มาเร็วเข้า	rêark mŏr/rót pa yar barn mar rehw kôw
Here's my driving licence.	นี่ใบขับขี่ของผม(ดิฉัน)	nêe bai kàp kèe kŏrng pŏm(dì chán)
What's your name and address?	คุณชื่ออะไรและอยู่บ้าน เลขที่เท่าไหร่?	kun chêur arai láih yòo bârn lêyk têe tôw rài
What's your insurance company?	บริษัทประกันของคุณ ชื่ออะไร?	bo ri sàt (b)pra gan kŏrng kun chêur arai

Road signs ป้ายจราจร

Most road signs are international pictographs.

หยุด	STOP
ระวัง ถนนกำลังซ่อม	CAUTION ROADWORKS
อันตราย	DANGER
ห้ามผ่าน	NO PASSING
ห้ามเข้า	NO ENTRY
ทางออก	EXIT
ขับช้าๆ	DRIVE SLOWLY
เปลี่ยนเส้นทาง	DIVERSION (DETOUR)
ทางโค้ง	BEND
ห้ามรถเข้า	NO VEHICLES
ห้ามเลี้ยว	NO TURNING
ห้ามจอด	NO PARKING

Sightseeing

The Head Office of the Tourist Authority of Thailand (TAT) is on Ratchadamnern Nok (*rârt cha dam nern nòrk*) Avenue, Bangkok 10100, and has leaflets, maps and an advice centre. TAT also has smaller offices in other provincial capitals of Thailand, with maps of the town frequently displayed outside.

Where's the tourist office?	สำนักงาน ท่องเที่ยวอยู่ที่ไหน?	sǎm nák ngarn tôrng têaw yòo têe nǎi
What are the main points of interest?	มีสถานที่ที่น่าสนใจหลักๆ อะไรบ้าง?	mee sa tǎrn têe nâr sǒn jai arai bârng
We're here for...	เราอยู่ที่นี่...	row yòo têe née
only a few hours	แค่ไม่กี่ชั่วโมง	kâir mâi gèe chûa moeng
a day	วันเดียว	wan deaw
a week	อาทิตย์หนึ่ง	ar tít nèuhng
Can you recommend a sightseeing tour/ an excursion?	คุณช่วยแนะนำทัวร์ นำเที่ยว/ รายการนำเที่ยว ให้หน่อยได้ไหม?	kun chûay náih nam tua nam têaw/rai garn nam têaw hâi nòy dâi mǎi
Where do we leave from?	เราจะออกเดินทาง จากที่ไหน?	row ja òrk dern tarng jàrk têe nǎi
Will the bus pick us up at the hotel?	รถจะมารับเรา ที่โรงแรมหรือเปล่า?	rót ja mar ráp row têe roeng rairm rěua (b)plòw
How much does the tour cost?	ค่าทัวร์เท่าไหร่?	kâr tua tôw rài
What time does the tour start?	รายการนำเที่ยวนี้จะ เริ่มตอนกี่โมง?	rai garn nam têaw née ja rêrm (d)torn gèe moeng
What time do we get back?	เราจะกลับมาถึง ที่นี่กี่โมง?	row ja glàp mar těuhng têe nêe gèe moeng
Do we have free time in...?	เรามีเวลาว่าง ที่...หรือเปล่า?	row ja mee wey lar wârng têe...rěua (b)plòw
Is there an English-speaking guide?	มีไก๊ด์ (มัคคุเทศก์) พูดภาษาอังกฤษ หรือเปล่า?	mee gái (mák ku têyt) pôot par sǎr ang grìt rěua (b)plòw

I'd like to hire a	ผม(ดิฉัน)ต้องการ	pŏm (di chán) (d)tôrng
private guide for...	ไกด์ส่วนตัวสัก...	garn gái sùan (d)tua sàk
half a day	ครึ่งวัน	krêuhng wan
a day	วันหนึ่ง	wan nèuhng
Where is/Where are the...?	...อยู่ที่ไหน?	... yòo têe năi
Ancient City	เมืองโบราณ	meuang borarn
art gallery	หอศิลป	hŏr sĭn
botanical gardens	สวนพฤกษชาติ	sŭan prúk sa chârt
building	อาคาร	ar karn
business district	ย่านธุรกิจ	yârn tu rá gìt
castle	ปราสาท	(b)prar sàrt
catacombs	อุโมงค์	u moeng
cathedral	วิหาร	wi hărn
cave	ถ้ำ	tâm
cemetery	ป่าช้า	(b)pàr chár
city centre	ใจกลางเมือง	jai glarng meuang
chapel	โรงสวด	roeng sùat
church	โบสถ์	bòet
concert hall	ที่แสดงดนตรี	têe sa dăirng don (d)tree
convent	คอนแวนท์	korn wairn
court house	ศาล	sărn
downtown area	ย่านในเมือง	yârn nai meuang
embankment	เขื่อน	kèuan
exhibition	นิทรรศการ	ní tát sa garn
factory	โรงงาน	roeng ngarn
fair	งานออกร้าน	ngarn òrk rárn
floating market	ตลาดน้ำ	(d)ta làrt nárm
fortress	ป้อมปราการ	pôrm prar garn
fountain	น้ำพุ	nárm pú
gardens	สวน	sŭan
harbour	ท่าจอดเรือ	tâ jòrt reua
lake	ทะเลสาบ	ta ley sàrp
library	ห้องสมุด	hôrng sa mùt
market	ตลาด	(d)ta làrt
memorial	อนุสรณ์สถาน	ar nú sŏrn sa tărn
monastery	วัด	wát
monument	อนุสาวรีย์	ar nú sŏw a ree
museum	พิพิธภัณฑ์	pi pít ta pan
old town	เมืองเก่า	meuang gòw
palace	วัง	wang
park	สวนสาธารณะ	sŭan săr tar ra ná
parliament building	ตึกรัฐสภา	(d)tèuhk rát ta sa par
planetarium	ท้องฟ้าจำลอง	tórng fár jam lorng
royal palace	พระราชวัง	prá rârt cha wang
ruins	โบราณสถาน	boe rarn sa tărn

shopping area	ย่านช้อปปิ้ง	yârn chóp (b)pîng
square	จตุรัส	jà (d)tu rát
stadium	สนามกีฬา	sa nǎrm gee lar
statue	รูปปั้น	rôop (b)pân
stock exchange	ตลาดหุ้น	(d)ta làrt hûn
temple	วัด	wát
theatre	โรงละคร	roeng la korn
tomb	สุสาน	su sǎrn
town hall	ศาลาว่าการจังหวัด	sǎr lar wâr garn jang wàt
university	มหาวิทยาลัย	ma hǎr wít ta yar lay
zoo	สวนสัตว์	sǔan sàt

Admission ค่าผ่านประตู

Museums, galleries and tourist attractions are often half price
or free on Sundays.

Is ... open on Sundays?	...เปิดวันอาทิตย์ไหม?	... (b)pèrt wan ar tít mǎi
What are the opening hours?	เปิดเวลาเท่าไหร่?	(b)pèrt wey lar tôw rài
When does it close?	ปิดตอนไหน?	(b)pìt (d)torn nǎi
How much is the entrance fee?	ค่าผ่านประตูเท่าไหร่?	kâr pàrn (b)pra (d)tòo tôw rài
Is there any reduction for (the) ...?	มีราคาพิเศษสำหรับ...ไหม?	mee rar kar pi sèyt sǎm ràp...mǎi
children	เด็ก	dèhk
disabled	คนพิการ	kon pi garn
groups	กลุ่ม	glùm
pensioners	ผู้ที่รับเงินบำนาญ	pôo têe ráp ngern bam narn
students	นักศึกษา	nák sèuhk sǎr
Do you have a guide-book (in English)?	คุณมีหนังสือนำเที่ยว (เป็นภาษาอังกฤษ)ไหม?	kun mee náng sěur nam têaw ((b)pehn par sǎr ang grìt) mǎi
Can I buy a catalogue?	ขอซื้อแคตตาล็อกหน่อย?	kǒr séur kâirt (d)tar lôk nòy
Is it all right to take pictures?	ถ่ายรูปที่นี่ได้ไหม?	tài rôop têe née dâi mǎi

| ไม่เก็บค่าผ่านประตู | ADMISSION FREE |
| ห้ามเอากล้องถ่ายรูปเข้าไป | NO CAMERAS ALLOWED |

| Is there easy access for the disabled? | มีสิ่งอำนวยความสะดวกสำหรับคนพิการไหม? | mee sìng am nuay kwarm sa dùak sǎm ràp kon pi garn mǎi |
| Are there facilities/ activities for children? | มีสิ่งอำนวยความสะดวก/ กิจกรรมสำหรับเด็กไหม? | mee sìng am nuay kwarm sa dùak/gìt ja gam sǎm ràp dèhk mǎi |

Who—What—When? ใคร-อะไร-เมื่อไหร่?

What's that building?	อาคารหลังนั้นคืออะไร?	ar karn lǎng nán keur arai
Who was the ...?	ใครเป็น...?	krai (b)pehn
architect	สถาปนิก	sa thǎr (b)pa ník
artist	ศิลปิน	sǐn la (b)pin
painter	จิตรกร	jìt ra gorn
sculptor	ประติมากร	(b)pra (d)tì mar gorn
Who built it?	ใครเป็นคนสร้าง?	krai (b)pehn kon sârng
Who painted that picture?	ใครเป็นคนวาดภาพนั้น?	krai (b)pehn kon wârt pârp nán
When did he live?	เขาเกิดสมัยไหน?	kow gèrt sa mǎy nǎi
When was it built?	อันนี้สร้างขึ้นมาเมื่อไหร่?	an nee sârng kêuhn mar mêua rài
We're interested in...	เราสนใจ...	row sǒn jai
antiques	โบราณวัตถุ	boe rarn wát tù
archaeology	โบราณคดี	boe rarn ka dee
art	ศิลปะ	sǐn la (b)pà
botany	พฤกษศาสตร์	prúk sa sârt
ceramics	เครื่องปั้นดินเผา/เซรามิค	krêuang (b)pân din pǒw/ sey rar mík
coins	เหรียญกษาปณ์	rěarn ga sàrp
fine arts	วิจิตรศิลป์	wi jìt sǐn
geology	ธรณีวิทยา	to ran ee wít ta yar
handicrafts	งานฝีมือ	ngarn fěe meur
history	ประวัติศาสตร์	(b)pra wát tì sàrt
medicine	เวชกรรม/การแพทย์	wêyt cha gam/garn pâirt
music	ดนตรี	don (d)tree
natural history	ธรรมชาติวิทยา	tam ma chârt wít ta yar
ornithology	ปักษีวิทยา	(b)pàk sěe wít ta yar
painting	จิตรกรรม	jìt ra gam
religion	ศาสนา	sàrt sa nǎr
sculpture	ประติมากรรม	(b)pra (d)tì mar gam
zoology	สัตววิทยา	sàt wít ta yar

Where's the...department?	แผนก...อยู่ที่ไหน?	pa nàirk...yòo têe nǎi
It's...	มัน...	man
amazing	น่าทึ่ง	nâr têuhng
awful	แย่มาก	yâir mârk
beautiful	สวย	sǔay
gloomy	น่าเศร้า	nâr sôw
impressive	น่าประทับใจ	nâr (b)pra táp jai
interesting	น่าสนใจ	nâr sǒn jai
magnificent	งดงามมาก	ngót ngarm mârk
pretty	น่ารักดี	nâr rák dee
strange	แปลก	plàirk
superb	เยี่ยมมาก	yêarm mârk
terrifying	น่ากลัว	nâr glua
ugly	น่าเกลียด	nâr glèart

Churches—Religious services โบสถ์

Buddhist temples (*wát*) proliferate in Thailand and almost all villages have a local temple. In the towns and cities temples may be much larger and ornate. The buildings within the temple complex include a chapel for prayer (*bòet*), a chapel for Buddha images (*wi hǎrn*) and cells (*gu (d)tì*) where the monks live.

While temples make popular tourist attractions, it should be remembered that they are places of worship where a certain etiquette must be obeyed. It is not appropriate to enter a temple in shorts or very informal clothing and you will be asked to remove your shoes. Feet are considered a debased part of the body and it causes offence to point them at people, and especially at Buddha images and monks.

Is there a... near here?	มี...แถวนี้ไหม?	mee...tǎiw née mǎi
temple	วัด	wát
Catholic church	โบสถ์คาทอลิค	bòet kàr tor lík
Protestant church	โบสถ์โปรแตสแตนท์	bòet proe tairt sa tairn
mosque	มัสยิด/สุเหร่า	mát sa yít/sù ròw
synagogue	สุเหร่ายิว	sú ròw yiw
What time is...?	เวลา...กี่โมง?	wey lar...gèe moeng
mass/the service	คนทั่วไป/สวดมนต์	kon tûa (b)pai/sùat mon
I'd like to visit the temple.	ผม(ดิฉัน)อยากจะแวะไปโบสถ์	pǒm (di chán) yàrk ja wéh (b)pai bòet

| Should I take off my shoes? | ต้องถอดรองเท้า ไหมครับ(คะ) | (d)tôrng tòrt rorng tów mái kráp (ká) |

In the countryside ในชนบท

How far is it to...?	ไป...ไกลไหม?	(b)pai...glai măi
Can we walk there?	เราสามารถเดินไป ได้ไหม?	row săr mârt dern (b)pai dâi măi
What kind of... is that?	นั้น...ประเภทไหน?	nân...(b)pra pêyt năi
animal	สัตว์	sàt
bird	นก	nók
flower	ดอกไม้	dòrk mái
tree	ต้นไม้	(d)tôn mái

Landmarks จุดสังเกตเห็นได้ชัด

bridge	สะพาน	sa parn
cliff	หน้าผา	nâr păr
farm	นา/ไร่	nar/râi
field	ทุ่ง	tûng
footpath	ทางเท้า	tarng tów
forest	ป่า	(b)pàr
garden	สวน	sŭan
hill	เนินเขา	nern kŏw
house	บ้าน	bârn
lake	ทะเลสาบ	ta ley sàrp
meadow	ทุ่งหญ้า	tûng yâr
mountain	ภูเขา	poo kŏw
(mountain) pass	ช่องเขา	chôrng kŏw
path	ทางเดิน	tarng dern
peak	ยอดเขา	yôrt kŏw
pond	บ่อน้ำ	bòr nárm
river	แม่น้ำ	mâir nárm
road	ถนน	ta nŏn
sea	ทะเล	ta ley
spring	บ่อน้ำแร่	bòr nárm râir
valley	หุบเขา	hùp kŏw
village	หมู่บ้าน	mòo bârn
wall	กำแพง	gam pairng
waterfall	น้ำตก	nárm (d)tòk
wood	ป่า	(b)pàr

ASKING THE WAY, see page 76

Relaxing

Cinema (movies)—Theatre โรงหนัง โรงละคร

The Thai word for film is *năng*, meaning leather, hide or skin, and is derived from traditional performances of shadow theatre in which leather cut-out puppets were shown against a lighted screen. Traditional shadow puppet performances are only to be found in Southern Thailand, having originated in Java.

There are several modern-day cinemas in Bangkok showing international films with Thai subtitles and other cinemas which show only Thai films. Cinema prices are cheap and advance bookings are not usually necessary. The national anthem is always played at the beginning of the programme as an accompaniment to pictures of the Thai Royal Family during which it is obligatory to stand. A film guide is given in the daily newspapers.

Traditional Thai masked drama, or *koen*, is performed at the National Theatre and performance details are given in the daily newspaper. *Koen* performances re-enact scenes from the Indian epic the Ramayana, known in Thai as the Ramakien.

Lí-gey or folk theatre is rather like pantomime and is often performed in dazzling costumes at night in side streets or night markets, particularly up country.

What's on at the cinema tonight?	คืนนี้มีหนังเรื่องอะไรฉาย?	keurn née mee năng rêuang arai chăi
What's playing at the... Theatre?	ที่โรงละคร...มีละคร เรื่องอะไรเล่น?	têe roeng la korn...mee la korn rêuang arai lêhn
What sort of play is it?	มันเป็นละครประเภทไหน?	man (b)pehn la korn (b)pra pêyt năi
Who's it by?	เป็นละครของใคร?	(b)pehn la korn kŏrng krai
Can you recommend a...?	ช่วยแนะนำ... ให้หน่อยได้ไหม?	chûay náih nam...hâi nòy dâi măi
good film	หนังดีๆ	năng dee dee
comedy	ละครตลก	la korn (d)ta lòk

masked drama	โขน	kŏen
musical	ละครเพลง	la korn pleyng
Where's that new film directed by... being shown?	หนังเรื่องใหม่ที่กำกับ โดย...ฉายที่ไหน?	năng rêuang mài têe gam gàp doey...chăi têe năi
Who's in it?	มีใครเล่นบ้าง?	mee krai lêhn bârng
Who's playing the lead?	ใครเล่นเป็นดารานำ?	krai lêhn (b)pehn dar rar nam
Who's the director?	ใครเป็นผู้กำกับ?	krai (b)pehn pôo gam gàp
At which theatre is that new play by... being performed?	ละครเรื่องใหม่ของ... เล่นที่ไหน?	la korn rêuang mài kŏrng...lêhn têe năi
Is there a shadow puppet show on somewhere?	มีการเล่นหนังตะลุง ที่ไหนบางไหม?	mee garn sadairng năng (d)talung têe năi bârng măi
What time does it begin?	เริ่มกี่โมง?	rêrm gèe moeng
Are there any seats for tonight?	มีที่นั่งสำหรับคืนนี้ หรือเปล่า?	mee têe nâng săm ràp kâm née rĕua plòw
How much are the seats?	ตั๋วใบละเท่าไหร่?	(d)tŭa bai lá tôw rài
I'd like to reserve 2 seats for the show on Friday evening.	ผม(ดิฉัน)อยากจะจองที่นั่ง ๒ที่สำหรับการแสดง เย็นวันศุกร์	pŏm (di chán) yàrk ja jorng têe nâng sŏrng têe săm ràp garn sa dairng yehn wan sùk
Can I have a ticket for the matinee on Tuesday?	ขอตั๋วใบหนึ่งสำหรับ รอบกลางวันวันอังคาร	kŏr tŭa bai nèuhng săm ràp rôrp glarng wan wan ang karn
I'd like a seat in the stalls (orchestra).	ผม(ดิฉัน)อยากได้ที่นั่ง ชั้นดีหน้าเวที	pŏm (di chán) yàrk dâi têe nâng chán dee nâr wey tee
Not too far back.	ไม่เอาที่ไกลเกินไป	mâi ow têe glai gern (b)pai
Somewhere in the middle.	เอาที่นั่งแถวกลางๆ	ow têe nâng tăiw glarng glarng
How much are the seats in the circle (mezzanine)?	ที่นั่งชั้นลอย?	têe nâng chán loy an lá tôw rài
May I have a programme, please?	ขอสูจิบัตรด้วย?	kŏr sŏo ji bàt dûay

DAYS OF THE WEEK, see page 151

ที่พักผ่อน

| Where's the cloakroom? | ห้องรับฝากเสื้อและสิ่งของอยู่ที่ไหน? | hôrng ráp fàrk sêua láih sìng kŏrng yòo têe năi |

| ขอโทษ ขายหมดแล้ว มีที่นั่งเหลืออยู่ไม่กี่ที่ บนชั้นลอย | I'm sorry, we're sold out. There are only a few seats left in the circle (mezzanine). |
| ขอดูตั๋วหน่อย? ที่นั่งคุณอยู่นี่ | May I see your ticket? This is your seat. |

Opera—Ballet—Concert อุปรากร บัลเล่ต์ คอนเสิร์ต

Can you recommend a(n)...?	ช่วยแนะนำ... ดีๆไหหนอยใดไหม?	chûay náih nam...dee dee hâi nòy dâi măi
ballet	บัลเล่ต์	ban lêy
concert	คอนเสิร์ต	kŏrn sèrt
opera	อุปรากร	ù (b)pa rar gorn
operetta	ละครรองขนาดสั้น	la korn rórng ka nàrt sân
Where's the concert hall?	ที่แสดงดนตรี	têe sa dairng don (d)tree
What's on at the opera tonight?	คืนนี้อุปรากรเล่น เรื่องอะไร?	keurn née ù (b)pa rar gorn lêhn rêuang arai
Who's singing/ dancing?	ใครร้อง/(เต้น)รำ?	krai rórng/((d)têhn) ram
Which orchestra is playing?	ออเคสตร้าวงไหนเล่น?	or key sa trăr wong năi lêhn
What are they playing?	พวกเขาเล่นเพลงอะไร?	pûak kŏw lêhn pleyng arai
Who's the conductor/ soloist?	ใครเป็นวาทยากร (คอนดักเตอร์)/ ใครเดี่ยว?	krai (b)pehn wârt ta yar gorn (kŏrn dàk ter)/ krai dèaw

Nightclubs—Discos ไนท์คลับ ดิสโก้

| Can you recommend a good nightclub? | ช่วยแนะนำไนท์คลับ ดีๆไหหนอยใดไหม? | chûay náih nam nai klàp dee dee hâi nòy dâi măi |

Is there a floor show?	มีฟลอร์โชว์ไหม?	mee flor choe măi
What time does the show start?	การแสดงจะเริ่มตอนกี่โมง?	garn sa dairng ja rêrm (d)torn gèe moeng
Is evening dress required?	ต้องแต่งชุดราตรีสโมสรไหม?	(d)tôrng (d)tàihng chút rar (d)tree sa mŏe sŏrn măi
Where can we go dancing?	เราจะไปเต้นรำได้ที่ไหนบ้าง?	row ja (b)pai têhn ram dâi têe năi bârng
Is there a disco-theque in town?	ในเมืองมีดิสโก้เธคไหม?	nai meuang mee dit sa gôe téhk măi
Would you like to dance?	คุณอยากไปเต้นรำไหม?	kun yârk (b)pai têhn ram măi

Sports กีฬา

Popular sports include Thai boxing (*muay tai*) which differs from Western-style boxing in that it permits the use of the feet. It can be seen in Bangkok at the city's two major stadium at Lumpini and Ratchadamnern.

Some sports organized for tourist participation include golf, water-skiing, windsurfing, scuba diving, sailing, fishing, swimming and tennis. Large hotels often have their own fitness centres with weight training facilities and saunas.

Is there a football (soccer) match anywhere this Saturday?	มีฟุตบอลแข่งที่ไหนบางไหมเสาร์นี้?	mee fút born kàihng têe năi bârng măi sŏw née
Which teams are playing?	ทีมไหนกับทีมไหนแข่งกัน?	teem năi gàp teem năi kàihng gan
Can you get me a ticket?	คุณช่วยซื้อตั๋วให้ไปหนึ่งหน่อยได้ไหม?	kun chûay séur tŭa hâi bai nèuhng nòy dâi măi
I'd like to see a kick boxing match.	ผม(ดิฉัน)อยากดูมวยไทยสักนัด	pŏm (di chán) yârk doo muay tai sàk nát
What's the admission charge?	ค่าผ่านประตูเท่าไหร่?	kâr pàrn (b)pra (d)tòo tôw rài
Where's the nearest golf course?	สนามกอล์ฟที่ใกล้ที่สุดอยู่ที่ไหน?	sa nărm gorf têe glâi têe sùt yòo têe năi

basketball	บาสเก็ตบอล	bàrt sa gèht born
boxing	ชกมวย	chók muay
car racing	แข่งรถ	kàihng rót
cycling	แข่งจักรยาน	kàihng jàk ra yarn
football (soccer)	ฟุตบอล	fút born
horse racing	แข่งม้า	kàihng már
(horse-back) riding	ขี่ม้า	kèe már
mountaineering	ปีนเขา	(b)peen kŏw
skiing	สกี	sa gee
swimming	ว่ายน้ำ	wâi nárm
tennis	เทนนิส	teyn nít
volleyball	วอลเลย์บอล	worn lêy born

Where are the tennis courts?	สนามเทนนิสอยู่ที่ไหน?	sa nǎrm teyn nít yòo têe nǎi
What's the charge per...?	ต้องเสียค่าเล่นเท่าไหรดอ...?	(d)tôrng sěar kâr lêhn tôw rài (d)tòr
day/round/hour	วัน/รอบ/ชั่วโมง	wan/rôrp/chûa moeng
Can I hire (rent) rackets?	ผมจะขอเช่าไม้แร็กเก็ตได้ไหม?	pǒm ja kŏr chôw mái râihk gèht dâi mǎi
Where's the race course (track)?	ลู่วิ่งอยู่ที่ไหน?	lôo wîng yòo têe nǎi
Is there any good fishing around here?	แถวนี้มีที่ตกปลาดีๆ ไหม?	tǎiw née mee têe (d)tòk (b)plar dee dee mǎi
Do I need a permit?	ผม(ดิฉัน)ต้องขออนุญาตหรือเปล่า?	pǒm (di chán) (d)tôrng kǒr an nú yârt rěua (b)plòw
Where can I get one?	ผม(ดิฉัน)จะขออนุญาตได้ที่ไหน?	pǒm (di chán) ja kǒr an nú yârt dâi têe nǎi
Can one swim in the lake/river?	ทะเลสาบ/แม่น้ำนี้ว่ายน้ำได้ไหม?	ta ley sàrp/mâir nárm née wâi nárm dâi mǎi
Is there a swimming pool here?	ที่นี่มีสระว่ายน้ำไหม?	têe nêe mee sà wâi nárm mǎi
Is it open-air or indoor?	อยู่กลางแจ้งหรืออยู่ในร่ม?	yòo glarng jâirng rěua yòo nai rôm
What's the temperature of the water?	น้ำอุณหภูมิเท่าไหร่?	nárm ùn a pǒom tôw rài

On the beach บนชายหาด

Thailand is well endowed with beautiful beaches, along the coast of the Gulf of Thailand, and with off-shore islands. The islands of Koh Samet (four hours by bus to the east of Bangkok) and Koh Samui, and Phuket in the far south, are popular tourist destinations.

Is there a sandy beach?	มีหาดทรายไหม?	mee hàrt sai mǎi
Is it safe to swim here?	ที่นี่ปลอดภัยพอที่จะว่ายน้ำได้ไหม?	têe nee (b)plòrt pai por têe ja wâi nárm dâi mǎi
Is there a lifeguard?	มียามคอยช่วยไหม?	mee yarm koy chûay mǎi
Is it safe for children?	ปลอดภัยสำหรับเด็กหรือเปล่า?	(b)plòrt pai sǎm ràp dèhk rěua (b)plòw
The sea is very calm.	ทะเลสงบมาก	ta ley sa ngòp mârk
There are some big waves.	มีคลื่นขนาดใหญ่บ้าง	mee klêurn ka nàrt yài bârng
Are there any dangerous currents?	มีกระแสน้ำที่อันตรายบางไหม?	mee gra sǎir nárm têe an ta rai bârng mǎi
What time is high tide/low tide?	น้ำขึ้น/น้ำลงตอนกี่โมง?	nárm kêuhn/nárm long (d)torn gèe moeng
I want to hire (rent) a/an/ some...	ผม(ดิฉัน)อยากเช่า...	pǒm (di chán) yàrk chôw
bathing hut (cabana)	ที่อาบน้ำ	têe àrp nárm
deck chair	เก้าอี้ผ้าใบ	gôw êe pâr bai
motorboat	เรือยนต์	reua yon
rowing-boat	เรือพาย	reua pai
sailing boat	เรือใบ	reua bai
skin-diving equipment	เครื่องมือดำน้ำ	krêuang meur dam nárm
sunshade (umbrella)	ร่มกันแดด	rôm gan dàirt
surfboard	กระดานโต้คลื่น	gra darn (d)tôe klêurn
water-skis	สกีน้ำ	sa gee nárm
windsurfer	วินด์เซิร์ฟ	win sêrf

ชายหาดส่วนตัว	PRIVATE BEACH
ห้ามว่ายน้ำ	NO SWIMMING

Making friends

Introductions   แนะนำตัว

On being introduced Thais will place both palms together beneath their chin, fingers pointing upwards. This guesture is known as ไหว้ —*wâi*. You will find most Thais very friendly and willing to strike up a conversation.

Smart, conservative dress is appreciated, particularly if you are invited to a Thai home. Do not touch anyone on the head, which is considered sacred, and avoid pointing your feet towards another's body.

The polite form of calling Thais by their name is the same whether speaking to a man or woman: the title *kun* followed by their first name.

May I introduce Mr./ Mrs/Miss...?	ขอแนะนำให้รู้จักคุณ...?	kŏr náih nam hâi róo jàk
John, this is Mr/Mrs/ Miss...	จอห์น นี่คุณ...	jorn née kun
My name is...	ผม(ดิฉัน)ชื่อ...	pŏm (di chán) chêur
Pleased to meet you!	ยินดีที่รู้จัก	yin dee têe róo jàk
What's your name?	คุณชื่ออะไร?	kun chêur arai
How are you?	เป็นยังไงบ้าง?	(b)pehn yang ngai bârng
Fine, thanks. And you?	สบายดี ขอบคุณ แล้วคุณละ?	sa bai dee kòrp kun láiw kun lâ
Where are you going?	ไปไหน	(b)pai năi
I'm going out.	ไปเที่ยว	(b)pai têaw
Where have you been?	ไปไหนมา	(b)pai năi mar
I've been out.	ไปเที่ยวมา	(b)pai têaw mar

Follow up   ติดตามคุณ

How long have you been here?	อยู่ที่นี่นานแค่ไหนแล้ว?	kun yòo têe nêe narn kâir năi láiw
We've been here a week.	เราอยู่ที่นี่ได้อาทิตย์ หนึ่งแล้ว	row yòo têe nêe dâi ar tít nèuhng láiw

Is this your first visit?	นี่เป็นครั้งแรกที่คุณมาที่นี่หรือเปล่า?	nêe (b)pehn kráng ráirk têe kun mar têe nêe rěua (b)plòw
No, we came here last year.	ไม่ใช่ เราเคยมาที่นี่แล้วเมื่อปีที่แลว	mâi châi row koey mar têe nêe láiw mêua (b)pee têe láiw
Are you enjoying your stay?	อยู่ที่นี่ชอบไหม?	yòo têe nêe chôrp mǎi
Yes, I like it very much.	ชอบ ผม(ดิฉัน)ชอบมาก	chôrp pǒm (di chán) chôrp mârk
Where do you come from?	คุณมาจากไหน?	kun mar jàrk nǎi
I'm from ...	ผม(ดิฉัน)มาจาก...	pǒm (di chán) mar jàrk
What nationality are you?	คุณเป็นคนชาติอะไร?	kun (b)pehn kon chârt arai
I'm ...	ผมเป็นคน...	pǒm (b)pehn kon
American	อเมริกัน	a mey rí gan
British	อังกฤษ	ang grìt
Canadian	แคนาดา	kǎir nar dar
English	อังกฤษ	ang grìt
Irish	ไอริช	ai rít
Where are you staying?	คุณพักที่ไหน?	kun pák têe nǎi
Are you on your own?	มาเที่ยวคนเดียวเหรอ?	mar têaw kon deaw rěr
I'm with my ...	ผม(ดิฉัน)มากับ...ของผม(ดิฉัน)	pǒm (di chán) mar gàp...kǒrng pǒm (di chán)
wife	ภรรยา	pan ra yar
husband	สามี	sǎr mee
family	ครอบครัว	krôrp krua
children	ลูกๆ	lôok lôok
parents	พ่อแม่	pôr mâir
boyfriend/girlfriend	แฟน	fairn

father/mother	พ่อ/แม่	pôr/mâir
son/daughter	ลูกชาย/ลูกสาว	lôok chai/lôok sǒw
brother/sister	พี่(น้อง)ชาย/พี่(น้อง)สาว	pêe (nórng) chai/pêe (nórng) sǒw
uncle/aunt	ลุง/ป้า	lung/(b)pâr
nephew/niece	หลานชาย/หลานสาว	lǎrn chay/lǎrn sǒw
cousin	ญาติ	yârt

COUNTRIES, see page 146

94

Are you married/ single?	คุณแต่งงานแล้วหรือยัง/ เป็นโสดอยู่หรือเปล่า?	kun tàihng ngarn láiw rĕua yang/(b)pehn sòet yòo rĕua (b)plòw
Do you have children?	คุณมีลูกแล้วหรือยัง?	kun mee lôok láiw rĕua yang
What do you do?	คุณทำงานอะไร?	kun tam ngan arai
I'm a student.	ผม(ดิฉัน)เป็นนักศึกษา	pŏm (di chán) (b)pehn nák sèuhk săr
What are you studying?	คุณกำลังศึกษาด้านไหน?	kun gam lang sèuhk săr dârn năi
I'm here on a business trip/on holiday.	ผม(ดิฉัน)มาธุระ/ เที่ยวพักผ่อน	pŏm (di chán) mar tu rá/têaw pák pòrn
Do you travel a lot?	คุณเดินทาง ท่องเที่ยวมากไหม?	kun dern tarng (d)tôrng têaw mârk măi
Do you play cards/ chess?	คุณเล่นไพ่/ หมากรุกเป็นไหม?	kun lêhn pâi/màrk rúk (b)pehn măi

The weather อากาศ

What a lovely day!	วันนี้อากาศดีจัง	wan née ar gàrt dee jang
What awful weather!	อากาศแย่จังเลย	ar gàrt yâir jang loey
Isn't it cold/ hot today?	วันนี้หนาว/ร้อนนะ?	wan née nŏw/rórn ná
Do you think it's going to ... tomorrow?	คิดว่าพรุ่งนี้...ไหม?	kit wâr prûng née...măi
be a nice day	อากาศดี	ar gàrt dee
rain	ฝนตก	fŏn (d)tòk
What's the weather forecast?	พยากรณ์อากาศ ว่ายังไงบ้าง?	pa yar gorn ar gàrt wâr yang ngai bâng

cloud	เมฆ	mêyk
fog	มีหมอก	mee mòrk
frost	น้ำค้างแข็ง	nárm kárng kăihng
lightning	ฟ้าแลบ	fár lâirp
monsoon	มรสุม	mo ra sŭm
rain	ฝนตก	fŏn (d)tòk
thunder	ฟ้าร้อง	fár rórng
thunderstorm	ฝนฟ้าคะนอง	fŏn fár ka norng
wind	ลม	lom

Invitations คำเชื้อเชิญ

Would you like to have dinner with us on...?	มากินอาหารเย็นกับเรา...ไหม?	mar gin ar hărn gàp row...măi
May I invite you to lunch?	อยากชวนไปกินอาหารเที่ยงด้วย?	yàrk chuan (b)pai gin ar hărn têarng dûay
Can you come round for a drink this evening?	แวะมาดื่มด้วยกันได้ไหมเย็นนี้?	wáih mar dèurm dûay gan dâi măi yehn née
There's a party. Are you coming?	มีงานปาร์ตี้ มาได้ไหม?	mee ngarn (b)par têe. mar dâi măi
That's very kind of you.	คุณใจดีจังเลย	kun jai dee jang loey
Great. I'd love to come.	ดีมาก ผม(ดิฉัน)อยากไปมาก	dee mârk. pŏm (di chán) yàrk (b)pai mârk
What time shall we come?	เราควรไปกี่โมง?	row kuan (b)pai gèe moeng
May I bring a friend?	ผม(ดิฉัน)พาเพื่อนไปด้วยคนหนึ่งได้ไหม?	pŏm (di chán) par pêuan (b)pai dûay kon nèuhng dâi măi
I'm afraid we have to leave now.	ขอโทษ เราต้องกลับแล้วละ	kŏr tôet row (d)tôrng glàp láiw lá
Next time you must come to visit us.	คราวหน้าคุณต้องมาเยี่ยมเรานะ	krow nâr kun (d)tôrng mar yêarm row ná
Thanks for the evening. It was great.	ขอบคุณสำหรับงานเลี้ยงเย็นนี้ ดีมากเลย	kòrp kun săm ràp ngarn léarng yehn née. dee mârk loey

Dating นัดหมาย

Do you mind if I smoke?	คุณจะรังเกียจไหมถ้าผม(ดิฉัน)จะสูบบุหรี่?	kun ja rang gèart măi târ pŏm (di chán) ja sòop bu rèe
Would you like a cigarette?	บุหรี่ไหม?	bu rèe măi
Do you have a light, please?	มีไฟแช็กไหม?	mee fai cháihk măi
Why are you laughing?	คุณหัวเราะอะไรเหรอ?	kun hŭa ró arai rĕr
Is my Thai that bad?	ภาษาไทยของผม(ดิฉัน)แย่ขนาดนั้นเลยเหรอ?	par săr tai kŏrng pŏm (di chán) yâir ka nàrt nán loey rĕr

DAYS OF THE WEEK, see page 151

Can I get you a drink?	ผม(ดิฉัน)ไปเอา เครื่องดื่มให้เอาไหม?	pǒm (di chán) (b)pai ow krèuang dèurm hâi ow mǎi
Are you waiting for someone?	รอใครอยู่หรือเปล่า?	ror krai yòo rěua (b)plòw
Are you free this evening?	คุณว่างไหมเย็นนี้?	kun wârng mǎi yehn née
Would you like to go out with me tonight?	อยากออกไปเที่ยวข้างนอก กับผม(ดิฉัน)ไหม?	yàrk òrk (b)pai têaw kârng nòrk gàp pǒm (di chán) mǎi
Would you like to go dancing?	อยากออกไปเต้นรำไหม?	yàrk òrk (b)pai (d)têhn ram mǎi
I know a good discotheque.	ผม(ดิฉัน)รู้จักดิสโก้เธคดีๆ อยู่ที่หนึ่ง	pǒm (di chán) róo jàk dìt sa gôe téhk dee dee têe nèuhng
Where shall we meet?	เราจะเจอกันที่ไหนดี?	row ja jer gan têe nǎi dee
I'll call for you at 8.	ผม(ดิฉัน)จะแวะ ไปหาตอนสองทุ่ม	pǒm (di chán) ja wáih (b)pai hǎr d(t)orn sǒrng tûm
May I take you home?	เดี๋ยวผม(ดิฉัน) ไปส่งที่บ้านให้นะ?	děaw pǒm (di chán) (b)pai sòng têe bârn hâi ná
Can I see you again tomorrow?	ผม(ดิฉัน)จะเจอคุณ อีกทีพรุ่งนี้ได้ไหม?	pǒm (di chán) ja jer kun èek tee prûng née dâi mǎi
I hope we'll meet again.	ผม(ดิฉัน)หวังว่าเราจะ ได้เจอกันอีก	pǒm (di chán) wǎng wâr row ja dâi jer gan èek

... and you might answer: ผม(ดิฉัน)สนใจมาก

I'd love to, thank you.	ขอบคุณ	pǒm (di chán) sǒn jai mârk kòrp kun
Thank you, but I'm busy.	ขอบคุณ แต่ว่าผม (ดิฉัน)ยุ่งมาก	kòrp kun (d)tàir wâr pǒm (di chán) yûng mârk
No, I'm not interested, thank you.	ไม่ละ ผม(ดิฉัน)ไม่สนใจ ขอบคุณ	mǎi lâ pǒm (di chán) mâi sǒn jai kòrp kun
Leave me alone, please!	ขอร้อง อย่ายุ่งได้ไหม	kǒr rórng yàr yûng dâi mǎi
Thank you, it's been a wonderful evening.	ขอบคุณ งานเลี้ยง เย็นนี้เยี่ยมจริงๆ	kòrp kun ngarn léarng yehn née yêarm jing jing
I've enjoyed myself.	ผม(ดิฉัน)รู้สึกสนุกมาก	pǒm (di chán) róo sèuhk sa nùk mârk

Shopping Guide

This shopping guide is designed to help you find what you want with ease, accuracy and speed. It features:

1. A list of all major shops, stores and services (p. 98).
2. Some general expressions required when shopping to allow you to be specific and selective (p. 100).
3. Full details of the shops and services most likely to concern you. Here you'll find advice, alphabetical lists of items and conversion charts listed under the headings below.

LAUNDRY, see page 29/HAIRDRESSER'S, see page 30

Shops, stores and services ร้านค้าและบริการ

Large department stores and shopping centres have shot up all over Bangkok and most provincial capitals. These stores open seven days a week, usually from 10am to 9pm or sometimes later. Traditional shop-houses which open onto the street are usually owned by Chinese Thais and are also open seven days a week, from early morning to last thing at night.

Local fresh food markets are at their busiest in the early morning and may only be open from 5am to 9am in smaller country towns. At night time the market place becomes a place for eating and drinking at food stalls and barrows, although curios, cassette tapes, clothes and so on may also be on sale. City pavements also become lined with stalls selling clothing, luggage and watches. The rock-bottom prices indicate that many of the goods are imitations of the brand names they bear.

Whenever you purchase goods (with the exception of food) from roadside stalls or markets, the price you are quoted will include an allowance for you to bargain down. As a general rule you can expect to purchase the item at 50–75% of the first price quoted to you. If you are not sure what the going rate is, shop around and enquire from several stallholders. However, it is not appropriate to bargain for goods in department stores or hotels.

Where's the nearest...?	...ที่ใกล้ที่สุดอยู่ที่ไหน?	...têe glâi têe sùt yòo têe nǎi
antique shop	ร้านขายโบราณวัตถุ	rárn kǎi boe rarn wát tù
art gallery	หอศิลป์	hǒr sǐn
baker's	ร้านขายขนมปัง	rárn kǎi ka nǒm (b)pang
bank	ธนาคาร	ta nar karn
barber's	ร้านตัดผม	rárn (d)tàt pǒm
beauty salon	ร้านเสริมสวย	rárn sěrm sǔay
bookshop	ร้านหนังสือ	rárn nǎng sěur
butcher's	ร้านขายเนื้อ	rárn kǎi néua
camera shop	ร้านขายกล้องถ่ายรูป	rárn kǎi glôrng tài rôop
chemist's	ร้านขายยา	rárn kǎi yar
dentist	ร้านหมอฟัน	rárn mǒr fan

department store	ห้างสรรพสินค้า	hârng sáp pa sĭn kár
drugstore	ร้านขายยา	rárn kăi yar
dry cleaner's	ร้านซักแห้ง	rárn sák hâirng
electrical goods shop	ร้านขายเครื่องไฟฟ้า	rárn kăi krêuang fai fár
fishmonger's	ร้านขายปลา	rárn kăi (b)plar
florist's	ร้านขายดอกไม้	rárn kăi dòrk mái
grocer's	ร้านขายของชำ	rárn kăi kŏrng cham
hairdresser's (ladies/ men)	ร้านทำผม	rárn tam pŏm
hardware store	ร้านขายเครื่องโลหะ	rárn krêuang loe hà
hospital	โรงพยาบาล	roeng pa yar barn
ironmonger's	ร้านขายเครื่องเหล็ก	rárn kăi krêuang lèhk
jeweller's	ร้านขายเครื่องประดับ	rárn kăi krêuang (b)pra dàp
launderette	ร้านซักผ้า	rárn sák pâr
library	ห้องสมุด	hôrng sa mùt
market	ตลาด	(d)ta làrt
newsstand	แผงขายหนังสือพิมพ์	păirng kăi năng sĕur pim
optician	ร้านตัดแว่น	rárn (d)tàt wăihn
pastry shop	ร้านขายขนม	rárn kăi ka nŏm
photographer	ร้านถ่ายรูป	rárn tài rôop
police station	สถานีตำรวจ	sa tăr nee (d)tam rùat
post office	ไปรษณีย์	(b)prai sa nee
shoemaker's (repairs)	ร้านซ่อมรองเท้า	rárn sôrm rorng tów
shoe shop	ร้านขายรองเท้า	rárn kăi rorng tów
shopping centre	ศูนย์การค้า	sŏon garn kár
souvenir shop	ร้านขายของที่ระลึก	rárn kăi kŏrng têe ra léuhk
sporting goods shop	ร้านขายเครื่องกีฬา	rárn kăi krêuang gee lar
stationer's	ร้านขายเครื่องเขียน	rárn kăi krêuang kĕarn
supermarket	ซุปเปอร์มาร์เก็ต	súp (b)per mar gêht
sweet shop	ร้านขายขนมหวาน	rárn kăi ka nŏm wărn
tailor's	ร้านตัดเสื้อ	rárn (d)tàt sêua
telegraph office	ที่ทำการโทรเลข	têe tam garn toe ra léyk
toy shop	ร้านขายของเล่น	rárn kăi kŏrng lêhn
travel agency	เอเยนต์ท่องเที่ยว	ey yêyn tôrng têaw
vegetable store	ร้านขายผัก	rárn kăi pàk
veterinarian	สัตวแพทย์	sàt pâirt

ทางเข้า	**ENTRANCE**
ทางออก	**EXIT**
ทางออกฉุกเฉิน	**EMERGENCY EXIT**

General expressions *การแสดงออกทั่วไป*

Where? *ที่ไหน?*

Where's there a good...?	มี...ที่ดีที่ไหนบ้าง?	mee... têe dee têe năi bârng
Where can I find a...?	ผม(ดิฉัน)จะ หา...ได้ที่ไหน?	pŏm (di chán) ja hăr... dâi têe năi
Where's the main shopping area?	ย่านการค้าสำคัญ อยู่ที่ไหน?	yârn garn kár săm kan yòo têe năi
Is it far from here?	ไกลจากที่นี่ไหม?	glai jàrk têe nêe măi
How do I get there?	ผม(ดิฉัน)จะไปที่นั่น ได้ยังไง?	pŏm (di chán) ja (b)pai têe nân dâi yang ngai

```
ลดราคา
SALE
```

Service *บริการ*

Can you help me?	ช่วยผม(ดิฉัน) หน่อยได้ไหม?	chûay pŏm (di chán) nòy dâi măi
I'm just looking.	ดูเฉยๆ	doo chŏey chŏey
Do you sell...?	คุณมี...ขายไหม?	kun... kăi măi
I'd like to buy...	ผม(ดิฉัน)อยากซื้อ...	pŏm (di chán) yàrk séur
I'd like...	ผม(ดิฉัน)ต้องการ...	pŏm (di chán) (d)tôrng garn
Can you show me some...?	ขอดู...หน่อยได้ไหม?	kŏr doo... nòy dâi măi
Do you have any...?	คุณมี...ไหม?	kun mee... măi
Where's the...?	...อยู่ที่ไหน?	... yòo têe năi
... department	แผนก...	pa nàirk
escalator	บันไดเลื่อน	ban dai lêuan
lift	ลิฟท์	lif

คู่มือซื้อของ

That one *อันนั้น*

Can you show me...?	ขอดู...หน่อยได้ไหม?	kŏr doo... nòy dâi măi
this/that	อันนี้ / อันนั้น	an née/an nán
the one in the window/in the display case	อันที่อยู่ในตู้โชว์ / ที่โชว์อยู่	an têe yòo nai (d)tôo choe/ têe choe yòo

Defining the article *อธิบายเกี่ยวกับสิ่งของ*

I'd like a... one.	ผมต้องการอัน...	pŏm (di chán) (d)tông garn an
big	ใหญ่	yài
cheap	(ที่)ราคาถูก	(têe) rar kar tòok
dark	สีเข้ม	sĕe kêhm
good	(ที่)ดี	(têe) dee
heavy	(ที่)หนัก	(têe) nàk
large	ใหญ่	yài
light (weight)	(ที่น้ำหนัก)เบา	(têe nárm nàk) bow
light (colour)	สีอ่อน	sĕe òrn
oval	รูปไข่	rôop kài
rectangular	สีเหลี่ยมผืนผ้า	sèe lèarm pĕurn pâr
round	กลม	glom
small	เล็ก	léhk
square	สีเหลี่ยมจัตุรัส	sèe lèarm jàt (d)tù rát
sturdy	(ที่)แข็งแรงทนทาน	(têe) kăihng rairng ton tarn

I don't want anything too expensive.	ผม(ดิฉัน)ไม่อยากได้ อะไรที่แพงเกินไป	pŏm (di chán) mâi yàrk dâi arai têe pairng gern (b)pai

Preference *ความชอบ*

Can you show me some others?	ขอดูอันอื่น อีกหน่อยได้ไหม?	kŏr doo an èurn èek nòy dâi măi
Don't you have anything...?	คุณมีอะไรที่...ไหม?	kun mee arai têe... măi
cheaper/better	ถูกกว่า / ดีกว่า	tòok gwàr/dee gwàr
larger/smaller	ใหญ่กว่า / เล็กกว่า	yài gwàr/léhk gwàr

How much? *เท่าไหร่*

How much is this?	อันนี้เท่าไหร่?	an née tôw rài
How much are they?	เท่าไหร่?	tôw rài
I don't understand.	ผม(ดิฉัน)ไม่เข้าใจ	pŏm (di chán) mâi kôw jai
Please write it down.	ช่วยเขียนให้ดูหน่อย	chûay kĕarn hâi doo nòy

COLOURS, see page 113

I don't want to spend more than... baht.	ผม(ดิฉัน)ไม่อยากจ่ายมากกว่า... บาท	pŏm (di chán) mâi yàrk jài mârk gwàr... bàrt
I'm afraid that's too much.	แพงไป	pairng (b)pai
OK, let's say... baht.	ตกลง ...บาทก็แล้วกัน	(d)tòk long... bàrt gôr láiw gan

Decision การตัดสินใจ

It's not quite what I want.	มันไม่ใช่สิ่งที่ผม(ดิฉัน)ต้องการเลยที่เดียว	man mâi châi sìng têe pŏm (di chán) (d)tôrng garn loey tee deaw
No, I don't like it.	ไม่ ผม(ดิฉัน)ไม่ชอบอันนี้เลย	mâi pŏm (di chán) mâi chôrp an née loey
I'll take it.	ผม(ดิฉัน)เอาอันนี้ละ	pŏm (di chán) ow an née lâ

Ordering การสั่ง

| Can you order it for me? | คุณช่วยสั่งให้ผม(ดิฉัน)หน่อยได้ไหม? | kun chûay sàng hâi pŏm (di chán) nòy dâi măi |
| How long will it take? | จะใช้เวลานานแค่ไหน? | ja châi wey lar narn kâir năi |

Delivery การส่ง

I'll take it with me.	ผม(ดิฉัน)จะเอาไปเอง	pŏm (di chán) ja ow (b)pai eyng
Deliver it to the... Hotel.	ช่วยส่งไปที่โรงแรม...ด้วย	chûay sòng (b)pai têe roeng rairm... dûay
Please send it to this address.	ช่วยส่งไปตามที่อยู่นี้ด้วย	chûay sòng (b)pai (d)tarm têe yòo née dûay
Will I have any difficulty with the customs?	ผม(ดิฉัน)จะมีปัญหายุ่งยากกับทางศุลกากรไหม?	pŏm (di chan) ja mee (b)pan hăr yûng yârk gàp tarng sŭn la gar gorn măi

Paying การจ่ายเงิน

How much is it?	เท่าไหร่?	tôw rài
Can I pay by traveller's cheque?	จ่ายด้วยเช็คเดินทางได้ไหม?	jài dûay chéhk dern tarng dâi măi
Do you accept dollars/pounds?	รับเงินดอลลาร์/ปอนด์ไหม?	ráp ngern dor lar/(b)porn măi
Do you accept credit cards?	รับบัตรเครดิตไหม?	ráp bàt krey dìt măi

Anything else? *รับอะไรอีกไหม?*

No, thanks, that's all.	ไม่ ขอบคุณ พอแล้ว	mâi kòrp kun por láiw
Yes, I'd like...	ครับ(ค่ะ) ผม(ดิฉัน) อยากได้...	kráp (kâ) pŏm (di chán) yàrk dâi
Can you show me...?	ช่วยบอก...หน่อยได้ไหม	chûay bòrk...nòy dâi mǎi
May I have a bag, please?	ผม(ดิฉัน) ขอถุงหน่อยได้ไหม	pŏm (di chán) kŏr tǔng nòy dâi mǎi
Could you wrap it up for me, please?	ช่วยห่อให้หน่อยได้ไหม?	chûay hòr hâi nòy dâi mǎi
May I have a receipt?	ขอใบเสร็จรับเงิน หน่อยได้ไหม?	kŏr bai sèht ráp ngern nòy dâi mǎi

Dissatisfied? *ไม่พอใจ?*

Can you exchange this, please?	ขอเปลี่ยนอันนี้ได้ไหม?	kŏr (b)plèarn an née dâi mǎi
I want to return this.	ผม(ดิฉัน)อยากคืนอันนี้	pŏm (di chán) yàrk keurn an née
I'd like a refund. Here's the receipt.	ขอเงินคืน นี้ใบเสร็จรับเงิน	kŏr ngern keurn. nêe bai sèht ráp ngern

---

มีอะไรจะให้ผมรับใช้ไหม?	Can I help you?
คุณอยากได้อะไร?	What would you like?
คุณต้องการ...อะไร(แบบไหน)?	What... would you like?
สี/รูปร่าง(แบบไหน)/ คุณภาพ(แบบไหน)	colour/shape/quality
ขอโทษด้วย เราไม่มีของเลย	I'm sorry, we don't have any.
ตอนนี้ไม่มีของเหลือเลย	We're out of stock.
จะให้เราสั่งของให้คุณไหม?	Shall we order it for you?
คุณจะเอาไปเองหรือจะ ให้เราส่งให้?	Will you take it with you or shall we send it?
รับอะไรอีกไหม?	Anything else?
อันนั้น...บาท	That's... baht, please.
ที่จ่ายเงินอยู่ที่โน่น	The cash desk is over there.

Bookshop—Stationer's ร้านหนังสือ ร้านขายเครื่องเขียน

Newspapers and magazines are for sale at bookshops as well as at some grocers' shops and stationers'. The two main English language newspapers—the *Bangkok Post* and the *Nation*—are not usually sold by roadside vendors. A number of publishing houses have begun to produce news and feature magazines in English.

Where's the nearest...?	...ที่ใกล้ที่สุดอยู่ที่ไหน?	...têe glâi têe sùt yòo têe nǎi
bookshop	ร้านหนังสือ	rárn nǎng sěur
stationer's	ร้านขายเครื่องเขียน	rárn kǎi krêuang kěarn
newsstand	แผงขายหนังสือพิมพ์	pǎirng kǎi nǎng sěur pim
Where can I buy an English-language newspaper?	ผม(ดิฉัน)จะหาซื้อหนังสือพิมพ์ภาษาอังกฤษได้ที่ไหน?	pǒm (di chán) ja hǎr séur nǎng sěur pim par sǎr ang grìt dâi têe nǎi
Where's the guide-book section?	แผนกหนังสือคู่มืออยู่ที่ไหน?	pa nàirk nǎng sěur kôo meur yòo têe nǎi
Where do you keep the English books?	ชั้นหนังสือภาษาอังกฤษอยู่ที่ไหน?	chán nǎng sěur par sǎr ang grìt yòo têe nǎi
Have you any of...'s books in English?	คุณมีหนังสือของ...เป็นภาษาอังกฤษบางไหม?	kun mee nǎng sěur kǒrng.... (b)pehn par sǎr ang grìt bârng mǎi
Do you have second-hand books?	คุณมีหนังสือมือสองบางไหม?	kun mee nǎng sěur meur sǒrng bârng mǎi
I want to buy a/an/some...	ผม(ดิฉัน)อยากซื้อ...	pǒm (di chán) yàrk séur
address book	สมุดจดที่อยู่	sa mùt jòt têe yòo
adhesive tape	เทปกาว	téyp gow
ball-point pen	ปากกาลูกลื่น	(b)pàrk gar lôok lêurn
book	หนังสือ	nǎng sěur
calendar	ปฏิทิน	pa tì tin
carbon paper	กระดาษอัดสำเนา	gra dàrt àt sǎm now
crayons	ดินสอสี	din sǒr sěe
dictionary	พจนานุกรม	po ja nar nú grom
Thai-English	ไทย-อังกฤษ	tai - ang grìt
pocket	ฉบับกระเป๋า	cha bàp gra (b)pǒw
drawing paper	กระดาษวาดเขียน	gra dàrt wârt kěarn

drawing pins	เข็มหมุดสำหรับวาดเขียน	kěhm mùt săm ràp wârt kĕarn
envelopes	ซองจดหมาย	sorng jòt măi
eraser	ยางลบ	yarng lóp
exercise book	สมุดแบบฝึกหัด	sa mùt bàirp fèukk hàt
felt-tip pen	ปากกาเมจิก	(b)pàrk gar mey jìk
fountain pen	ปากกาหมึกซึม	(b)pàrk gar mèuhk seuhm
glue	กาว	gow
grammar book	หนังสือไวยากรณ์	náng sěur wai yar gorn
guidebook	หนังสือคู่มือ	náng sěur kôo meur
ink	หมึก	mèuhk
black/red/blue	ดำ/ แดง/ น้ำเงิน	dam/dairng/nárm ngern
(adhesive) labels	ป้ายสติ๊กเกอร	(b)pâi sa (d)tík ger
magazine	วารสาร	wa ra sărn
map	แผนที่	păirn têe
street map	แผนที่ถนน	păirn têe ta nŏn
road map of...	แผนที่ถนนของ...	păirn têe ta nŏn kŏrng
mechanical pencil	ดินสอกด	din sŏr gòt
newspaper	หนังสือพิมพ์	náng sěur pim
American/English	อเมริกัน/ อังกฤษ	a mey ri gan/ang grìt
notebook	สมุดโน๊ต	sa mùt nóht
note paper	กระดาษจดบันทึก	gra dàrt jòt ban téuhk
paintbox	กล่องสี	glòrng sěe
paper	กระดาษ	gra dàrt
paperback	หนังสือปกอ่อน	náng sěur (b)pòk òrn
paperclips	กิ๊ปหนีบกระดาษ	gíp nèep gra dàrt
paper napkins	กระดาษเช็ดปาก	gra dàrt chéht (b)pàrk
paste	แป้งเปียก	(b)pâirng (b)pèark
pen	ปากกา	(b)pàrk gar
pencil	ดินสอ	din sŏr
pencil sharpener	ที่เหลาดินสอ	têe lŏw din sŏr
playing cards	ไพ่	pâi
postcard	โปสการ์ด	(b)poe sa gàrt
propelling pencil	ดินสอกด	din sŏr gòt
refill (for a pen)	หมึก	mèuhk
rubber	ยางลบ	yarng lóp
ruler	ไม้บรรทัด	mái ban tát
staples	ที่เย็บกระดาษ	têe yéhp gra dàrt
string	เชือกเย็บกระดาษ	kěhm yéhp gra dàrt
thumbtacks	เป๊กติดกระดาษ	(b)péhk (d)tìt gra dàrt
travel guide	หนังสือคู่มือ	náng sěur kôo meur
typewriter ribbon	ผ้าเทปพิมพ์ดีด	pâr téyp pim dèet
typing paper	กระดาษพิมพ์ดีด	gra dàrt pim dèet
writing pad	กระดาษเขียนหนังสือ	gra dàrt kěarn náng sěur

Camping and sports equipment แค้มป์ปิ้งและเครื่องกีฬา

I'd like a/an/some …	ผม(ดิฉัน)อยากได้…	pŏm (di chán) yàrk dâi
I'd like to hire a(n)/ some …	ผม(ดิฉัน)อยากเช่า…	pŏm (di chán) yàrk chôw

air bed (mattress)	ที่ปูนอน	têe (b)poo norn
backpack	เป้หลัง	(b)pêy lăng
butane gas	ก๊าซบิวเทน	gárt biw teyn
campbed	เตียงสนาม	(d)tearng sa nǎrm
(folding) chair	เก้าอี้(พับ)	gôw êe (páp)
charcoal	ถาน	tàrn
compass	เข็มทิศ	kěhm tít
cool box	กระติกน้ำแข็ง	gra (d)tìk nárm kǎihng
deck chair	เก้าอี้ผ้าใบ	gôw êe pâr bai
fire lighters	เครื่องจุดไฟ	krêuang jùt fai
fishing tackle	คันเบ็ดชนิดมีรอก	kan bèht cha nít mee rôrk
flashlight	ไฟกระพริบ	fai gra príp
groundsheet	ผ้ายางปูพื้น	pâ yarng (b)poo péurn
hammock	เปลญวน	(b)pley yuan
ice pack	น้ำแข็ง	nárm kǎihng
insect spray (killer)	ยาฉีดกันยุง	yar chèet gan yung
kerosene	น้ำมันก๊าด	nám man gárt
lamp	ตะเกียง	(d)ta gearng
lantern	โคมไฟ	koem fai
mallet	ฆ้อนไม้	kórn mái
matches	ไม้ขีด	mái kèet
(foam rubber) mattress	ที่นอน(ยาง)	têe norn (yarng)
mosquito net	มุ้ง	múng
paraffin	น้ำมันก๊าด	nám man gárt
picnic basket	ตะกร้าปิคนิค	(d)ta grâr (b)pìk ník
pump	ที่สูบลม	têe sòop lom
rope	เชือก	chêuak
rucksack	เป้หลัง	(b)pêy lăng
screwdriver	ไขควง	kǎi kuang
skin-diving equipment	เครื่องประดาน้ำ	krêuang (b)pra dar nárm
sleeping bag	ถุงนอน	tǔng norn
(folding) table	โต๊ะ(พับ)	(d)tóh (páp)
tent	เตนท์	(d)têyn
tent pegs	หมุดปักเต็นท์	mùt (b)pàk (d)têyn
tent pole	เสากระเตนท์	sǒw (d)têyn
torch	ไฟฉาย	fai chǎi
windsurfer	กระดานโต้คลื่น	gra darn (d)tôe klêurn
water flask	กระติกน้ำ	gra (d)tìk nárm

Chemist's (drugstore) ร้านขายยา

Chemist's, like other shop-houses, are open seven days a week from early morning till late at night. There are few laws restricting across-the-counter sales of drugs in Thailand and antibiotics, penicillin etc. do not require a prescription. If you purchase drugs from a shop within a department store or shopping complex you are more likely to receive the advice of a qualified chemist. The word for a chemists' shop is *rárn yar* or *rárn kǎi yar*.

General ทั่วไป

Where's the nearest (all-night) chemist's?	ร้านขายยา(ที่เปิดตลอด คืน)ที่ใกล้ที่สุดอยู่ที่ไหน?	rárn kǎi yar (têe (b)pèrt (d)ta lòrt keurn) têe glâi têe sùt yòo têe nǎi
What time does the chemist's open/ close?	ร้านขายยาเปิด/ ปิดกี่โมง?	rárn kǎi yar (b)pèrt/(b)pìt gèe moeng

1—Pharmaceutical เกี่ยวกับยา

I'd like something for...	ผม(ดิฉัน)อยากได้ยา สำหรับแก...	pǒm (di chán) yàrk dâi yar sǎm ràp gâir...
a cold/a cough	หวัด/ไอ	wàt/ai
hay fever	โรคแพ้อากาศ	rôek páir ar gàrt
insect bites	แมลงกัดต่อย	ma lairng gàt (d)tòy
sunburn	แดดเผา	dàirt pǒw
travel/altitude sickness	เมารถเมาเรือ/ แพ้ความสูง	mow rót mow reua/páir kwarm sǒong
an upset stomach	ท้องเสีย	tórng sěar
Can you prepare this prescription for me?	ช่วยเขียนใบสั่งยานี้ ให้หน่อยได้ไหม?	chûay kěarn bai sàng yar née hâi nòy dâi mǎi
Can I get it without a prescription?	ผม(ดิฉัน)ซื้อยานี้ โดยไม่ใช้ใบสั่งยาได้ไหม?	pǒm (di chán) séur yar née doy mâi chái bai sàng yar dâi mǎi
Shall I wait?	ให้ผม(ดิฉัน)คอยไหม?	hâi pǒm (di chán) koy mǎi

Can I have a/an/some...?	ขอซื้อ...หน่อย?	kŏr séur... nòy
adhesive plaster	พาสเต้อร์	plar sa (d)têr
analgesic	ยาแก้ปวด	yar gâir (b)pùat
antiseptic cream	ครีมแก้อักเสบ	kreem gâir àk sèyp
aspirin	แอสไพริน	àirt sa pai rin
bandage (elastic)	ผ้าพันแผล	pâr pan plâir
Band-Aids®	พลาสเตอร์ปิดแผล	plar sa (d)ter (b)pèet plǎir
condoms	ถุงยางอนามัย	tǔng yarng a nar mai
contraceptives	คุมกำเนิด	kum gam nért
corn plasters	พาสเตอร์สำหรับติดตาปลา	plar sa (d)têr sǎm ràp (d)tit (d)tar (b)plar
cotton wool (absorbent cotton)	สำลี	sǎm lee
cough drops	ยาแก้ไอ	yar gâir ai
disinfectant	ยาฆ่าเชื้อ(สำหรับใช้กับสิ่งของ)	yar kâr chéua (sǎm ràp chái gàp sìng kǒrng)
ear drops	ยาหยอดหู	yar yòrt hǒo
eye drops	ยาหยอดตา	yar yòrt (d)tar
first-aid kit	เครื่องมือปฐมพยาบาล	krêuang meur (b)pa tom pa yar barn
gauze	ผ้าก๊อซ	pâr gòrs
insect repellent/spray	ยากันแมลง / สเปรย์ฉีดกันแมลง	yar gan ma lairng/sa (b)prey chèet gan ma lairng
iodine	ไอโอดีน	ai oe deen
laxative	ยาระบาย	yar ra bai
mouthwash	น้ำยาบ้วนปาก	nárm yar bûan (b)pàrk
nose drops	ยาหยอดจมูก	yar yòrt ja mòok
sanitary towels (napkins)	ผ้าอนามัย	pâr a nar mai
sleeping pills	ยานอนหลับ	yar norn làp
suppositories	ยาเหน็บทวาร	yar nèhp ta warn
... tablets	...เม็ด	... méht
tampons	ผ้าอนามัยชนิดสอด	pâr a nar mai cha nít sod
thermometer	ปรอท	(b)pròrt
throat lozenges	ยาอม	yar om
tranquillizers	ยากล่อมประสาท	yar glòrm (b)pra sàrt
vitamin pills	วิตามิน	wi (d)tar min

	ยาพิษ	POISON
	สำหรับใช้ภายนอกเท่านั้น	FOR EXTERNAL USE ONLY

DOCTOR, see page 137

2—Toiletry เครื่องใช้ในห้องน้ำ

I'd like a/an/some . . .   ผม(ดิฉัน)อยากได้...   pŏm (di chán) yàrk dâi

after-shave lotion	โลชั่นสำหรับทาหลังโกนหนวด	loe chân sǎm ràp tar lǎng goen nùat
astringent	ยามาสมาน	yar sa màn
blusher (rouge)	รูจทาแก้ม	rôot tar gâirm
bubble bath	บับเบิ้ลบาธ	báp bêrl bàrt
cream	ครีม	kreem
cleansing cream	ครีมล้างหน้า	kreem lárng nâr
foundation cream	ครีมรองพื้น	kreem rorng péurn
moisturizing cream	ครีมบำรุงผิว	kreem bam rung pǐw
night cream	ครีมบำรุงผิวตอนกลางคืน	kreem bam rung pǐw (d)torn glarng keurn
cuticle remover	ที่แต่งโคนเล็บ	têe (d)tàihng koen léhp
deodorant	ยาดับกลิ่นตัว	yar dàp glìn (d)tua
emery board	ตะไบเล็บ(ไม้)	(d)ta bai léhp (mái)
eyebrow pencil	ดินสอเขียนคิ้ว	din sŏr kěarn kíw
eyeliner	ที่เขียนขอบตา	têe kěarn kòrp (d)tar
eye shadow	ที่ทาตา	têe tar (d)tar
face powder	แป้งผัดหน้า	(b)pâihng pàt nâr
foot cream	ครีมทาเท้า	kreem tar tów
hand cream	ครีมทามือ	kreem tar meur
lipsalve	ขี้ผึ้งทาปาก	kêe pêuhng tar (b)pàrk
lipstick	ลิปสติก	líp sa (d)tìk
make-up remover pads	แผ่นเช็ดเครื่องสำอางค์	pàirn chéht krêuang sǎm arng
mascara	ที่ปัดขนตา	têe (b)pat kŏn (d)tar
nail brush	แปรงขัดเล็บ	(b)prairng kàt léhp
nail clippers	กรรไกรขลิบเล็บ	gan grai klip léhp
nail file	ตะไบขัดเล็บ	(d)ta bai kàt léhp
nail polish	ยาทาเล็บ	yar tar léhp
nail polish remover	น้ำยาล้างเล็บ	nárm yar lárng léhp
nail scissors	กรรไกรตัดเล็บ	gan grai (d)tàt léhp
perfume	น้ำหอม	nárm hǒrm
powder	แป้ง	(b)pâirng
powder puff	แป้งพลัฟ	(b)pâirng plàp
razor	มีดโกน	mêet goen
razor blades	ใบมีดโกน	bai mêet goen
rouge	รูจ	rôot
safety pins	เข็มกลัด	kěhm glàt
shaving brush	แปรงสำหรับโกนหนวด	(b)prairng sǎm ràp goen nùat
shaving cream	ครีมสำหรับโกนหนวด	kreem sǎm ràp goen nùat

soap	สบู่	sa bòo
sponge	ฟองน้ำขัดตัว	forng nárm kàt (d)tua
sun-tan cream	ครีมกันแดด	kreem gan dàirt
sun-tan oil	น้ำมันกันแดด	nám man gan dàirt
talcum powder	แป้งโรยตัว	(b)pâirng roey (d)tua
tissues	กระดาษทิชชู่	gra dàrt tít sôo
toilet paper	กระดาษชำระ	gra dàrt cham rá
toilet water	โอดิโคโลญจน์	oe di koe loen
toothbrush	แปรงสีฟัน	(b)praing sĕe fan
toothpaste	ยาสีฟัน	yar sĕe fan
towel	ผ้าขนหนู	pâr kŏn nŏo
tweezers	แหนบ	nàirp

For your hair สำหรับเส้นผม

bobby pins	กิ๊บ	gíp
colour shampoo	แชมพูย้อมผม	chairm poo yórm pŏm
comb	หวี	wĕe
curlers	เครื่องมือดัดผม	krêuang meur dàt pŏm
dry shampoo	แชมพูผง	chairm poo pŏng
dye	ยาย้อมผม	yar yórm pŏm
hairbrush	หวีแปรงผม	wĕe (b)prairng pŏm
hair gel	เยลใส่ผม	yeyl sài pŏm
hairgrips	กิ๊บติดผม	gíp (d)tìt pŏm
hair lotion	โลชั่นใส่ผม	loe chân sài pŏm
hairpins	ปิ่นปักผม	(b)pìn (b)pàk pŏm
hair spray	สเปรย์ฉีดผม	sa (b)prĕy chèet pŏm
setting lotion	โลชั่นสำหรับเซ็ทผม	loe chân sǎm ràp séht pŏm
shampoo	แชมพู	chairm poo
for dry/greasy (oily) hair	สำหรับผมแห้ง/ผมมัน	sǎm ràp pŏm hâirng/ pŏm man
tint	ยาย้อมผม	yar yórm pŏm
wig	วิกผม	wík pŏm

For the baby สำหรับเด็กอ่อน

baby food	อาหารเด็ก	ar hǎrn dèhk
dummy (pacifier)	จุกนม	jùk nom
feeding bottle	ขวดนมน้ำ	kùat nárm
nappies (diapers)	ผ้าอ้อม	pâr ôrm

Clothing เสื้อผ้า

If you want to buy something specific, prepare yourself in advance. Look at the list of clothing on page 115. Get some idea of the colour, material and size you want. They're all listed on the next few pages.

General ทั่วไป

I'd like...	ผม(ดิฉัน)อยากได้...	pŏm (di chán) yàrk dâi
I'd like... for a 10-year-old boy/girl.	ผม(ดิฉัน)อยากได้... สำหรับเด็กผู้ชาย/ เด็กผู้หญิงอายุ ๑๐ขวบ	pŏm (di chán) yàrk dâi... săm ràp dèhk pôo chai/ dèhk pôo yĭng ar yú sìp kùap
I'd like something like this.	ผม(ดิฉัน)อยากได้ อะไรเหมือนกับอันนี้	pŏm (di chán) yàrk dâi arai mĕuan gàp an née
I like the one in the window.	ผม(ดิฉัน)อยากได้ อันที่อยู่ในตู้โชว์	pŏm (di chán) yàrk dâi an têe yòo nai (d)tôo choe
How much is that per metre?	อันนี้เมตรละเท่าไหร่?	an née méht la tôw rài

1 centimetre (cm)	= 0.39 in.	1 inch = 2.54 cm
1 metre (m)	= 39.37 in.	1 foot = 30.5 cm
10 metres	= 32.81 ft.	1 yard = 0.91 m.

Colour สี

I'd like something in...	ผม(ดิฉัน)อยากได้สี...	pŏm (di chán) yàrk dâi sĕe
I'd like a darker/lighter shade.	ผม(ดิฉัน)อยากได้ สีเข้มกว่านี้/ อ่อนกว่านี้	pŏm (di chán) yàrk dâi sĕe kêhm gwàr née/òrn gwàr née
I'd like something to match this.	ผม(ดิฉัน)อยากได้อันที่ เข้ากับอันนี้	pŏm (di chán) yàrk dâi an têe kôw gàp an née
I don't like the colour.	ผม(ดิฉัน)ไม่ชอบสีเลย	pŏm (di chán) mâi chôrp sĕe loey

beige	สีทราย	sĕe sai
black	สีดำ	sĕe dam
blue	สีน้ำเงิน	sĕe nárm ngern
brown	สีน้ำตาล	sĕe nárm (d)tarn
fawn	สีเทาแกมเหลือง	sĕe tow gairm lĕuang
golden	สีทอง	sĕe torng
green	สีเขียว	sĕe kĕaw
grey	สีเทา	sĕe tow
mauve	สีม่วงสด	sĕe mûang sòt
orange	สีส้ม	sĕe sôm
pink	สีชมพู	sĕe chom poo
purple	สีม่วง	sĕe mûang
red	สีแดง	sĕe dairng
scarlet	สีเลือดหมู	sĕe lêuat mŏo
silver	สีเงิน	sĕe ngern
turquoise	สีเทอร์คอยส์	sĕe ter koyt
white	สีขาว	sĕe kŏw
yellow	สีเหลือง	sĕe lĕuang
light...	สี...อ่อน	sĕe... òrn
dark...	สี...เข้ม	sĕe... kêhm

สีเรียบ	ลายทาง	ลายจุด	ลายหมากรุก	ลวดลาย
(rêarp)	(lai tarng)	(lai jùt)	(lai màr krúk)	(lûat lai)

Fabric เนื้อผ้า

Do you have any-thing in...?	คุณมีอะไร ที่ทำด้วยผ้า...ไหม?	kun mee arai tée tam dûay pâr... măi
Is that...?	นั่น...ใช่ไหม?	nân... châi mâi
handmade	ทำด้วยมือ	tam dûay meur
imported	นำเข้าจากต่างประเทศ	nam kôw jàrk (d)tàrng (b)pra téyt
made here	ทำที่นี่	tam têe nêe
I'd like something thinner.	ผม(ดิฉัน)อยากได้ ที่บางกว่านี้	pŏm (di chán) yàrk dâi têe barng gwàr née
Do you have anything of better quality?	คุณมีอะไรที่ คุณภาพดีกว่านี้ไหม?	kun mee arai tée kun a pârp dee gwàr née măi
What's it made of?	อันนี้ทำด้วยอะไร?	an née tam dûay arai

cambric	ผ้าลินินขาว	pâr li nin kŏw
camel-hair	ขนอูฐ	kŏn òot
chiffon	แพรชีฟอง	prair chee forng
corduroy	ผ้าริ้ว	pâr ríw
cotton	ผ้าฝ้าย	pâr fâi
crepe	แพรยอน	prair yôn
denim	ผ้ายีนส์	pâr yeen
felt	ผ้าสักหลาด	pâr sàk làrt
flannel	ผ้าสักหลาดอ่อนนุ่น	pâr sàk làrt òrn
gabardine	ผ้าลายสูงหน้าเดียว	pâr lai sŏrng nâr deaw
lace	ผ้าลูกไม้	pâr lôok mái
leather	หนัง	nǎng
linen	ผ้าลินิน	pâr li nin
poplin	ผ้าแพรป๊อปลิน	pâr prair (b)pohp lin
satin	ผ้าซาติน	pâr sar (d)tin
silk	ผ้าไหม	pâr mǎi
suede	หนังกลับ	nǎng glàp
towelling	ผ้าขนหนู	pâr kŏn nǒo
velvet	ผ้ากำมะหยี่	pâr gam ma yèe
velveteen	ผ้ากำมะหยี่เทียม	pâr gam ma yèe tearm
wool	ผ้าขนแกะ	pâr kŏn gàih
worsted	ไหมพรม	mǎi prom

Is it...?	อันนี้...หรือเปล่า?	an née...rěur (b)plòw
pure cotton/wool	ผ้าฝ้าย/ ผ้าขนแกะแท้	pâr fâi/ pâr kŏn gàih táir
synthetic	ผ้าใยสังเคราะห์	pâr yai sǎng kró
colourfast	สีตก	sěe (d)tòk
crease (wrinkle) resistant	กันยับ	gan yáp
Is it hand washable/Is it machine washable?	อันนี้ซักด้วยมือ/ อันนี้ซัก ด้วยเครื่องซักได้ไหม?	an née sák dûay meur/an née sák dûay krêuang sák pâr dâi mǎi
Will it shrink?	มันจะหดหรือเปล่า?	man ja hòt rěur (b)plow

Size ขนาด

I take size 38.	ผม(ดิฉัน)เอาเบอร์ ๓๘	pǒm (di chán) ow ber sǎrm sìp pàirt
Could you measure me?	ช่วยวัดตัวผม(ดิฉัน) หน่อยได้ไหม?	chûay wát (d)tua pǒm (di chán) nòy dâi mǎi
I don't know the Thai sizes.	ผม(ดิฉัน)ไม่รู้จัก ขนาดของไทย	pǒm (di chán) mâi róo jàk ka nàrt kǒrng tai

NUMBERS, see page 147

Sizes can vary somewhat from one manufacturer to an-other, so be sure to try on shoes and clothing before you buy.

small (S)	เล็ก	léhk
medium (M)	กลาง	glarng
large (L)	ใหญ่	yài
extra large (XL)	ใหญ่พิเศษ	yài pi sèyt
larger/smaller	ใหญ่กว่า / เล็กกว่า	yài gwàr/ léhk gwàr

A good fit? พอดีไหม?

Can I try it on?	ขอลองหน่อยได้ไหม?	kŏr lorng nòy dâi măi
Where's the fitting room?	ห้องลองอยู่ที่ไหน?	hôrng lorng yòo têe năi
Is there a mirror?	มีกระจกไหม?	mee gra jòk măi
It fits very well.	กำลังพอดี	gam lang por dee
It doesn't fit.	มันไม่พอดี	man mâi por dee

Tailor—Dressmaker ช่างตัดเสื้อผ้า

I'd like to have a ... made.	ผม(ดิฉัน) อยากตัด...สักตัว	pŏm (dichán) yàrk (d)tàt ... sàk (d)tua
dress	ชุดเสื้อกระโปรงติดกัน	chút sêua gra(b)proeng (d)tìt gan
shirt	เสื้อเชิ้ต	sêua chért
suit	สูท	sòot
Can I see some patterns?	ขอดูแบบหน่อย	kŏr doo bàirp nòi
I'd like it the same ... as this.	อยากได้...เหมือนตัวนี้	yàrk dâi....měuan (d)tua née
colour	สี	sĕe
style	สไตล์	sa(d)tai
When can I collect it?	จะให้มารับได้เมื่อไหร่	ja hâi mar ráp dâi mêua rài
Will it be ready by Wednesday?	วันพุธจะเสร็จไหม	wan pút ja sèht mái
It's too ...	มัน...เกินไป	man ... gern (b)pai
short/long	สั้น / ยาว	sân/yow
tight/loose	คับ / หลวม	káp/lŭam
How long will it take to alter?	ใช้เวลาแก้นานแค่ไหน?	chái wey lar gâir narn kâir năi

Clothes and accessories เสื้อผ้าและของที่ไปกับเสื้อผ้า

I would like a/an/ some...	ผม(ดิฉัน)อยากได้...	pǒm (di chán) yàrk dâi
bathing cap	หมวกอาบน้ำ	mùak àrp nárm
bathing suit	ชุดว่ายน้ำ	chút wâi nárm
bathrobe	เสื้อคลุมอาบน้ำ	sêua klum àrp nárm
blouse	เสื้อผู้หญิง	sêua pôo yǐng
bow tie	หูกระต่าย	hǒo gra (d)tài
bra	ยกทรง	yók song
braces	สายโยงกางเกง	sǎi yoeng garng geyng
cap	หมวกแกป	mùak gáihp
cardigan	คาร์ดิกัน	kar di gan
coat	เสื้อโคท	sêua kóet
dress	เสื้อกระโปรงชุด	sêua gra (b)proeng chùt
with long sleeves	แขนยาว	kǎirn yow
with short sleeves	แขนสั้น	kǎirn sân
sleeveless	ไม่มีแขน	mâi mee kǎirn
dressing gown	เสื้อคลุมอาบน้ำ	sêua klum àrp nárm
evening dress (woman's)	ชุดราตรี	chút rar (d)tree
girdle	เข็มขัด/ผ้าคาดเอว	kěhm kàt/ pâr kârt ew
gloves	ถุงมือ	tǔng meur
handbag	กระเป๋าถือ	gra (b)pǒw těur
handkerchief	ผ้าเช็ดหน้า	pâr chéht nâr
hat	หมวก	mùak
jacket	เสื้อแจ็กเก็ต	sêua jàirk gèht
jeans	ยีนส์	yeens
jersey	เสื้อไหมพรม	sêua mǎi prom
jumper (Br.)	เสื้อไหมพรม	sêua mǎi prom
kneesocks	ถุงเท้ายาวถึงเข่า	tǔng tów yow těuhng kòw
nightdress	ชุดนอน	chút norn
pair of...	...คู่	... kôo
panties	กางเกงรัดรูป	garng geyng rát rôop
pants (Am.)	กางเกงขายาว	garng geyng kǎr yow
panty girdle	ถุงนอง	tǔng nông
panty hose	ถุงนอง	tǔng nông
pullover	เสื้อไหมพรม	sêua mǎi prom
polo (turtle)-neck	คอโปโล	kor (b)poe loe
round-neck	คอกลม	kor glom
V-neck	คอวี	kor wee
with long/short sleeves	แขนยาว/ แขนสั้น	kǎirn yow/kǎirn sân
without sleeves	ไม่มีแขน	mâi mee kǎirn

pyjamas	เสื้อกางเกงนอน	sêua garng geyng norn
raincoat	เสื้อกันฝน	sêua gan fŏn
scarf	ผ้าพันคอ	pâr pan kor
shirt	เสื้อเชิร์ต	sêua chért
shorts	กางเกงขาสั้น	garng geyng kăr sân
skirt	กระโปรง	gra (b)proeng
slip	กางเกงอาบน้ำผู้ชาย	garng geyng àrp nárm pôo chai
socks	ถุงเท้า	tŭng tów
stockings	ถุงน่อง	tŭng nôong
suit (man's)	ชุดสากล(ของผู้ชาย)	chút săr gon (kŏrng pôo chai)
suit (woman's)	ชุดสากล(ของสุภาพสตรี)	chút săr gon (kŏrng sŭ pârp sa (d)tree)
suspenders (Am.)	สายที่แขวนกางเกง	săi têe kwăirn garng geyng
sweater	เสื้อไหมพรม	sêua măi prom
sweatshirt	เสื้อกีฬาคอกลมแขนยาว	sêua gee lar kor glom kăirn yow
swimming trunks	กางเกงว่ายน้ำ	garng geyng wâi nárm
swimsuit	ชุดว่ายน้ำ	chút wâi nárm
T-shirt	เสื้อคอกลม	sêua kor glom
tie	เนคไท	néhk tai
tights	ถุงน่อง	tŭng nôong
tracksuit	ชุดวอร์ม	chút worm
trousers	กางเกงขายาว	garng geyng kăr yow
umbrella	ร่ม	rôm
underpants	กางเกงใน	garng geyng nai
undershirt	เสื้อยืด	sêua yêurt
vest (Am.)	เสื้อกั๊ก	sêua gák
vest (Br.)	เสื้อกล้าม	sêua glârm
waistcoat	เสื้อกั๊ก	sêua gák

belt	เข็มขัด	kĕhm kàt
buckle	หัวเข็มขัด	hŭa kĕhm kàt
button	กระดุม	gra dum
collar	คอเสื้อ	kor sêua
pocket	กระเป๋า	gra (b)pŏw
press stud (snap fastener)	แปะติดเสื้อ	(b)páih (d)tìt sêua
zip (zipper)	ซิป	síp

Shoes รองเท้า

I'd like a pair of...	ผม(ดิฉัน)อยากได้...คู่หนึ่ง	pŏm (di chán) yàrk dâi... kôo nèuhng
boots	รองเท้าบู๊ท	rorng tów bôot
plimsolls (sneakers)	รองเท้าผ้าใบ	rorng tów pâr bai
sandals	รองเท้าแตะ	rorng tów (d)tàih
shoes	รองเท้า	rorng tów
flat	พื้นราบ	péurn rârp
with (high) heels	สูนสูง	sôn sŏong
with leather soles	พื้นหนัง	péurn nǎng
with rubber soles	พื้นยาง	péurn yarng
slippers	รองเท้าแตะ	rorng tów (d)tàih
These are too...	มัน...เกินไป	man... gern (b)pai
narrow/wide	แคบ/ กว้าง	kâirp/gwârng
big/small	ใหญ่/ เล็ก	yài/léhk
Do you have a larger/ smaller size?	คุณมีขนาดใหญ่กว่า/ เล็กกว่านี้ไหม?	kun mee ka nàrt yâi gwàr/ léhk gwar née măi
Do you have the same in black?	มีสีดำแบบเดียวกันนี้?	mee sěe dam bàirp deaw gan née
cloth	ผ้า	pâr
leather	หนัง	nǎng
rubber	ยาง	yarng
suede	หนังกลับ	nǎng glàp
Is it real leather?	อันนี้หนังแท้หรือเปล่า?	an née nǎng táir rěur (b)plòw
I need some shoe polish/shoelaces.	ผม(ดิฉัน)อยากได้ยาง ขัดรองเท้า/ เชือกผูกรองเท้า	pŏm (di chán) yàrk dâi yarng kàt rorng tów/chêuak pòok rorng tów

Shoes worn out? Here's the key to getting them fixed again:

Can you repair these shoes?	ช่วยซ่อมรองเท้า คู่นี้ได้ไหม?	chûay sôrm rorng tów kôo née dâi măi
Can you stitch this?	ช่วยเย็บอันนี้ ให้หนอยได้ไหม?	chûay yéhp an née hâi nòy dâi măi
I want new soles and heels.	ช่วยเปลี่ยนพื้นและส้น รองเท้าให้หนอย	chûay (b)plèarn péurn láih sôn rorng tów hâi nòy
When will they be ready?	จะเสร็จเมื่อไหร่?	ja sèht mêua rài

COLOURS, see page 113

Electrical appliances *เครื่องใช้ไฟฟ้า*

The standard current is 220 volts, 50-cycle AC with two-pin plugs and sockets. Most hotels have a point for shavers.

What's the voltage?	ที่นี่ใช้ไฟฟ้ากี่โวลท์?	têe nêe chái fai fár gèe woel
Do you have a battery for this?	คุณมีถ่านไฟฉายสำหรับอันนี้ไหม?	kun mee tàrn fai chái săm ràp an née măi
This is broken. Can you repair it?	อันนี้มันเสีย ช่วยซ่อมให้หน่อยได้ไหม?	an née man sĕar. chûay sôrm hâi nòy dâi măi
Can you show me how it works?	ช่วยแสดงให้ดูหน่อยว่ามันทำงานยังไง?	chûay sa dairng hâi doo nòy wâr man tam ngarn yang ngai
I'd like (to hire) a video cassette.	ผม(ดิฉัน)อยากได้ (อยากเช่า)ม้วนเทปวีดีโอ	pǒm (dì chán) yàrk dâi (yàrk chôw) múan téyp wee dee oe
I'd like a/an/ some ...	ผม(ดิฉัน)อยากได้...	pǒm (dì chán) yàrk dâi...
adaptor	ปลั๊กแปลงไฟฟ้า	blák (b)plairng fai fár
amplifier	เครื่องขยายเสียง	krêuang ka yǎi sĕarng
bulb	หลอดไฟฟ้า	lòrt fai fár
CD player	เครื่องเลนซีดี	krêuang lêhn see dee
clock-radio	วิทยุ-นาฬิกา	wít ta yú - nar̀ lí gar
electric toothbrush	แปรงสีฟันไฟฟ้า	(b)prairng sěe fan fai fár
extension lead (cord)	สายตอด(ไฟฟ้า)	sǎi (d)tòr (fai fár)
hair dryer	เครื่องเป่าผม	krêuang (b)pòw pǒm
headphones	หูฟัง	hŏo fang
(travelling) iron	เตารีด(สำหรับเดินทาง)	(d)tow rêet (sǎm ràp dern tarng)
lamp	โคมไฟ	koem fai
plug	ปลั๊ก	(b)plák
portable ...	...กระเป๋าหิ้ว	... gra (b)pǒw hîw
radio	วิทยุ	wít ta yú
car radio	วิทยุรถยนต์	wít ta yú rót yon
(cassette) recorder	เครื่องอัดเทป	krêuang àt téyp
record player	เครื่องเล่นเทป	krêuang lêhn téyp
shaver	เครื่องโกนหนวดไฟฟ้า	krêuang goen nùat fai fár
speakers	ลำโพง	lam poeng
(colour) television	โทรทัศน์(สี)	toe ra tát (sěe)
transformer	หม้อแปลงไฟฟ้า	môr (b)plairng fai fár
video-recorder	เครื่องอัดวีดีโอ	krêuang àt wee dee oe

Grocery ร้านขายของชำ

Thais measure in kilograms and kilometres. They have a 100g measure too, called a *kèet*— ขีด .

I'd like some bread, please.	ผม(ดิฉัน)อยากได้ขนมปัง	pŏm (di chán) yàrk dâi ka nŏm (b)pang
What sort of cheese do you have?	คุณ มีเนยแข็งแบบไหนบ้าง?	kun mee noey kǎihng bàirp nǎi bârng
A piece of...	...ชิ้นหนึ่ง	... chín nèuhng
that one	อันนั้น	an nán
the one on the shelf	อันที่อยู่บนชั้นนั้น	an têe yòo bon chán nán
I'll have one of those, please.	ผม(ดิฉัน)อยากได้อันนั้น อันหนึ่ง	pŏm (di chán) yàrk dâi an nán an nèuhng
May I help myself?	ผม(ดิฉัน)หยิบเองได้ไหม?	pŏm (di chán) yìp eyng dâi mǎi
I'd like...	ผม(ดิฉัน)อยากได้...	pŏm (di chán) yàrk dâi
a kilo of oranges	ส้มหนึ่งกิโล	sôm nèuhng gi loe
half a kilo of tomatoes	มะเขือเทศครึ่งกิโล	ma kěua téyt krêuhng gi loe
100 grams of chillies	พริกขีดหนึ่ง/๑๐๐กรัม	prík kèet nèuhng/rói gram
a litre of milk	นมหนึ่งลิตร	nom nèuhng lít
half a dozen eggs	ไข่ครึ่งโหล	kài krêuhng lòe
4 slices of ham	แฮมสี่แผ่น	hairm sèe pàirn
a packet of tea	ชาหนึ่งกลอง	char nèuhng glòrng
a jar of jam	แยมหนึ่งขวด	yairm nèuhng kùat
a tin (can) of peaches	ลูกท้อหนึ่งกระป๋อง	lôok tór nèuhng gra (b)pǒrng
a box of chocolates	ช็อกโกแล็ตหนึ่งกลอง	chôk goe lâiht nèuhng glòng

1 kilogram or kilo (kg.) = 1000 grams (g.)	
100 g. = 3.5 oz.	½ kg. = 1.1 lb.
200 g. = 7.0 oz.	1 kg. = 2.2 lb.
1 oz. = 28.35 g.	
1 lb. = 453.60 g.	

1 litre (l.) = 0.88 imp. quarts = 1.06 U.S. quarts	
1 imp. quart = 1.14 l.	1 U.S. quart = 0.95 l.
1 imp. gallon = 4.55 l.	1 U.S. gallon = 3.8 l.

FOOD, see also page 63

Household articles ของใช้ในบ้าน

bottle opener	ที่เปิดขวด	têe (b)pèrt kùat
bucket (pail)	ถังน้ำ	tăng nárm
can opener	ที่เปิดกระป๋อง	têe (b)pèrt gra (b)pŏrng
candles	เทียน	tearn
clothes pegs (pins)	ไม้หนีบผ้า	mái nèep pâr
dish detergent	น้ำยาล้างจาน	nám yar lárng jarn
food box	อาหารกลอง	ar hărn glòng
frying pan	กะทะแบน	gà tá bairn
matches	ไม้ขีด	mái kèet
paper napkins	กระดาษเช็ดปาก	gra dàrt chéht (b)pàrk
plastic bags	ถุงพลาสติก	tŭng plar sa (d)tìk
saucepan	หม้อ	môr
tin opener	ที่เปิดกระป๋อง	têe (b)pèrt gra (b)pŏrng
tea towel	ผ้าเช็ดจาน	pâr chéht jarn
vacuum flask	กระติกสูญญากาศ	gra (d)tìk sŏon yar gàrt
washing powder	ผงซักฟอก	pŏng sák fôrk
washing-up liquid	น้ำยาล้างจาน	nám yar lárng jarn

Tools เครื่องมือ

hammer	ฆ้อน	kórn
nails	ตะปู	(d)tà (b)poo
penknife	มีดพับ	mêet páp
pliers	คีม	keem
scissors	กรรไกร	gan grai
screws	ตะปูควง	(d)tà (b)poo kuang
screwdriver	ไขควง	kăi duang
spanner	กุญแจเลื่อน	gun jair lêuan

Crockery ถ้วยชาม

cups	แก้ว	gâiw
mugs	เหยือก	yèuak
plates	จาน	jarn
saucers	จานรองถ้วย	jarn rorng tûay
tumblers	ถ้วยแก้ว	tûay gâiw

Cutlery (flatware) ช้อน-ส้อม

forks	ส้อม	sôrm
knives	มีด	mêet
spoons	ช้อน	chórn
teaspoons	ช้อนชา	chórn char

Jeweller's—Watchmaker's ร้านขายเครื่องรูปพรรณ ร้านนาฬิกา

Could I see that, please?	ขอดูอันนั้นหน่อยได้ไหม?	kŏr doo an nán nòy dâi măi
Do you have anything in gold?	มีอะไรที่ทำจากทองไหม?	mee arai têe tam jàrk torng măi
How many carats is this?	อันนี้กี่กะรัต?	an née gèe ga rát
Is this real silver?	อันนี้เงินแท้หรือเปล่า?	an née ngern táir rĕur (b)plòw
Can you repair this watch?	ช่วยซ่อมนาฬิกาเรือนนี้ หน่อยได้ไหม?	chûay sôrm nar lí gar reuan née nòy dâi măi
I'd like a/an/some ...	ผม(ดิฉัน)อยากได้...	pŏm (di chán) yàrk dâi

alarm clock	นาฬิกาปลุก	nar lí gar (b)plùk
bangle	กำไล	gam lai
battery	ถ่านไฟฉาย	tàrn fai chăi
bracelet	สร้อยข้อมือ	sôy kôr meur
chain bracelet	สร้อยข้อมือ	sôy kôr meur
charm bracelet	สร้อยข้อมือ ที่มีเครื่องราง	sôy kôr meur têe mee krêuang rarng
brooch	เข็มกลัด	kĕhm glàt
chain	สร้อย	sôy
charm	เครื่องราง	krêuang rarng
cigarette case	ตลับใส่บุหรี่	(d)ta làp sài bu rèe
cigarette lighter	ไฟแช็ก	fai cháihk
clip	เข็มกลัดหนีบ	kĕhm glàt nèep
clock	นาฬิกา	nar lí gar
cross	ไม้กางเขน	mái garng kĕyn
cuckoo clock	นาฬิกานกร้อง	nar lí nok rórng
cuff-links	กระดุมข้อมือเสื้อ	gra dum kôr meur sêua
earrings	ตุ้มหู	(d)tûm hŏo
gem	เพชรพลอย	péht ploy
jewel box	ตู้เครื่องเพชร	(d)tôo krêuang péht
mechanical pencil	ดินสอกด	din sŏr gòt
music box	กล่องดนตรี	glòrng don (d)tree
necklace	สร้อยคอ	sôy kor
pendant	จี้	jêe
pin	เข็มหมุด	kĕhm mùt
pocket watch	นาฬิกาพก	nar lí gar pók
powder compact	ตลับแป้ง	(d)ta làp (b)pâirng
propelling pencil	ดินสอกด	din sŏr gòt

ring	แหวน	wăirn
engagement ring	แหวนหมั้น	wăirn mân
signet ring	แหวนรุน	wăirn rûn
wedding ring	แหวนแดงงาน	wăirn (d)tàirng ngarn
rosary	ลูกประคำ	lôok (b)pra kam
silverware	เครื่องเงิน	krêuang ngern
tie clip	ที่หนีบเนคไท	têe nèep néyk tai
tie pin	เข็มกลัดเนคไท	kăihm glàt néyk tai
watch	นาฬิกาขอมือ	nar lí gar kôr meur
automatic	อัตโนมัติ	àt noe mát
digital	ดิจิตอล	(d)ti jí (d)torn
quartz	ควอทซ์	kẁort
with a second hand	มีอสูง	meur sŏrng
waterproof	กันน้ำ	gan nárm
watchstrap	สายนาฬิกาขอมือ	săy na lí gar kôr meur
wristwatch	นาฬิกาขอมือ	nar lí gar kôr meur

amber	อ่ำพัน	am pan
amethyst	เขียวหนุมาน	kêaw ha nŭ marn
chromium	โครเมี่ยม	kroe mêarm
copper	ทองแดง	torng dairng
coral	หินปะการัง	hĭn (b)pà gar rang
crystal	แก้วผลึก/คริสตัล	gâiw plèuhk/kri sa (d)tăn
cut glass	แกวเจียรใน	gâiw jea ra nai
diamond	เพชร	péht
emerald	มรกต	mo ra gòt
enamel	ลงยา/เคลือบ	long yar/klêuap
gold	ทองคำ	torng kam
gold plate	ชุบทอง	chúp torng
jade	หยก	yòk
onyx	หินจำพวกโมรา	hĭn jam pûak moe rar
pearl	ไข่มุก	kài múk
pewter	พิวเตอร์	piw (d)ter
platinum	แพลตตินั่ม	plairt (d)ti nâm
ruby	ทับทิม	táp tim
sapphire	ไพลิน/บุษราคัม/มรกต	pai lin/bùt rar kam/mo ra gòt
silver	เงิน	ngern
silver plate	ชุบเงิน	chúp ngern
stainless steel	สเตนเลส	sa (d)tăirn léyt
topaz	บุษราคัม	bùt sa rar kam
turquoise	เทอรคอยส์/พลอยสีฟ้า	ter kôyt/ploy sĕe fár

Optician ร้านตัดแว่น

I've broken my glasses.	แว่นผม(ดิฉัน)แตก	wâirn pŏm (di chán) (d)tàirk
Can you repair them for me?	ช่วยซ่อมแว่นให้ผม(ดิฉัน) หน่อยได้ไหม?	chûay sôrm wâirn hâi pŏm (di chán) nòy dâi măi
When will they be ready?	จะเสร็จเมื่อไหร่?	ja sèht mêua rài
Can you change the lenses?	ช่วยเปลี่ยนเลนส์ ให้หน่อยได้ไหม?	chûay (b)plèarn leyns hâi nòy dâi măi
I'd like tinted lenses.	เลนส์สี	leyns sĕe
The frame is broken.	กรอบแว่นหัก	gròrp wâirn hàk
I'd like a spectacle case.	ผม(ดิฉัน)อยากได้ ซองใส่แว่น	pŏm (di chán) yàrk dâi sorng sài wâirn
I'd like to have my eyesight checked.	ช่วยตรวจสายตาให้ผม (ดิฉัน)หน่อย	chûay (d)truat săi (d)tar pŏm (di chán) nòy
I'm short-sighted/ long-sighted.	สายตาผม(ดิฉัน)สั้น/ ยาว	săi (d)tar pŏm (di chán) sân/yow
I'd like some contact lenses.	ผม(ดิฉัน)อยากได้ คอนแท็กต์เลนส์	pŏm (di chán) yàrk dâi korn táihk leyns
I've lost one of my contact lenses.	คอนแท็กต์เลนส์ผม(ดิฉัน) หายไปข้างหนึ่ง	korn táihk leyns pŏm (di chán) hăi (b)pai kârng nèuhng
Could you give me another one?	ขอซื้อข้างเดียวได้ไหม?	kŏr séur kârng deaw dâi măi
I have...	ผม(ดิฉัน)ใช้ประเภท...	pŏm (di chán) chái (b)pra péyt
hard/soft lenses	ฮาร์ทเลนส์/ ซ็อฟเลนส์	hârt leyns/sóf leyns
Do you have any contact-lens fluid?	มีน้ำยาล้างคอนแท็กต์ เลนส์ไหม?	mee nám yar lárng korn táihk leyns măi
I'd like to buy a pair of sunglasses.	ผม(ดิฉัน)อยากจะ ได้แว่นตาดำ	pŏm (di chán) yàrk ja dâi wâirn (d)tar dam
May I look in a mirror?	ขอดูกระจกหน่อยได้ไหม?	kŏr doo gra jòk nòy dâi măi
I'd like to buy a pair of binoculars.	ผม(ดิฉัน)อยากได้ กล้องสองทางไกล	pŏm (di chán) yàrk dâi glôrng sòrng tarng glai

Photography   *การถ่ายรูป*

I'd like a(n) ... camera.	ผม(ดิฉัน)อยากได้ กล้องถ่ายรูป... ตัวหนึ่ง	pŏm (di chán) yàrk dâi glôrng tài rôop ... (d)tua nèuhng
automatic	อัตโนมัติ	àt noe mát
inexpensive	ไม่แพง	mâi pairng
simple	แบบธรรมดา	bàirp tam ma dar
Can you show me some..., please?	ขอดู...หน่อยได้ไหม?	kŏr doo....nòy dây măi
cine (movie) cameras	กล้องถ่ายหนัง	glôrng tài năng
video cameras	กล้องวีดีโอ	glôrng wee dee oe
I'd like to have some passport photos taken.	ผม(ดิฉัน) อยากถ่ายรูปขนาดติด พาสปอร์ต/ หนังสือเดินทาง	pŏm (di chán) yàrk tài rôop ka nàrt (d)tìt par sa (b)pòrt/náng sěur dern tarng

Film   *ฟิล์ม*

I'd like a film for this camera.	ผม(ดิฉัน)อยากได้ฟิล์ม สำหรับกล้องตัวนี้สักม้วน	pŏm (di chán) yàrk dâi feem săm ràp glôrng (d)tua née sàk múan
black and white	ขาวดำ	kŏw dam
colour	สี	sěe
colour negative	ฟิล์มสีที่ล้างแล้ว	feem sěe têe lárng láiw
colour slide	ฟิล์มสไลด์	feem sa lai
cartridge	กล้องฟิล์มขนาดใหญ่	glòrng feem ka nàrt yài
disc film	ฟิล์มดูสลับ	feem (d)ta làp
roll film	ฟิล์มม้วน	feem múan
video cassette	ม้วนเทปวีดีโอ	múan téyp wee dee oe
24/36 exposures	๒๔/๓๖ รูป	yêe sìp sèe/ sărm sìp hòk rôop
this size	ขนาดนี้	ka nàrt née
this ASA/DIN number	เอเอสเอ/ ความไวแสงของฟิล์มเท่านี้	ey eys ey/kwarm wai săirng kŏrng feem tôw née
artificial light type	ชนิดแสงไม่ธรรมชาติ	cha nít săirng mâi tam ma chârt
daylight type	ชนิดแสงธรรมชาติ	cha nít săirng tam ma chârt
fast (high-speed)	ความเร็วสูง	kwarm rehw sŏong
fine grain	เนื้อละเอียด	néua lá èart

Processing การล้างรูป

How much do you charge for processing?	ค่าล้างรูปที่นี่คิดเท่าไหร่?	kâr lárng rôop têe nêe kít tôw rài
I'd like ... prints of each negative.	ผม(ดิฉัน)อยากได้รูป...ชุด	pǒm (di chán) yàrk dâi rôop ...chút
with a matt finish	กระดาษด้าน	gra dàrt dârn
with a glossy finish	กระดาษมัน	gra dàrt man
Will you enlarge this, please?	ช่วยขยายรูปนี้ให้หน่อยได้ไหม?	chûay ka yǎi rôop nêe hâi nòy dâi mǎi
When will the photos be ready?	รูปจะเสร็จเมื่อไหร่?	rôop ja sèht mêua rài

Accessories and repairs อุปกรณ์ถ่ายรูปและการซ่อม

I'd like a/an/some ...	ผม(ดิฉัน)อยากได้...	pǒm (di chán) yàrk dâi
battery	แบตเตอรี่	bàirt (d)ter rêe
cable release	สายกดชัตเตอร์	sǎi gòt chát (d)ter
camera case	กระเป๋าใส่กล้อง	gra (b)pǒw sài glôrng
(electronic) flash	แฟลช	flàirt
filter	ฟีลเตอร์	fil (d)ter
for black and white	สำหรับฟิล์มขาวดำ	sǎm ràp feem kǒw dam
for colour	สำหรับฟิล์มสี	sǎm ràp feem sěe
lens	เลนส	leyns
telephoto lens	เลนส์เทเล	leyns tey lêy
wide-angle lens	เลนส์มุมกว้าง	leyns mum gwârng
lens cap	ฝาครอบเลนส์	fǎr krôrp leyns
Can you repair this camera?	ช่วยซ่อมกล้อง ถ่ายรูปนี้ให้หน่อย ได้ไหม?	chûay sôrm glôrng tâi rôop nêe hâi nòy dâi mǎi
The film is jammed.	ฟิล์มเลื่อนไม่ไป	feem lêuan mâi (b)pai
There's something wrong with the ...	มีปัญหาบางอย่างกับ...	mee (b)pan hǎr barng yàrng gàp
exposure counter	ที่บอกจำนวนรูปที่ถ่าย	têe bòrk jam nuan rôop têe tài
film winder	ตัวขึ้นฟิล์ม	(d)tua kêuhn feem
flash attachment	แป้นแฟลช	(b)pâirn flâirt
lens	เลนส์	leyns
light meter	เครื่องวัดแสง	krêuang wát sǎirng
rangefinder	เครื่องวัดระยะ	krêuang wát rá yá
shutter	ชัตเตอร์	chát (d)ter

NUMBERS, see page 147

Tobacconist's ร้านขายบุหรี่และยาสูบ

Thai cigarettes and tobacco are on sale at most general purpose stores and at restaurants. The most commonly smoked are the filtered *krorng típ* although mentholated cigarettes called *săi fŏn* are also available. International cigarettes are more costly and can be bought in department stores and from roadside vendors.

A packet of cigarettes, please.	ขอบุหรี่ซองหนึ่ง	kŏr bu rèe sorng nèuhng
Do you have any... cigarettes?	คุณมีบุหรี่...ไหม?	kun mee bu rèe... măi
American/English	อเมริกัน/อังกฤษ	a mey ri gan/ang grìt
I'd like a carton.	ผม(ดิฉัน)อยากได้ บุหรี่คอตตอนหนึ่ง	pŏm (di chán) yàrk dâi bu rèe kârt (d)torn nèuhng
Give me a/some..., please.	ผม(ดิฉัน)อยากได้...	pŏm (di chán) yàrk dâi
candy	ลูกกวาด	lôok gwàrt
chewing gum	หมากฝรั่ง	màrk fa ràng
chewing tobacco	ยาเส้น	yar sêhn
chocolate	ช็อคโกแล็ต	chôk goe láiht
cigarette case	ตลับบุหรี่	(d)ta làp bu rèe
cigarette holder	ที่คาบบุหรี่	têe kârp bu rèe
cigarettes	บุหรี่	bu rèe
filter-tipped/ without filter	กันกรอง/ไม่มีก้นกรอง	gôn grorng/ mâi mee gôn grorng
light/dark tobacco	ยาเส้นอ่อน/เข้ม	yar sêhn òrn/ kêym
mild/strong	รสอ่อน/จัด	rót òrn/jàt
menthol	รสเมนทอล	rót meyn torl
cigars	ซิการ์	si gar
lighter	ไฟแช็ก	fai châihk
matches	ไม้ขีด	mái kèet
pipe	ไปป์	(b)pai
pipe cleaners	ที่ทำความสะอาด ไปป์	têe tam kwarm sa àrt (b)pai
pipe tobacco	ยาเส้นสำหรับไปป์	yar sêyn săm ràp (b)pai
postcard	โปสการ์ด	(b)poe sa gàrt
snuff	ยานัตถุ์	yar nát
stamps	แสตมป์	sa (d)tairm
sweets	ลูกกวาด	lôok gwàrt
wick	ไส้ตะเกียง	sâi (d)tà gearng

Miscellaneous เบ็ดเตล็ด

Souvenirs ของที่ระลึก

Thailand is an emporium of handicrafts which makes souvenir shopping an irresistible temptation. The country is famed for its silk, most of which comes from the North-East, and tends to be rather thick and heavy. It can be bought from the roll or made up by one of Bangkok's speedy and efficient tailoring services concentrated along the Sukumwit Road and in most shopping arcades.

Other souvenirs include antiques (export permission is required for genuine antiques), hand-made flowers, bronze, niello and lacquer ware, wooden elephants, brightly coloured kites, dolls in hill tribe costume, hill tribe clothes and fabrics, gemstones, jewellery and ceramics. It is illegal to take Buddha images out of Thailand unless prior permission had been sought.

ของเก่า	kŏrng gòw	antiques
ดอกไม้ประดิษฐ์	dòrk mái (b)pra dìt	hand-made flowers
ทองสัมฤทธิ์	torng săm rít	bronze ware
เครื่องถม	krêuang tŏm	niello ware
เครื่องเขิน	krêuang kĕrn	lacquer ware
ว่าวสีสด	wôw sĕe sòt	brightly coloured kites
อัญมณี	an ya ma nee	gemstones
เครื่องรูปพรรณ	krêuang rôop pan	jewellery
พระพุทธรูป	prá pút tá rôop	Buddha images
เครื่องเงิน	krûeang ngern	silver ware
ผ้าไหม	pâr măi	silk
ช้างไม้	chárng mái	wooden elephant
ชุดชาวเขา	chút chow kŏw	hill tribe clothes
เซรามิค	sey rar mík	ceramics

Records—Cassettes แผ่นเสียง เทปคาคาเซ็ท

I'd like a...	ผม(ดิฉัน)อยากได...	pŏm (di chán) yàrk dâi
cassette	เทปคาคาเซ็ท	téyp kârt séht
video cassette	ม้วนเทปวีดีโอ	múan téyp wee dee oe
compact disc	ซีดี	see dee

L.P.(33 rpm)	แผ่นเสียง(๓๓รอบ ต่อนาที)	pàirn sĕarng (sărm sìp sărm rôrp (d)tòr nar tee)
E.P.(45 rpm)	แผ่นเสียง(๔๕รอบ ต่อนาที)	pàirn sĕarng (sèe sìp hâr rôrp (d)tòr nar tee)
single	แผ่นซิงเกิ้ล	pàirn sing gêrl

Do you have any records by ...?	มีแผ่นเสียงของ...ไหม?	mee pàirn sĕarng kŏrng... mǎi
Can I listen to this record?	ขอฟังแผ่นนี้ หน่อยได้ไหม?	kŏr fang pàirn née nòy dâi mǎi
classical music	ดนตรีคลาสสิค	don (d)tree klârt sìk
folk music	ดนตรีพื้นบ้าน	don (d)tree péurn bârn
folk song	เพลงพื้นบ้าน/โฟล์คซอง19	pleyng péurn bârn/fôek sorng
jazz	แจ๊ส	jáiht
light music	ดนตรีเบาๆ	don (d)tree bow bow
orchestral music	ดนตรีออเคสตร้า	don (d)tree or key sa (d)trâr
pop music	ดนตรีป๊อบ	don (d)tree (b)pôrp

Toys ของเล่น

I'd like a toy/game...	ผม(ดิฉัน)อยากได้ ของเล่น/เกม	pŏm (di chán) yàrk dâi kŏrng lêhn/ geym
for a boy	สำหรับเด็กผู้ชาย	săm ràp dèhk pôo chai
for a 5-year-old girl	สำหรับเด็กผู้หญิงอายุ ๕ขวบ	săm ràp dèhk pôo yǐng ar yú hâr kùap
(beach) ball	ลูกบอลชายหาด	lôok born (chai hàrt)
bucket and spade (pail and shovel)	ถังและพลั่ว	tăng láih plûa
card game	ไพ่	pâi
chess set	หมากรุก	màrk rúk
colouring book	สมุดระบายสี	sa mùt ra bai sĕe
doll	ตุ๊กตา	(d)túk a (d)tar
electronic game	เกมไฟฟ้า	geym fai fár
hill tribe doll	ตุ๊กตาชาวเขา	(d)túk a (d)tar chow kŏw
roller skates	สเก็ต	sa gèht
snorkel	ท่อดำน้ำ	tôr dam nárm
teddy bear	ตุ๊กตาหมี	(d)túk a (d)tar mĕe
toy car	รถของเล่น	rót kŏrng lêhn

Your money: banks—currency

Banks are open between 8.30am and 3.30pm from Monday to Friday but their currency exchanges often stay open for longer hours, seven days a week.

The unit of Thai currency is the baht (บาท—*bàrt*). The smallest coins are the copper 25 and 50 satang (ห้าตางค์—*sa (d)tàrng*) pieces and there are 100 satang in one baht. Silver coins are used for 1, 5 and 10 baht, while bank notes cover 10 (brown), 20 (green), 50 (blue), 100 (red) and 500 (purple) baht denominations.

Thais do not tend to pay for goods by cheque but credit cards and traveller's cheques will be accepted as a method of payment in most large restaurants and hotels.

Where's the nearest bank?	ธนาคารที่ใกล้ที่สุดอยู่ที่ไหน?	ta nar karn têe glâi têe sùt yòo têe nǎi
Where's the nearest currency exchange office?	ที่รับแลกเงินที่ใกล้ที่สุดอยู่ที่ไหน?	têe ráp lâirk ngern têe glâi têe sùt yòo têe nǎi

At the bank ที่ธนาคาร

I want to change some dollars/pounds.	ผม(ดิฉัน)อยากแลกเงินดอลลาร์/ปอนด์หน่อย	pǒm (di chán) yàrk lâirk ngern dorn lar/(b)porn nòy
I want to cash a traveller's cheque.	ผม(ดิฉัน)อยากแลกเช็คเดินทางเป็นเงินสด	pǒm (di chán) yàrk lâirk chéhk dern tarng (b)pehn ngern sòt

What's the exchange rate?	ยัตราแลกเปลี่ยนเท่าไหร่?	at (d)tra lâirk (b)plèarn tôw rài
How much commission do you charge?	คิดค่าบริการเท่าไหร่?	kit kàr boe ri garn tôw rài
Can you cash a personal cheque?	เช็คส่วนตัว ใช้เบิกเงินสดได้ไหม?	chéhk sùan tua chái bèrk ngern sòt dâi mǎi
Can you telex my bank in London?	ช่วยเทเล็กซ์ไปที่ ธนาคารของผม(ดิฉัน) ที่ลอนดอนได้ไหม?	chûay tey léhk (b)pai têe ta nar karn kǒng pǒm (di chán) têe lorn dorn dâi mǎi
I have a/an/some...	ผม(ดิฉัน)มี...	pǒm (di chán) mee
credit card	บัตรเครดิต	bàt krey dìt
Eurocheques	ยูโรเช็ค	yoo roe chéhk
letter of credit	แอล.ซี.	airl see
I'm expecting some money from New York. Has it arrived?	ผม(ดิฉัน) คอยเงินจากนิวยอร์กอยู่ ไม่ทราบว่ามาถึงแล้วยัง?	pǒm (di chán) koy ngern jàrk niw yôrk yòo mâi sarp wâr mar těuhng láiw yang
Please give me... notes (bills) and some small change.	ขอเป็นแบงค์/ใบ...และ เงินยอยอีกนิดหนอย	kǒr (b)pehn bairng/bai... láih ngern yôy èek nít nòy
Give me... large notes and the rest in small notes.	ขอเป็นแบงค์ใหญ่...ใบ และที่เหลือเป็นแบงค์ยอย	kǒr (b)pehn bairng yài...bai láih têe lěua (b)pehn bairng yôy

Deposits—Withdrawals ฝาก ถอน

I want to...	ผม(ดิฉัน)อยากจะ...	pǒm (di chán) yàrk ja
open an account	เปิดบัญชี	(b)pèrt ban chee
withdraw... baht	ถอนเงิน...บาท	tǒrn ngern...bàrt
Where should I sign?	เซ็นชื่อตรงไหน?	sehn chêur (d)trong nǎi
I'd like to pay this into my account.	ผม(ดิฉัน)อยากจะ ให้หจายเข้าบัญชี ของผม(ดิฉัน)	pǒm (di chán) yàrk ja hâi jài kôw ban chee kǒng pǒm (di chán)

NUMBERS, see page 147

Business terms เงื่อนไขทางธุรกิจ

My name is...	ผมชื่อ...	pŏm chêur
Here's my card.	นี่นามบัตรของผม(ดิฉัน)	nêe narm bàt kŏrng pŏm (di chán)
I have an appointment with ...	ผม(ดิฉัน)มีนัดกับ...	pŏm (di chán) mee nát gàp
Can you give me an estimate of the cost?	ช่วยประเมินค่าใช้จ่ายคราวๆได้ไหม?	chûay (b)pra mern kâr chái jài krŏw krŏw dâi măi
What's the rate of inflation?	อัตราเงินเฟ้อเท่าไหร่?	a (d)tra ngern fér tôw rài
Can you provide me with ...?	ช่วยจัดหา...ให้หน่อย?	chûay jàt hăr ... hâi nòy
an interpreter	ล่าม	lârm
a personal computer	คอมพิวเตอร์(พี.ซี.)	korm piw (d)ter (pee see)
a secretary	เลขานุการ	lêy kăr nú garn
Where can I make photocopies?	ผม(ดิฉัน)จะถ่ายเอกสารได้ที่ไหน?	pŏm (di chán) ja tài èyk ga sărn dâi têe năi

amount	จำนวน	jam nuan
balance	ดุล	dun
capital	ทุน	tun
cheque	เช็ค	chéhk
contract	สัญญา	săn yar
discount	ส่วนลด	sùan lót
expenses	ค่าใช้จ่าย	kâr chái jài
interest	ดอกเบี้ย	dòrk bêar
investment	การลงทุน	garn long tun
invoice	ใบเรียกเก็บเงิน	bai rêark gèhp ngern
loss	ขาดทุน	kàrt tun
mortgage	จำนอง	jam norng
payment	จ่าย	jài
percentage	เปอร์เซนต์	(b)per sehn
profit	กำไร	gam rai
purchase	ซื้อ	séur
sale	ขาย	kăi
share	หุ้น	hûn
transfer	โอนเงิน	oen ngern
value	มูลค่า	moon kâr

At the post office

Bangkok's Central Post Office on Charoen Krung Road is open from 8am to 8pm on weekdays and from 8am to 1pm at weekends and on public holidays. It operates a busy but efficient poste restante service and a packing and parcelling service for those wishing to send excess luggage home.

Branch post offices are open from 8am to 6pm on weekdays and from 8am to 1pm on Saturdays.

Mail can be posted in the red letter boxes along the roadside but it is more reliable to post your mail at the post office itself as box collections are sometimes irregular.

The Central Post Office in Bangkok has a 24-hour international telephone exchange although since the introduction of direct dialling international calls can now be made from some branch post offices.

Where's the nearest post office?	ที่ทำการไปรษณีย์ที่ใกล้ที่สุดอยู่ที่ไหน?	têe tam garn (b)prai sa nee têe glâi têe sùt yòo têe nǎin
What time does the post office open/close?	ที่ทำการไปรษณีย์เปิด/ปิดกี่โมง?	têe tam garn (b)prai sa nee (b)pèrt/(b)pìt gèe moeng
A stamp for this letter/postcard please.	ขอซื้อแสตมป์สำหรับจดหมาย/โปสการ์ดอันนี้	kǒr séur sa (d)tairm sǎm ràp jòt mǎi/(b)pòe sa gàrt an née
A...-baht stamp, please.	ขอแสตมป์...บาทดวงหนึ่ง	kǒr sa (d)tairm ... bàrt duang nèuhng
What's the postage for a letter to London?	ค่าแสตมป์เท่าไหร่สำหรับจดหมายส่งไปลอนดอน?	kâr sa (d)tairm tôw rài sǎm ràp jòt mǎi sòng (b)pai lorn dorn
What's the postage for a postcard to Los Angeles?	ค่าแสตมป์เท่าไหร่สำหรับโปสการ์ดส่งไปลอสแองเจลิส?	kâr sa (d)tairm tôw rài sǎm ràp (b)pòe sa gàrt sòng (b)pai lót airng jeh lít
Where's the letter box (mailbox)?	ตู้ไปรษณีย์อยู่ที่ไหน?	(d)tôo (b)prai sa nee yòo têe nǎi
I want to send this parcel.	ผม(ดิฉัน)อยากส่งพัสดุห่อนี้	pǒm (di chán) yàrk sòng pát sa du hòr née

I'd like to send this (by)...	ผม(ดิฉัน)อยากส่ง อันนี้ทาง/โดย...	pŏm (di chán) yàrk sòng an née tarng/doey
airmail	ไปรษณีย์อากาศ	(b)prai sa nee ar gàrt
express (special delivery)	ไปรษณีย์ด่วน	(b)prai sa nee dùan
registered mail	ลงทะเบียน	long ta bearn
At which counter can I cash an international money order?	ผม(ดิฉัน)จะเอาตั๋ว แลกเงินนะหว่างประเทศ ไปขึ้นเงินได้ที่ช่องไหน?	pŏm (di chán) ja ow (d)tŭa lăirk ngern ra wàrng (b)pra têyt (b)pai kêuhn ngern dâi têe chông năi
Where's the poste restante (general delivery)?	ส่งทั่วไปช่องไหน?	sòng tûa (b)pai chông năi
Is there any post (mail) for me? My name is...	มีจดหมายมาถึงผม (ดิฉัน)บ้างไหม? ผมชื่อ...	mee jòt măi mar tĕuhng pŏm (di chán) bârng măi. pŏm chêur

แสตมป์/ดวงตราไปรษณียากร	STAMPS
พัสดุ	PARCELS
ตั๋วแลกเงิน/ธนาณัติ	MONEY ORDERS

Telegrams—Telex—Fax *โทรเลข เทเล็กซ แฟ็กซ*

Telegrams and facsimile messages can be sent from Bangkok's Central Post Office. Telegrams can also be sent from branch post offices. Most large hotels and shops specializing in communications also have fax facilities.

I'd like to send a telegram/telex.	ผม(ดิฉัน)อยากส่ง โทรเลข/เทเล็กซ	pŏm (di chán) yàrk sòng toe ra lêyk/tey léhk
May I have a form, please?	ขอแบบฟอร์มหน่อย?	kŏr bàirp form nòy
How much is it per word?	ค่าส่งเท่าไหร่ต่อคำ?	kâr sòng tôw rài (d)tòr kam
How long will a cable to Boston take?	โทรเลขไปบอสตัน ใช้เวลานานแค่ไหน?	toe ra lêyk (b)pai bòrt sa (d)tan chái wey lar narn kâir năi
How much will this fax cost?	ค่าแฟกซ์อันนี้เท่าไหร่?	kâr fáihk an née tôw rài

Telephoning โทรศัพท์

Most roadside telephone booths have red telephones and are for local calls only. The boxes take 1-baht coins. Booths for long distance internal calls (including Malaysia) also exist, and have turquoise telephones taking 5-baht coins. In addition airports and some department stores and shopping complexes have telephones taking phone cards which can be used for direct dialling overseas. Telephone cards can be purchased from special desks in department stores.

Where's the telephone?	โทรศัพท์อยู่ที่ไหน?	toe ra sàp yòo têe nǎi
I'd like a telephone card.	ขอซื้อการ์ดโฟนหน่อย	kǒr séur gàrt foen nòy
Where's the nearest telephone booth?	ตู้โทรศัพท์ที่ใกล้ที่สุดอยู่ที่ไหน?	(d)tôo toe ra sàp têe glâi têe sùt yòo têe nǎi
May I use your phone?	ขอใช้โทรศัพท์หน่อยได้ไหม?	kǒr chái toe ra sàp nòy dâi mǎi
Do you have a telephone directory for Chiang Mai?	คุณมีสมุดโทรศัพท์สำหรับเชียงใหม่ไหม?	kun mee sa mùt toe ra sàp sǎm ràp chearng mài mǎi
I'd like to call ... in England.	ผมอยากจะโทรถึง...ที่อังกฤษ	pǒm yàrk ja toe těuhng...têe ang grìt
What's the dialling (area) code for	รหัสพื้นที่ของ...รหัสอะไร?	ra hàt péurn têe kǒrng...ra hàt arai
How do I get the international operator?	โอเปอเรเต้อร์ระหว่างประเทศ หมายเลขอะไร?	oe (b)per rey (d)têr ra wàrng (b)pra têyt mǎi lêyk arai

Operator โอเปอเรเต้อร์

I'd like Khon Khan 23 45 67.	ช่วยต่อขอนแก่น หมายเลข ๒๓ ๔๕ ๖๗ ให้หน่อย	chûay (d)tòr kǒrn gàihn mǎi lêyk sǒrng sǎrm sèe hâr hòk jèht
Can you help me get this number?	ช่วยต่อหมายเลขนี้ให้หน่อย?	chûay (d)tòr mǎi lêyk née hâi nòy

NUMBERS, see page 147

| I'd like to place a personal (person-to-person) call. | ผม(ดิฉัน)อยากจะ ขอโทรสวนตัวหนอย | pǒm (di chán) yàrk ja kǒr toe sùan (d)tua nòy |
| I'd like to reverse the charges (call collect). | ผม(ดิฉัน)อยากขอ โทรเก็บเงินปลายทาง | pǒm (di chán) yàrk kǒr toe gèh ngern (b)plai tarng |

Speaking กำลังพูด

Hello. This is...	สวัสดี/ฮัลโหล นี่...	sa wàt dee/hǎn lǒe. nêe
I'd like to speak to...	ขอพูดกับคุณ...	kǒr pôot gàp kun
Extension...	ตอหมายเลข...	(d)tòr mǎi lêyk
Speak louder/more slowly, please.	ช่วยพูดดังขึ้น/ช้าลง หนอยได้ไหม	chûay pôot dang kêuhn/ chár long nòy dâi mǎi

Bad luck โชคไม่ดี

Would you try again later, please?	กรุณาโทรมาใหมอี กครั้ง?	ga ru nar toe mar mài èek kráng
Operator, you gave me the wrong number.	โอเปอเรเดอร์ คุณ ตอให้ผม(ดิฉัน)ผิด	oe (b)per rey (d)têr kun (d)tòr hâi pǒm (di chán) pìt
Operator, we were cut off.	โอเปอเรเดอร์ สายมันขาด	oe (b)per rey (d)têr sǎi man kàrt

Not there ไม่อยู่ที่นั่น

When will he/she be back?	เขา/เธอจะกลับ มาตอนไหน?	kǒw/ter ja glàp mar (d)torn nǎi
Will you tell him/her I called? My name is...	ฝากบอกเขา/ เธอดวยวาผม(ดิฉัน) โทรมา ผม(ดิฉัน)ชื่อ...	fàrk bòrk kǒw/ter dûay wâr pǒm (di chán) toe mar. pǒm (di chán) chêur
Would you ask him/her to call me? My number is...	ฝากบอกให้เขา/ เธอโทรกลับดวย หมายเลข...?	fàrk bòrk hâi kǒw/ter toe glàp dûay. mǎi lêyk

| Would you take a message, please. | ฝากข้อความถึงเขา/เธอได้ไหม | fàrk kôr kwarm těuhng kŏw/ter dâi mǎi |

Charges ค่าโทรศัพท์

| What was the cost of that call? | ค่าโทรศัพท์เมื่อสักครู่เท่าไหร? | kâr toe ra sàp mêua sàk krôo tôw rài |
| I want to pay for the call. | ขอจ่ายค่าโทรศัพท์เมื่อสักครู่ | kôr jài kâr toe ra sàp mêua sàk krôo |

มีโทรศัพท์ถึงคุณ	There's a telephone call for you.
คุณจะโทรไปหมายเลขอะไร?	What number are you calling?
สายไม่ว่าง	The line's engaged.
ไม่มีคนรับ	There's no answer.
คุณโทรผิด	You've got the wrong number.
โทรศัพท์เสีย	The phone is out of order.
รอเดี๋ยว	Just a moment.
กรุณารอสักครู่	Hold on, please.
ตอนนี้เขา/เธอไม่อยู่	He's/She's out at the moment.

Doctor

Health care is not free in Thailand and you are strongly advised to take out health insurance before travelling. Clinics are often open 24 hours a day and since they are private there is no need to register with any particular one.

Be careful of having injections as many doctors, especially in the provinces, rely upon sterilizing needles in boiling water rather than using disposable ones and rates of HIV infection are very high in Thailand.

General ทั่วไป

Can you get me a doctor?	ช่วยตามหมอมาให้หน่อย ได้ไหม?	chûay (d)tarm mŏr mar hâi nòy dâi măi
Where can I find a doctor who speaks English?	ผมจะหาหมอที่พูดภาษา อังกฤษได้ที่ไหน?	pŏm ja hăr mŏr têe pôot par săr ang grìt dâi têe năi
Where's the surgery (doctor's office)?	คลีนิคหมออยู่ที่ไหน?	klee ník mŏr yòo têe năi
What are the surgery (office) hours?	เวลาทำการของคลีนิค หมอกี่โมงถึงกี่โมง?	wey lar tam garn kŏrng klee ník mŏr gèe moeng tĕuhng gèe moeng
Could the doctor come to see me here?	ให้หมอมาที่นี่ได้ไหม?	hâi mŏr mar têe nêe dâi măi
What time can the doctor come?	หมอจะมาได้กี่โมง?	mŏr ja mar dâi gèe moeng
Can you recommend a/an...?	คุณช่วยแนะนำ ...ให้หน่อยได้ไหม?	kun chûay náih nam...hâi nòy dâi măi
general practitioner	หมอ/แพทย์	mŏr/pâirt
children's doctor	กุมารแพทย์	gu marn a pâirt
eye specialist	จักษุแพทย์	jàk sù pâirt
gynaecologist	นรีแพทย์	na ree pâirt
Can I have an appointment...?	ขอนัด...ได้ไหม?	kŏr nát...dâi măi
tomorrow	พรุ่งนี้	prûng née
as soon as possible	เร็วที่สุดเท่าที่จะเร็วได้	rehw têe sùt tôw têe ja rehw dâi

CHEMIST'S, see page 107

138

Parts of the body ส่วนต่างๆของร่างกาย

appendix	ไส้ติ่ง	sâi (d)ting
arm	แขน	kǎirn
back	หลัง	lǎng
bladder	กระเพาะปัสสาวะ	gra po (b)pàt sǎr wá
bone	กระดูก	gra dòok
bowel	ภายในของท้อง	pai nai chông tórng
breast	หน้าอก	nâr òk
chest	หน้าอก	nâr òk
ear	หู	hǒo
eye(s)	ตา	(d)tar
face	หน้า	nâr
finger	นิ้ว	níw
foot	เท้า	tów
genitals	อวัยวะเพศ	a way a wá péyt
gland	ตอม	(d)tòrm
hand	มือ	meur
head	หัว	hǔa
heart	หัวใจ	hǔa jai
jaw	ขากรรไกร	kǎr gan grai
joint	ข้อต่อ	kôr (d)tòr
kidney	ไต	(d)tai
knee	เข่า	kòw
leg	ขา	kǎr
ligament	เอ็น	ehn
lip	ริมฝีปาก	rim fěe (b)pàrk
liver	ตับ	(d)tàp
lung	ปอด	(b)pòrt
mouth	ปาก	(b)pàrk
muscle	กล้ามเนื้อ	glârm néua
neck	คอ	kor
nerve	เส้นประสาท	sêhn (b)pra sàrt
nose	จมูก	ja mòok
rib	ซี่โครง	sêe kroeng
shoulder	ไหล่	lài
skin	ผิวหนัง	pǐw nǎng
spine	กระดูกสันหลัง	gra dòok sǎn lǎng
stomach	ท้อง	tórng
tendon	เอ็นในร่างกาย	ehn nai rârng gai
thigh	ต้นขา/ ขาอ่อน	(d)tôn kǎr/kǎr òrn
throat	ลำคอ	lam kor
thumb	นิ้วหัวแม่มือ	níw hǔa mâir meur
toe	นิ้วเท้า	níw tów
tongue	ลิ้น	lín
tonsils	ตอมทอนซิล	(d)tòrm torn sin
vein	เส้นเลือด	sêhn lêuat

Accident—Injury อุบัติเหตุ บาดเจ็บ

There's been an accident.	เกิดอุบัติเหตุ	gèrt u bàt (d)tì hêyt
My child has had a fall.	ลูกผม(ดิฉัน)ตกจากที่สูง/หกล้ม	lôok pŏm (di chán) (d)tòk jàrk têe sŏong/hòk lóm
He/She has hurt his/her head.	เขา/เธอได้รับบาดเจ็บที่หัว	kŏw/ter dâi ráp bàrt jèhp têe hŭa
He's/She's unconscious.	เขา/เธอหมดสติ	ków/ter mòt sa (d)tì
He's/She's bleeding (heavily).	เลือดเขา/เธอออก(มาก)	lêuat kŏw/ter òrk (mârk)
He's/She's (seriously) injured.	เขา/เธอได้รับบาดเจ็บ(ร้ายแรง)	kŏw/ter dâi ráp bàrt jèhp (rái rairng)
His/Her arm is broken.	แขนเขา/เธอหัก	kăirn kŏw/ter hàk
His/Her ankle is swollen.	ข้อเท้าเขา/เธอบวม	kôr tów kŏw/ter buam
I've been stung.	ผม(ดิฉัน)ถูกแมลงต่อย	pŏm (di chán) tòok ma lairng (d)tòy
I've got something in my eye.	มีอะไรเข้าไปในตาของผม(ดิฉัน)	mee arai kôw (b)pai nai (d)tar kôrng pŏm (di chán)
I've got a/an...	ผม(ดิฉัน)มีปัญหา...	pŏm (di chán) mee (b)pan hăr
boil	ถูกน้ำร้อนลวก	tòok nárm rórn lûak
bruise	เป็นรอยช้ำ	(b)pehn roy chám
burn	ถูกไฟไหม้	tòok fai mâi
cut	ถูกมีดบาด	tòok mêet bàrt
graze	เป็นแผลถลอก	(b)pehn plăir ta lòrk
insect bite	ถูกแมลงต่อย	tòok ma lairng (d)tòy
lump	บวม/ใน	buam/noe
rash	เป็นผื่นคัน	(b)pehn pèurn kan
sting	ถูกแมลงต่อย	tòok ma lairng (d)tòy
swelling	บวม	buam
wound	ได้รับบาดเจ็บ	dâi ráp bàrt jèhp
Could you have a look at it?	ช่วยดูให้หน่อยได้ไหม?	chûay doo hâi nòy dâi măi
I can't move my ...	ผม(ดิฉัน)ขยับ...ไม่ได้	pŏm (di chán) ka yàp...mâi dâi
It hurts.	มันเจ็บ	man jèhp

เจ็บตรงไหน?	Where does it hurt?
เจ็บแบบไหน?	What kind of pain is it?
เจ็บไม่มาก/แปลบ/ตุ๊บๆ	dull/sharp/throbbing
ตลอดเวลา/เป็นๆ หายๆ	constant/on and off
มัน...	It's...
หัก/เคล็ด	broken/sprained
เคลื่อน/ฉีก	dislocated/torn
ผม(ดิฉัน)อยากให้คุณ ฉายเอ็กซเรย์	I'd like you to have an X-ray.
เราจะต้องใส่เฝือก	We'll have to put it in plaster.
มันติดเชื้อ	It's infected.
คุณได้ฉีดวัคซีนป้องกัน บาดทะยักหรือเปล่า?	Have you been vaccinated against tetanus?
ผม(ดิฉัน)จะให้ยาแก้ปวดคุณ	I'll give you a painkiller.

Illness เจ็บป่วย

I'm ill.	ผม(ดิฉัน)ไม่สบาย	pŏm (di chán) mâi sabay
I feel...	ผม(ดิฉัน)รู้สึก...	pŏm (di chán) róo sèuhk
dizzy	เวียนศีรษะ	wearn sĕe sà
nauseous	คลื่นไส้	klêurn sâi
shivery	หนาวสั่น	nŏw sàn
I have a temperature (fever).	เป็นไข้	(b)pehn kâi
My temperature is 38 degrees.	อุณหภูมิของผมสูง ๓๘ องศา	un a poom kŏrng pŏm sŏong sǎrm sìp (b)pàirt ong sǎr
I've been vomiting.	ผม(ดิฉัน)เพิ่งอาเจียนมา	pŏm (di chán) pêuhng ar jearn mar
I'm constipated/ I've got diarrhoea.	ผม(ดิฉัน) มีอาการท้องผูก/ ผม(ดิฉัน)มีอาการท้องร่วง	pŏm (di chán) mee ar gàrn tórng pòok/pŏm (di chán) mee ar gàrn tórng rûang
My ... hurt(s).	...ของผม(ดิฉัน)เจ็บ	... kŏrng pŏm (di chán) jèhp

I've got (a/an) …	ผม(ดิฉัน)เป็น…	pŏm (di chán) (b)pehn
asthma	เป็นโรคหืด	(b)pehn rôek hèurt
backache	เป็นโรคปวดหลัง	(b)pehn rôek (b)pùat lăng
cold	เป็นหวัด	(b)pehn wàt
cough	ไอ	ai
cramps	เป็นตะคริว	(b)pehn (d)ta kriw
earache	ปวดหู	(b)pùat hŏo
hay fever	แพ้อากาศ	páir ar gàrt
headache	ปวดหัว	(b)pùat hŭa
indigestion	ท้องผูก	tórng pòok
nosebleed	เลือดกำเดาไหล	lêuat gam dow lăi
palpitations	ใจสั่น	jai sàn
rheumatism	เป็นโรคปวดในข้อ	(b)pehn rôek (b)pùat nai kôr
sore throat	เจ็บคอ	jèhp kor
stiff neck	คอแข็ง	kor kăihng
stomach ache	ปวดท้อง	(b)pùat tórng
sunstroke	เป็นลมแดด	(b)pehn lom dàirt
I have difficulties breathing.	หายใจขัดๆ	hăi jai kàt kàt
I have chest pains.	เจ็บที่หน้าอก	jèhp têe nâr òk
My blood pressure is …	ความดันโลหิตของ ผม(ดิฉัน)…	kwarm dan loe hìt kŏrng pŏm (di chán)
too high/too low	สูงเกินไป/ต่ำเกินไป	sŏong gern (b)pai/(d)tàm gern (b)pai
I'm allergic to …	ผม(ดิฉัน)แพ้…	pŏm (di chán) páir
I'm diabetic.	ผม(ดิฉัน)เป็นโรค เบาหวาน	pŏm (di chán) (b)pehn rôek bow wărn

Women's section ส่วนที่เกี่ยวกับผู้หญิง

I have period pains.	ดิฉันปวดประจำเดือน	di chán (b)pùat (b)pra jam deuan
I have a vaginal infection.	ดิฉันติดเชื้อที่อวัยวะเพศ	di chán (d)tit chéua têe a way ya wá péyt
I'm on the pill.	ดิฉันกินยาคุมอยู่	di chán gin yar kum yòo
I haven't had a period for 2 months.	ประจำเดือนของดิฉัน ไม่มาสองเดือนแล้ว	(b)pra jam deuan kŏrng di chán mâi mar sŏrng deuan láiw
I'm (3 months') pregnant.	ดิฉันตั้งท้อง(สามเดือน) แล้ว	di chán (d)tâng tórng (sărm deuan) láiw

☞ 🔙

คุณรู้สึกอย่างนี้ มานานเท่าไหร่แล้ว?	How long have you been feeling like this?
นี่เป็นครั้งแรกหรือเปล่า ที่คุณเป็นโรคนี้?	Is this the first time you've had this?
ผม(ดิฉัน)จะวัดอุณหภูมิ/ ความดันดูหน่อย	I'll take your temperature/ blood pressure.
ถลกแขนเสื้อขึ้นหน่อย	Roll up your sleeve, please.
ช่วยถอดเสื้อออกด้วย	Please undress (down to the waist).
ช่วยนอนราบลงตรงนั้นด้วย	Please lie down over here.
อ้าปากหน่อย	Open your mouth.
หายใจลึกๆ	Breathe deeply.
ไอให้ฟังหน่อย	Cough, please.
เจ็บที่ตรงไหน?	Where does it hurt?
คุณเป็น...	You've got (a/an) ...
โรคไส้ติ่งอักเสบ	appendicitis
กระเพาะปัสสาวะอักเสบ	cystitis
โรคกระเพาะอักเสบ	gastritis
ไข้	flu
...อักเสบ	inflammation of...
อาหารเป็นพิษ	food poisoning
โรคดีซ่าน	jaundice
กามโรค	venereal disease
ปอดบวม	pneumonia
โรคหัด	measles
มัน(ไม่)เป็นโรคติดต่อ	It's (not) contagious.
มันเป็นโรคภูมิแพ้	It's an allergy.
ผม(ดิฉัน)จะ ฉีดยาให้เข็มหนึ่ง	I'll give you an injection.
ผมอยากได้ตัวอย่างเลือด/ อุจจาระ/ ปัสสาวะของคุณ	I want a specimen of your blood/stools/urine.
คุณจะต้องนอนพักสัก ...วัน	You must stay in bed for... days.
ผม(ดิฉัน)อยากให้คุณไปโรงพย าบาลเพื่อตรวจเช็คร่างกาย	I want you to go to the hospital for a general check-up.

Prescription—Treatment ใบสั่งยา การรักษา

This is my usual medicine.	นี่เป็นยาที่ผม(ดิฉัน)กินเป็นประจำ	nêe (b)pehn yar têe pŏm (di chán) gin (b)pehn (b)pra jam
Can you give me a prescription for this?	ช่วยเขียนใบสั่งยาตัวนี้ให้ผม(ดิฉัน)หน่อยได้ไหม?	chûay kěarn bai sàng yar (d)tua née hâi pŏm (di chán) nòy dâi mǎi
Can you prescribe a/an/some...?	ช่วยสั่ง...ให้หน่อยได้ไหม?	chûay sàng...hâi nòy dâi mǎi
antidepressant	ยาบรรเทาอาการหดหู่	yar ban tow ar garn hòt hòo
sleeping pills	ยานอนหลับ	yar norn làp
tranquillizer	ยากล่อมประสาท	yar glòm (b)pra sàrt
Are you using a sterilized needle?	คุณใช้เข็มฉีดยาที่ฆ่าเชื้อหรือเปล่า	kun chái kěm chèet yar têe kâr chéua rěua (b)plòw
I'm allergic to...	ผม(ดิฉัน)แพ้...	pŏm (di chán) páir
certain antibiotics/penicillin	ยาปฏิชีวนะบางตัว/เพนนีซิลิน	yar (b)pa (d)tí chi wa ná barng (d)tua/peyn ni si lin
How many times a day should I take it?	ต้องกินวันละกี่ครั้ง?	(d)tôrng gin wan lá gèe kráng

ตอนนี้คุณกินยาอะไรอยู่?	What medicine are you taking?
ฉีดหรือกิน?	By injection or orally?
กินยานี้...ช้อนชา	Take... teaspoons of this medicine...
กินยานี้หนึ่งเม็ดกับน้ำแก้วหนึ่ง	Take one pill with a glass of water...
ทุก...ชั่วโมง	every... hours
วันละ...ครั้ง	... times a day
ก่อน/หลังอาหาร	before/after each meal
ตอนเช้า/ตอนกลางคืน	in the morning/at night
ถ้ามีอาการเจ็บ	if there is any pain
เป็นเวลา...วัน	for... days

CHEMIST'S, see page 107

144

Fee ค่ารักษา

How much do I owe you?	เท่าไหร่?	tôw rài
May I have a receipt for my health insurance?	ขอใบเสร็จรับเงินไปให้ประกันสุขภาพด้วยได้ไหม?	kŏr bai sèht ráp ngern (b)pai hâi (b)pra gan sùk ka pârp dâi mǎi
Can I have a medical certificate?	ขอใบรับรองแพทย์หน่อยได้ไหม?	kŏr bai ráp rorng pâirt nòy dâi mǎi
Would you fill in this health insurance form, please?	ช่วยกรอกแบบฟอร์มประกันสุขภาพนี้ด้วยได้ไหม?	chûay gròrk bairp form (b)pra gan sùk ka pârp née dûay dâi mǎi

Hospital โรงพยาบาล

Please notify my family.	ช่วยแจ้งให้ครอบครัวของผม(ดิฉัน)ทราบด้วย	chûay jâirng hâi krôrp krua kŏrng pŏm (di chán) sârp dûay
What are the visiting hours?	เวลาเปิดทำการจากกี่โมงถึงกี่โมง?	wey lar (b)pèrt tam garn jàrk gèe moeng těung gèe moeng
When can I get up?	เมื่อไหร่ผม(ดิฉัน)ถึงจะลุกได้?	mêua rài pŏm (di chán) těuhng ja lúk dâi
When will the doctor come?	คุณหมอจะมาเมื่อไหร่?	kun mŏr ja mar mêua rài
I'm in pain.	ผม(ดิฉัน)รู้สึกปวดมาก	pŏm (di chán) róo sèuhk (b)pùat mârk
I can't eat/sleep.	ผม(ดิฉัน)กินไม่ได้/นอนไม่หลับ	pŏm (di chán) gin mái dâi/norn mâi làp
Where is the bell?	กระดิ่งอยู่ที่ไหน?	gra dìng yòo têe nǎi

nurse	พยาบาล	pa yar barn
patient	คนไข้	kon kâi
anaesthetic	ยาๆ	yar char
blood transfusion	การถ่ายเลือด	garn tài lêuat
injection	ฉีดยา	chèet yar
operation	ผ่าตัด	pàr (d)tàt
bed	เตียง	(d)tearng
bedpan	กระโถนปัสสาวะ	gra tǒen (b)pàt sǎr wá
thermometer	ปรอท	(b)pròrt

Dentist *หมอฟัน/ ทันตแพทย์*

Dental treatment is available on a private basis either at dental clinics or in hospitals. Costs vary according to the standard of clinic attended. Again, be wary of inadequately sterilized dental equipment.

Can you recommend a good dentist?	ช่วยแนะนำหมอฟันดีๆ	chûay náih nam mŏr fan dee dee
Can I make an (urgent) appointment to see Dr...?	ขอนัดเจอหมอ... (เป็นการด่วน)ได้ไหม?	kŏr nát jer mŏr... ((b)pehn garn dùan) dâi măi
Couldn't you make it earlier?	นัดเร็วกว่านี้หน่อย ได้ไหม?	nát rehw gwar née dâi mâi
I have a broken tooth.	ฟันผม(ดิฉัน)หัก	fan pŏm (di chán) hàk
I have toothache.	ผม(ดิฉัน)ปวดฟัน	pŏm (di chán) (b)pùat fan
I have an abscess.	ผม(ดิฉัน)เป็นหนอง	pŏm (di chán) (b)pehn nŏrng
This tooth hurts.	ปวดฟันซี่นี้	(b)pùat fan sêe née
at the top	ด้านบน	dârn bon
at the bottom	ด้านล่าง	dârn lârng
at the front	ด้านหน้า	dârn nâr
at the back	หน้าหลัง	nâr lăng
Can you fix it temporarily?	ช่วยอุดชั่วคราวได้ไหม?	chûay ùt chûa krow dâi mâi
I don't want it pulled out.	ผม(ดิฉัน)ไม่อยากให้ถอน	pŏm (di chán) mâi yàrk hâi tŏrn
Could you give me an anaesthetic?	ช่วยให้ยาชาผม (ดิฉัน)ได้ไหม?	chûay hâi yar char pŏm (di chán) dâi mâi
I've lost a filling.	ที่อุดหลุดหายไป	têe ùt lùt hăi (b)pai
My gums...	เหงือกผม(ดิฉัน)...	ngèuak pŏm (di chán)
are very sore	ปวดมาก	(b)pùat mârk
are bleeding	เลือดไหล	lêuat lăi
I've broken my dentures.	ฟันปลอมของผม(ดิฉัน)หัก	fan (b)plorm kŏrng pŏm (di chán) hàk
Can you repair my dentures?	ช่วยซ่อมฟันปลอม ของผม(ดิฉัน) หน่อยได้ไหม?	chûay sôrm fan (b)plorm kŏrng pŏm (di chán) nòy dâi mâi
When will they be ready?	จะเสร็จเมื่อไหร่?	ja sèht mêua rài

Reference section

Where do you come from? คุณมาจากไหน?

Africa	อาฟริกา	ar fri gar
Asia	เอเชีย	ey sear
Australia	ออสเตรเลีย	or sa (d)trey lear
Europe	ยุโรป	yu roep
North America	อเมริกาเหนือ	a mey rí gar něua
South America	อเมริกาใต้	a mey rí gar (d)tâi
Austria	ออสเตรีย	òrt sa (d)trear
Belgium	เบลเยี่ยม	ben yêarm
Canada	แคนาดา	kair nar dar
China	จีน	jeen
Denmark	เดนมาร์ก	deyn mârk
England	อังกฤษ	ang grìt
Finland	ฟินแลนด์	fin lairn
France	ฝรั่งเศส	fa ràng sèyt
Germany	เยอรมันนี	yer ra man nee
Great Britain	อังกฤษ/ สหราชอาณาจักร	ang grìt/sa hăr rârt cha ar nar jàk
Greece	กรีซ	grèek
India	อินเดีย	in dear
Indonesia	อินโดนีเซีย	in doe nee sear
Ireland	ไอรแลนด์	ai lairn
Israel	อิสราเอล	ìt sa rar eyn
Italy	อิตาลี	ìt (d)tar lee
Japan	ญี่ปุ่น	yêe (b)pùn
Laos	ลาว	low
Luxembourg	ลักเซมเบิร์ก	lák seym bèrk
Myanmar	พมา	pa mâr
Netherlands	เนเธอรแลนด์	ney ter lairn
New Zealand	นิวซีแลนด์	niw see lairn
Norway	นอรเวย	nor wey
Philippines	ฟิลิปปินส	fi li peen
Portugal	โปรตุเกส	(b)poer (d)tù gèyt
Russia	รัสเซีย	rát sear
Scotland	สกอตแลนด์	sa gót lairn
South Africa	อาฟริกาใต้	ar frík gar (d)tâi
Spain	สเปน	sa (b)peyn
Sweden	สวีเดน	sa wěe deyn
Switzerland	สวิสเซอรแลนด์	sa wít ser lairn
Thailand	ไทย	tai
United States	สหรัฐ	sa hăr rát
Vietnam	เวียดนาม	wêart narm
Wales	เวลส	weyl

Numbers *ตัวเลข*

0	๐	sŏon
1	๑	nèuhng
2	๒	sŏrng
3	๓	sǎrm
4	๔	sèe
5	๕	hâr
6	๖	hòk
7	๗	jèht
8	๘	(b)pàirt
9	๙	gôw
10	๑๐	sìp
11	๑๑	sìp èht
12	๑๒	sìp sŏrng
13	๑๓	sìp sǎrm
14	๑๔	sìp sèe
15	๑๕	sìp hâr
16	๑๖	sìp hòk
17	๑๗	sìp jèht
18	๑๘	sìp (b)pàirt
19	๑๙	sìp gôw
20	๒๐	yêe sìp
21	๒๑	yêe sìp èht
22	๒๒	yêe sìp sŏrng
23	๒๓	yêe sìp sǎrm
24	๒๔	yêe sìp sèe
25	๒๕	yêe sìp hâr
26	๒๖	yêe sìp hòk
27	๒๗	yêe sìp jèht
28	๒๘	yêe sìp (b)pàirt
29	๒๙	yêe sìp gôw
30	๓๐	sǎrm sìp
31	๓๑	sǎrm sìp èht
32	๓๒	sǎrm sìp sŏrng
33	๓๓	sǎrm sìp sǎrm
40	๔๐	sèe sìp
41	๔๑	sèe sìp èht
42	๔๒	sèe sìp sŏrng
43	๔๓	sèe sìp sǎrm
50	๕๐	hâr sìp
51	๕๑	hâr sìp èht
52	๕๒	hâr sìp sŏrng
53	๕๓	hâr sìp sǎrm
60	๖๐	hòk sìp
61	๖๑	hòk sìp èht
62	๖๒	hòk sìp sŏrng

REFERENCE SECTION

63	๖๓	hòk sìp sǎrm
70	๗๐	jèht sìp
71	๗๑	jèht sìp èht
72	๗๒	jèht sìp sǒrng
73	๗๓	jèht sìp sǎrm
80	๘๐	(b)pàirt sìp
81	๘๑	(b)pàirt sìp èht
82	๘๒	(b)pàirt sìp sǒrng
83	๘๓	(b)pàirt sìp sǎrm
90	๙๐	gôw sìp
91	๙๑	gôw sìp èyt
92	๙๒	gôw sìp sǒrng
93	๙๓	gôw sìp sǎrm
100	๑๐๐	róy
101	๑๐๑	róy èht
102	๑๐๒	róy sǒrng
110	๑๑๐	róy sìp
120	๑๒๐	róy yêe sìp
130	๑๓๐	róy sǎrm sìp
140	๑๔๐	róy sèe sìp
150	๑๕๐	róy hâr sìp
160	๑๖๐	róy hòk sìp
170	๑๗๐	róy jèht sìp
180	๑๘๐	róy (b)pàirt sìp
190	๑๙๐	róy gôw sìp
200	๒๐๐	sǒrng róy
300	๓๐๐	sǎrm róy
400	๔๐๐	sèe róy
500	๕๐๐	hâr róy
600	๖๐๐	hòk róy
700	๗๐๐	jèyt róy
800	๘๐๐	(b)pàirt róy
900	๙๐๐	gôw róy
1000	๑๐๐๐	pan
1100	๑๑๐๐	pan nèuhng róy
1200	๑๒๐๐	pan sǒrng róy
2000	๒๐๐๐	sǒrng pan
5000	๕๐๐๐	hâr pan
10,000	๑๐,๐๐๐	mèurn
50,000	๕๐,๐๐๐	hâr mèurn
100,000	๑๐๐,๐๐๐	sǎirn
1,000,000	๑,๐๐๐,๐๐๐	lárn

first	ที่หนึ่ง	têe nèuhng
second	ที่สอง	têe sŏrng
third	ที่สาม	têe sărm
fourth	ที่สี่	têe sèe
fifth	ที่ห้า	têe hâr
sixth	ที่หก	têe hòk
seventh	ที่เจ็ด	têe jèht
eighth	ที่แปด	têe (b)pàirt
ninth	ที่เก้า	têe gôw
tenth	ที่สิบ	têe sip

| once/twice | ครั้งหนึ่ง/สองครั้ง | kráng nèuhng/sŏrng kráng |
| three times | สามครั้ง | sărm kráng |

a half	ครึ่งหนึ่ง	krêuhng nèuhng
half a...	ครึ่ง...	krêuhng
half of...	ครึ่งหนึ่งของ...	krêuhng nèuhng kŏrng
half (adj.)	ครึ่ง	krêuhng
a quarter/one third	หนึ่งในสี่/หนึ่งในสาม	nèuhng nai sèe/nèuhng nai sărm

| a pair of | หนึ่งคู่ | nèuhng kôo |
| a dozen | หนึ่งโหล | nèuhng lŏe |

| one per cent | หนึ่งเปอร์เซนต์/ร้อยละหนึ่ง | nèuhng (b)per seyn/róy la nèuhng |
| 3.4% | ร้อยละ๓.๔ | róy la sărm jùt sèe |

Year and age ปีและอายุ

1981	๑๙๘๑	pan gôw róy jèht sìp èht
1993	๑๙๙๓	pan gôw róy gôw sìp sărm
2005	๒๐๐๕	sŏrng pan hâr
year	ปี	(b)pee

| leap year | ปีอธิกสุรทิน | (b)pee ar tí gà sù ra tin |

decade	ทศวรรษ	tót sa wát
century	ศตวรรษ	sà ta wát
this year	ปีนี้	(b)pee née
last year	ปีที่แล้ว	(b)pee têe láiw
next year	ปีหน้า	(b)pee nâr
each year	แต่ละปี	(d)tàir lá (b)pee

2 years ago	๒ปีที่แล้ว	sŏrng (b)pee têe láiw
in one year	ในหนึ่งปี	nai nèuhng (b)pee
in the eighties	ในทศวรรษที่ ๘๐	nai tót sa wát tée (b)pàirt sìp
in the 20th century	ในศตวรรษที่ ๒๐	sà ta wát têe yêe sìp

How old are you?	คุณอายุเท่าไหร่?	kun ar yú tôw rài
I'm 30 years old.	ผม(ดิฉัน)อายุ ๓๐ปี	pŏm (di chán) ar yú sǎrm sìp (b)pee
He/She was born in 1960.	เขาเกิดปี ๑๙๖๐	kǒw gèrt (b)pee pan gòw róy hòk sìp
What is his/her age?	เขาอายุเท่าไหร่?	kǒw ar yú tôw rài
Children under 16 are not admitted.	เด็กอายุต่ำกว่า ๑๖ปีห้ามเข้า	déhk ar yú (d)tàm gwàr sìp hòk (b)pee hârm kǒw

Seasons ฤดู/หน้า

spring/summer	ใบไม้ผลิ/ร้อน	bai mái plì/rórn
autumn/winter	ใบไม้รวง/หนาว	bai mái rûang/nǒw
in spring	ในฤดูใบไม้ผลิ	nai ri doo bai mái plì
during the summer	ในช่วงฤดูร้อน	nai chûang ri doo rórn
in autumn (fall)	ในฤดูใบไม้รวง	nai ri doo bai mái rûang
during the winter	ในช่วงฤดูหนาว	nai chûang ri doo nǒw
high season	ฤดูท่องเที่ยว	ri doo tông têaw
low season	นอกฤดูท่องเที่ยว	nôrk ri doo tông têaw

Months เดือน

January	มกราคม	mók ga rar kom
February	กุมภาพันธ์	gum par pan
March	มีนาคม	mee nar kom
April	เมษายน	mey sǎr yon
May	พฤษภาคม	prút sa pǎr kom
June	มิถุนายน	mí tu nar yon
July	กรกฎาคม	ga rák ga (d)tar kom
August	สิงหาคม	sǐng hǎr kom
September	กันยายน	kan yar yon
October	ตุลาคม	(d)tu lar kom
November	พฤศจิกายน	prút sa jìk gar yon
December	ธันวาคม	tan war kom
in September	ในเดือนกันยายน	nai deuan gan yar yon
since October	ตั้งแต่เดือนตุลาคม เป็นต้นมา	(d)tâng tàir deuan (d)tu lar kom (b)pehn (d)tôn mar
the beginning of January	ต้นเดือนมกราคม	(d)tôn deuan mók ga rar kom
the middle of February	กลางเดือนกุมภาพันธ์	glarng deuan gum par pan
the end of March	ปลายเดือนมีนาคม	(b)plai deuan mee nar kom

หมวดอ้างอิง

Days and date วันและ วันที่

What day is it today?	วันนี้วันอะไร?	wan née wan arai
Sunday	วันอาทิตย์	wan ar tìt
Monday	วันจันทร	wan jan
Tuesday	วันอังคาร	wan ang karn
Wednesday	วันพุธ	wan pút
Thursday	วันพฤหัสบดี	wan pá rú hàt
Friday	วันศุกร์	wan sùk
Saturday	วันเสาร์	wan sŏw
It's...	มันเป็น/ คือ...	man (b)pehn/keur
July 1	วันที่ ๑ กรกฎาคม	wan têe nèuhng ga rák ga (d)tar kom
March 10	วันที่ ๑๐ มีนาคม	wan têe sìp mee nar kom
in the morning	เวลาเช้า	wey lar chów
during the day	เวลากลางวัน	wey lar glarng wan
in the afternoon	เวลาบ่าย	wey lar bài
in the evening	เวลาเย็น	wey lar yehn
at night	เวลากลางคืน	wey lar glarng keurn
the day before yesterday	เมื่อวานซืน	mêua warn seurn
yesterday	เมื่อวาน	mêua warn
today	วันนี้	wan née
tomorrow	พรุ่งนี้	prûng née
the day after tomorrow	มะรืนนี้	ma reurn née
the day before	วันก่อน	wan gòrn
the next day	วันถัดไป	wan tàt (b)pai
two days ago	สองวันก่อน	sŏrng wan gòrn
in three days' time	ในอีกสามวันข้างหน้า	nai èek sărm wan kârng nâr
last week	อาทิตย์ที่แล้ว	ar tìt têe láiw
next week	อาทิตย์หน้า	ar tìt nâr
for a fortnight (two weeks)	เป็นเวลาสองอาทิตย์	(b)pehn wey lar sŏrng ar tìt
birthday	วันเกิด	wan gèrt
day off	วันหยุด	wan yùt
holiday	วันหยุดพักผ่อน	wan yùt pák pòrn
holidays/vacation	วันหยุดพักผ่อน	wan yùt pák pòrn
week	อาทิตย์/ สัปดาห์	ar tìt/sàp pa dar
weekend	สุดสัปดาห์	sùt sàp pa dar
working day	วันทำงาน	wan tam ngarn

Public holidays *วันหยุดประจำปี*

The dates for some public holidays differ each year since they are calculated by the lunar calendar. Although banks and government offices close on these days, shops remain open and public transport is unaffected. Chinese New Year, which is not a national holiday, does mean that many of the smaller shops close for two or three days, but department stores are largely unaffected.

วันขึ้นปีใหม่	wan kéuhn (b)pee mài	New Year's Day
วันจักรี	wanjàkgree	April 6, Chakri Day, in memory of Rama I
สงกรานต์	sŏng grarn	April 13–15, Songkran, or the traditional Thai New Year
วันแรงงาน	wan rairng ngarn	May 1, Labour Day
วันฉัตรมงคล	wan chàt mongkon	May 5, Coronation Day, in memory of the coronation in 1946 of the present king, Rama IX
วันเฉลิมพระชนมพรรษา สมเด็จพระบรมราชินีนาถ	wan chalĕrm práchanom pansăr	August 12, H.M. Queen's Birthday (Mother's Day)
วันปิยะมหาราช	wan (b)pee-yámahăr rârt	October 23, Chulalongkorn Day, in memory of King Rama V
วันเฉลิม พระชนมพรรษา พระบาทสมเด็จ พระเจ้าอยู่หัว	wan chalĕrm práchanom pansăr prábàrt sŏmdèht prá jôw yoo hŭa	December 5, H.M. King's Birthday (National Day)
วันรัฐธรรมนูญ	wan rát-tá-tam-má-noon	December 10, Constitution Day

Movable holidays

มาฆบูชา (marká boochar)	February, commemorating the day which the Buddha taught the key tenets of Buddhism. Thais celebrate this with a *wearn tearn* ceremony in which people walk round the temple chapel with lighted candles.
วิสาขบูชา (wisărkà boochar)	May, commemorating the Buddha's birth, enlightenment and death with a *wearn tearn* ceremony.
อาสาฬหบูชา (arsărláhà boochar)	July, commemorating the first sermon of the Buddha.
เข้าพรรษา (kôw pansăr)	Late July, the first day of Buddhist Lent and the time when Thai men traditionally become ordained as monks.
ลอยกระทง (loi gratong)	The Festival of Lights. Praise is given to the Goddess of the Waters, *mâir prá kongkăr*, in the form of banana leaf (or polystyrene) boats filled with flowers, incense and candles.

Greetings and wishes คำทักทายและอวยพร

Merry Christmas!	สุขสันต์วันคริสต์มาส!	sùk săn wan krít sa mârt
Happy New Year!	สวัสดีปีใหม่	sa wàt dee (b)pee mài
Happy birthday!	สุขสันต์วันเกิด	sùk săn wan gèrt
Best wishes!	โชคดี	chôek dee
Congratulations!	ขอแสดงความยินดีด้วย	kŏr sa dairng kwarm yin dee dûay
Good luck/ All the best!	โชคดี	chôek dee
Have a good trip!	เที่ยวให้สนุก	têaw hâi sa nùk
Have a good holiday!	พักผ่อนให้สนุก	pák pòrn hâi sa nùk
Best regards from …	ด้วยความปรารถนาดีจาก…	dûay kwarm (b)pràt ta năr dee jàrk
My regards to …	ฝากความคิดถึง/เคารพถึง…	fàrk kwarm kít tĕuhng/kow róp tĕuhng

REFERENCE SECTION

What time is it? ตอนนี้กี่โมง/เวลาเท่าไหร่?

Telling the time in Thai can be a complicated business. The twenty four hours of the day and night are divided into four six-hour time periods, as follows: midnight to 6am (ตี —(d) tee), 7am to 1pm (เช้า —chów), 1pm to 6pm(บ่าย —bai) and 7pm to midnight (ทุ่ม —tûm). Each time span begins again at one, so that 7am becomes not "seven hours morning" but '"one hour morning". The word "one" is often omitted.

Excuse me. Can you tell me the time?	ขอโทษ, ตอนนี้เวลา เท่าไหร่?	kŏr tôet (d)torn née wey lar tôw rài
It's...	ตอนนี้...	(d)torn née
five past one (13.05)	บ่ายโมงห้านาที	bài moeng hâr nar tee
ten past two (14.10)	บ่ายสองโมงสิบนาที	bài sŏrng moeng sìp nar tee
a quarter past three (15.15)	บ่ายสามโมงสิบห้านาที	bài sărm moeng sìp hâr nar tee
twenty past four (16.20)	บ่ายสี่โมงยี่สิบนาที	bài sèe moeng yêe sìp nar tee
twenty-five past five (17.25)	ห้าโมงยี่สิบห้านาที	hâr moeng yêe sìp hâr nar tee
half past six (18.30)	หกโมงครึ่ง	hòk moeng krêuhng
twenty-five to seven (18.35)	หกโมงสามสิบห้านาที	hòk moeng sărm sìp hâr nar tee
twenty to eight (19.40)	ทุ่มสี่สิบนาที	tûm sèe sìp nar tee
a quarter to nine (20.45)	สองทุ่มสี่สิบห้านาที	sŏrng tûm sèe sìp hâr nar tee
ten to ten (21.50)	สามทุ่มห้าสิบนาที	sărm tûm hâr sìp nar tee
five to eleven (22.55)	สี่ทุ่มห้าสิบห้านาที	sèe tûm hâr sìp hâr nar tee
twelve o'clock (noon/ midnight)	เที่ยงวัน/เที่ยงคืน	têarng wan/têarng keurn
in the morning	ตอนเช้า	(d)torn chów
in the afternoon	ตอนบ่าย	(d)torn bài
in the evening	ตอนเย็น	(d)torn yehn
The train leaves at...	รถไฟออกเวลา...	rót fai òrk wey lar
13.04 (1.04 p.m.)	บ่ายโมงสี่นาที	bài moeng sèe nar tee
0.40 (0.40 a.m.)	เที่ยงคืนสี่สิบนาที	têarng keurn sèe sìp nar tee
in five minutes	ในอีกห้านาทีข้างหน้า	nai èek hâr nar tee kârng nâr

ไทย/อังกฤษ

in a quarter of an hour	ในอีกสิบห้านาที	nai èek sìp hâr nar tee
half an hour ago	เมื่อครึ่งชั่วโมงที่แล้ว	mêua krèuhng chûa moeng têe láiw
about two hours	ประมาณสองชั่วโมง	(b)pra marn sŏrng chûa moeng
more than 10 minutes	กว่าสิบนาที	gwàr sìp nar tee
less than 30 seconds	ไม่ถึงสามสิบวินาที	mâi tĕuhng sărm sìp wí nar tee
The clock is fast/slow.	นาฬิกาเดินเร็วไป/ช้าไป	nar li gar dern rehw (b)pai/chár (b)pai

Common abbreviations *คำย่อที่พบเห็นบ่อยๆ*

พ.ศ.	พุทธศักราช	Buddhist Era*
ค.ศ.	คริสต์ศักราช	Christian Era, AD
กทม.	กรุงเทพมหานคร	Bangkok Metropolitan District
บขส.	บริษัทขนส่งจำกัด	The National Transport Company Limited
รฟท.	การรถไฟแห่งประเทศไทย	The National Railway of Thailand
ขสมก.	ขนส่งมวลชนกรุงเทพมหานคร	The Bangkok Metropolitan Public Transport Company
ก.ก.	กิโลกรัม	kilograms
ก.ม.	กิโลเมตร	kilometres
น.	นาฬิกา	o'clock
พ.ร.ก.	พระราชกำหนด	Decree
พ.ร.บ.	พระราชบัญญัติ	an Act of legislation
ด.ช.	เด็กชาย	boy
ด.ญ.	เด็กหญิง	girl
น.ส.	นางสาว	Miss
ดร.	ดอกเตอร์	Doctor of Philosophy
ส.ส.	สมาชิกสภาผู้แทนราษฎร	Member of Parliament
ครม.	คณะรัฐมนตรี	Cabinet

---

*The Thais count their years not from the birth of Christ but from the birth of the Buddha, 543 years earlier. They are consequently 543 years ahead of the West.

Signs and notices *เครื่องหมายและสัญญาณ*

ระวังสุนัขดุ	Beware of the dog
รับ-จ่ายเงิน	Cash desk
โปรดระวัง	Caution
อันตราย(แก่ชีวิต)	Danger (of death)
โปรดอย่าจอดรถขวางประตู	Do not block entrance
ห้ามรบกวน	Do not disturb
ห้ามจับ	Do not touch
ลง	Down
ทางออกฉุกเฉิน	Emergency exit
เข้ามาได้โดยไม่ต้องเคาะประตู	Enter without knocking
ทางเข้า	Entrance
ทางออก	Exit
ให้เช่า	For hire
สำหรับขาย	For sale
ห้าม...	... forbidden
เข้าฟรี	Free admittance
สุภาพบุรุษ/ชาย	Gentlemen
ร้อน	Hot
ขอมูล	Information
สุภาพสตรี/หญิง	Ladies
ลิฟท์	Lift
ห้ามเข้า	No admittance
ห้ามทิ้งขยะ	No littering
ห้ามสูบบุหรี่	No smoking
ไม่ว่าง	No vacancies
เปิด	Open
เต็ม/จองแล้ว	Occupied
เสีย	Out of order
โปรดกดกระดิ่ง	Please ring
โปรดรอ	Please wait
ถนนส่วนบุคคล	Private road
ดึง	Pull
ผลัก	Push
จอง	Reserved
ขาย/ลดราคา	Sale
ขายหมด	Sold out
ให้เช่า	To let
ห้ามบุกรุก	Trespassers will be prosecuted
ขึ้น	Up
ว่าง	Vacant
สีไม่แห้ง	Wet paint

Emergency ฉุกเฉิน

Call the police	ช่วยเรียกตำรวจให้หน่อย	chûay rêark (d)tam rûat hâi nòy
Consulate	กงสุล	gong sǔn
DANGER	อันตราย	an (d)ta rai
Embassy	สถานทูต	sa tǎrn tôot
FIRE	ไฟไหม้	fai mâi
Gas	กาซ	gárt
Get a doctor	เรียกหมอให้หน่อย	rêark mǒr hâi nòy
Go away	ไปให้พ้น	(b)pai hâi pón
HELP	ช่วยด้วย	chûay dûay
Get help quickly	หาคนมาช่วยเร็วเข้า	hǎr kon mar chûay rehw kôw
I'm ill	ผม(ดิฉัน)ป่วย	pǒm (di chán) (b)pùay
I'm lost	ผม(ดิฉัน)หลงทาง	pǒm (di chán) lǒng tarng
LOOK OUT	ระวัง	ra wang
Poison	ยาพิษ	yar pít
POLICE	ตำรวจ	(d)tam rûat
Stop that man/ woman	ช่วยหยุดคนนั้นด้วย	chûay yùt kon nán dûay

Emergency telephone numbers หมายเลขโทรศัพท์ฉุกเฉิน

The all purpose emergency telephone number is 191. Hospitals and many clinics are open for emergencies 24 hours a day.

Lost property—Theft ของหาย ขโมย

Where's the ...?	...อยู่ที่ไหน?	... yòo têe nǎi
lost property (lost and found) office	ฝ่ายจัดการเรื่องของหาย	fài jàt garn rêuang kòrng hǎi
police station	สถานีตำรวจ	sa tǎr nee (d)tam rûat
I want to report a theft.	ผม(ดิฉัน)จะ ขอแจ้งความเรื่องขโมย	pǒm (di chán) ja kǒr jâirng kwarm rêuang ka moey
My ... has been stolen.	...ของผม(ดิฉัน)ถูกขโมย	... kòrng pǒm (di chán) tòok ka moey
I've lost my ...	...ของผม(ดิฉัน)หาย	... kòrng pom (di chán) hǎi
handbag	กระเป๋ามือถือ	gra (b)pǒw meur těur
passport	หนังสือเดินทาง	nǎng sěur dern tarng
wallet	กระเป๋าใส่เงิน	gra (b)pǒw sài ngern

CAR ACCIDENTS, see page 78

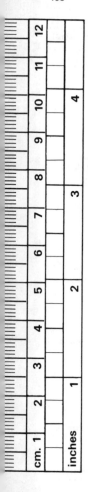

Conversion tables

Centimetres and inches

To change centimetres into inches, multiply by .39.

To change inches into centimetres, multiply by 2.54.

	in.	feet	yards
1 mm	0.039	0.003	0.001
1 cm	0.39	0.03	0.01
1 dm	3.94	0.32	0.10
1 m	39.40	3.28	1.09

	mm	cm	m
1 in.	25.4	2.54	0.025
1 ft.	304.8	30.48	0.304
1 yd.	914.4	91.44	0.914

(32 metres = 35 yards)

Temperature

To convert Centigrade into degrees Fahrenheit, multiply Centigrade by 1.8 and add 32.

To convert degrees Fahrenheit into Centigrade, subtract 32 from Fahrenheit and divide by 1.8.

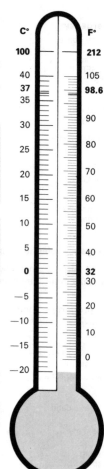

Kilometres into miles

1 kilometre (km.) = 0.62 miles

km.	10	20	30	40	50	60	70	80	90	100	110	120	130
miles	6	12	19	25	31	37	44	50	56	62	68	75	81

Miles into kilometres

1 mile = 1.609 kilometres (km.)

miles	10	20	30	40	50	60	70	80	90	100
km.	16	32	48	64	80	97	113	129	145	161

Fluid measures

1 litre (l.) = 0.88 imp. quart or 1.06 U.S. quart
1 imp. quart = 1.14 l.   1 U.S. quart = 0.95 l.
1 imp. gallon = 4.55 l.   1 U.S. gallon = 3.8 l.

litres	5	10	15	20	25	30	35	40	45	50
imp. gal.	1.1	2.2	3.3	4.4	5.5	6.6	7.7	8.8	9.9	11.0
U.S. gal.	1.3	2.6	3.9	5.2	6.5	7.8	9.1	10.4	11.7	13.0

Weights and measures

1 kilogram or kilo (kg.) = 1000 grams (g.)

100 g. = 3.5 oz.   ½ kg. = 1.1 lb.
200 g. = 7.0 oz.   1 kg. = 2.2 lb.
1 oz. = 28.35 g.
1 lb. = 453.60 g.

A very basic grammar

At first sight Thai appears to have very little in the way of strict grammar rules and it certainly cannot be explained in the terms we might use for European languages. There are no declensions of nouns or conjugations of verbs to remember and the simplest of rules are used to create past and future tenses. This can give the initial impression of Thai being a very simple language but the fact that sentences are structured in such a different way from English, with very little to follow for actual grammar rules, can end up making it much more difficult.

Parts of speech are not nearly so clearly defined in Thai as they are in Western languages. Nevertheless, a few helpful indicators can be given with reference to nouns, verbs and adjectives.

Nouns

There is no word for *the* or *a* in Thai so the word หมอ *(mŏr)*, for example, can mean "a doctor", "the doctor", "doctors" (in general) or "the doctors". The plural is *only* indicated when it is essential and not evident in the context. This can be done by the addition of the prefix พวก *(pûak)*, making พวกหมอ *(pûak mŏr)*. For example:

| หมอไปทำงานที่กรุงเทพฯ | *mŏr (b)pai tam ngarn têe grung têyp* | The doctor went to work in Bangkok |
| พวกหมอไปทำงานที่กรุงเทพฯ | *pûak mŏr (b)pai tamngarn têe grungtêyp* | The doctors went to work in Bangkok |

The second sentence above would only be used, if it was not obvious in the context that there was more than one doctor involved in going to work in Bangkok.

Adjectives

Adjectives always follow the noun. In order to say "the clever doctor", it is หมอฉลาด *(mŏr chalàrt)*. This phrase can also be a complete sentence, meaning "the doctor is clever". When adjectives are used with a noun the verb "to be" ((b)pehn) is dropped: Therefore:

| เขาฉลาด | ków chalàrt | He is clever. |

but

| เขาเป็นหมอ | ków (b)pehn mŏr | He is a doctor. |

Adjectives can be doubled for emphasis. Some adjectives lend themselves to this more readily than others. For example, ใกล้ (glâi) meaning "near" is often doubled to ใกล้ๆ (glâi glâi) meaning "quite near" or "close at hand", whereas ไกล (glai) meaning "far" is never doubled. Sometimes the tone changes on the first word of the pair double to give extra emphasis. For example,

| ซ้วยสวย | sùai suai | extremely beautiful |
| ว้านหวาน | wàrn warn | incredibly sweet |

Verbs

Verbs do not conjugate in Thai so whatever subject they are attached to they do not change in form.

The **past tense** can be indicated by the addition of either แล้ว (láiw—already) after the verb, or of ได้ (dâi—to get or receive) immediately in front of the verb. However, these are used only sparingly, and are not necessary if the past tense is implicit in the context. Sentences beginning with เมื่อ (mêua— when), for example, are automatically past tense.

The **future tense** is indicated by the addition of จะ (ja) immediately in front of the verb.
For example:

หมอไปทำงานแล้ว	mŏr (b)pai tam ngarn láiw	The doctor has gone to work (already).
หมอได้ไปทำงานที่ กรุงเทพฯ	mŏr dâi (b)pai tam ngarn têe grungtêyp	The doctor went to work in Bangkok.
หมอจะไปทำงาน ที่กรุงเทพฯ	mŏr ja (b)pai tam ngarn têe grungtêyp	The doctor will go to work in Bangkok.

Classifiers

Counting nouns is a rather complicated process and involves the use of noun "classifiers". Each noun has a "classifier", which is a term of measurement appropriate to the noun in question. The word คน (*kon*), for example, is used to classify all nouns referring to people.

When the number of a certain noun is to be specified, the word order is as follows: noun + number + classifier. For example, หมอห้าคน (*mŏr hâr kon*) would mean "five doctors". The only exception to this rule occurs with the number one, in which case the word order is noun + classifier + one, for example: หมอคนหนึ่ง (*mŏr kon nèuhng*—one doctor).

A list of useful classifiers is given below:

คน	*kon*	for people
ตัว	*tua*	for animals, tables, chairs and items of clothing
ลูก	*lôok*	for fruit and eggs
ชิ้น	*chín*	meaning a "piece" can be used for anything served/sold in pieces, for example cake, sweetmeats, paper
ใบ	*bai*	for fruit, paper and banknotes
ฉบับ	*chabàp*	for letters and newspapers
เล่ม	*lêhm*	for books

Portions of food and drink are classified according to the dishes in which they are served. Therefore fried rice would be classified by the word plate, coffee by cup, noodle soup by bowl and so forth:

ข้าวผัดจานหนึ่ง	*kôw pàt jarn nèuhng*	one plate of fried rice
กาแฟถ้วยหนึ่ง	*gar fair tûay nèuhng*	one cup of coffee
ก๋วยเตี๋ยวชามหนึ่ง	*guáy-těaw charm nèuhng*	one bowl of noodles

Questions and Answers

There are a number of ways of asking questions.

1. The words ใช่ไหม (*châi mǎi*) or หรือ (*rěua*) can be placed at the end of a phrase or sentence to verify that the statement made is true. For example:

คุณเป็นหมอ	*kun (b)pehn mǒr*	You are a doctor.
คุณเป็นหมอใช่ไหม	*kun (b)pehn mǒr châi mǎi*	You are a doctor, aren't you?

This kind of question is answered in the positive with ใช่ (*châi*) and in the negative with ไม่ใช่ (*mâi châi*). There is no single word for "yes" in Thai. The word for "no" is ไม่ (*mâi*).

2. Questions can also be asked by adding *mǎi* to the end of a phrase. For example:

คุณชอบอาหารไทยไหม	*kun chôrp ar hǎrn tai mǎi*	Do you like Thai food?

With this kind of verbal based question the verb is repeated in the answer. In the case of the example it is either ชอบ (*chôrp*) for a positive answer or ไม่ชอบ (*mâi chôrp*) for a negative response. The word ไม่ (*mâi*) is used directly in front of the verb to negate its meaning.

หมอทำงานไหม	*mǒr tam ngarn mǎi*	Does the doctor work?
ทำงาน	*tam ngarn*	Yes.
ไม่ทำงาน	*mâi tam ngarn*	No.
หมอไม่ทำงาน	*mǒr mâi tam ngarn*	The doctor does not work.
เขาทำงานที่กรุงเทพฯ ใช่ไหม	*kǒw tam ngarn têe grungtêyp châi mǎi*	He works in Bangkok, doesn't he?
ใช่ เขาทำงาน ที่กรุงเทพฯ	*châi kǒw tam ngarn têe grungtêyp*	Yes, he works in Bangkok.
ไม่ใช่ เขาไม่ทำงาน ที่กรุงเทพฯ เขาทำงานที่ลอนดอน	*mâi châi kǒw mâi tam ngarn têe grungtêyp kǒw tam ngarn têe lorndorn*	No, he doesn't work in Bangkok, he works in London.

หลักไวยากรณ์

Dictionary
and alphabetical index

English—Thai

A

abbreviation คำย่อ kam yôr 155
about *(approximately)* ประมาณ (b)pra marn 155
above บน bon 15
abscess ฝี fèe 145
absorbent cotton สำลี săm lee 108
accessories เครื่องประดับ krêuang (b)pra dàp 115, 125
accident อุบัติเหตุ u ba ti hèyt 79, 139
account บัญชี ban chee 130
ache ปวด (b)pùat 141
adaptor ปลั๊กแปลงไฟฟ้า (b)plàk (b)plairng fai fár 118
address ที่อยู่ têe yòo 21, 31, 77, 79, 102
address book สมุดจดที่อยู่ sa mùt jòt têe yòo 104
adhesive กาว gow 105
adhesive tape เทปกาว têyp gaw 104
admission ผ่านประตู pàrn (b)pra (d)too 82, 89
aeroplane เครื่องบิน krêuang bin 65
Africa อาฟริกา ar fri gar 146
after หลัง(จาก) lăng (jàrk) 15
after-shave lotion โลชั่นทาหลังโกนหนวด loe chăn tar lăng goen nùat 109
afternoon, in the ตอนบ่าย (d)torn bài 151; เวลาบ่าย wey lar bài 153
again อีกครั้ง èek kráng 96, 135
against ต่อต้าน (d)tòr (d)tărn 140
age อายุ ar yú 149
ago ที่แล้ว têe láiw 149
air bed ที่ปูนอน têe (b)poo norn 106
air conditioning แอร์ air 23, 28
air mattress ที่ปูนอน têe (b)poo norn 106
airmail จดหมายอากาศ jot măi ar gàrt 133
airport สนามบิน sa nărm bin 21, 65
aisle seat ที่นั่งติดทางเดิน têe nâng (d)tìt tarng dern 65
alarm clock นาฬิกาปลุก nar lí gar (b)plòok 121
alcohol อัลกอฮอล์ al gor horl 38, 60
alcoholic เกี่ยวกับอัลกอฮอล์ glaw gàp al

kor horl 60
allergic แพ้ páir 141, 143
almond อัลมอนด์ a la morn 56
alphabet อักษร ak kà rà 9
alter, to *(garment)* แก gâir 114
altitude sickness แพ้ความสูง páir kwarm sŏong 107
amazing น่าทึ่ง năr têuhng 84
amber อำพัน am pan 122
ambulance รถพยาบาล rót pa yar barn 79
American อเมริกัน a mey ri gan 93, 105, 126
American plan รวมอาหารทุกมื้อ ruam ar hărn túk méur 24
amethyst เขียวหนุมาน kĭaw ha nŭ marn 122
amount จำนวน jam nuan 131
amplifier เครื่องขยายเสียง krêuang ka yăi sĕarng 118
anaesthetic ยาชา yar char 144, 145
analgesic ยาแก้ปวด yar kăir (b)puat 108
Ancient City เมืองโบราณ meung borarn 81
and และ láih 15
animal สัตว์ sàt 85
aniseed โป๊ยกั๊ก (b)póey gák 55
ankle ข้อเท้า kôr tów 139
another อีก èek 60
answer ตอบ (d)tòrp 136
antibiotic ปฏิชีวนะ (b)pa (d)ti chee wa ná 143
antidepressant ยาบรรเทาอาการหดหู่ yar ban tao ar garn hòt hòo 143
antique shop ร้านขายของโบราณ rárn kăi kŏrng boe rarn 98
antiques โบราณวัตถุ boe rarn wát tù 83
antiseptic cream ครีมแกล้งเสบ kreem gâir àk sèyp 108
anyone ใคร krai 11, 17
anything อะไร arai 18, 24, 25, 101, 112
anywhere ที่ไหน têe năi 90
apartment อพาร์ตเมนต์ a part méhnt 23
appendicitis ไส้ติ่ง sâi (d)tìng 142

appetizer อาหารเรียกน้ำย่อย ar hărn rêark nárm yôi 42
apple แอปเปิ้ล áihp (b)pêrn 56, 64
appliance เครื่องใช้ krêuang chái 118
appointment นัดหมาย nát măi 131, 137, 145
April เมษายน mey sǎr yon 150
archaeology โบราณคดี boe rarn ka dee 83
architect สถาปนิก sa thǎr (b)pa ník 83
area code รหัสพื้นที่ ra hàt péurn têe 134
arm แขน kǎirn 138, 139
arrival ขาเข้า kǎr kâo 16, 66
arrive, to มาถึง ma těuhng 65, 69
art ศิลปะ sǐn la (b)pa 83
art gallery หอศิลป์ hǒr sǐn 81, 98
article มาตรา mar (d)tra 101
artificial light แสงเมธรรมชาติ sáirng mâi tam ma chârt 124
artist ศิลปิน sǐn la (b)pin 83
ashtray ที่เขี่ยบุหรี่ têe kear bu rèe 37
Asia เอเชีย ey sear 146
ask for, to ขอ kǒr 25
asparagus หน่อไม้ฝรั่ง nòr mái fa ràng 53
aspirin แอสไพริน àirt sa pai rin 108
asthma โรคหืด rôek hèurt 141
astringent ยาสมาน yar sa mǎrn 109
at ที่ têe 15
at least อย่างน้อย yàrng nói 24
aubergine มะเขือยาว ma kěua yow 53
August สิงหาคม sǐng hǎr kom 150
aunt ป้า (b)pâr 93
Australia ออสเตรเลีย òr sa (d)trey lear 146
Austria ออสเตรีย òrt sa (d)trear 146
automatic อัตโนมัติ àt noe mát 20, 122, 124
autumn ฤดูใบไม้ร่วง ri doo bai mái rûang 150
average เฉลี่ย cha lìa 91
awful แย่ yâir 84, 94

B

baby เด็กอ่อน dèhk òrn 24, 110
baby food อาหารเด็ก ar hărn dèhk 110
babysitter คนเลี้ยงเด็ก kon léang dèhk 27
back หลัง lǎng 138
back, to be/to get กลับมา glàp mar 21, 80
backache ปวดหลัง (b)pùat lǎng 141
backpack เป๋หลัง (b)pěy lǎng 106
bacon เบคอน bey korn 41
bacon and eggs เบคอนกับไข่ bey korn gàp kài 41
bad เลว lehw 14
bag กระเป๋า gra (b)pǒw 18
baggage check ตรวจกระเป๋า (d)trùat gra (b)pǒw 68, 71

baked อบ òp 46, 47
baker's ร้านขายขนมปัง rárn kǎi ka nǒm (b)pang 98
balance (finance) ดุล dun 131
balcony ระเบียง ra beang 23
ball (inflated) ลูกบอล lôok born 128
ball-point pen ปากกาลูกลื่น (b)pàrk gar lôok lêurn 104
ballet บัลเล่ต์ ban lêy 88
banana กล้วย glûay 56, 64
Band-Aid® พลาสเตอรปิดแผล plar sa (d)ter (b)pìt plǎir 108
bandage ผ้าพันแผล pâr pan plǎir 108
bangle กำไล gam lai 121
bangs ผมม้า pom mâr 30
bank (finance) ธนาคาร ta nar karn 98, 129, 130
barber's ร้านตัดผม rárn (d)tàt pǒm 30, 98
basil โหระพา hǒe ra par 55
basketball บาสเก็ตบอล bàrt sa gèht born 90
bath อาบน้ำ àrp nárm 23, 25, 27
bath towel ผ้าขนหนู pâr kǒn nǒo 27
bathing cap หมวกคลุมผมอาบน้ำ mùak klum pǒm àrp nárm 115
bathing hut ที่อาบน้ำ têe àrp nárm 91
bathing suit ชุดอาบน้ำ chút àrp nárm 115
bathrobe เสื้อคลุมอาบน้ำ sêua klum àrp nárm 115
bathroom ห้องอาบน้ำ hôrng àrp nárm 27
battery แบตเตอรี่ bairt ter rêe 75, 78, 125; ถ่านไฟฉาย tàrn fai chǎi 118, 121
beach หาดทราย hàrt sai 90
beach ball ลูกบอลชายหาด lôok born chai hàrt 128
bean ถั่ว tùa 53
beard เครา krow 31
beautiful สวย sǔay 14, 84
beauty salon ห้องเสริมสวย rórng sěrm sǔay 30, 98
bed เตียง (d)tearng 24, 28, 142, 144
bed and breakfast ค่าที่พักและอาหารเช้า kâr têe pák láir ar hărn chów 24
bedpan กระโถนปัสสาวะ gra tǒen (b)pàt sa wá 144
beef เนื้อ néua 47
beer เบียร์ bear 59, 64
before (time) ก่อน gòrn 15
beginning เริ่มต้น rêrm (d)tôn 150
behind หลัง lǎng 15, 77
beige สีทราย sěe sai 112
Belgium เบลเยี่ยม ben yârm 146
bell (electric) กระดิ่งไฟฟ้า gra dìng fai fár 144
bellboy เด็กรับใช้ dèk ráp chái 26
below ต่ำกว่า, ใต้ (d)tàm gwàr, (d) tǎi 15
belt เข็มขัด kěhm kàt 116
bend (road) โค้ง kóeng 79

berth ที่นอน têe norn 70, 71
better ดีกว่า dee gwàr 14, 25, 101
between ระหว่าง ra wàrng 15
bicycle จักรยาน jàk ra yarn 74
big ใหญ่ yài 14, 101
bill ใบเสร็จ bai sèht 31, 63
bill (banknote) ธนบัตร ta na bàt 130
billion (Am.) พันล้าน pan lárn 148
binoculars กล้องสองทางไกล glông sòng tarng glai 123
bird นก nók 85
birth เกิด kèrt 25
birthday วันเกิด wan gèrt 151, 153
biscuit (Br.) ขนมปังกรอบ ka nŏm (b)pang gròrp 64
bitter ขม kŏm 62
black ดำ dam 112
black and white (film) ขาวดำ kŏw dam 124, 125
black coffee กาแฟดำ gar fair dam 41, 61
bladder กระเพาะปัสสาวะ gra po (b)pàt săr wa 138
blade ใบมีด bai mêet 109
blanket ผ้าห่ม pâr hòm 27
bleach กัดสีผม gàt sĕe pŏm 30
bleed, to เลือดออก lêuat òrk 139, 145
blind (window shade) มูลี่ môo lêe 29
blocked ตัน (d)tan 28
blood เลือด lêuat 142
blood pressure ความดันโลหิต kwarm dan loe hìt 141, 142
blood transfusion การถ่ายเลือด garn tài lêuat 144
blouse เสื้อผู้หญิง sêua pôo yĭng 115
blow-dry เป่า (b)pòw 30
blue น้ำเงิน nárm ngern 112
blusher รูจทาแก้ม rôot tar gâirm 109
boat เรือ reua 73, 74
bobby pin กิ๊บติดผม gíp (d)tìt pŏm 110
body รางกาย rárng gai 138
boiled egg ไข่ต้ม kài (d)tôm 41
bone กระดูก gra dòok 138
book หนังสือ năng sĕur 12, 104
booking office ที่ของตั๋วลวงหน้า têe jorng (d)tŭa lûang nâr 19, 67
bookshop ร้านหนังสือ rárn náng sĕur 98, 104
boot รองเท้าบูท rorng táw bóot 117
born เกิด gèrt 150
botanical gardens สวนพฤกษชาติ sŭan prúk sa chàrt 81
botany พฤกษศาสตร prúk sa sàrt 83
bottle ขวด kùat 17, 59
bottle-opener ที่เปิดขวด têe (b)pèrt kùat 120
bottom ด้านล่าง dârn lârng 145
bow tie หูกระต่าย hŏo gra (d)tai 115
bowel ภายในของท้อง pai nai chông tórng 138

box กล่อง glòng 120
boxing ชกมวย chók muay 90
boy เด็กชาย dèhk chai 111, 112, 128
boyfriend แฟนหนุ่ม fairn nùm 93
bra เสื้อยกทรง ,sêua yók song 115
bracelet สร้อยข้อมือ sôy kôr meur 121
braces (suspenders) สายโยงกางเกง săi yeong garng geyng 115
brake เบรก breyk 78
brake fluid น้ำมันเบรก nám man breyk 75
bread ขนมปัง ka nŏm (b)pang 37, 41, 64
break down, to เสีย sĕar 78
breakdown เสีย sĕar 78
breakdown van รถลาก rót lârk 79
breakfast อาหารเช้า ar hărn chów 24, 27, 35, 41
breast หน้าอก nâr òk 138
breathe, to หายใจ hăi jai 141, 142
bridge สะพาน sa parn 85
British อังกฤษ ang grìt 93
broken เสีย sĕar 118; หัก hàk 123, 139, 140
brooch เข็มกลัด kĕhm glàt 121
brother พี่ชายน้องชาย pêe chai nórng chai 93
brown น้ำตาล nárm (d)tarn 112
brush แปรงผม (b)prairng pŏm 110
bubble bath บับเบิลบาธ báp bêrl bàrt 109
bucket ถัง tăng 120, 128
buckle หัวเข็มขัด hŭa kĕhm kàt 116
Buddha image พระพุทธรูป prá pút tá rôop 127
build, to สร้าง sârng 83
building อาคาร ar karn 81, 83
bulb (light) หลอดไฟ lòrt fai 28, 76, 118
Burma (Myanmar) พม่า pa mâr 146
burn ไหม้ mâi 139
burn out, to (bulb) ไฟขาด fai kàrt 28
bus รถ rút 18, 19, 65, 72, 80
bus stop ป้าย(รถเมล์) (b)pâi (rót mey) 73
business ธุรกิจ tú ra gìt 16, 131
business class ชั้นธุรกิจ chán tú ra gìt 65
business district ย่านธุรกิจ yârn tú rá gìt 81
business trip ไปติดต่อธุระ (b)pai (d)tìt (d)tòr tú rá 94
busy ยุ่ง yûng 96
but แต่ (d)tàir 15
butane gas กาซบิวเทน gárt biw teyn 32, 106
butcher's ร้านขายเนื้อ rárn kăi néua 98
butter เนย noey 37, 41, 64
button กระดุมเสื้อ gra dum sêua 29, 116
buy, to ซื้อ séur 82, 100, 104

c

cabana ที่อาบน้ำ têe àrp nárm 91

cabbage กระหล่ำ gra làm 53

cabin (ship) ห้องนอนในเรือ hông norn nai reua 74

cable release สายกดชัตเตอร์ sǎi gòt chát (d)têr 125

cake ขนมเค้ก ka nŏm kéhk 38, 64

calendar ปฏิทิน pa tì tin 104

call (phone) โทรศัพท์ toe.ra sàp 136

call, to (give name) เรียกว่า rêark wâr 11; (phone) โทร toe 134, 136; (summon) เรียก rêark 79, 157

call back, to กลับไปใหม่ glàp (b)pai mài 136

calm สงบ ,sa ngòp 91

cambric ผ้าลินินขาว păr li nin kŏw 112

camel-hair ขนอูฐ kŏn òot 112

camera กล้องถ่ายรูป glôrng tài rôop 124, 125

camera case กระเป๋าใส่กล้อง gra (b)pŏw sài glôrng 125

camera shop ร้านขายกล้อง rárn kǎi glôrng 98

camp site ที่ตั้งแคมป์ têe (d)tăng káirm 32

camp, to ตั้งแคมป์ (d)tăng káirm 32

campbed เตียงสนาม (d)tearng sa nǎrm 106

camping แค้มปิ้ง káirm (b)pîng 32

camping equipment เครื่องมือแคมปิ้ง krêuang meur káirm (b)pîng 106

can (container) กระป๋อง gra (b)pŏng 120

can opener ที่เปิดกระป๋อง têe (b)pèrt gra (b)pŏrng 106

Canada แคนาดา kair nar dar 146

Canadian แคนาดา kàir nar dar 93

cancel, to ยกเลิก yók lêrk 66

candle เทียน tearn 120

candy ลูกกวาด lôok gwàrt 120

cap หมวกแก๊ป mùak gáihp 115

capital (finance) ทุน tun 131

car รถ rót 19, 20, 75, 78

car hire รถเช่า rót chôw 20

car park ที่จอดรถ têe jòrt rót 78

car racing แข่งรถ kàihng rót 90

car radio วิทยุรถยนต์ wít.ta yú rót yon 118

car rental รถเช่า rót chôw 20

carafe คาราฟ kar rârf 60

carat กะรัต ga rát 121

caraway ยี่หร่า yêe rár 55

carbon paper กระดาษอัดสำเนา gra dàrt àt sǎmnow 104

carbonated (fizzy) ชนิดที่มีก๊าซ cha nít tée mee gárt 61

carburettor คาร์บิวเรเตอร์ kar bi wrey têr 78

card นามบัตร ,narm bàt 131

card game ไพ่ pâi 128

cardigan คาร์ดิก้น kar di gan 115

carrot แครอต kair rót 53

cart รถเข็น rót kĕhn 18.

carton (of cigarettes) ห่อ hòr 17; คาร์ตตอน kàrt (d)torn 126

cartridge (camera) กล่องใส่ฟิล์มขนาดใหญ่ glôrng feem ka nàrt yài 124

case กระเป๋า gra (b)pŏw 125

cash desk ที่รับเงิน têe ráp ngern 103, 156

cash, to เบิกเงิน bèrk ngern 130, 133

cassette เทปคาสเซ็ท téyp kar sèht 118, 127

cassette recorder เครื่องอัดเทป krêuang àt téyp 118

castle ปราสาท (b)pra sàrt 81

catacombs อุโมงค์ u moeng 81

catalogue แคตตาล็อก kàirt (d)tar lók 82

catfish ปลาดุก (b)plar dùk 45

cathedral วิหาร wi hǎrn 81

Catholic คาทอลิค kar tor lík 84

cauliflower กระหล่ำดอก gra làm dòrk 53

caution ระมัดระวัง ramát rawang 156

cave ถ้ำ tâm 81

celery คืนฉ่ายฝรั่ง kêuhn chài fa ràng 53

cemetery ป่าช้า (b)pàr chár 81

centimetre เซ็นติเมตร sehn (d)tí meht 111

centre ใจกลาง jai glarng 19, 21, 77, 81

century ศตวรรษ sàt tá wát 149

ceramics เซรามิค sey rar mík 83

cereal ซีเรียล see rearl 41

certificate ใบรับรองแพทย์ bai ráp rorng pàirt 144

chain (jewellery) สร้อย sôy 121

chain bracelet สร้อยข้อมือ sôy kôr meur 121

chair เก้าอี้ kôw êe 106

chamber music ดนตรีที่เล่นในห้อง don (d)tree têe lêhn nai hông 128

change, to เปลี่ยน (b)plearn 62, 66, 68, 76, 123

change, to (money) แลกเงิน lâirk ngern 18, 129

change (money) แลกเงิน lâirk ngern 63, 129

chapel โรงสวด roeng sùat 81

charge คิดเงิน kít kâr 20, 78, 90, 136

charge, to คิดค่า kít kâr 24, 130

charm (trinket) เครื่องราง krêuang rarng 121

charm bracelet สร้อยข้อมือที่มีเครื่องราง sôy kôr meur têe mee krêuang rarng 121

cheap ถูก tòok 14, 24, 25, 101

check (restaurant) เก็บเงิน gèhp ngern 63

check (bank) เช็ค chéhk 130, 131

check, to ตรวจ (d)trùat 123

check, to (luggage) ตรวจดู(กระเป๋า) fàrk

พจนานุกรม

(gra (b)pōw) 71
check in, to *(airport)* เช็คอิน chék in 65
check out, to เช็คเอาท์ chék ōw 31
check-up *(medical)* ตรวจร่างกาย (d)trùat rầrng gai 142
cheese เนยแข็ง noey kǎihng 64
chemist's ร้านขายยา rárn kǎi yar 98, 107
cheque เช็ค chéck 130, 131
cherry เชอรี่ cher rêe 56
chess หมากรุก mǎrk rúk 94
chess set หมากรุก mǎrk rúk 128
chest หน้าอก nâr òk 138, 141
chestnut เกาลัด gow lát 56
chewing gum หมากฝรั่ง mǎrk fa ràng 126
chewing tobacco ยาเส้น yar sêhn 126
chicken ไก่ gài 63
chicken breast อกไก่ òk gài 49
chiffon แพรชีฟอง prair chee forng 113
child เด็ก dèhk 24, 62, 82, 150
children's doctor กุมารแพทย์ gu marn pǎirt 137
China จีน jeen 146
chips มันทอด man tôrt 64
chocolate ช็อกโกแล็ต chók goe láiht 119, 126
chocolate (hot) ช็อกโกแล็ต(ร้อน) chók goe láiht (rórn) 41, 61
chopstick ตะเกียบ (d)ta gèap 37
Christmas คริสต์สมาสต์ krít sa mǎrt 153
chromium โครเมี่ยม kroe mêarm 122
church โบสถ์ bòet 81, 84
cigar ซิการ์ si gar 126
cigarette บุหรี่ bu rèe 17, 95, 126
cigarette case ตลับบุหรี่ (d)tal àp bu rèe 121, 126
cigarette holder ที่คาบบุหรี่ têe kàrp bu rèe 126
cigarette lighter ไฟแช็ก fai cháihk 121, 126
cine camera กล้องถ่ายหนัง glôrng tài nǎng 124
cinema หนัง nǎng 86
cinnamon อบเชย òp choey 55
circle *(theatre)* ชั้นลอย chán loy 87, 88
city เมือง meuang 81
city centre ใจกลางเมือง jai glarng meuang 81
classical คลาสสิก klàrt sìk 128
clean สะอาด sa àrt 62
clean, to ทำความสะอาด tam kwarm sa àrt 76; ซักแห้ง sák hâirng 29
cleansing cream ครีมล้างหน้า kreem lárng nâr 109
cliff หน้าผา nâr pǎr 85
clip เข็มกลัดหนีบ kěhm glàt nèep 121
cloakroom ห้องรับฝากของ hôrng ráp fàrk kǒrng 88
clock นาฬิกา nar lí gar

clock-radio วิทยุ-นาฬิกา wít ta yú nar lí gar 118
close, to ปิด (b)pìt 107, 132
cloth ผ้า pâr 117
clothes เสื้อผ้า sêua pâr 29, 115
clothes peg/pin ไม้หนีบผ้า mái nèep pâr 120
clothing เสื้อผ้า sêua pâr 111
cloud เมฆ mêyk 94
clove กานพลู garn ploo 55
coach *(bus)* รถทัวร์ rót tua 72
coat เสื้อโค้ท sêua kóet 115
coconut มะพร้าว ma prów 56
coffee กาแฟ gar fair 41, 61, 64
cognac *(brandy)* คอนยัค korn yák 60
coin เหรียญ(กษาปณ์) rearn (ga sàrp) 83
cold หนาว nǒw 25, 94; เย็น yehn 14, 61
cold *(illness)* หวัด wàt 108, 141
collar คอเสื้อ kor sêua 116
colour สี sěe 103, 111, 124, 125
colour chart ตารางสี (d)tar rarng sěe 30
colour rinse ทำสีผม tam sěe pǒm 30
colour shampoo แชมพูย้อมผม chairm poo yórm pǒm 110
colour slide ฟิลมสไลด์ feem sa lai 124
colourfast สีตก sěe (d)tòk 113
comb หวี wěe 110
come, to มา mar 16, 95, 137, 144, 146
comedy ละครตลก la korn (d)ta lòk 86
commission *(fee)* ค่าบริการ kâr bo ri garn 130
common *(frequent)* บ่อย bòy 155
compact disc ซีดี see dee 127
compartment *(train)* ห้องวาง nông wǎrng 70
compass เข็มทิศ kěhm tít 106
complaint ตอบว่า (d)tòr wâr 62
concert คอนเสิร์ต korn sèrt 88
concert hall ที่แสดงดนตรี têe sa dairng don (d)tree 81, 88
condom ถุงยางอนามัย tǔng yarng a nar mai 108
conductor *(orchestra)* วาทยากร wârt ta yar gorn 88
conference room ห้องประชุม hôrng (b)pra chum 23
confirm, to ยืนยัน yeurn yan 66
confirmation คำยืนยัน kam yeurn yan 23
congratulation ขอแสดงความยินดีด้วย kǒr sa dairng kwarm yin dee dûay 153
connection *(transport)* ต่อ (d)tòr 65
constipated ท้องผูก tórng pòok 140
consulate กงสุล gong sǔn 157
contact lens คอนแท็คเลนส์ korn tàihk leyns 123
contagious โรคติดต่อ rôek (d)tìt (d)tòr 142
contain, to มี mee 38

DICTIONARY

contraceptive ยากำเนิด kum gam nèrt 108

contract สัญญา săn yar 131

control ควบคุม kùap kum 16

convent คอนแวนต์ korn wairn 81

cookie คุกกี้ kúk gêe 64

cool box กระติกน้ำแข็ง gra (d)tìk nárm kăihng 106

copper ทองแดง torng dairng 122

coral หินปะกวารัง hĭn (b)pa gar rang 122

corduroy ผ้าริ้ว pâr ríw 113

corn (foot) ตาปลา (d)tar (b)plar 108

corn plaster พลาสเตอร์สำหรับปิดตาปลา plar sa ter sǎm ràp (b)pìt (d)tar (b)plar 108

corner มุม mum 21, 36, 77

cost ค่าใช้จ่าย kâr chái jài 131

cost, to เท่าไหร่ tôwrài 11, 80, 133

cot อู่นอน òp norn 24

cotton ผ้าฝ้าย pâr fâi 113

cotton wool สำลี săm lee 108

cough ไอ ai 108, 141

cough drops ยาแก้ไอ yar gâir ai 108

cough, to ไอ ai 142

countryside ชนบท chon a bòt 85

court house ศาล sărn 81

cousin ญาติ yârt 93

cover charge ค่าบริการต่อหัว kâr boe ri garn (d)tòr hŭa 63

crab ปูทะเล (b)poo ta ley 45

cramp ตะคริว (d)tà kríw 141

crayon ดินสอสี din sŏr sĕe 104

cream ครีม kreem 61

cream (toiletry) ครีม kreem 109

crease resistant กันยับ gan yáp 113

credit เครดิต krey dìt 130

credit card บัตรเครดิต bàt krey dìt 20, 31, 63, 102, 130

crepe แพรยับ prair yôn 113

crockery ถ้วยชาม tûay charm 120

cross ไม้กางเขน mái garng kĕyn 121

crossing (maritime) ข้ามฟาก kârm fârk 74

crossroads สี่แยก sèe yâirk 77

cruise ล่องเรือ lông reua 74

crystal แก้วผลึก , คริสตัล gâiw pléuhk, krí sa (d)tan 122

cucumber แตงกวา (d)tairng gwar 53

cuisine อาหาร ar hărn 35

cup ถ้วย tûay 37; แก้ว gâiw 120

curler เครื่องม้วนผม krêuang meur dàt pŏm 110

currency เงิน ngern 129

currency exchange office ที่รับแลกเงิน têe ráp lâirk ngern 19, 68, 129

current กระแสน้ำ gra săir nárm 91

curried แกง gairng 46

curtain ผ้าม่าน pâr mârn 28

customs ศุลกากร sŭn la gar gorn 17, 102

cut (wound) บาด bàrt 139

cut glass แก้วเจียรนัย gâiw jea ra nai 122

cut, to (with scissors) ตัด (d)tàt 30

cut off, to (interrupt) (สาย)ขาด (sǎi) kàrt 135

cuticle remover ที่แต่งโคนเล็บ têe (d)tàihng kŏn léhp 109

cutlery ช้อน-ส้อม chórn sôm 120, 121

cycling แข่งจักรยาน kàihng jàk ra yarn 90

cystitis กระเพาะปัสสาวะอักเสบ gra póh (b)pàt sa wá ak sèyp 142

D

dance, to เต้นรำ (d)têhn ram 88, 96

danger อันตราย an (d)ta rai 156, 157

dangerous อันตราย an (d)ta rai 91

dark มืด mêurt 25; เข้ม kêhm 101, 111, 112

date (appointment) นัดหมาย nát măi 95; (day) วันที่ wan têe 25, 151; (fruit) อินทผลัม in ta păr lam 56

daughter ลูกสาว lôok sŏw 93

day วัน wan 20, 24, 32, 80, 94, 151

day off วันหยุด wan yùt 151

daylight แสงธรรมชาติ săirng tam ma chàrt 124

decade ทศวรรษ tót sa wát 149

decaffeinated ชนิดไม่มีคาเฟอีน chanít mâi mee kar fey een 41, 61

December ธันวาคม tan war kom 150

decision ตัดสินใจ (d)tàt sĭn jai 25, 102

deck (ship) ดาดฟ้าเรือ dàrt fár reua 74

deck chair เก้าอี้ผ้าใบ gôw êe pâr bai 91, 106

declare, to (customs) แสดงรายการสิ่งของ sa dairng rai garn sìng kŏng 17

deep ลึก léuhk 142

degree (temperature) องศา ong săr 140

delay ช้า chár 69

delicious อร่อย a ròy 63

deliver, to ส่ง sòng 102

delivery การส่ง garn sòng 102

denim ผ้ายีนส์ pâr yeen 113

Denmark เดนมาร์ก deyn mârk 146

dentist หมอฟัน mŏr fan 98, 145

denture ฟันปลอม fan (b)plorm 145

deodorant ยาดับกลิ่นตัว yar dàp glìn (d)tua 109

department (museum) แผนก pa nàirk 84; (shop) ร้าน rárn 99

department store ห้างสรรพสินค้า hârng sàp pá sĭn kár 99

departure ขาออก kàr òrk 66

deposit (down payment) เงินมัดจำ ngern mát jam 20; (bank) ธนาคาร ta nar karn 130

dessert ของหวาน kŏrng wărn 38, 57

diabetic โรคเบาหวาน rôek bow wărn 38, 141

dialling code รหัสพื้นที่ ra hàt péurn têe 134

diamond เพชร péht 122

diaper ผ้าอ้อม păr ôrm 110

diarrhoea ท้องร่วง tórng rûang 140

dictionary พจนานุกรม po ja nar nú grom 104

diesel ดีเซล dee seyn 75

diet อาหาร ar hărn 38

difficult ยาก yărk 14

difficulty ยุ่งยาก yûng yărk 28, 102

digital ดิจิตอล di jì l (d)torn 122

dining car รถเสบียง rót sa bearng 68, 71

dining room ห้องอาหาร hôrng ar hărn 27

dinner อาหารเย็น ar hărn kăm 35, 95

dinner, to have กินอาหารเย็น gin ar hărn yehn 95

direct ตรง (d)trong 65

direct, to บอก(ทาง) bòrk (tarng) 13

direction ทิศ tít 76

director (theatre) ผู้กำกับ pôo gam gàp 87

directory (phone) สมุดโทรศัพท์ sa mùt toe ra sàp 134

disabled คนพิการ kon pi garn 83

discotheque ดิสโกเธค dìt sa gôe táihk 88, 96

discount ส่วนลด sùan lót 131

disease โรค rôeg 142

dish จาน jarn 36

dishwashing detergent น้ำยาล้างจาน nám lárng jarn 120

disinfectant ยาฆ่าเชื้อ yar kăr chéua 108

dislocated เคลื่อน kêuan 140

display case โชว์อยู่ choe yòo 101

dissatisfied ไม่ชอบใจ măi chôrp jai 103

district (of town) ย่าน yârn 81

disturb, to รบกวน róp guan 156

dizzy เวียนศีรษะ wearn sĕe sà 140

doctor หมอ mŏr 79, 137, 144, 145

doctor's office คลีนิคหมอ klee ník mŏr 137

dog สุนัข su nák 156

doll ตุ๊กตา (d)túk a (d)tar 128

dollar ดอลลาร์ dorn lar 19, 102, 129

door ประตู (d)pra.(d)too 156

double bed เตียงคู่ (d)teang kòo 23

double room ห้องคู่ hôrng kòo 19, 23

down ลง long 15

downtown ในเมือง nai meuang 81

dozen โหล lŏe 149

drawing paper กระดาษวาดเขียน gra dàrt wărt kĕarn 104

drawing pins เข็มหมุดสำหรับวาดเขียน kĕhm mùt săm ràp wărt kĕarn 105

dress เสื้อกระโปรงชุด sêua gra (b)proeng

dressing gown เสื้อคลุมอาบน้ำ sêua klum àrp nárm 115

drink เครื่องดื่ม krêuang dèurm 59, 60, 61, 95

drink, to ดื่ม dèurm 36, 38

drinking water น้ำดื่ม nárm dèurm 32

drip, to หยด yòt 28

driving licence ใบขับขี่ bai kàp kèe 20, 79

drop (liquid) ยาหยอด yar yòrt 108

drugstore ร้านขายยา rárn kăi yar 99, 107

dry แห้ง hâirng 30, 110; (wine) ครา da rai 60

dry cleaner's ร้านซักแห้ง rárn sák hâirng 29, 99

dry shampoo แชมพูผง chairm poo pŏng 110

duck เป็ด (b)pèht 50

dummy (baby's) จุกนม jùk nom 110

during ระหว่าง ra wàrng 15

duty (customs) ภาษีศุลกากร parsăr sŭn la gar gorn 18

duty-free shop ร้านค้าปลอดภาษี rárn kár (b)plòrt par sĕe 19

dye ยาย้อมผม yar yórm pŏm 30, 111

E

ear หู hŏo 138

ear drops ยาหยอดหู yar yòrt hŏo 108

earache ปวดหู (b)pùat hŏo 141

early เช้า ,chów 14, 31

earring ตุ้มหู (d)tûm hŏo 121

east ทิศตะวันออก tít (d)tawan òrk 77

easy ง่าย ngăi 14

eat, to กิน gin 36, 38; ทาน tarn 144

eel ปลาไหล (b)plar lăi 45

egg ไข่ kài 41, 64

eggplant มะเขือยาว ma kĕua yow 53

eight แปด (b)pàirt 147

eighteen สิบแปด sìp (b)pàirt 147

eighth ที่แปด têe (b)pàirt 149

eighty แปดสิบ (b)pàirt sìp 148

elastic bandage ผ้าพันแผล păr pan plàir 108

electric(al) ไฟฟ้า fai fár 118

electrical appliance เครื่องใช้ไฟฟ้า krêuang chái fai fár 118

electrical goods shop ร้านขายเครื่องไฟฟ้า rárn kăi krêuang fai fár 99

electricity ไฟฟ้า fai fár 32

electronic ไฟฟ้า fai fár 128

elevator ลิฟท์ líf 27, 100

eleven สิบเอ็ด sìp èht 147

embarkation point ท่าเรือ tăr reua 74

embassy สถานทูต sa tărn tôot 157

emerald มรกต mo ra gòt 122

emergency ฉุกเฉิน chùk chĕrn 157

emergency exit ทางออกฉุกเฉิน tarng òrk chùk chěrn 27, 100

emery board ตะไบเล็บ (d)tà bai léhp 109

empty วาง wârng 14

enamel ลงยา, เคลือบ long yar, klêuap 122

end ปลาย (b)plai 150

engaged (phone) ติด(สาย) (d)tìt (sǎi) 136

engagement ring แหวนหมั้น wǎirn mân 122

engine (car) เครื่องยนต์ krêuang yon 78

England อังกฤษ ang grìt 134, 146

English อังกฤษ ang grìt 11, 17, 80, 82, 93, 104, 105, 126

enjoy oneself, to รู้สึกสนุก róo sèuhk sa nùk 96

enjoyable สนุก sa nùk 31

enlarge, to ขยาย ka yǎi 125

enough พอ por 14

entrance ทางเข้า tarng kôw 67, 100, 156

entrance fee ค่าผ่านประตู kâr pàrn (b)pra (d)tòo 82

envelope ซองจดหมาย sorng jot mǎi 105

equipment ยางลบ krêuang meur 91, 106

eraser ยางลบ yarng lóp 105

escalator บันไดเลื่อน ban dai lêuan 100

estimate (cost) ประเมิน (b)pra mern 131

Eurocheque ยูโรเช็ค yoo roe chéhk 130

Europe ยุโรป yu ròep 146

evening เย็น yehn 95, 96

evening dress ชุดราตรีสโมสร chút rar (d)tree sa mõe sõrn 89

evening dress (woman's) ชุดราตรี chút rar (d)tree 115

evening, in the ตอนเย็น (d)torn yehn 151; เวลาเย็น wey lar yehn 153

every ทุก túk 143

everything ทุกอย่าง túk yàrng 31, 63

exchange rate อัตราแลกเปลี่ยน a (d)tra làirk (b)plèarn 19

excursion รายการนำเที่ยว rai garn nam têaw 80

excuse, to แก้ตัว kâir (d)tua 10

excuse me ขอโทษ kŏr tôet 154

exercise book สมุดแบบฝึกหัด sa mùt bàirp fèuhk hàt 105

exhaust pipe ท่อไอเสีย tôr ai sěar 79

exhibition นิทรรศการ ni tát sa garn 81

exit ทางออก tarng òrk 67, 100, 156

expenses ค่าใช้จ่าย kâr chái jài 131

expensive แพง pairng 14, 19, 24, 101

exposure (photography) รูป rôop 124

exposure counter ที่บอกจำนวนรูปที่ถ่าย têe bòrk jam nuan rôop têe tài 125

express ด่วน dùan 133

expression แสดงออก sa dairng òrk 10, 100

expressway ทางด่วน tarng dùan 76

extension (phone) ต่อ (d)tòr 135

extension cord/lead สายต่อ(ไฟฟ้า) sǎi (d)tòr (fai fár) 118

extra เพิ่ม pêrm 27

eye ตา (d)tar 138, 139

eye drops ยาหยอดตา yar yòrt (d)tar 108

eye shadow ที่ทาตา têe tar (d)tar 109

eye specialist จักษุแพทย์ jàk sù pàirt 137

eyebrow pencil ดินสอเขียนคิ้ว din sŏr kěarn kíw 109

eyesight สายตา sǎi (d)tar 123

F

fabric (cloth) เนื้อผ้า néua pâr 112

face หน้า nâr 138

face pack พอกหน้า fôrk nâr 30

face powder แป้งผัดหน้า (b)pâirng pàt nâr 109

factory โรงงาน roeng ngarn 81

fair งานออกร้าน ngarp òrk rárn 81

fall (autumn) ฤดูใบไม้ร่วง ri doo bai mái rûang 150

fall, to หกล้ม hòk lóm 139

family ครอบครัว krôrp krua 93, 144

fan พัดลม pát lom 28

fan belt สายพานพัดลม sǎi parn pát lom 76

far ไกล glai 14, 100

fare (ticket) ค่า kâr 68, 73

farm นา, ไร่ nar, râi 85

fast เร็ว rehw 124

fat (meat) มัน man 38

father พ่อ pôr 93

faucet ก๊อกน้ำ gók nárm 28

fax แฟ็กซ์ fáihk 133

February กุมภาพันธ์ gum par pan 150

fee (doctor's) ค่ารักษา kâr rák sǎr 144

feeding bottle ขวดนม kùat nárm 110

feel, to (physical state) รู้สึก róo sèuhk 140, 142

felt ผ้าสักหลาด pâr sàk làrt 113

felt-tip pen ปากกาเมจิก (b)pàrk gar meyjìk 105

ferry เรือข้ามฟาก reua kârm fârk 74

fever ไข้ kâi 140

few น้อย nóy 14

few (a few) ไม่กี่ mâi gèe 14

field ทุ่ง tûng 85

fifteen สิบห้า sìp hâr 147

fifth ที่ห้า têe hâr 149

fifty ห้าสิบ hâr sìp 147

file (tool) ตะไบเล็บ (d)ta bai kàt léhp 109

fill in, to กรอก gròrk 26, 144

filling (tooth) อุด ùt 145

filling station ปั๊มน้ำมัน (b)pám nárm man

75
film หนัง nǎng 86; ฟิล์ม feem 124, 125
film winder ตัวขึ้นฟิล์ม (d)tua kéuhn feem 125
filter ฟิลเตอร์ ,fil (d)ter 125
filter-tipped กันกรอง gôn grorng 126
find, to หา hǎr 11, 12, 100
fine (OK) สบายดี sa bai dee 10, 92
fine arts วิจิตรศิลป์ wi jìt ra sǐn 83
finger นิ้ว níw 138
Finland ฟินแลนด์ fin lairn 146
fire ไฟ fai 157
first แรก ráirk 68, 73, 77; ที่หนึ่ง têe nèuhng 149
first class ชั้นหนึ่ง chán nèuhng 69
first name ชื่อ, chêur 25
first-aid kit เครื่องมือปฐมพยาบาล krêuang meur (b)pa tǒm pa yar barn 108
fish ปลา (b)plar 45
fishing ตกปลา (d)tòk (b)plar 90
fishing permit ขออนุญาตตกปลา kǒr an nú yârt (d)tòk (b)plar 90
fishing tackle คันเบ็ดชนิดมีรอก kan bèht cha nít mee (d)ork 106
fishmonger's ร้านขายปลา rárn kǎi (b)plar 99
fit, to พอดี por dee 114
fitting room ห้องลอง hôrng lorng 114
five ห้า hâr 147
fix, to ปะ (b)pà 76; ดู, ด้ ùt 145
fizzy (mineral water) ชนิดที่มีก๊าซ cha nít têe mee gárt 61
flannel ผ้าสักหลาดอ่อน pǎr sàk làrt òrn 113
flash (photography) แฟลช fláirt 125
flash attachment แป้นแฟลช (b)pâirn fláirt 125
flashlight ไฟกระพริบ fai gra príp 106
flat (apartment) แฟลต fláiht 23
flat (shoe) พื้นราบ péurn ràrp 117
flat tyre ยางแบน yarng bairn 76
flight เที่ยวบิน têaw bin 65
floating market ตลาดน้ำ (d)ta làrt nárm 81
floor show ฟลอร์โชว์ ,flor choe 89
florist's ร้านขายดอกไม้ rárn kǎi dòrk mái 99
flour แป้ง (b)pâirng 38
flower ดอกไม้ dòrk mái 85
flu ไข้ kâi 142
fluid (brake) น้ำมัน(เบรก) nárm man (breyk) 75; น้ำยาล้าง nárm yar lárng 123
foam rubber mattress ที่นอนยาง têe norn yarng 106
fog หมอก mòrk 94
folding chair เก้าอี้พับ gôw wêe páp 106
folding table โต๊ะพับ (d)tóh páp 106

folk song เพลงพื้นบ้าน pleyng péun bârn 128
follow, to ตาม (d)tarm 77
food อาหาร ,ar hǎrn 37, 38, 62, 110
food box กล่องอาหาร glòrng ar hǎrn 120
food poisoning อาหารเป็นพิษ ,ar hǎrn (b)pehn pít 142
foot เท้า tów 138
foot cream ครีมทาเท้า kreem tar tów 109
football ฟุตบอล, fút born 89, 90
footpath ทางเท้า tarng tów 85
for เพื่อ, สำหรับ pêua, sǎm ràp 15
forbidden ห้าม ,hârm 156
forecast พยากรณ์ pa yar gorn 94
forest ป่า (b)pàr 85
fork ส้อม sôrm 37, 62, 120,
form (document) แบบฟอร์ม bàirp form 26, 133, 144
fortnight สองอาทิตย์ sǒrng ar tít 151
fortress ป้อมปราการ (b)pôrm (b)pra garn 81
forty สี่สิบ sèe sìp 147
foundation cream ครีมรองพื้น kreem rorng péurn 109
fountain น้ำพุ nárm pú 81
fountain pen ปากกาหมึกซึม (b)pàrk gar mèuhk seuhm 105
four สี่ sèe 147
fourteen สิบสี่ sìp sèe 147
fourth ที่สี่ têe sèe 149
frame (glasses) กรอบ(แว่น) gròrp (wàirn) 123
France ฝรั่งเศส fa ràng sèyt 146
free ว่าง wârng 14, 80, 96, 155
fresh สด sòt 56
Friday วันศุกร์ wan sùk 151
fried egg ไข่ดาว kài dow 41
friend เพื่อน pêuan 95
fringe ผมม้า pǒm már 30
from จาก jàrk 15
front ด้านหน้า dârn nâr 76
frost น้ำค้างแข็ง nárm kárng kǎihng 94
fruit ผลไม้ pǒn la mái 56
fruit cocktail ค็อกเทลผลไม้ kók teyn pǒn la mái 56
fruit juice น้ำผลไม้ nárm pǒn la mái 41, 61
frying pan กะทะ gà tá 120
full เต็ม (d)tehm 14
full board รวมอาหารทุกมื้อ ruam ar hǎrn túk méur 24
full insurance ประกันเต็มที่ (b)pra gan (d)tehm têe 20

G

gabardine ผ้าลายสองหน้าเดียว pǎr lai sǒrng nǎr deaw 113

DICTIONARY

gallery หอศิลป์ hŏr sĭn 81, 98
game เกม geym 128
garage โรงรถ roeng rót 26
garden สวน sŭan 85
gardens สวน sŭan 81
gas ก๊าซ gárt 157
gasoline เบนซิน beyn sin 76; น้ำมัน nám man 78
gastritis โรคกระเพาะอักเสบ rôeg gra póh àk sèyp 142
gauze ผ้าก๊อซ păr górt 108
gem เพชรพลอย péht ploy 121
general ทั่วไป tûa (b)pai 27, 100, 137
general delivery ส่งทั่วไป sòng tûa (b)pai 133
general practitioner หมอ mŏr 137
genitals อวัยวะเพศ a way a wá pêyt 138
gentleman สุภาพบุรุษ su pârp bù rùt 156
geology ธรณีวิทยา to ra nee wít ta yar 83
Germany เยอรมันนี yer ra man nee 146
get, to หา hăr 11, 32; เรียก rêark 19, 21, 31; ซื้อ séur 108
get off, to ลง(รถ) long (rót) 74
get past, to (ผ่าน)ไป pàrn (b)pai 70
get to, to ไป (b)pai 19, 76, 100
get up, to ลุก lúk 144
gift ของฝาก kŏrng fàrk 17
gin จิน jin 60
gin and tonic จินโทนิค jin toe ník 60
ginger ขิง kĭng 55
girdle เพชรรัดเอว, ผ้าคาดเอว kêhm kàt, păr kàrt ew 115
girl เด็กหญิง (d)èhk yĭng 111, 112, 128
girlfriend แฟนสาว fairn sŏw 93
give, to ให้ hâi 13
give way, to (traffic) ให้ทาง hâi tarng 79
gland ต่อม (d)tòrm 138
glass แก้ว gâiw 37, 60, 62, 143
glasses แว่นตา wâirn (d)tar 123
gloomy หน้าเศร้า năr sôw 84
glove ถุงมือ tŭng meur 115
glue กาว gow 105
go, to ไป (b)pai 21, 72, 77, 96
go away! ไปให้พ้น (b)pai hâi pón 157
go back, to กลับไป glàp (b)pai 77
go out, to ไปข้างนอก (b)pai kârng nôrk 96
gold ทอง torng 121, 122
gold plate ชุบทอง chúp torng 122
golden สีทอง see torng 112
golf กอล์ฟ gorf 89
golf course สนามกอล์ฟ sa nàrm gorf 89
good ดี dee 14, 86, 101
good afternoon สวัสดี sa wàt dee 10
good evening สวัสดี sa wàt dee 10
good morning สวัสดี sa wàt dee 10
good night ราตรีสวัสดิ์ rar tree sa sàt dee 10
goodbye สวัสดี sa wàt dee 10

goose ห่าน hàrn 49
gram กรัม gram 120
grammar ไวยากรณ์ wai ya gorn 160
grammar book หนังสือไวยากรณ์ năng sĕur wai ya gorn 160
grape องุ่น a ngùn 56, 64
gray สีเทา see tow 112
graze แผลถลอก plăir ta lòrk 139
greasy มัน man 30, 111
great (excellent) ดีมาก dee mârk 95
Great Britain สหราชอาณาจักร sa har rârt ar nar jàk 146
Greece กรีก grèek 146
green สีเขียว see kĕaw 112
greeting ทักทาย ták tay 10, 153
grey สีเทา see tow 112
grilled ปิ้ง, ย่าง (b)píng, yârng 46, 47
grocer's ร้านขายของชำ rárn kăi kŏrng cham 99, 119
groundsheet ผ้ายางปูพื้น păr yarng (b)poo péurn 106
group กลุ่ม glùm 82
guesthouse เกสต์เฮาส์ géyt hówt 20, 23
guide ไกด์ gai 80
guidebook หนังสือคู่มือ năng sĕur kôo meur 82, 104, 105
guinea fowl ไก่ตอก gài (d)tók 49
gum (teeth) เหงือก ngèuak 145
gynaecologist นรีแพทย์ na ree pâirt 137

H

hair ผม pŏm 30, 111
hair dryer เครื่องเป่าผม krêuang (b)pòw pŏm 118
hair gel เยลใส่ผม yehl sài pŏm 30, 111
hair lotion โลชั่นใส่ผม loe chân sài pŏm 110
hair spray สเปรย์ฉีดผม sa (b)prey chèet pŏm 30, 111
hairbrush หวีประจำผม wĕe (b)prairng pŏm 110
haircut ตัดผม (d)tàt pŏm 30
hairdresser ร้านทำผม rárn tam pŏm 30, 99
hairgrip กิ๊บติดผม gíp (d)tìt pŏm 110
hairpin ปิ่นปักผม (b)pìn (b)pàk pŏm 110
half ครึ่ง krêuhng 149
half an hour ครึ่งชั่วโมง krêuhng chûa moeng 155
half price ครึ่งราคา krêuhng rar kar 69
hall porter พนักงานยกกระเป๋า pa nák ngarn yók gra (b)pŏw 26
ham แฮม hairm 41, 64
ham and eggs แฮมกับไข่ดาว hairm gàp kài dow 41
hammer ฆ้อน kórn 120
hammock เปลญวน (b)pley yuan 106

DICTIONARY

พจนานุกรม

hand มือ meur 138
hand cream ครีมทามือ kreem tar meur 109
hand washable ซักด้วยมือ sák dûay meur 113
handbag กระเป๋ามือถือ gra (b)pǒw meur tĕur 115, 157
handicrafts งานฝีมือ ngarn fěe meur 83
handkerchief ผ้าเช็ดหน้า pâr chéht nâr 115
handmade ทำด้วยมือ tam dûay meur 112
hanger ไม้แขวนเสื้อ mái kwǎirn sêua 27
happy สุขสันต์ sùk sǎn 153
harbour ท่าจอดเรือ târ jòrt reua 74, 81
hard (lens) ฮาร์ด(เลนส์) hàrt (leyns) 123
hard-boiled (egg) ไข่ต้มสุก kài tôm sùk sùk 41
hardware store ร้านขายเครื่องโลหะ rárn kǎi krêuang loh ha 99
hat หมวก mùak 115
have to (must) ต้อง (d)tôrng 18, 69, 77, 95
hay fever โรคแพ้อากาศ rôek páir ar gàrt 108, 141
head หัว hǔa 138, 139
head waiter หัวหน้าบ๋อย hǔa nâr bǒy 62
headache ปวดหัว (b)pùat hǔa 141
headphones หูฟัง hǒo fang 118
health insurance form แบบฟอร์มประกันสุขภาพ bàirp form (b)pra gan sùk ka pârp 144
heart หัวใจ hǔa jai 138
heating เครื่องทำความร้อน krêuang tam kwarm rórn 28
heavy หนัก nàk 139
heel ส้น sôn 117
helicopter เฮลิคอปเตอร์ hey li kòrp (d)ter 75
hello สวัสดี sa wàt dee 10, 135
help ช่วย chûay 157
help! ช่วยด้วย chûay dûay 157
help, to ช่วย chûay 12, 71, 100, 134
help, to (oneself) ช่วย(ตัวเอง) chûay ((d)tua eyng) 119
herb tea ชาสมุนไพร char sa mǔn prai 61
herbs สมุนไพร sa mǔn prai 55
here ที่นี่ têe nêe 14
hi สวัสดี sa wàt dee 10
high สูง sǒong 141
high season ฤดูท่องเที่ยว ri doo tông têaw 150
high tide น้ำขึ้น nárm kéuhn 91
hill เนินเขา nern kǒw 85
hire เช่า chôw 20, 74
hire, to เช่า chôw 19, 20, 74, 90, 91, 118, 156
history ประวัติศาสตร์ (b)pra wàt tí sàrt 83
hitchhike, to โบกรถ bòek rót 75

hold on! (phone) รอสักครู่ ror sák krôo 136
hole รู roo 30
holiday(s) วันหยุดพักผ่อน wan yùk pák pòrn 151, 153
home บ้าน bârn 96
home address ที่อยู่ têe yòo 31
home town บ้านเกิด bârn gèrt 25
honey น้ำผึ้ง nárm pêuhng 41
hope, to หวัง wǎng 96
horse racing แข่งม้า kàihng már 90
horseback riding ขี่ม้า kèe már 90
hospital โรงพยาบาล roeng pa yar barn 99, 142, 144
hot ร้อน rórn 14, 25, 94
hot (spicy) รสชาติ rót jàt 37
hot water น้ำร้อน nárm rórn 24, 28
hot-water bottle ถุงน้ำร้อน tǔng nárm rórn 27
hotel โรงแรม roeng rairm 19, 21, 22, 26, 80, 102
hotel directory/guide สมุดรายชื่อโรงแรม sa mùt rai chêur roen grairm 19
hotel reservation จองโรงแรม jorng roengrairm 19
hour ชั่วโมง chûa moeng 80, 143
house บ้าน bârn 85
household article ของใช้ในบ้าน kǒrng chái nai bârn 120
how อย่างไร yàng ngai 11
how far ไกลไหม glai mái 11, 76, 85
how long นานไหม narn mái 11, 24
how many เท่าไหร่ tôw rài 11
how much เท่าไหร่ tôw rài 11, 24
hundred ร้อย róy 148
hungry หิว hǐw 13, 36
hurt, to เจ็บ jèhp 139, 140, 142
husband สามี sǎr mee 93

I
ice cream ไอศครีม ai sa kreem 57
ice cube น้ำแข็ง nárm kǎihng 27
ice pack น้ำแข็ง nárm kǎihng 106
iced tea ชาเย็น char yehn 61
if ถ้า târ 143
ill ไม่สบาย mǎi sa bai 140
illness เจ็บป่วย jèhp (b)pùay 140
important สำคัญ sǎm kan 13
imported นำเข้า nam kôw 112
impressive น่าประทับใจ nâr (b)pra táp jai 84
in ใน nai 15
include, to รวม ruam 24, 31, 32
included บวก bùak 20; ruam 31, 32
India อินเดีย jn dear 146
indigestion ท้องผูก tórng pòok 141
Indonesia อินโดนีเซีย in doe nee sear 146

indoor ในร่ม nai rôm 90
inexpensive ไม่แพง mâi pairng 36, 124
infected ติดเชื้อ (d)tìt chéua 140
infection ติดเชื้อ (d)tìt chéua 141
inflammation อักเสบ àk sèyp 142
inflation rate อัตราเงินเฟ้อ a (d)tra ngern fér 131
information ข้อมูล kôr moon 67, 156
injection ฉีดยา chèet yar 142, 143, 144
injured (ได้รับ)บาดเจ็บ (dâi ráp) bàrt jèhp 139
injury บาดเจ็บ bàrt jèhp 139
ink หมึก mèuhk 105
inquiry สอบถาม sòrp tärm 68
insect bite แมลงกัดต่อย ma lairng gàt (d)tòy 108, 139
insect repellent ยากันแมลง yar gan ma lairng 108
insect spray ยาฉีดกันยุง yar chèet gan yung 106
inside ข้างใน kârng nai 15
instead of แทน tairn 37
insurance ประกันภัย (b)pra gan pai 20, 144
insurance company บริษัทประกันภัย bo ri sàt (b)pra gan pai 79
interest (finance) ดอกเบี้ย dòrk bêar 131
interested, to be สนใจ sôn jai 83, 96
interesting น่าสนใจ nâr sôn jai 84
international ระหว่างประเทศ ra wàrng (b)pra têyt 133, 134
interpreter ล่าม lârm 131
intersection สี่แยก sèe yâirk 77
introduce, to แนะนำ náih nam 92
introduction (social) การแนะนำตัว garn náih nam (d)tua 92
investment ลงทุน long tun 131
invitation คำเชื้อเชิญ kam chéua cheurn 95
invite, to ชวน chuan 95
invoice ใบเรียกเก็บเงิน bai rêark gèhp ngern 131
iodine ไอโอดีน ai oe deen 108
Ireland ไอร์แลนด์ ai lairn 146
Irish ไอริช ai rít 93
iron (for laundry) เตารีด (d)tow rêet 118
iron, to รีด rêet 29
ironmonger's ร้านขายเครื่องเหล็ก rárn kâi krêuang lèhk 99
Israel อิสราเอล it sa rar eyn 146
Italy อิตาลี it (d)tar lêe 146

J
jacket เสื้อแจ็กเก็ต sêua jáihk gàiht 115
jade หยก yòk 122
jam (preserves) แยม yairm 41
jam, to เป็ดไม่ได้ (b)pèrt mâi dâi 28;

เลื่อนไม่ไป lêuan mâi (b)pai 125
January มกราคม mok ga rar kom 150
Japan ญี่ปุ่น yêe (b)pùn 146
jar (container) ขวด kùat 119
jaundice โรคดีซ่าน rôeg dee sârn 142
jaw ขากรรไกร kâr gan grai 138
jazz แจ๊ส jáiht 128
jeans ยีนส์ yeens 115
jersey เสื้อไหมพรม sêua mâi prom 115
jewel box ตู้เครื่องเพชร (d)tôo krêuang péht 121
jeweller's ร้านขายเครื่องประดับ rárn kâi krêuang (b)pra dàp 99, 121
joint ข้อต่อ kôr (d)tòr 138
journey การเดินทาง Jar dern tarng 72
juice (fruit) น้ำ(ผลไม้) nárm (pôn la mái) 38, 41, 61
July กรกฎาคม ga rák ga (d)tar kom 150
jumper เสื้อไหมพรม sêua mâi prom 115
June มิถุนายน gní tú nar yon 150
just (only) เท่านั้น tôw nán 16

K
keep, to เก็บ gèhp 63
kerosene น้ำมันก๊าด nám man gárt 106
key กุญแจ gun jair 27
kick boxing มวยไทย muay tai 89
kidney ไต (d)tai 138
kilo(gram) กิโล(กรัม) gi loe (gram) 119
kilometre กิโลเมตร gi loe méyt 20, 79
kind ใจดี jai dee 95
kind (type) ประเภท (b)pra pêyt 85, 140
knee เข่า kòw 138
kneesocks ถุงเท้ายาวถึงเข่า tǔng tów yow tǔng kòw 115
knife มีด mêet 37, 62, 120
knock, to เคาะ kóh 156
know, to รู้จัก róo jàk 16, 96, 114

L
label ป้าย (b)pâi 105
lace ผ้าลูกไม้ pâr lôok mái 113
lacquer ware เครื่องเขิน krêuang kěrn 127
lake ทะเลสาบ ta ley sàrp 81, 85, 90
lamb (meat) เนื้อแกะ néua gàih 47
lamp หลอดไฟ lòrt fai 29; ตะเกียง (d)ta gearng 106; โคมไฟ koem fai 118
language ภาษา par sǎr 104
lantern โคมไฟ koem fai 106
large ใหญ่ yài 20, 101, 130
last ที่แล้ว têe láiw 14, 149, 151; สุดท้าย sút tái 68, 73
late สาย sǎi 14
laugh, to หัวเราะ hǔa ró 95
launderette ร้านซักผ้า rárn sák pâr 99
laundry (clothes) ซักรีด sák rêet 29

laundry (place) ร้านซักรีด rárn sák pår 29, 99
laundry service บริการซักรีด bo ri garn sák rêd 24
laxative ยาระบาย yar ra bai 108
lead (metal) ตะกั่ว (d)ta gùa 75
lead (theatre) (ดารา)นำ (dar rar) nam 87
leap year ปีอธิกสุรทิน (b)pèe ar tí kà sù ra tin 149
leather หนัง năng 113, 117
leave, to ออก(จาก) òrk (jàrk) 31, 69
leave, to (deposit) ฝาก fàrk 26; (leave behind) ทิ้ง tíng 20
left ซ้าย sái 21, 69, 77
left-luggage office ตรวจกระเป๋า (d)trùat gra (b)pŏw 68, 71
leg ขา kăr 138
lemon มะนาว ma now 37, 41, 56, 61
lemonade เล็มมะเนด lehm ma nèyd 61
lens (camera) เลนส์ leyns 125
lens (glasses) เลนส์ leyns 123
lentils ถั่วแขก tùa kàirk 53
less น้อยกว่า nóy gwàr 14
let, to (hire out) ให้เช่า hâi chôw 156
letter จดหมาย jòt măi 132
letter box ตู้จดหมาย (d)tôo jòt mǎi 132
letter of credit แอลซี airl see 130
lettuce ผักสลัด pàk sa làt 53
library ห้องสมุด hŏrng sa mùt 81, 99
licence (driving) ใบขับขี่ bai kàp kèe 20, 79
lie down, to นอนราบ norn rârp 142
life belt เข็มขัดนิรภัย kěhm kàt ni rá pai 74
life boat เรือชูชีพ reua choo chêep 74
life belt เข็มขัดนิรภัย kěhm kàt ni rá pai 74
life boat เรือชูชีพ reua choo chêep 74
life guard (beach) ยาม yarm 91
lift (elevator) ลิฟท์ lif 27, 100
light (weight) เบา bow 14, 101
light ไฟฟ้า fai fár 28; สง săirng 124
light (colour) ออน òrn 101, 111, 112
light (for cigarette) ไฟ fai 95
light meter เครื่องวัดแสง krêuang wát săirng 125
lighter ไฟแช็ก fai chéhk 126
lightning ฟ้าแลบ fár lâirp 94
like เหมือนกับ měuan gàp 111
like, to อยาก(ได้) yàrk (dâi) 96, 103, 112
like, to (please) ชอบ chôrp 25, 93, 102
linen (cloth) ลินิน li nin 113
lip ฝีปาก rim fěe (b)pàrk 138
lipsalve ขี้ผึ้งทาปาก kêe pêuhng tar (b)pàrk 109
lipstick ลิปสติก líp sa (d)tìk 109
liqueur เหล้าชนิดหวาน lôw cha nít wǎrn 60
listen, to ฟัง fang 128
litre ลิตร lít 75, 119
little (a little) น้อย nóy 14

liver ตับ (d)tàp 138
lobster ล็อบสเตอร์ lób sa (d)têr 45
local พื้นบ้าน péurn bârn 37
long ยาว yow 115
long-sighted สายตายาว săi (d)tar yow 123
look for, to หา hăr 13
look out! ระวัง ra wang 157
look, to ดู doo 100, 123, 139
loose (clothes) หลวม lǔam 114
lose, to หาย hǎi 123, 157
loss ขาดทุน kàrt tun 131
lost หลงทาง lŏng tarng 13
lost and found office/lost property office ฝ่ายจัดการเรื่องของหาย fài jàk ra yarn rêuang kŏrng hǎi 157
lot (a lot) มาก mârk 14
lotion โลชั่น loe chàn 110
loud (voice) ดัง dang 135
love, to อยาก(ไป) yàrk 95
low ต่ำ (d)tàm 141
low season นอกฤดูของเที่ยว nôrk ri doo tông têaw 150
low tide น้ำลง nárm long 90
lower ชั้นล่าง chán lârng 70, 71
luck โชค chôek 153
luggage กระเป๋า gra (b)pŏw 18, 26, 31, 71
luggage locker ตู้เก็บของ (d)tôo gèhp kŏrng 68, 71
luggage trolley รถเข็นกระเป๋า rót kěhn gra (b)pŏw 18, 71
luggage/baggage กระเป๋า gra (b)pŏw 18, 26, 31, 71
lump (bump) บวม, โน buam, noe 139
lunch อาหารเที่ยง/กลางวัน ar hărn glarng wan 35, 80, 95
lung ปอด (b)pòrt 138
lychee ลิ้นจี่ lín jèe 56

M

machine (washable) (ซัก)เครื่อง(ได้) (sák) krêuang (dûay) 113
mackerel ปลาทู (b)plar too 45
magazine วารสาร wa ra sărn 105
magnificent งดงามมาก ngót ngarm mârk 84
maid พนักงานดูแลห้องพัก sŏw chái 26
mail จดหมาย jòt măi 28, 133
mail, to (post) สง(จดหมาย) sòng (jòt măi) 28
mailbox ตู้จดหมาย (d)tôo jòt măi 132
main สำคัญ săm kan 100
make, to (photocopies) ถาย(เอกสาร) tài (èyk ga sǎrn) 131
make-up เครื่องสำอางค์ krêuang sǎ marng 109
make-up remover pad แผ่นเช็ดเครื่องสำอางค์ pàihn chéhk

krêuang sǎm arng 109
mallet ฆอนไม้ kórn mái 106
manager ผู้จัดการ pôo jàt garn 26
mango มะม่วง ma mûang 56
manicure แต่งเล็บ (d)tàirng léhp 30
many หลาย lǎi 14
map แผนที่ pǎirn tée 77, 155
March มีนาคม mee nar kom 150
market ตลาด (d)ta làrt 81, 99
marmalade แยมเปลือกส้ม yairm (b)plèuak sôm 41
married แต่งงาน (d)tàihng ngarn 94
masked drama โขน kǒen 87
mass (church) คนเข้าไป kon tûa (b)pai 84
mat/matt (finish) ด้าน dǎrn 125
match ไม้แขงขัน nát kàirng kán 106 ; ไม้ขีด mái kèet 126
match, to (colour) เข้ากับ... kôw gàp 111
matinée รอบกลางวัน rôrp glarng wan 87
mattress ที่นอน têe norn 106
May พฤษภาคม prút sa pår kom 150
may (can) ขอ kǒr 12
meadow ทุ่งหญ้า tûng yàr 85
meal อาหาร ar hǎrn 24, 35, 143
mean, to มีความหมายว่า mee kwarm mǎi wâr 11, 26
means วิธี wi tee 75
measles โรคหัด rôek hàt 142
measure, to วัดตัว wát (d)tua 113
meat เนื้อ néua 38, 47, 48, 62
meatball ลูกชิ้น lôok chín 47
mechanic ช่าง chârng 78
mechanical pencil ดินสอกด din sŏr gòt 105, 121
medical certificate ใบรับรองแพทย์ bai ráp rorng pàirt 144
medicine เวชกรรม, การแพทย์ wêyt cha gam, garn pàirt 83
medicine (drug) ยา yar 143
medium (meat) สุกปานกลาง sùk (b)parn glarng 47
medium-sized ขนาดกลาง ka nàrt glarng 20
melon แตงไทย (d)tairng tai 56
memorial อนุสรณ์สถาน ar nú sŏrn sa tǎrn 81
mend, to ปะ(ยาง) (b)pà (yarng) 75
mend, to (clothes) ซ่อม sôrm 29
menthol (cigarettes) รสเมนทอล rót meyn torl 126
menu รายการอาหาร rai garn ar hǎrn 37, 39, 40
merry สุขสันต์ sùk sǎn 153
mesh screen มุ้งลวด múng lûat 28
message ข้อความ kôr kwarm 28, 136
metre เมตร mèyt 111
mezzanine (theatre) ชั้นลอย chán loy 87, 88

middle ตรงกลาง (d)trong glarng 69, 150
midnight เที่ยงคืน têarng keurn 154
mild (light) รสอ่อน rót òrn 126
mileage ระยะทาง rá yá tarng 20
milk นม nom 41, 61, 64
milkshake มิลค์เชค milk chéyk 61
million ล้าน lárn 148
mineral water น้ำแร่ nárm râir 61
minister (religion) พระ prá 84
mint สะระแหน่ sà rá nàir 55
minute นาที nar tee 21, 69, 154
mirror กระจก gra jòk 114, 123
miscellaneous เบ็ดเตล็ด bèht (d)talèht 127
miss, to หาย hǎi 18, 30
mistake ผิดพลาด pìt plârt 62, 63
moisturizing cream ครีมบำรุงผิว kreem bam rung pǐw 109
moment สักครู่ sák krôo 12, 136
monastery วัด wát 81
Monday วันจันทร์ wan jan 151
money เงิน ngern 18, 130
money order ธนาณัติ tha nar nát 133
monsoon มรสุม mora sǔm 94
month เดือน deuan 16, 150
monument อนุสาวรีย์ ar nú sǒw a ree 81
more มากกว่า mârk gwàr 14
morning, in the ในตอนเช้า nai (d)torn chów 143, 153 ; เวลาเช้า wey lar chów 151
mortgage จำนอง jam norng 131
mosquito net มุ้ง múng 106
motel โรงแรม roen grairm 22
mother แม่ mâir 93
motorbike จักรยานยนต์ jàk ra yarn 74
motorboat เรือยนต์ reua yon 91
motorway ทางด่วน tarng dùan 76
mountain ภูเขา poo kǒw 85
mountaineering ปีนเขา (b)peen kǒw 90
moustache หนวด nùat 31
mouth ปาก (b)pàrk 138, 142
mouthwash น้ำยาล้างปาก nárm yar lárng (b)pàrk 108
move, to ขยับ ka yàp 139
movie หนัง nǎng 86
movie camera กล้องถ่ายหนัง glông tài nǎng 124
movies หนัง nǎng 86
much มาก mârk 14
mug เหยือก yèuak 120
muscle กล้าม glârm 138
museum พิพิธภัณฑ์ pi pít ta pan 81
mushroom เห็ด hèht 53
music คนตรี don (d)tree 83, 128
musical เพลง pleyng 87
mussel หอยแมลงภู่ hǒy mairng pôo 45
must (have to), ต้อง (d)tôrng 38, 95, 142
mustard มัสตาร์ด mát sa tàrt 55, 64

myself ผม(ดิฉัน)เอง pŏm (di chán) eyng 119

N

nail *(human)* เล็บ léhp 109
nail brush แปรงขัดเล็บ (b)prairng kàt léhp 109
nail clippers กรรไกรขลิบเล็บ gan grai klip léhp 109
nail file ตะไบขัดเล็บ (d)tà bai kàt léhp 109
nail polish ยาทาเล็บ yar tar léhp 109
nail polish remover น้ำยาลางเล็บ nám yar lárng léhp 109
nail scissors กรรไกรตัดเล็บ gan grai (d)tàt léhp 109
name ชื่อ chêur 23, 25, 79, 92, 131
name *(surname)* นามสกุล narm 25
napkin กระดาษเช็ดปาก gra dàrt chét (b)pàak 37, 105
nappy ผาออม pâr ôrm 110
narrow แคบ kâirp 117
nationality สัญชาติ săn chàrt 25, 93
natural ธรรมชาติ tam ma hàrt 83
natural history ธรรมชาติวิทยา tam ma hàrt wít ta yar 83
nauseous คลื่นไส้ klêuhn sâi 140
near ใกล้ glâi 14, 15
near(by) ใกลๆแถวนี้ glâi glâi tâew née 32, 78
nearest ใกล้ที่สุด glâi têe sùt 75, 78, 98
neat *(drink)* เพียว peaw 60
neck คอ kor 30, 138
necklace สรอยคอ sôy kor 121
need, to ตองการ (d)tôrng garn 90
needle เข็ม kĕhm 27
negative ฟิลมลางแลว feem lárng láiw 124
nephew หลานชาย lărn chay 93
nerve เสนประสาท sêhn (b)pra sàrt 138
Netherlands เนเธอรแลนด ney ter lairn 146
never ไมเคย mâi koei 15
new ใหม mâi 14
New Year ปใหม (b)pee mài 152
New Zealand นิวซีแลนด niw see lairn 146
newspaper หนังสือพิมพ náng sĕur pim 104, 105
newsstand แผงขายหนังสือพิมพ pâirng kăi náng sĕur pim 19, 67, 99, 104
next หนา nâr 14, 76, 149, 151; ตอไป (d)tòr (b)pai 65,,68, 73
next time คราวหนา krow nâr 95
next to ติดกับ (d)tìt gàp 15, 77
nice *(beautiful)* ดี dee 94
niece หลานสาว lărn sŏw 93
niello ware เครื่องถม krêuang tŏm 127

night กลางคืน glarng keurn 151
night, at เวลากลางคืน wey lar glarng keurn 151
night cream ครีมบำรุงผิวตอนกลางคืน kreem bam rung piw (d)torn glarng keurn 109
nightclub ไนทคลับ nai klàp 88
nightdress/-gown ชุดนอน chút norn 115
nine เกา gôw 147
nineteen สิบเกา sìp gôw 147
ninety เกาสิบ gôw sìp 148
ninth ที่เกา têe gôw 149
no ไม mâi 10
noisy เสียงดัง sĕarng dang 25
non-smoking หามสูบบุหรี่ hârm sòop bu rèe 36, 70
nonalcoholic ไมมีอัลกอฮอล mâi mee alkorhorl 61
none ไมเลย mâi loei 15
noodle กวยเตี๋ยว gúay tĕaw 50
noon เที่ยง têarng 31, 154
normal ธรรมดา tam ma dar 30
north เหนือ nĕua 77
North America อเมริกาเหนือ a mey ri gar nĕua 146
Norway นอรเวย nor wey 146
nose จมูก ja mòok 138
nose drops ยาหยอดจมูก yar yòrt ja mòok 108
nosebleed เลือดกำเดาไหล lêuat gam dow lăi 141
not ไม mâi 15
note paper กระดาษจดบันทึก gra dàrt jòt ban téuhk 105
notebook สมุดโนต sa mùt nóht 105
nothing ไมมีอะไร mâi mee arai 15, 17
notice *(sign)* ปาย săn yarn 156
notify, to แจง jâirng 144
November พฤศจิกายน prút sa jìk gar yon 150
now ตอนนี้ (d)torn née 15
number หมายเลข mâi lêyg 26, 135, 136, 147
nurse พยาบาล pa ya barn 144
nutmeg ลูกจันทร lôok jan 55

O

o'clock โมง moeng 154
occupation *(profession)* อาชีพ archêep 25
occupied ไมวาง mâi wârng 14, 156
October ตุลาคม (d)tù lar kom 150
office ที่(ทำการ) têe (tam garn) 19, 67, 80, 99, 132
oil น้ำมัน nám man 37, 75, 110
oily *(greasy)* มัน man 30, 111
old เกา gòw 14

DICTIONARY

old town เมืองเก่า meuang gòw 81
on บน bon 15
on foot เดินไป dern (b)pai 77
on time ตรงเวลา (d)trong wey lar 68
once ครั้งหนึ่ง kráng nèuhng 149
one หนึ่ง nèuhng 147
one-way (traffic) วันเวย wan wey 77
one-way ticket เที่ยวเดียว têaw deaw 65, 69
onion หอมหัวใหญ่ hörm hŭa yài 53
only เท่านั้น tôw nàn 15, 88
onyx หินจำพวกโมรา hĭn jam pûak moe rar 122
open เปิด (b)pèrt 14, 156
open, to เปิด (b)pèrt 11, 18, 82, 107, 130, 132, 142
open-air กลางแจ้ง glarng jâirng 90
opera อุปรากร ù (b)pa rar gorn 88
operation ผ่าตัด pàr (d)tàt 144
operator โอเปอเรเตอร์ oe (b)per rey (d)ter 134
operetta ละครร้องขนาดสั้น la korn rórng ka nàrt săn 88
opposite ตรงข้าม (d)trong kârm 77
optician ร้านตัดแว่น rárn (d)tàt wăihn 99, 123
or หรือ rěua 15
orange ส้ม sôm 56, 64
orange (colour) สีส้ม sěe sôm 112
orange juice น้ำส้ม nárm sôm 41, 61
orchestra ออเคสตรา or.key sa trár 88
orchestra (seats) ที่นั่งชั้นดีหน้าเวที têe nâng chán dée wey tee 87
order, to (goods, meal) สั่ง sàng 62, 102, 103
ornithology ปักษีวิทยา (b)pàk sěe wít ta yar 83
other อื่นๆ èurn èurn 75, 101
out of order เสีย sěar 156
out of stock ไม่มีของเหลือ măi mee kŏrng lĕua 103
outlet (electric) ปลั๊ก(ไฟฟ้า) (b)plàk (fai fár) 27,
outside ข้างนอก kârng nôrk 15; ด้านนอก dârn nôrk 36
oval รูปไข่ rôop kài 101
overdone (meat) สุกเกินไป sùk gern (b)pai 62
overheat, to (engine) ร้อนเกินไป rórn gern (b)pai 78
oyster หอยนางรม hŏy nang rom 45

P

pacifier (baby's) จุกนม jùk nom 110
packet ซอง sorng 126
pail ถัง tăng 120, 128
pain เจ็บ jèhp 140, 144; ปวด (b)pùat

141
painkiller ยาแก้ปวด yar găir (b)pùat 140
paint สี sěe 156
paintbox กล่องสี glôrng sěe 105
painter จิตรกร jìt ra gorn 83
painting จิตรกรรม jìt ra gam 83
pair คู่ kôo 115, 117, 149
pajamas เสื้อกางเกงนอน sêua garng geyng norn 116
palace วัง wang 81
palpitations ใจสั่น jai sàn 141
panties กางเกงรัดรูป garng geyng rát rôop 116
panty girdle กางเกงรัดรูป garng geyng rát rôop 116
panty hose ถุงน่อง tŭng nông 116
paper กระดาษ gra dàrt 105
paper napkin กระดาษเช็ดปาก gra dàrt chéhk (b)pàrk 105 , 120
paperback หนังสือปกอ่อน náng sěur (b)pòk òrn 105
paperclip กิ๊บหนีบกระดาษ gíp nèep gra dàrt 105
paraffin (fuel) น้ำมันก๊าด nám man gárt 106
parcel พัสดุ pát sa du 132, 133
pardon, I beg your อะไรนะ arai ná 10
parents พ่อแม่ pôr mâir 93
park สวนสาธารณะ sŭan sär tar ra ná 81
park, to จอดรถ jòrt rót 26, 78
parking การจอดรถ garn jòrt rót 77, 78
parliament building ตึกรัฐสภา (d)tèuhk rát ta sa par 81
parsley ผักชีฝรั่ง pàk chee far àng 55
part ส่วน sùan 138
partridge นกกระทา nók gra tar 49
party (social gathering) งานปาร์ตี้ ngarn (b)pàr (d)têe 95
pass (mountain) ช่องเขา chông kŏw 85
pass through, to แวะผ่าน wáih pàrn 16
pass, to (driving) ขับผ่าน (kàp) pàrn 79
passport พาสปอร์ต pàrs (b)pòrt 16, 17, 25, 26; หนังสือเดินทาง náng sěur dern tarng 156
passport photo รูปติดพาสปอร์ต rôop (d)tìt pà sa (b)pòrt 124
paste (glue) แป้งเปียก (b)pâirng (b)pèark 105
pastry shop ร้านขายขนม rárn kăi ka nŏm 99
patch, to (clothes) ปะ (b)pà 29
path ทางเดิน tarng dern 85
patient คนไข้ kon kâi 144
patterned ลวดลาย lûat lai 112
pay, to จ่าย jài 18, 31, 102, 136
payment จ่าย jài 131

พจนานุกรม

peach ลูกท้อ lôok tór 56
peak ยอดเขา yôrt kŏw 85
peanut ถั่วลิสง tùa li song 56
pear ลูกแพร lôok pair 56
pearl ไข่มุก kài múk 122
peg *(tent)* หมุด(ปักเตนท) mùt ((b)pàk tôyn) 106
pen ปากกา (b)pàrk gar 105
pencil ดินสอ din sŏr 105
pencil sharpener ที่เหลาดินสอ tôe lŏw din sŏr 105
pendant จี้ jêe 121
penicillin เพนนิซิลิน peyn ni si lin 143
penknife มีดพับ mêet páp 120
pensioner ผู้ที่รับเงินบำนาญ pôo tôe ráp ngern bam narn 82
pepper พริกไทย prík tai 37, 41, 55, 64
per cent เปอรเซนต (b)per sehn 149
per day ต่อวัน (d)tòr wan 20, 32, 90
per hour ต่อชั่วโมง (d)tòr chûa moeng 78, 89
per person ต่อคน ,(d)tòr kon 32
per week ต่ออาทิตย (d)tòr ar tít 20, 24
percentage เปอรเซนต (b)per sehn 131
perfume น้ำหอม nárm hŏrm 109
perhaps บางที barng tee 15
period *(monthly)* ประจำเดือน (b)pra jam deuan 141
period pains ปวดประจำเดือน (b)pùat (b)pra jam deuan 141
permanent wave ดัดถาวร dàt tăr worn 30
permit อนุญาต an nú yârt 90
person คน kon 32
personal ส่วนตัว sùan (d)tua 17
personal call/person-to-person call โทรส่วนตัว toe sùan (d)tua 135
personal cheque เช็คส่วนตัว chéhk sùan (d)tua 130
petrol เบนซิน beynsin 75; น้ำมัน nám man 78
pewter พิวเตอร piw (d)ter 122
Philippines ฟิลิปปินส fi li peen 146
photo รูป rôop 124, 125
photocopy ถ่ายเอกสาร tài èyk ga sărn 131
photographer ร้านถ่ายรูป rárn tài rôop 99
photography การถ่ายรูป garn tài rôop 124
phrase วลี wa lee 12
pick up, to *(person)* รับ ráp 80
picnic ปิคนิค (b)pík,ník 64
picnic basket ตะกร้าปิคนิค (d)ta grâr (b)pík ník 106
picture *(painting)* วาดภาพ wârt pârp 83
picture *(photo)* รูป rôop 82
piece ชิ้น chín 18, 119
pig หมู mŏo 47
pigeon นกพิราบ nók pi rârp 49

pill ยาคุม yar kum 141
pillow หมอน mŏrn 27
pin เข็ม(กลัด) kěhm (glàt) 107, 121; กิ๊บ gíp 110
pineapple สับประรด sàp (b)pa rót 56
pink สีชมพู sĕe chom poo 112
pipe ไปป (b)pái 126
pipe cleaner ที่ทำความสะอาดไปป tôe tam kwarm sa àrt (b)pái 126
pipe tobacco ยาเส้นสำหรับไปป yar sêhn săm ràp (b)pái 126
place สถานที่ sa tărn tôe 25
place of birth สถานที่เกิด sa tărn tôe gért 25
place, to ขอ(โทร) kŏr (toe) 135
plain *(colour)* สีเรียบ rêarp 112
plane เครื่องบิน krêuang bin 65
planetarium ท้องฟ้าจำลอง tórng fár jam lorng 81
plaster เฝือก fèuak 140
plastic พลาสติก plar sa (d)tìk 120
plastic bag ถุงพลาสติก tŭng plar sa (d)tìk 120
plate จาน jarn 37, 62, 120
platform *(station)* ชานชลา charn cha lar 67, 68, 69, 70
platinum แพลตตินั่ม plàirt (d)ti năm 122
play *(theatre)* เลน(ละคร) (b)plêhn (la korn) 86
play, to เลน lêhn 87, 88, 94; แข่ง kàihng 89
playground สนามวิ่งเลน sa nărm wîng lêhn 32
playing card ไพ pài 105, 128
please กรุณา ga rú nar
plimsolls รองเทาผาใบ rorng tów par bai 117
plug *(electric)* ปลั๊กไฟ (b)plàk fai 29, 118
plum ลูกพลัม lôok plam 56
pneumonia ปอดบวม (b)pòrt buam 142
pocket กระเป๋า gra (b)pŏw 116
pocket watch นาฬิกาพก na lí gar pók 121
point of interest *(sight)* สถานที่น่าสนใจ sa tărn tôe tôe năr sŏn jai 80
point, to ชี้ chée 12
poison ยาพิษ yar pít 109, 157
poisoning (อาหาร)เป็นพิษ (ar hărn) (b)pehn pít 142
pole *(tent)* เสา(เตนท) sŏw ((d)tehn) 106
police ตำรวจ (d)tam rùat 79, 156, 157
police station สถานีตำรวจ sa tărn tee (d)tam rùat 99, 157
pond บ่อน้ำ bòr nárm 85
poplin ผาแพรปอปลิน pàr prair (b)póhp lin 113
pork เนื้อหมู néua mŏo 47
port ท่าเรือ târ reua 74
portable กระเป๋าหิ้ว gar (b)pŏw hîw 118

porter คนยกกระเป๋า kon yók gra (b)pŏw
18, 26, 71
portion ที่ tée 38, 57, 62
Portugal โปรตุเกส (b)pòer (d)tu gèyt 146
post *(mail)* จดหมาย jòt mǎi 28, 133
post office ที่ทำการไปรษณีย์ tée tam garn
(b)prai sa nee 99, 132
post, to ส่ง(จดหมาย) sòng (jòt mǎi) 28
postage ค่าแสตมป์ kâr sa (d)tairm 132
postage stamp แสตมป์ sa (d)tairm 28,
126, 132, 133
postcard โปสการ์ด (b)pòe sa gàrt 105,
126, 132
poste restante ส่งทั่วไป sòng tûa (b)pai
133
pottery เครื่องปั้นดินเผา krêuang (b)pân
din pǒw 83
poultry เป็ดไก่ (b)pèht gài 49
pound *(เงิน)*ปอนด์ (ngern)(b)porn 19, 102,
129
powder แป้ง (b)pâirng 109
powder compact ตลับแป้ง (d)ta làp
(b)pâirng 121
powder puff แป้งพัฟ (b)pâirng pláp 109
prawn กุ้ง gûng 45
pregnant ตั้งท้อง (d)tâng tórng 141
premium *(gasoline)* ซุปเปอร์(เบนซิน) súp
per (beynsin) 75
prescribe, to สั่ง(ยา) sàng (yar) 143
prescription ใบสั่งยา bai sàng yar 108,
143
press stud แป๊ะติดเสื้อ (b)páih (d)tìt sêua
116
pressure ลม(ยางรถ) lom (yarng rót) 76;
ความดัน kwarm dan 141
pretty น่ารักดี nâr rák dee 84
price ราคา rar kar 69
private ส่วนตัว sùan (d)tua 24, 81, 91,
156
process, to *(film)* ล้าง(รูป) lárng (rôop)
125
processing *(photo)* การล้างรูป garn lárng
rôop 125
profession อาชีพ ar chêep 25
profit กำไร gam rai 131
programme สูจิบัตร sǒo ji bàt 87
pronounce, to ออกเสียง òrk sěarng 12
pronunciation การออกเสียง garn òrk
sěarng 6
propelling pencil ดินสอกด din sǒr gòt
105, 121
Protestant โปรเตสแตนท์ (b)proe tairt sa
tairn 84
provide, to จัดหา jàt hǎr 131
prune ลูกพรุน lôok prun 56
pub ผับ pàp 34
public holiday วันหยุดประจำปี wan yùt
(b)pra jam (b)pee 152

pull, to ดึง deuhng 156
pull, to *(tooth)* ถอน tǒrn 145
pullover เสื้อไหมพรม sêua mǎi prom 115
pump ที่สูบลม tée sòop lom 106
puncture ยางรั่ว yarng rûa 76
purchase ซื้อ séur 131
pure แท้ táir 113
purple สีม่วง sěe mûang 112
push, to ผลัก plàk 156
put, to ใส่ sài 24
pyjamas เสื้อกางเกงนอน sêua garng geyng
norn 116

Q

quality คุณภาพ kun la pàrp 103, 112, 113
quantity ปริมาณ (b)pa ri marn 103
quarter of an hour สิบห้านาที sìp hâr nar
tee 155
quartz ควอตซ์ kwòrt 122
question คำถาม kam tǎrm 11
quick(ly) เร็ว rehw 14, 79
quiet เงียบ ngêarp 23, 25

R

race แข่ง kàihng 90
race course/track ลู่วิ่ง lôo wîng 90
racket *(sport)* ไม้แร็กเก็ต mái ráihk gèht 90
radio วิทยุ wít ta yú 24, 28, 118
raft แพ pair 2, 3
railway station สถานีรถไฟ sa tǎr nee rót
fai 19, 21, 67
rain ฝน fǒn 94
rain, to ฝนตก fǒn (d)tòk 94
raincoat เสื้อกันฝน sêua gan fǒn 116
raisin ลูกเกด lôok gèyt 56
rangefinder เครื่องวัดระยะ krêuang wát ra
yá 125
rare *(meat)* ไม่ค่อยสุก mâi ow sùk 48
rash เป็นผื่นคัน (b)pehn pèurn kan 139
rate *(inflation)* อัตรา(เงินเฟ้อ) a (d)tra
(ngern fér) 131
rate *(price)* ราคา rar kar 20
rate *(of exchange)* อัตรา(แลกเปลี่ยน) a
(d)tra (lâirk (b)plèarn) 19
razor มีดโกน mêet goen 109
razor blades ใบมีดโกน bai mêet goen 109
read, to อ่าน àrn 40
reading lamp โคมไฟหัวเตียง koem fai hǔa
(d)teang 27
ready เสร็จ sèht 29, 117, 123, 125, 145
real *(genuine)* แท้ táir 117
rear ท้าย tái 69; หลัง lǎng 75
receipt ใบเสร็จรับเงิน bai sèht ráp ngern
103, 144
reception แผนกต้อนรับ pa nàirk (d)tôrn
ráp 23

DICTIONARY

receptionist พนักงานต้อนรับ pa nák ngarn (d)tôrn ráp 26

recommend, to แนะนำ náih nam 80, 86, 88, 137, 145

record (disc) แผ่นเสียง pàihn sěarng 128, 129

record player เครื่องเล่นเทป krêuang lêhn téyp 118

recorder เครื่องอัดเทป krêuang àt téyp 118

rectangular สี่เหลี่ยมผืนผ้า sèe lèarm pěurn pâr 101

red สีแดง sěe dairng 105, 112

red (wine) (ไวน์)แดง (wai) dairng 59, 60

reduction ส่วนลด sùan lót 24

refill (pen) หมึก mèuhk 105

refund (to get a) ขอเงินคืน kŏr ngern keurn 103

regards คิดถึง, เคารพ kít těuhng, kow róp 153

register, to (luggage) ฝาก(กระเป๋า) fàrk (gra (b)pŏw) 71

registered mail จดหมายลงทะเบียน jòt mǎi long ta bearn 133

registration ลงทะเบียน long tabearn 25

registration form แบบฟอร์มลงทะเบียน bàirp form long ta bearn 25, 26

regular (petrol) ธรรมดา tam ma dar 75

religion ศาสนา sàrt sa nǎr 83

religious service สวดมนต์ sùat mon 84

rent, to เช่า chôw 19, 20, 90, 91

rental เช่า chôw 20

repair ซ่อม sórm 125

repair, to ซ่อม sórm 29, 117, 118, 121, 123, 125, 145

repeat, to พูดอีกที pôot èek tee 12

report, to (a theft) แจ้งความ jâirng kwarm 157

required ต้อง (d)tôrng 89

requirement ความต้องการ kwarm (d)tôrng garn 27

reservation การจอง garn jorng 19, 23, 66, 69

reservations office แผนกสำรองที่นั่งล่วงหน้า pa nàirk sǎm rorng têe nâng lûang nâr 67

reserve, to จอง jorng 19, 23, 36, 87

reserved จอง jorng 156

rest ที่เหลือ têe lěua 130

restaurant ร้านอาหาร rárn ar hǎrn 32, 34, 68; ภัตตาคาร pát (d)ta karn 36

return ticket ตั๋วไปกลับ tǔa (b)pai glàp 65, 69

return, to (come back) กลับ glàp 80

return, to (give back) คืน keurn 103

rheumatism โรคปวดในข้อ rôeg (b)pùat nai kôr 141

rib ซี่โครง sêe kroeng 138

ribbon ผ้าเทป pâr téyp 105

rice ข้าว kôw 50

right (correct) ถูก tòok 14

right (direction) ขวา kwar 21, 69, 77

ring (jewellery) แหวน wǎirn 122

ring, to (doorbell) กดกระดิ่ง gòt gra dìng 156

river แม่น้ำ mâir nárm 85, 90

river cruise ล่องแม่น้ำ lôhng mâir nárm 74

road ถนน ta nǒn 76, 77, 85

road assistance ความช่วยเหลือบนถนน kwarm chûay lěua bon tanǒn 78

road map แผนที่ถนน pǎirn têe ta nǒn 105

road sign ป้ายจราจร (b)pâi ja rar jorn 79

roasted อบ,ปิ้ง àp,(b)pîng 47

roll ขนมปังก้อน ka nǒm (b)pang gôn 41, 64

roll film ฟิล์มม้วน feem múan 124

roller skate สเก็ต da gèht 128

room ห้อง hôrng 19, 23, 24, 25, 27, 29

room number หมายเลขห้อง mǎi lêyg hôrng 26

room service บริการรูมเซอร์วิส bo ri garn room ser wít 24

rope เชือก chêuak 106

rosary ลูกประคำ lôok (b)pra kam 122

rouge รูจ rôot 109

round กลม glom 101

round (golf) รอบ rôrp 90

round up, to รวมทั้งหมด ruam táng mòt 63

round-neck คอกลม kor glom 116

round-trip ticket ตั๋วไปกลับ tǔa (b)pai glàp 65, 69

rowing boat เรือพาย reua pai 91

royal พระราช pra rârt 81

rubber (eraser) ยางลบ yarng lóp 105

rubber (material) ยาง yarng 117

ruby ทับทิม, táp tim 122

rucksack เป๋หลัง (b)pêy lǎng 106

ruin โบราณสถาน boe raṇ sa tǎrn 81

ruler (for measuring) ไม้บรรทัด mái ban tát 105

rum เหล้ารัม lôw ram 60

running water น้ำประปา nárm (b)pra (b)par 24

Russia รัสเซีย rát sear 146

S

safe ตู้เซฟ (d)tôo séyf 26

safe (free from danger) ปลอดภัย (b)plòrt pai 91

safety pin เข็มกลัด kěhm glàt 109

saffron หญ้าฝรั่น yǎr fa ràn 55

sailing boat เรือใบ reua bai 91

sale ขาย kǎi 131

sale (bargains) ลดราคา lót rarkar 100

DICTIONARY

salt เกลือ gleua 37, 41, 64
salty เค็ม kehm 62
same แบบเดียวกัน bàirp deaw gan 117
sand ทราย sai 90
sandal รองเท้าแตะ rorng tów (d)tàih 117
sandwich แซนด์วิช sairn wít 64
sanitary napkin/towel ผ้าอนามัย pàr a nar mai 108
sapphire ไพลิน, บุษราคัม pai lin, bùt rar kam 122
satin ผ้าซาติน pàr sar(d)tin 113
Saturday วันเสาร์ wan sǒw 151
sauce ซอส, น้ำจิ้ม sórt, nárm jîm 52
saucepan หม้อ ,mòr 120
saucer จานรองถ้วย jarn rorng tûay 120
sausage ไส้กรอก sài gròrk 47, 64
scalded ลวก lûak 46
scalded eggs ไข่ลวก kài lûak 41
scarf ผ้าพันคอ pàr pan kor 116
scarlet สีเลือดหมู sěe lêuat mǒo 112
scissors กรรไกร, gang rai 109
Scotland สก็อตแลนด์ sa gót lairn 146
scooter สกูตเตอร์ sa góot têr 75
scrambled eggs ไข่คน kài kon 41
screwdriver ไขควง kǎi duang 120
sculptor ประติมากร (b)pra (d)tì mar gorn 83
sculpture ประติมากรรม (b)pra (d)tì mar gam 83
sea ทะเล ta ley 85, 91
seafood อาหารทะเล ar hǎrn ta ley 45
season ฤดู, หน้า rí doo, nàr 150
seasoning เครื่องปรุง krêuang (b)prung 37
seat ที่นั่ง têe nâng 65, 70, 87
second ที่สอง têe sǒrng 149; วินาที wi nar tee 155 ,
second class ชั้นสอง chán sǒrng 69
second hand (on watch) มือสอง meur sǒrng 122
secretary เลขานุการ ley kǎ rnú garn 27, 131
section แผนก pa nàirk 104
see, to ดู doo 25, 26, 89, 121
sell, to ขาย kǎi 100
send, to ส่ง sòng 78, 102, 103, 132, 133
sentence ประโยค (b)pra yòek 12
separately แยกกัน yàirk gan 63
September กันยายน kan yar yon 150
seriously รุนแรง rái rairng 139
service บริการ bo ri garn 24, 63, 98, 100
service (church) สวดมนต์ sùat mon 84
serviette กระดาษเช็ดปาก gra dàrt chét (b)pàak 37
set (hair) เซ็ท séht 30
set menu อาหารชุด ar hǎrn chút 37
setting lotion น้ำยาเซ็ทผม náim yar séht pom 30; โลชั่นสำหรับเซ็ทผม loe chǎn sǎm ràp séht pǒm 111

seven เจ็ด jèht 147
seventeen สิบเจ็ด sìp jèht 147
seventh ที่เจ็ด têe jèht 149
seventy เจ็ดสิบ jèht sìp 148
sew, to เย็บ yéhp 29
shade (colour) สี sěe 111
shampoo แชมพู chairm poo 30, 111
shampoo and set สระเซ็ท sà séht 30
shape รูปร่าง rôop rǎrng 103
share (finance) หุ้น hûn 131
sharp (pain) แปลบ (b)plàirp 140
shave โกนหนวด goen nùat 31
shaver เครื่องโกนหนวดไฟฟ้า krêuang goen nùat fai fár 27, 118
shaving brush แปรงสำหรับโกนหนวด (b)prairng sǎm ràp goen nùat 109
shaving cream ครีมสำหรับโกนหนวด kreem sǎm ràp goen nùat 109
shelf ชั้น chán 119
ship เรือกำปั่น, เรือทะเล reua gam (b)pàn, reua ta ley 74
shirt เสื้อเชิร์ต sêua chért 116
shivery หนาวสั่น nǒw sàn 140
shoe รองเท้า rorng tów 117
shoe polish ยาขัดรองเท้า yarng kàt rong tów 117
shoe shop ร้านขายรองเท้า rárn kǎi rorng tów 99
shoelace เชือกผูกรองเท้า chêuak pòok rorng tów 117
shoemaker's ร้านซ่อมรองเท้า rárn sôrm rorng tǒw 99
shop ร้านค้า rárn kár 98
shop window ตู้โชว์ (d)tôo choe 101, 112
shopping ช้อปปิ้ง chóp (b)pîng 97
shopping area ย่านช้อปปิ้ง yàrn chóp (b)pîng 82; ย่านการค้า yàrn garn kár 100
shopping centre ศูนย์การค้า sǒon garn kár 99
shopping facilities/mall ที่ช้อปปิ้ง, ร้านขายของ têe chórp (b)pîng, rárn kǎi kǒng 32
short สั้น sǎn 30, 115
short-sighted สายตาสั้น sǎi (d)tar sǎn 123
shorts กางเกงขาสั้น garng geyng kǎr sǎn 116
shoulder ไหล่ lài 138
shovel พลั่ว plûa 128
show การแสดง garn sa dairng 87
show, to บอก bòrk 12, 13, 103; (แสดง)ให้ดู (sa dairng) hâi doo 118
shower ฝักบัว fàk bua 23, 32
shrink, to หด hòt 113
shut ปิด (b)pit 14
shutter (camera) ชัตเตอร์ chát (d)têr 125
shutter (window) หน้าต่างบานเกล็ด nàr (d)tàrng barn glèht 29

sick (ill) ไม่สบาย mǎi sabay 140
sickness (illness) เจ็บปวด jèhp (b)pùay 140.
side ด้านข้าง dǎrn kàrng 30
sideboards/-burns จอน jorn 31
sightseeing เที่ยวชมเมือง têaw chom meuang 97
sightseeing tour ทัวร์นำเที่ยว tûa nam têaw 80
sign (notice) ป้าย (b)pâi 77, 79, 155
sign, to เซ็นชื่อ sehn chêur 26, 130
signature ลายมือชื่อ lai meur chêur 25
signet ring แหวนรูน wǎirn rûn 122
silk ผ้าไหม pâr mǎi 113
silver เงิน ngern 121, 122
silver (colour) สีเงิน sěe ngern 112
silver plate ชุบเงิน chúp ngern 122
silverware เครื่องเงิน krêuang ngern 122, 127
simple แบบธรรมดา bàirp tam ma dar 124
since ตั้งแต่ (d)tâng (d)tàir 15, 150
sing, to ร้อง(เพลง) rórng (pleyng) 88
single (ticket) เที่ยวเดียว têaw deaw 65, 69
single (unmarried) เป็นโสด (b)pehn sòet 94
single cabin ห้องนอนเดี่ยว(ในเรือ) hông norn dèaw (nai reua) 74
single room ห้องเดี่ยว hôrng dèaw 19, 23
sister พี่(น้อง)สาว pêe (nórng) sǒw 93
six หก hòk 147
sixteen สิบหก sìp hòk 147
sixth ที่หก têe hòk 149
sixty หกสิบ hòk sip 148
size ขนาด ka nàrt 124
size (clothes) ขนาด, เบอร์ ka nàrt, ber 113
size (shoes) ขนาด ka nàrt 117
skiing สกี sa gee 90
skin ผิวหนัง pǐw nǎng 138
skin-diving ดำน้ำ dam nárm 91
skirt กระโปรง gra (b)proeng 116
sleep, to นอน norn 144
sleeping bag ถุงนอน tǔng norn 106
sleeping car ตู้นอน rót norn 66, 69, 70
sleeping pill ยานอนหลับ yar norn làp 109, 143
sleeve แขน(เสื้อ) kǎirn (sêua) 115, 142
sleeves, without ไม่มีแขน mǎi mee kǎirn 116
slice แผ่น pàihn 119
slide (photo) ฟิล์มสไลด์ feem sa lai 124
slip (underwear) กางเกงอาบน้ำผู้ชาย garng geyng àrp párm pôo chai 116
slipper รองเท้าแตะ rorng tów (d)tàih 117
slow(ly) ช้า chár 14, 135
small เล็ก léhk 14, 20, 25, 101, 118
smoke, to สูบบุหรี่ sòob bu rèe 95

smoked รมควัน rom kwan 46
smoker สูบบุหรี่ได้ sòob bu rèe dâi 70
snack อาหารว่าง ar hǎrn wârng 64
snap fastener แปะติดเสื้อ (b)páih (d)tìt sêua 116
sneaker รองเท้าผ้าใบ rorng tów pâr bai 117
snorkel ท่อดำน้ำ tôr dam nárm 128
snuff ยานัตถุ์ yar nát 126
soap สบู่ sa bòo 27, 111
soccer ฟุตบอล fút born 89, 90
sock ถุงเท้า tǔng tów 116
socket (electric) ปลั๊กไฟฟ้า (b)plàk fai fár 27
soft ซ็อฟต์(เลนส) sóf (leyn) 123
soft-boiled (egg) ไข่ต้มไม่สุกมาก ki (d)tôm mǎi sùk mârk 41
sold out ขายหมด kǎi mòt 87
sole (shoe) พื้น(รองเท้า) péurn (rorng tów) 117
soloist เดี่ยว dèaw 88
some บาง barng 14
someone ใคร krai 96
something อะไร arai 36, 57, 139; (อัน)ที่ (an) têe 113
somewhere ที่ têe 88
son ลูกชาย lôok chai 93
song เพลง pleyng 128
soon ในเมชา nai mǎi chár 15
sore (painful) ปวด (b)pùat 145
sore throat เจ็บคอ jèhp kor 141
sorry ขอโทษ kǒr tôet 10, 17, 88, 103
sort (kind) แบบ bàirp 119
soup ซุป súp 43
south ทิศใต้ tít (d)tâi 77
South Africa อาฟริกาใต้ ar fri gar (d)tâi 146
South America อเมริกาใต้ a mey ri gar (d)tâi 146
souvenir ของที่ระลึก kǒrng têe raléuk 127
souvenir shop ร้านขายของที่ระลึก rárn kǎi kǒrng têe ra léuk 99
spade พลั่ว plûa 128
Spain สเปน sa (b)peyn 146
spare tyre ยางสำรอง yarng sǎm rorng 76
spark(ing) plug หัวเทียน bǔa tearn 76
sparkling (wine) สปาร์กลิ้ง sa (b)par gîng 60
speak, to พูด pôot 11, 16, 135
speaker (loudspeaker) ลำโพง lam poeng 118
special พิเศษ pi sèyt 20,
special delivery ไปรษณีย์ด่วน (b)prai sa nee dùan 133
specimen (medical) ตัวอย่าง (d)tua yàrng 142
spectacle case ซองใส่แว่น sorng sài wǎihn 123

spell, to สะกด sa gòt 12

spend, to จาย jài 102

spice เครื่องเทศ krêuang téyp 53

spicy รสจัด rót yàt 37

spinach ผักขม pàk kŏm 53

spine กระดูกสันหลัง gra dùk săn lăng 138

sponge ฟองน้ำซักตัว forng nárm kàt (d)tua 110

spoon ช้อน chórn 37, 62, 120

sport กีฬา gee lar 89

sporting goods shop ร้านขายเครื่องกีฬา rárn kăi krêuang gee lar 99

sprained เคล็ด klèht 140

spring (season) ฤดูใบไม้ผลิ ri doo bai mái plì 150

spring (water) บอน้ำแร่ bor nárm ràir 85

square สี่เหลี่ยมจัตุรัส sèe lèarm jàt(d)tù rát 101

square (town) จัตุรัส jàt(d)tù rát 82

squid ปลาหมึก (b)plar mèuhk 45

stadium สนามกีฬา sa nărm gee lar 82

staff (personnel) พนักงาน pa nák ngarn 26

stain รอยคราบ roy krârp 29

stainless steel สแตนเลส sa (d)tairn léyt 122

stalls (theatre) ที่นั่งชั้นดีหน้าเวที têe nâng chán dee năr wey tee 87

stamp (postage) แสตมป์ sa (d)tairm 28, 126, 132, 133

staple เย็บกระดาษ têe yéhp gra dàrt 105

start, to (begin) เริ่ม rêrm, 80, 87

starter (meal) อาหารเรียกน้ำย่อย ar hărn rêark nárm yôi 42

station (railway) สถานี(รถไฟ) sa tăr nee (rót fai) 19, 21, 67

stationer's ร้านขายเครื่องเขียน rárn kăi krêuang kĕarn 99, 104

statue รูปปั้น rôop (b)pân 82

stay อยู่ yòo 31, 93

stay, to อยู่ yòo 16, 24, 26, 142

steal, to ขโมย ka moey 157

steamed นึ่ง nêuhng 46

stewed ตุ๋น, (d)tŭn 47

sticky rice ข้าวเหนียว kôw něaw 50

stiff neck คอแข็ง kor kăihng 141

still (mineral water) ชนิดไม่มีก๊าซ cha nít mâi mee gárt 61

sting ถูกแมลงต่อย tòok ma lairng (d)tòy 139

sting, to แมลงต่อย ma lairng (d)tòy 139

stitch, to สอย sŏy 29

stock exchange ตลาดหุ้น (d)ta làrt hûn 82

stocking ถุงน่อง tŭng nông 116

stomach ท้อง tórng 138

stomach ache ปวดท้อง (b)pùat tórng 141

stools อุจจาระ ùt jar rá 142

stop (bus) ป้าย(รถเมล์) (b)pâi (rót mey) 73

stop, to จอด jòrt 21, 70, 72; หยุด yùt 69

stop! หยุด yùt 157

store (shop) ร้านค้า rárn kár 98

straight (drink) เพียว peaw 59, 64

straight ahead ตรงไป (d)trong bpai 21, 77

strange แปลก (b)plàirk 84

strawberry สตรอเบอร์รี่ sa (d)tror ber rêe 56

street ถนน ta nŏn 25, 77

street map แผนที่ถนน pàirn têe ta nŏn 20, 105

string เข็มเย็บกระดาษ kĕhm yéhp gra dàrt 105

strong (รส)จัด (rót) jàt 126

student นักศึกษา nák sèuhk săr 82, 94

study, to ศึกษา sèuhk săr 94

stuffed ยัดไส้ yát sâi 42

sturdy แข็งแรงทนทาน kăihng rairng ton tarn 101

suede หนังกลับ năng glàp 113, 117

sugar น้ำตาล nárm (d)tarn 37, 64

suit (man's) ชุดสากล chút săr gon 116

suit (woman's) ชุดสตรี chút săr gon 116

suitcase กระเป๋า gra (b)pŏw 18

summer ฤดูร้อน ri doo rórn 150

sun-tan cream ครีมกันแดด kreem gan dàirt 110

sun-tan oil น้ำมันกันแดด nám man gan dàirt 110

sunburn แดดเผา, dàirt pŏw 107

Sunday วันอาทิตย์ wan ar tít 151

sunglasses แว่นกันแดด wâirn dar dam 123

sunshade (beach) ร่มกันแดด rôm gan dàirt 91

sunstroke (เป็น)ลมแดด ((b)pehn) lom dàirt 141

superb เยี่ยมมาก yêarm màrk 84

supermarket ซุปเปอร์มาร์เกต súp (b)per mar géht 99

suppository ยาเหน็บทวาร yar nèhp ta warn 108

surgery (consulting room) คลีนิคหมอ kleeník mŏr 137

surname นามสกุล narm sagun 25

suspenders (Am.) สายขวนกางเกง săi kwâirn garng geyng 116

swallow, to กลืน kleurn 143

sweater เสื้อไหมพรม sêua măi prom 116

sweatshirt เสื้อกีฬาคอกลมแขนยาว sêua geelar kor glom kăirn yow 116

Sweden สวีเดน sa wee deyn 146

sweet หวาน wărn 60; (wine) สวีท wèet 62

sweet (confectionery) ลูกกวาด lôok gwàrt 126

sweet corn ข้าวโพด kôw pòet 53

sweet shop ร้านขายขนมหวาน rárn kǎi ka nǒm wǎrn 99

sweetener น้ำตาลเทียม nárm (d)tarn team 38

swelling บวม buam 139

swim, to ว่ายน้ำ wâi nárm 90

swimming ว่ายน้ำ wâi nárm 90, 91

swimming pool สระว่ายน้ำ sà wâi nárm 32, 90

swimming trunks กางเกงว่ายน้ำ garng geyng wâi nárm 116

swimsuit ชุดว่ายน้ำ chút wâi nárm 116

switch (electric) สวิทช์ไฟ sa wít,faj 29

switchboard operator โอเปอเรเตอร์ oe (b)per rey (d)tèr 26

Switzerland สวิตเซอร์แลนด์ sa wít ser lairn 146

swollen บวม buam 139

synagogue สุเหร่ายิว sú,ròw yiw 84

synthetic ผ้าใยสังเคราะห์ pǎr yai sǎng kró 113

T

T-shirt เสื้อคอกลม sêua kor glom 116

table โต๊ะ (d)tóh 36, 106

tablet (medical) ยาเม็ด yar méht 108

tailor's ร้านตัดเสื้อ rárn (d)tàt sêua 99

take, to ยก yók 18; เอา ow 25, 102

take away, to หอไปกินบ้าน hòr (b)pai gin bârn 64

take pictures, to (photograph) ถ่ายรูป tài rôop 82

take to, to ไปส่งที่ (b)pai sòng têe 21, 67

taken (occupied) มีคนนั่ง mee kon nâng 70

talcum powder แป้งโรยตัว (b)pâirng roey (d)tua 110

tampon ผ้าอนามัยชนิดแท่ง pǎr a nar mai cha nít tâjhng 108

tangerine ส้มจีน sôm jeen 56

tap (water) ก๊อกน้ำ gók nárm 28

tax ภาษี par sěe 32

taxi แท็กซี่ táihk sêe 19, 21, 31, 67

taxi rank/stand ที่จอดรถแท็กซี่ têe jòrt rót táihk sêe 21

tea ชา char 41, 61, 64

teaspoon ช้อนชา chórn char 120, 143

team ทีม teem 89

tear, to (muscle) ฉีก chèek 140

teaspoon ช้อนชา chórn char 120, 143

telegram โทรเลข toe ra lêyk 133

telegraph office ที่ทำการโทรเลข têe tam garn toe ra lêyk 99

telephone โทรศัพท์ toe ra sàp 28, 79, 134

telephone booth ตู้โทรศัพท์ (d)tôo toe ra sàp 134

telephone call โทรศัพท์ toe ra sàp 136

telephone directory สมุดโทรศัพท์ sa mút

telephone number หมายเลขโทรศัพท์ mǎi lêyk toe ra sàp 135, 136, 157

telephone, to (call) โทร toe 134

telephoto lens เลนส์เทเลโฟโต้ leyn tey tey lêy 125

television โทรทัศน์ toe ra tát 24, 28, 118

telex เทเล็กซ์ tey léhk 133

telex, to เทเล็กซ์ tey léhk 130

tell, to บอก bòrk 73, 76

temperature อุณหภูมิ u na ha poom 90, 140, 142

temporarily ชั่วคราว chûa krow 145

ten สิบ sìp 147

tendon เอ็นในรางกาย ehn nai rǎrng gai 138

tennis เทนนิส teyn nít 90

tennis court สนามเทนนิส sa nǎrm teyn nít 90

tennis racket ไม้แร็กเก็ต mái rǎirk gèht 90

tent เต้นท์ (d)téyn 32, 106

tent peg หมุดปักเต้นท์ mùt (b)pàk (d)téhn 106

tent pole เสาเต้นท์ sǒw (d)téhn 106

tenth ที่สิบ têe sìp 149

term (word) เงื่อนไข ngêuan kǎi 131

terrace ระเบียง rá beang 36

terrifying น่ากลัว nâr glua 84

tetanus บาดทะยัก bàrt ta yák 140

Thai ไทย tai 11, 95, 113

Thailand ไทย tai 146

than กว่า gwàr 14

thank you ขอบคุณ kòrp kun 10

thank, to ขอบคุณ kòrp kun 10, 96

that นั้น nán 11; นั่น nán 101

theatre โรงละคร roeng la korn 82, 86, 87

theft ขโมย ka moey 157

then แล้วก็ láiw gô 15

there ที่นั่น têe nân 14

thermometer ปรอท (b)pròrt 109, 144

thigh ต้นขา (d)tôn kǎr 138

thin บาง barng 112

think, to (believe) คิดว่า kít wâr 31, 63, 94

third ที่สาม têe sǎrm 149

thirsty, to be หิวน้ำ hǐw nárm 13, 36

thirteen สิบสาม sìp sǎrm 147

thirty สามสิบ sǎrm sìp 147

this นี่ nêe 11; อันนี้ an née 101

thousand พัน pan 148

thread ด้าย dâi 27

three สาม sǎrm 147

throat ลำคอ lam kor 138, 141

throat lozenge ยาอม yar om 108

through ผ่าน pàรn 15

through train รถไฟที่ไม่ต้องเปลี่ยน mâi (d)tôrpg plèarn rót fai 68

thumb นิ้วหัวแม่มือ níw hǔa mǎir meur 138

thumbtack เป๊กติดกระดาษ (b)péhk (d)tìt

gra dàrt 105
thunder ฟ้าร้อง fár, rórng 94
thunderstorm ฝนฟ้าคะนอง fŏn fár ka norng 94
Thursday วันพฤหัสบดี wan pá rú hàt 151
ticket ตั๋ว tŭa 65, 69, 87, 89
ticket office แผนกจำหน่ายตั๋ว pa nàirk jam nài (d)tŭa 68
tie เนคไท nêhk tai 116
tie clip ที่หนีบเนคไท têe nèep néhk tai 122
tie pin เข็มกลัดเนคไท kăihm glàt néhk tai 122
tight (close-fitting) คับ káp 116
tights ถุงน่อง tŭng nông 115
time เวลา wey yar 68, 80, 153
time (occasion) ครั้ง kráng 143
timetable (trains) ตารางเดินรถ (d)tar rarng dern rót 69
tin (container) กระป๋อง gra (b)pŏrng 119
tin opener ที่เปิดกระป๋อง têe (b)pèrt gra (b)pŏrng 120
tint ยายยอมผม yar yórm pŏm 110
tinted สี sĕe 123
tire (vehicle) ยาง(รถ) yarng (rót) 76
tired เหนื่อย nèuay 13
tissue (handkerchief) กระดาษทิชชู่ gra dàrt tít sôo 110
to ถึง tĕuhng 15
toast ขนมปังปิ้ง ka nŏm (b)pang (b)pîng 41
tobacco ยาเส้น yar sêhn 126
tobacconist's ร้านขายบุหรี่และยาสูบ rárn kăi burèe láih yar sòop 126
today วันนี้ wan née 29, 151
toe นิ้วเท้า níw tów 138
toilet paper กระดาษชำระ gra dàrt cham rá 110
toilet water โอดิโคโลญจ์ oe do koe loen 110
toiletry เครื่องใช้ในห้องน้ำ krêuang chái nai hông,nárm 110
toilets ห้องน้ำ hông nárm 24, 27, 32, 37, 68
tomato มะเขือเทศ ma kĕua têyt 53
tomato juice น้ำมะเขือเทศ nárm ma kĕua têyt 61
tomb สุสาน su sărn 82
tomorrow วันพรุ่งนี้ wan prûng née 29, 96, 151
tongue ลิ้น lín 138
tonic water โทนิค toe ník 61
tonight คืนนี้ keurn née 29, 86
tonsils ทอนซิล (d)tòrm torn sin 138
too เกินไป gern (b)pai 15
too (also) เหมือนกัน mĕuan gan 15
too much มากเกินไป mârk gern (b)pai 14
tools เครื่องมือ krêuang meur 120
tooth ฟัน fan 145

toothache ปวดฟัน (b)pùat fan 145
toothbrush แปรงสีฟัน (b)prairng sĕe fan 110, 118
toothpaste ยาสีฟัน yar sĕe fan 110
toothpick ไม้จิ้มฟัน mái jîm fân 37
top, at the ข้างบน kârng bon 30; ด้านบน dârn bon 145
torch (flashlight) ไฟฉาย fai chăi 106
torn (muscle) ฉีก chèek 140
touch, to จับ jàp 156
tough (meat) เหนียว nĕaw 62
tour เที่ยว têaw 74, 80
tourist office สำนักงานท่องเที่ยว săm nák ngarn tông têaw 80
tourist tax ภาษีนักท่องเที่ยว par sĕe nák tông têaw 32
tow truck รถลาก rót lârk 78
towards ตรงไปที่ (d)trong (b)pai têe 15
towel ผ้าขนหนู păr kŏn,nŏo 27, 111
towelling (terrycloth) ผ้าขนหนู păr kŏn nŏo 113
town เมือง meuang 19, 77, 89
town center ใจกลางเมือง jai glarng meuang 21, 77; ในเมือง nai meuang 72
town hall ศาลาว่าการจังหวัด săr lar wâr garn jang wàt 82
toy ของเล่น kŏrng lêhn 128
toy shop ร้านขายของเล่น rárn kăi kŏrng lêhn 99
tracksuit ชุดวอร์ม chút worm 116
traffic light แยกไฟแดง yâirk fai dairng 77
trailer จุดรถนอน jòrt rót norm 32
train รถไฟ rót fai 66, 68, 69, 70, 153
tranquillizer ยากล่อมประสาท yar glòrm (b)pra sàrt 109, 143
transfer (finance) โอนเงิน oen ngern 131
transformer หม้อแปลงไฟฟ้า môr (b)plairng fai fár 118
translate, to แปล (b)plair 12
transport, means of การเดินทาง garn dern tarng 75
travel agency เอเยนต์ท่องเที่ยว ey yêhn tôrng têaw 99
travel guide หนังสือคู่มือ náng sĕur kôo meur 105
travel sickness เมารถเมาเรือ mow rót mow reua 107
travel, to เดินทางท่องเที่ยว dern tarng (d)tôrng têaw 94
traveller's cheque เช็คเดินทาง chéhk dern tarng 19, 63, 102, 129
travelling bag กระเป๋า(เดินทาง) gra (b)pŏw,dern tarng 18
tree ต้นไม้ (d)tôn mái 85
trim, to (a beard) เล็ม lehm 31
trip การเดินทาง garn dern tarng 72
trolley รถเข็น rót kĕhn 18, 71
trousers กางเกงขายาว garng keyng kăr

yow 116

try on, to ลอง lorng 114

Tuesday วันอังคาร wan ang karn 151

tuk tuk ตุ๊กตุ๊ก (d)túk (d)túk 21

tumbler ถ้วยแก้ว tûay gãiw 120

turkey ไก่งวง gài nguang 49

turn, to *(change direction)* เลี้ยว léaw 21, 77

turquoise เทอรคอยส teŗ koys 122

turquoise *(colour)* สีเทอรคอยส sẽe ter koys 122

turtleneck คอโปโล kor (b)poe loe 116

tweezers แหนบ nàirp 110

twelve สิบสอง sìp sŏrng 147

twenty ยี่สิบ yêe sìp 147

twice สองครั้ง sŏrng kráng 149

two สอง sŏrng 147

typewriter เครื่องพิมพ์ดีด krêuang pim dèet 27

typing paper กระดาษพิมพ์ดีด gra dàrt pim dèet 105

tyre ยาง(รถ) yarng (rót) 76

U

ugly น่าเกลียด nâr glèart 14, 84

umbrella ร่ม rôm 116

umbrella *(beach)* ร่มกันแดด rôm gan dàirt 91

uncle ลุง lung 93

unconscious หมดสติ mòt sa(d)tì 139

under ใต้ (d)tâi 15

underpants กางเกงใน garng geyng nai 116

undershirt เสื้อยืด sêua yêurt 116

understand, to เข้าใจ kôw jai 12, 17

undress, to ถอดเสื้อ tôrt sêua 142

United States สหรัฐ sa har rát 146

university มหาวิทยาลัย ma hăr wít ta yar lai 82

unleaded ไร้สารตะกั่ว rái sărn (d)ta gùa 75

until กระทั่ง gra tâng 15

up ขึ้น kêun 14

upper ชั้นบน chán bon 70

upset stomach ท้องเสีย tórng sĕar 107

upstairs ชั้นบน chán bon 15

urgent ด่วน dùan 13, 145

urine ปัสสาวะ (b)pàt săr wá 142

use ใช้ chái 108

use, to ใช้ chái 134

useful เป็นประโยชน์ (b)pehn (b)pra yòet 15

usual เป็นประจำ (b)pehn (b)pra jam 143

V

V-neck คอวี kor wee 115

vacant ว่าง wârng 14, 23, 156

vacation วันหยุดพักผ่อน wan yùt pák pòrn 151

vaccinate, to ฉีดวัคซีน chèet wák seen 140

vacuum flask กระติกสุญญากาศ gra (d)tik sŏon yar gàrt 120

valley หุบเขา hùp kŏw 85

value มูลค่า moon kâr 131

vanilla วานิลา war ni lar 55

veal เนื้อลูกวัวอ่อน néua lôok wua òrn 47

vegetable ผัก pàk 53

vegetable store ร้านขายผัก rárn kăi pàk 99

vegetarian มังสวิรัติ mang sa wi rát 38

vegetarian เสบเสียด sèhn lèuat 138

velvet ผ้ากำมะหยี่ pâr gam ma yêe 113

velveteen ผ้ากำมะหยี่เทียม pâr gam ma yêe tearm 113

venereal disease กามโรค garm ma rôek 142

vermouth เวอมัธ wer mát 60

very มาก mârk 15

vest เสื้อกล้าม sêua glârm 116

vest *(Am.)* เสื้อกั๊ก sêua gák 116

veterinarian สัตวแพทย์ sàt pâirt 99

video camera กล้องวีดีโอ glông wee dee oe 124

video cassette ม้วนเทปวีดีโอ múan téyp wee dee oe 118, 124, 127

video recorder เครื่องอัดวีดีโอ krêuang àt wee dee oe 118

view *(panorama)* วิว wiw 23, 25

village หมู่บ้าน mòo bârn 76, 85

vinegar น้ำส้มสายชู nárm sôm săi choo 37

visit มาที่นี่ mar têe nêe 93

visit, to เยี่ยม yêarm 95

visiting hours เวลาเปิดทำการ wey lar (b)pèrd tam garn 144

vitamin pill วิตามิน wi (d)tar min 108

vodka วอดก้า wód gâr 60

volleyball วอลเลย์บอล worn lêy born 90

voltage โวลต์ wóel 27, 118

vomit, to อาเจียน ar jearn 140

W

waist เอว ew 142

waistcoat เสื้อกั๊ก sêua gák 116

wait, to รอ ror 21; คอย koy 107

waiter บอย bŏy 26, 36; พนักงานเสิร์ฟ pa nák ngarn sèrp 26

waiting room ห้องพักผู้โดยสาร hôrng pák pôo doey sărn 68

waitress พนักงานเสิร์ฟ pa nák ngarn sèrp 26; คุณ kun 36

wake, to ปลุก (b)plùk 27, 71

Wales เวลส weyls 146

walk, to เดิน dern 75, 85

wall กำแพง gam pairng 85
wallet กระเป๋าใส่เงิน gra (b)pǒw sài ngern 160
want, to ต้องการ gra (b)pǒw sài ngern 13; อยาก(ได้) yàrk (dâi) 101, 102
warm อุ่น ùn 94
wash, to ซัก sák 29, 113
washable ซักได้ sák dûay 113
washbasin อ่างล้างหน้า àrng lárng nàr 28
washing powder ผงซักฟอก pŏng sák fôrk 120
washing-up liquid น้ำยาล้างจาน nárm yar lárng jarn 120
watch นาฬิกาข้อมือ nar lí gar kôr meur 121, 122
watchmaker's ร้านนาฬิกา rárn nar li gar 121
watchstrap สายนาฬิกาข้อมือ sǎi na li gar kôr meur 122
water น้ำ nárm 24, 28, 32, 41, 75, 90
water flask กระติกน้ำ gra dtìk nárm 106
water melon แตงไม (d)tairng moe 56
water-skis สกีน้ำ sa gee nárm 91
waterfall น้ำตก nárm (d)tòk 85
waterproof กันน้ำ gan nárm 122
wave คลื่น klêurn 91
way ทาง tarng 76
weather อากาศ ar gàrt 94
weather forecast พยากรณ์อากาศ pa yar gorn ar gàrt 94
wedding ring แหวนแต่งงาน wǎirn (d)tàihng ngarn 122
Wednesday วันพุธ wan pút 151
week อาทิตย์ ar tít 16, 20, 24, 80, 92, 151
well (สบาย ดี) (sa bai) dee 10
well-done (meat) สุกๆ sùk sùk 47
west ทิศตะวันตก tít (d)tawan (d)tòk 77
what อะไร arai 11
wheel ล้อรถ lór rót 78
when เมื่อไหร่ mêua rài 11
where ที่ไหน têe nǎi 11
where from มาจากไหน mar jàrk nǎi 93, 146
which อันไหน an nǎi 11
whisky วิสกี้ wít sa gêe 17, 60
white สีขาว sěe kǒw 59, 112
who ใคร krai 11
whole ทั้งหมด táng mòt 143
why ทำไม tam mai 11
wick ไส้ตะเกียง sâi (d)ta gearng 126
wide กว้าง gwârng 117
wide-angle lens เลนส์มุมกว้าง leyn mum gwǎrng 125
wife ภรรยา pan ra yar 93
wig วิกผม wík pǒm 110
wild boar หมูป่า mǒo (b)pàr 49
wind ลม lom 94
window หน้าต่าง nàr (d)tàrng 28, 36, 65, 70

window (shop) ตู้โชว์ (d)tôo choe 101, 112
windscreen/shield กระจกหน้ารถยนต์ gra jòk nàr rót yon 76
windsurfer วินด์เซิร์ฟ win sêrf 91
wine เหล้าไวน์ lôw wai 59, 62
wine list รายการเหล้าไวน์ rai garn lôw wai 59
winter ฤดูหนาว rí doo nǒw 150
wiper (car) ที่ปัดน้ำฝน têe (b)pàt nárm fǒn 76
wish อวยพร uay porn 153
with กับ, ด้วย gàp, dûay 15
withdraw, to (from account) ถอนเงิน tǒrn ngern 130
withdrawal ถอน tǒrn 130
without ไม่มี, mâi mee 15
wonderful เยี่ยม yêarm 96
wood ป่า (b)pàr 85
wool ผ้าขนแกะ pâr kǒn gàih 113
word คำ kam 12, 15, 133
work, to ทำงาน tam ngarn 28, 118
working day วันทำงาน wan tam ngarn 151
worse เลวกว่า leyw gwàr 14
worsted ไหมพรม mǎi prom 113
wound ได้รับบาดเจ็บ dâi ráp bàrt jèhp 139
wrap up, to ห่อ hòr 103
wrinkle-free กันยับ gan yáp 113
wristwatch นาฬิกาข้อมือ na li gar kôr meur 122
write, to เขียน kěarn 12, 101
writing pad กระดาษเขียนหนังสือ gra dàrt kěarn náng sěur 105
writing paper กระดาษเขียนหนังสือ gra dàrt kěarn náng sěur 105
wrong ผิด pìt 14, 77, 135

Y

year ปี (b)pee 149
yellow สีเหลือง sěe lěuang 112
yes ครับ (คะ) kráp (kà) 10
yesterday เมื่อวาน mêua warn 151
yet ยัง yang 15, 16, 25
yoghurt โยเกิร์ต yoe gèrt 41, 64
young เด็ก dèhk 14
youth hostel ที่พักเยาวชน têe pák yo wa chon 32

Z

zero ศูนย์ sǒon 147
zip(per) ซิป, síp 116
zoo สวนสัตว์ suan sàt 82
zoology สัตววิทยา sàt wít ta yar 83

ดัชนีภาษาไทย